Mur

Murder Files

Richard Whittington-Egan

Magpie Books, London

Constable & Robinson Ltd
3 The Lanchesters
162 Fulham Palace Road
London W6 9ER

This edition published by Magpie Books,
an imprint of Constable & Robinson Ltd 2006

A copy of the British Library Cataloguing in
Publication Data is available from the British Libary

ISBN-10: 1-84529-435-1
ISBN-13: 978-1-84529-435-9

Printed and bound in the European Union

1 3 5 7 9 10 8 6 4 2

Contents

Acknowledgment

A number of these pieces first appeared in the *New Law Journal*,
to whose editor I am grateful for permitting their second bow.

The House in Euston Square

The next time business or pleasure takes you through the renovated portals and air-terminal-like concourse of Euston Station, spare a moment's thought for the old-world, tree-lined London square which it has engulfed, and the strange business which, in the late 'seventies of Queen Victoria's golden age, came to be known, not without delicious *frisson*, as the Euston Square Mystery.

One could not in the good old days of freely – well, considering the going rate of pay, *almost* freely – available domestic help, be too careful in the matter of selecting one's maid, tweeny, slavey, butler, valet, pantryboy, or cook. Mostly they were suitably cowed, docile, respectful, and domesticated, but the odd maverick could prove not only disagreeable to have about the place, but even positively lethal.

Best remembered, perhaps, of these ferocious "undomestics", is that terrible Irish tigress, Kate Webster, the cook-general who ended up with her mistress simmering in the pot at No 2 Mayfield Cottages, in leafy Richmond.

Less well remembered – in fact hardly remembered at all – but certainly no less worthy of recall, is one Hannah Dobbs.

The riddle surrounds the murder of an aged Canterbury *belle*, Matilda Hacker, a well-to-do spinster, who, because of a streak of aversion to the spending of money in general and the paying of rates in particular, absconded from her Canterbury home, leaving her rates bill unpaid. Calling herself Huish, this strange old bird came to roost among the trees of Euston Square, taking the second floor front at No 4, the tall Bloomsbury lodging-house kept by Mr and Mrs Severin Bastindoff.

That was in August, 1877. On an October Sunday she vanished from the face of the earth.

The Bastindoffs were out. Miss Hacker was left alone in the house with their maid, 24-year-old Hannah Dobbs.

On Monday – October 15 – morning, Mr Bastindoff sent Hannah up for some overdue rent. She returned with a five-pound note saying Miss Huish had just given it to her. Two days later, the Bastindoffs were told their lodger had left. Well . . . she was an eccentric old woman . . . they shrugged . . . set to work preparing her room for the next lodger. Mrs Bastindoff did notice a large, partly washed-out stain on the carpet. Later analysis showed it to be blood.

Life settled down, like the London dust on the plane-tree leaves, to cover and blot out with its fine powder every last trace and memory of the mysteriously vanished lodger.

Then, 18 months later, what the newspapers called a "shocking discovery".

On May 9, 1879, Mr Bastindoff had the cellar cleared out. A new lodger wanted it for coals. And there was Miss Huish. What remained of her.

Hannah Dobbs was charged with the murder. The case against her was entirely circumstantial, but pretty damning. Shortly after Miss Hacker/Huish's "departure", Hannah gave the old lady's cash-box to one of the Bastindoff children as a plaything. She showed another child a book of dreams which had belonged to Miss Hacker. And the Bastindoffs noticed she was wearing a watch and chain and some rings they had not seen previously. Left to her by an uncle who had recently died at Bideford, she explained.

The police investigated. There was no dead uncle at Bideford. Miss Hacker's watch and chain were found in a pawnshop. Hannah was picked out at an identity parade as the pledger thereof.

In July, 1879, she was tried before the fearsome Mr Justice Hawkins in the New Court at the Old Bailey. The defence relied upon the improbability of a young woman's being able, in the short time available, to commit the murder, remove unassisted a heavy body down to the cellar, and obliterate all traces of the crime.

The Bastindoffs were most unsatisfactory witnesses. Severin vehemently denied immoral intercourse with Hannah.

Hawkins J., most uncharacteristically, summed up for an acquittal.

The jury acquitted.

An end to the affair? Not quite.

Mr Purkiss, proprietor of the *Police News*, published a pamphlet on the career of Hannah Dobbs. It alleged immoralities between her and Severin Bastindoff before and after entering his service. Bastindoff applied for an injunction against further publication, swore an affidavit denying intimacy with Dobbs, and instituted an action for libel against the publisher. In retaliation, a summons was taken out against Bastindoff for perjury. The magistrate committed him for trial.

So it was, by an odd quirk of chance, that Severin Bastindoff came to stand in the identical place, in the identical court, before the identical judge, where Hannah Dobbs had fought for her life.

Prosecuted by Montagu Williams, QC – Harry Poland, who, incidentally, believed that Severin killed Miss Hacker and gave the stolen items to Dobbs, was in the defence team – he cut a poor figure.

Hannah Dobbs did not come out of it too well, either. In cross-examination she was forced to admit previous conviction for theft. "A most infamous person," observed Hawkins J.

Severin Bastindoff proved equally infamous and considerably less adroit. His defence was that when he was claimed to have been staying with Hannah at an inn at Redhill, Surrey, he was with a fishing party in quite another district. It was actually his brother, Peter Bastindoff, who was with Hannah. He was very like him in appearance. Severin's principal witness was his mother-in-law!

Neither judge nor jury swallowed the bait. Severin Bastindoff was trundled off to serve 12 months' hard labour.

But what about the murder of Miss Hacker? To this day the riddle remains. Did Hannah Dobbs contrive it as a sole personal enterprise? Or in felonious partnership with either Severin or Peter Bastindoff? Surely the Bastindoffs must have known more than they pretended?

Something to think about next time you are waiting for a train – late, of course – at Euston . . .

The Stella Maris Case

Alfonso Francis Austin-Smith had been born under an initially benevolent stellar constellation. His was a pampered childhood, followed by Eton, Trinity College, Cambridge, and a commission in the 4th Dragoon Guards.

When, in 1910, he came of age, legacies from his Canadian grandparents totalling half a million pounds descended in a golden shower about his head. He resigned his commission in the guards to become a full-time playboy. And a pretty good fist he made of it, wining, dining, gambling and wenching. He owned racehorses, a large yacht, even his own private aeroplane.

In October, 1912, he married Ruth Wynne, the daughter of an American Government official. It didn't work out. They were to divorce in 1922.

On the outbreak of the Great War, Frank joined up, serving throughout as a private in the Sutherland Highlanders. He fought well and bravely, and was badly gassed.

During the war he met a young London office worker, Rosina Ivy Wright. Her friends called her Kathie. After his divorce came through, he married her. She bore him three children, and although Frank, as he liked to be, and habitually was, called, had by this time spent all of his half-million except £10,000, that residuum he responsibly settled on Kathie.

The marriage had not proved entirely happy. There were periodic furious quarrels, caused in part by his drinking, followed by fervent reconciliations. All might well have straightened itself out and settled down had it not been for the appearance on the scene, in February, 1926, of John Tyler Derham.

Not surprisingly, since the two men had much in common – Eton, Cambridge, the army, and wealth, which Derham, however, had held on to – they got along well together. It was when Frank invited his new friend home to the furnished bungalow at Herne Bay, where he and his family were now living, that the trouble started.

At forty, three years older than Frank, John Derham, an international rink hockey player who had represented England, was an attractive man. Separated for some years from his wife, he fell deeply in love with the vivacious, amusing, and very pretty, 27-year-old Kathie Smith. And his love was returned.

Several scenes ensued between the two men. They even exchanged blows. Towards the end of June, Frank and Kathie's constant quarrelling over Derham became mutually intolerable. Frank moved out, betaking himself off to London, where he found a kind of consolation in the whisky bottle. Kathie packed up her and the children's things and went to stay at a house named Claverhouse, owned by Derham's father. Derham, observing punctiliously conventional correctness, did not spend any night there with her, but he did come to see her every day.

Persuaded no doubt by Derham, Kathie had her solicitor draw up a deed of separation. She also moved out of Claverhouse and rented a rather dreary looking Edwardian villa, named, somewhat inappropriately, Stella Maris, in St. Anne's Road, in Tankerton, a suburb of Whitstable.

Meanwhile, Frank, who was staying with a friend in Maida Vale, obtained from him the loan of a loaded Webley revolver. Clearly, he intended to use it in an attempt to solve the perpetual problem of the eternal triangle. But how? To shoot himself, as he afterwards claimed? Or to kill Derham and Kathie, as witnesses were to testify to hearing him say? This is the fulcrum of the Stella Maris case.

On August 9th, Frank travelled down to Stella Maris. He stayed there three nights, and on the last two shared his wife's bed. Consequently emboldened to believe that a satisfactory resolution might be brought about, Derham persuaded to see sense, he optimistically despatched a telegram to him in his wife Kathie's name, inviting him to Stella Maris. And on August 12th – the glorious grouse-shooting twelfth – Derham, equally optimistic, turned up.

After some reasonably restrained conversation, the trio, overcome by hunger, traipsed off to the nearby Marine Hotel for some dinner. But Smith's appetite deserted him. He just drank some champagne. Then back to Stella Maris they wended their disputatious way.

Both men were passionately in love with Kathie. Her feelings were never made clear. The exchanges there grew heated. Exploded.

That loud explosion brought Kathie's 16-year-old sister, Lily, who was staying with her, tumbling down from her bedroom. From the bottom of the stairs, she saw the two men struggling on the floor.

So did John Browning Barton, a local builder, who, night-strolling, happened at 11 p.m. to be walking along St. Anne's Road. As he was passing Stella Maris, the light in the front room was on, and the curtains drawn back, so that all inside was visible, brightly illuminated like a stage set. He glimpsed briefly a tableau of three people. One of them, a man, was standing in the bay-window, his back to the street. The other two, a man and a woman, stood facing him, a few feet away.

Momentarily, Barton's gaze shifted. He heard a shot, and, looking swiftly back, saw the other two hurl themselves at the man in the window, bearing him to the ground. He crashed against the bay-window, which broke.

Barton watched the male assailant's arm rising and falling, as if he were striking the prostrate man with the gun in his hand. The woman, shouting, "Don't! Don't! Give me the revolver," struggled with him, but he eluded her, staggered out into the road, still clutching the gun, and collapsed. It was Derham. Shot through the stomach, within twenty-four hours he was dead.

Arrested, Smith told the police: "I intended to shoot myself, but in the struggle for the revolver it went off and shot Derham."

Facing a charge of murder, Frank Smith retained Sir Edward Marshall Hall to represent him at Maidstone Assizes that November. As it happened, this was to be the last capital case in which Marshall Hall appeared, and there was a poetic rightness in the fact that this, his final murder case, involved the same sort of allegedly involuntary killing, arising out of a sexual entanglement and a death during a struggle for a loaded weapon, as did his first.* Three months later, at the age of sixty-eight, the Great Defender would be dead.

In his defence of Alfonso Smith, Hall played every card that forty years' forensic experience had put into his hands – a brilliant performance, aided by the gun expert, Robert Churchill, of a mock struggle, to demonstrate the absolute possibility of a revolver's having been fired by accident in the course thereof; the reading out of heart-rending letters from Smith to his wife that reduced many of those in court and on the jury, but not the judge, to tears; a superb, vintage Marshall Hall closing peroration. The jury were won over.

Not so Mr. Justice Avory, the acid drop. Barely disguising his dissatisfaction with the verdict, he proceeded to sentence Smith to twelve months' imprisonment with hard labour for possessing firearms and ammunition with intent to endanger life.

There was no happy hearts and flowers ending to the once charmed life of Alfonso Smith. He came out of prison to find his wife and children had moved away to start anew without him. They had gone to live in Paris. She obtained a decree of nullity, the grounds being that he was not legally married to her. His American divorce was invalid, as he had not been domiciled in America. His little son was burnt to death in a school fire. Smith took up farming in Devonshire, but his last years were ruined by the shadows of debt and litigation. He died, poor and forgotten, in November, 1944, in a furnished room in Ilfracombe.

*See "The Great Defender's First Murder Case", page 256.

The Awful Advent of Bible John

Sudden as a gusting wind that bowls the tumbleweed, sadistic slayer Bible John literally danced his psychopathic way through the Glasgow badlands, a quotation from the Good Book ever-ready on the trigger of his tongue and a strangler's ligature in his holster.

At his high noon – the late 1960s – the rampaging throttler squeezed the tough heart of Scotland's wild west town – "Taggart-land" – into a panic that edged it towards a Yorkshire Ripper style terror *Fest*. His killing ground was the brassy Barrowland Ballroom, just east of the city's High Street, and his partners had a way of ending up naked and very dead, garrotted with their own tights.

Bible John's *danse macabre* began in February, 1968. The first to whirl away the last waltz of her life in his arms was Patricia Docker. Twenty-five years old, she worked as a nursing auxiliary at Mearnskirk Hospital. Her five-year marriage to an R.A.F. corporal had broken down, and she and her four-year-old son were living with her parents. On Thursday night – February 22nd, 1968 – she went along for a harmless evening out at the Barrowland.

When the blue of the night met the gold of the next day, they found her stripped and strangled in the door recess of a back lane garage, barely 200 yards from her Langdale Place home.

Police descended on the Barrowland in droves. But neither the Thursday night hoppers, nor anyone else, it seemed, could help. The strangler had vanished into the sunrise.

Then, one August Saturday eighteen months later, Bible John reached for his dancing pumps again.

Like Patricia Docker, 32-year-old Jemima McDonald was dancing mad. Mima, as she was generally called, had produced and brought up three children without benefit of spouse. Life had not been easy. The soft lights, sweet music, swirl and excitement of the dance-hall added up to a welcome make-believe luxury halt for her on a stony road. The Barrowland was her 'local'. Bible John was waiting there for his next dance.

For Mima, her dancing years ended in a derelict tenement, not twenty yards from her home in Bridgeton, whence she had set out merrily so few short hours before with her dancing shoes in a brown paper parcel. Like Patricia Docker, she had been raped and strangled.

But this time the police had something to go on. A sketchy description. Mima had been seen dancing with a man – 6 feet 2 in. tall, slim, aged 25–35, short reddish hair, blue suit, white shirt. For the first time in a Scottish murder hunt an artist's impression was issued.

All was optimism. Then the trail went cold.

The third partner whom destiny had written on Bible John's dance card was 29-year-old Helen Puttock. She, too, was a mother – married, with two children.

On Thursday, October 30th, 1969, she and her sister, Jeannie, went to the Barrowland. Helen was soon being whisked round the floor by a handsome six-footer. Bit of a dude. Beautifully cut, short red hair. Nice manners. Said his name was John.

She had kept her appointment with Fate.

Between dances, Jeannie was introduced to him. After the ball was over, Helen and John went off together. When next seen she was alone – a crumpled corpse in a back court near her Scotstoun home, raped, one of her own stockings biting deep into the flesh of her neck.

But now the police had a solid lead. Helen's sister was still alive to tell the tale. John, she said, had told her that his parents were strictly religious, and fervent teetotallers. They had brought him and his sister up that way. He could recite whole passages of the Bible by heart. He proved it. Kept on coming up with apt quotations from the Good Book all evening.

A beaming Chief Superintendent Joe Beattie, spearheading the manhunt, was confident. "We now know so much about the man, it's just a matter of time till we pull him in."

Time passed. Nothing happened. The Dutch clairvoyant, Gerard Croiset, was consulted. It was a measure of despair that failed.

The most widely held theory was that Bible John was a serviceman, a prison officer, or a policeman, because of his, then, unfashionably neat and tidy short-back-and-sides hair-cut. Another suggestion was that he was a member of a religious order or a fanatic sect determined to punish "sinful" dancing women.

Without doubt, the killer's motive was murder for sexual pleasure. He was a serial killer. Why, though, did he suddenly stop killing – and vanish into thin air? Did he die? Was he jailed for some other offence? Had he satisfied his blood lust? We face here the same sort of riddle as bedevils the Jack the Ripper affair.

The search for Bible John dragged on for years, and extended as far afield as Ulster, Germany, Hong Kong and Zambia. Incredibly, the dancing psychopath never tripped into the net. His foot-work – and his luck – held.

Then, in 1983, something very exciting happened. A man who had just returned to this country after living for the last ten years in Australia, came forward saying that he recognised Bible John as a friend of his with whom he used to go dancing at the Barrowland. This friend was traced to a village near Amsterdam. He bore a quite remarkable likeness to the identikit picture and the artist's impression of Bible John. Everything, in fact, seemed to fit . . . except for one thing. There was not the tiniest scrap of evidence to tie him to the Glasgow dance of death killings.

At the time of the great manhunt, a young soldier named John Irvine McInnes had been a prime suspect. The circumstantial evidence surrounding him seemed persuasive. He had red hair. He had had a strict religious upbringing by Plymouth Brethren parents. He had been at the Barrowland on the night of Helen Puttock's murder.

He was pulled in four times to take part in identity parades. But Jeannie had not identified him, and he had been finally eliminated from the inquiry by Joe Beattie. However, 27 years later, he was to become the prime suspect again.

In the 1990s the new scientific technique of genetic profiling had been developed and police decided to compare McInnes' DNA with that yielded by a semen stain which had been preserved on Helen Puttock's skirt.

McInnes was no longer alive. He had committed suicide on April 29th, 1980, at the age of forty-one, and been laid to rest in the Lanarkshire village of Stonehouse's hillside cemetery.

Permission was sought and granted for his exhumation. A sampling of his DNA was taken. It did not accord with that on Helen's skirt.

Bible John remains as intangible as the gust of killer wind that blew him into town.

The Scholar Murderer of Knaresborough

Among the equitable maxims of criminology is the one which affirms that murder will out.

Nowhere is this comforting tenet more convincingly validated than by the curious case of Eugene Aram – a multifold cautionary tale which, *inter alia*, demonstrates also the perils of conspiracy, the lethal power of the "squealer", and the irrebuttable veracity of the venerable saw which warns against scorned women and wives.

In the days before Harrogate was on the map, and Knaresborough was a centre of the Yorkshire universe, returning two members to Parliament, there dwelt in those parts a respected and seemingly respectable dominie, Eugene Aram.

The gifted son of a gardener to the nobility, Aram had been cradle-blessed with a taste for learning and the intellectual equipment where-with to indulge it. Born in 1704, at Ramsgill, in Upper Nidderdale, he had come with his wife, Anna, to Knaresborough in 1734, and commenced as schoolmaster. The marriage had not prospered. Although he manfully overcame his distaste for Anna sufficiently to permit her seven or eight children, his conduct outside the confines of the marital bed was distinctly unfriendly. If he met Anna in the street, he would conspicuously ignore her. It was his pleasure to torment her by pretending that a comely boy, dressed as a girl, was his latest light o' love. Anna would repay!

A scholar, but not quite a gentleman, his especial gift was for languages, all self-taught – Latin, Greek, French, Hebrew, the Celtic tongues, Sanskrit, and even Aramaic, spoken of Jesus. In other circumstances he could well have become a philologist of worldwide repute. Instead . . .

In 1745 Aram conspired with three friends – Daniel Clark, cordwainer or shoemaker; Richard Houseman, heckler or flax-dresser; and Henry Terry, ale-draper or innkeeper – to carry out an 18th-century version of the long-firm fraud.

Clark, recently married to a passing rich wife who imported a passable dowry, seized of two freeholds, and keeping a horse at bait, was a person of good credit. This brotherhood of boon and bent com-panions used purse-proud Clark's sound name to order large quantities of goods and to acquire jewellery and plate.

On February 8, 1745, Clark – and the goods – mysteriously disappeared. The tricked tradesmen were beside themselves. With Daniel gone, Aram and Houseman were left in the lion's den. Terry was somehow overlooked.

Under the trim flower-beds of Aram's schoolhouse were discovered bales of velvet and other cloths. Beneath the flax in

Houseman's warehouse were leather goods. But jewellery and plate had, like Daniel Clark, evaporated.

Efforts were made to charge Aram and Houseman, but they failed. Then Aram disappeared – leaving wife and children behind to fend for themselves. Thirteen years went by . . .

In August, 1758, a workman dug up human bones on Thistle Hill, overlooking Knaresborough. Long memories instantly connected the find with the vanishing of Dan Clark. An inquest was held, and Anna Aram came forward with a scorned wife's tale of her errant husband and Houseman's having murdered Clark.

How did Houseman earn his niche in *Wills on Circumstantial Evidence*? Taking up one of the disinterre: arm-bones, "This is no more Daniel Clark's bone than it is mine", quoth he.

"From which it was concluded, that if he was so certain that the bones before him were not those of Clark, he could give some account of him", quoth Wills. And, pressed, outside court, Houseman subsequently stated that he had seen Aram strike Clark down and bury the body in St Robert's Cave.

That cave, the legendary cell of a medieval hermit, stood – and still stands – in the same cliff terrace wherein was the des. res. of Mother Shipton, prophetess of the time of Henry VIII. And close by is the Petrifying or Dropping well.

Sure enough, exactly as Houseman said, there they found the remains of Daniel Clark. Houseman agreed to turn King's Evidence. By pure chance, a travelling stallion man from near Knaresborough had recently recognised Aram at Lynn, in Norfolk, where he was employed as an usher at the Free School. Two constables went and fetched him back.

Tried at York Assizes in 1759, he was prosecuted by the celebrated, hectoring Fletcher Norton KC. Aram defended himself, making a finely-wrought but, forensically speaking, pretty useless, closing speech. Unswayed by his crocket and finialed rhetoric, a stolid Yorkshire jury found him guilty. He received both verdict and sentence with philosophic composure.

An English – but lethal – Deacon Brodie figure, he was hanged on August 6, 1759, but not before he had admitted his guilt and, on the night before his execution, attempted suicide with a razor. After hanging he was gibbeted, his corpse left caged in chains, and ultimately losing its head when a local doctor named Hutchinson clambered up a ladder and sawed the skull off to take home to his private collection of curiosities.

Aram's career is commemorated in a poem, "The Dream of Eugene Aram" by Thomas Hood, the metre of which is effectively echoed in Oscar Wilde's *Ballad of Reading Gaol*. There is a novel by Bulwer Lytton, and a play in which Sir Henry Irving took the part of the Yorkshire scholiast at the Lyceum in 1873.

Eugene Aram is represented, too, in the murderer's equivalent of Poets' Corner; not in the Abbey of Westminster, but in the museum of the Royal College of Surgeons in Lincoln's Inn Fields. His cranium, rescued from the hands of Dr Hutchinson, has joined there such other delectable medico-legal picked plums as the skeletons of Jonathan Wild and William Corder, of the Red Barn, and the skull of John Thurtell, who, with Joseph Hunt, murdered Mr Weare at Elstree. In such distinguished black calendar company Aram
". . . Stands on a shelf,
A venerable monument raised to himself"

The Christmas Apple

In a swift and bloody moment one wild December night, 27-year-old Harriet Buswell ceased to exist. It was she herself who brought Death in out of the darkness, and, all unknowingly, made him welcome in the poor little room which she occupied in Great Coram Street, Bloomsbury.

Like Harriet, Great Coram Street no longer exists. The dreary thoroughfare of out-at-elbows Victorian hotels and flyblown lodging-houses that ran straight as a dagger through the seedy heart of Bloomsbury, has vanished beneath the breakers' hammers. If Harriet's outraged ghost walks, it walks the concrete ways of the new Brunswick shopping precinct. Her only other memorial, a shrivelled, half-eaten apple, preserved once in the Black Museum at Scotland Yard, has also disappeared.

But let us go back to the time when the apple – and Harriet – were glossy and appetising. Back to the terrible, mystifying events of December, 1872.

Harriet Buswell aka Clara Burton, was a young and not very

successful actress, who, in the quaint phrase of our great-grand-fathers, was "no better than she ought to be." Not to put too fine a point on it, when she could find no berth in the theatre, she played out her romances on the streets, seeking her leading men at such haunts of talent as the Alhambra and the Argyll Rooms, and whisking them home to her second-floor back at No 12 Great Coram Street – a discreet lodging-house presided over by a discreet Mrs Wright.

On Christmas Eve, after a lengthy period of "resting", Harriet's cupboard was bare. Painting a smile on her wan face, putting on her prettiest skirt and pertest bonnet, she stepped out into the wintry darkness of the shrouded Bloomsbury streets, and headed for the gas flare and warmth of the golden-paved West End.

At midnight she returned to Great Coram Street, escorted by a gentleman. Mrs Wright, who saw her arrival, was afterwards to say that Mr Wrong – as he proved to be – "appeared like a foreigner".

The last time the landlady saw Harriet, the last time anyone saw her, alive – was when she emerged to ask for some stout to be brought up. It could not be done. By then all the public-houses had closed. Disappointed, Harriet withdrew up the gloomy stairs, and into the long darkness of oblivion.

Gradually, the noises of the late revellers in the streets faded away. The house in Great Coram stood gaunt and silent under the frosty glitter of the stars. But, stealthily in that black pool of silence, a murderer's hand moved . . . and swiftly slashed away the sleeping girl's life.

As the first grey light of Christmas dawn filtered dustily into the shabby room, the assassin, leaving a half-eaten apple on the wash-stand, quit the scene of his ferocious pleasure. Locking the door to delay discovery of the thing he left behind him on the bed, and pocketing the key, he tiptoed down the creaking stairs and softly let himself out of the house.

The sun rose. The church bells rang. All over Victorian England Christmas gifts were being exchanged and steaming, festive lunches being prepared. But up in the second-floor back in Bloomsbury, Harriet Buswell slept on. A bluebottle buzzed.

It was later that day that other lodgers broke open the door of the locked and silent room and made their appalling discovery. The task of Superintendent Thompson of E Division was unenviable. The casual Romeo of the "Juliet of a night" was the proverbial Anonymous Man.

But . . . there was the apple. It became the subject of one of the pioneering exercises in forensic odontology. A careful cast was made of the bite marks. They did not fit the dead girl's teeth. They were the teeth marks of the killer.

Superintendent Thompson's inquiries fanned out. George Fleck, a Compton Street fruiterer, remembered selling the couple apples, oranges and nuts. William Stalker, a waiter at the Cavour Restaurant, remembered serving them. Both thought, like Mrs Wright, that the man was a German.

Inquiries about aliens led Thompson to Ramsgate, where, after running on to the Goodwin Sands, the German brig *Wangerland* had put in for repairs two weeks before Christmas.

Soon he had a suspect in his spyglass. A surgeon's assistant, Karl Whollebe, had been behaving suspiciously. He was arrested. Fleck and Stalker attended an identification parade. Neither picked out Whollebe. Both identified the *Wangerland*'s chaplain, Dr Gottfried Hessel, from the line-up of ship's personnel. Whollebe was released, Pastor Hessel arrested.

Hessel, it transpired, had accompanied Whollebe to London on December 22. He, Mrs Hessel, Whollebe, and a ship-owner, Mr Hermes, had all stayed at Kroll's Hotel in the City.

At Bow Street Magistrates' Court, Fleck and Stalker stuck to their identification. A maid-servant said Hessel looked like a man she saw leaving No 12 on Christmas morning. Jane Somers, housemaid at Hiscock's Royal Hotel, where the pastor stayed when he returned to Ramsgate shortly after Christmas, said he had asked for turpentine and a brush to clean his clothing, and had sent half-a-dozen badly bloodstained handkerchiefs to the laundry.

But the magistrate chose to believe Hessel's alibi. Whollebe testified that when he and Hermes went out at 10 pm on December 24, Hessel was in the dining-room at Kroll's Hotel looking very unwell. Mr Kroll, the hotel proprietor, said that Hessel was heard coughing in his room during the night, and that his only pair of boots were seen outside his bedroom door.

Pastor Hessel was set triumphantly free – with a letter of apology from Mr Gladstone and a solatium of £1,225.8s.11d., subscribed by the British public, Queen Victoria herself contributing £30.

And so the good pastor slipped away from our shores, dento-logically unassailed, having, one feels, escaped detection by, shall we say, the skin of his teeth . . .

A Black Magic Christmas

For most of us Christmas was, when we were young – and still is, even when we are, perhaps, not so young – a magic time. It certainly was for a young man named Eric Willmot, even though, at 36, he was well past believing in Santa Claus, and had, indeed, very valid reasons for doubting the existence of his "good fairy". All of which adds up to the fact that Eric Willmot had proved unable to do anything more than eke out a narrow, spare-ribbed and precarious living, drubbing his Irish blarney into service selling pots and pans at country fairs in and around Dublin.

Well . . . the great Christmas festival was just two days away as Thomas Gilligan, full of merry Yuletide thoughts, chugged homewards in his aged truck along a country road outside Cork. The inner eye's vision of turkey and plum-pudding and a long, long row of miraculously ever-replenishing bottles of Guinness, was suddenly – rudely and alarmingly – extinguished by the outer eye's extremely unwelcome perception of a shoe, sticking in a most provocatively suspicious fashion out of the rough-turned earth of a nearside stretch of barren field.

Never a man to resist the temptation of challenge, Tom Gilligan seized hold of the semi-submerged shoe and gave it an almighty tug. It wouldn't budge. He investigated more closely and saw why. It was attached to the foot, leg, and the rest of the body of a dead man. Gilligan did what "sure any dacent man would do" in the circumstances: went off in search of the "polis".

The detectives accompanied Gilligan back to where the shoe marked the spot. And the first thing that, somewhat puzzled, they observed was scuff marks in the earth, plainly showing that a sizeable group of people had been dancing on the dead man's grave. They noted, too, the extraordinary shallowness of that grave. The body had been stowed away no more than six inches below the surface of the ground. Six inches more and the shoe would have been completely covered – and quite possibly the body never discovered.

There had, of course, to be a post-mortem that Christmas Eve of 1979. The doctors declared that the man had been dead only a very short time; killed as recently, they thought, as the night before. That would have been Saturday, December 22. The corpse had been tied hand and foot. The skull was fractured, the ribcage smashed. Sharp spikes of rib had penetrated vital organs. In short, the manner of the man's death had been extremely brutal. Thanks to that dependable factor of the volatile Irish, voluble free speech, especially free when the vocal organs are well oiled, the detectives did not take too long in unearthing the dead man's identity and fullish life history.

It seemed that one fine day in 1973, Eric Willmot had had the misfortune to wander into 43-year-old Phoebe Brady's fair-ground tent to have his fortune told in her crystal ball. She, it transpired, when not thus gainfully employed in scrying for palm-crossing silver, functioned as High Priestess of a cult of some 30 tatterdermalion lost sheep, who passed themselves off as Devil Worshippers.

Phoebe had had previous misfortunate marital experience – misfortunate at any rate for her whilom husband, who had, as a result of magnificent persistence, succeeded ultimately in deserting her – and at the age of 16 she had been delivered of a daughter, Verren, who was now 27 and her mother's Satanic acolyte. No matter. Eric was smitten with Phoebe, and the pair "married" at a ceremony performed by the High Priestess herself.

Alas! the union did not prosper. It proved no marital bed of shamrock. The trouble seems to have been that for Phoebe every moon was a honeymoon, and Eric simply could not keep up – or down! – with her. Eventually, by the light of the moon, he did a flit. That was definitely not permitted. It was an insult to the High Priestess and her fertility rites; an act crying out for punishment. Phoebe and her devils went in full pursuit, tracked Eric down, and beat him up.

The desperate, hapless, exhausted bedfellow of the high performing priestess attempted the divorce of distance twice more. Third time fatally unlucky They caught up with him on the night of the winter solstice – December 22.

Phoebe, Verren and all the members of the Devil cult could provide alibis. It was verified that they had been enacting a special dance in honour of the solstice. But that was at 10 pm. So, for the rest of the night, that was no alibi at all. However; in the course of persistent questioning of everyone in the bar where Eric had spent the last evening of his life, the detectives found that the name Mike Harmsworth kept coming up.

A hard man with a lengthy police record, including grievous assault, he met them wooden-faced. Frustrated, the police decided to cut corners, deploy a Jesuitical end-justifies-the-means tactic. They charged him with murder, hoping the shock would crack his insouciance. The sham worked. He sang like a Kilkenny canary.

Yes, he *did* know Phoebe. He had met her while having his fortune told, and had revealed to her during that sitting that he was broke. She had offered him £800 if he would render a man named Eric Willmot helpless and deliver him to a field outside the city She had given him a photograph of the man. He had recognised him, followed him out of the pub, felled him with a massive blow on the back of the neck from his clenched ham fists, and carried him senseless through the streets of Cork. Folk who saw him simply thought that he was charitably carrying home a drunken comrade. At the appointed rural spot, he had duly delivered Eric up to the High Priestess and her daughter, who were waiting on the windswept moor, iron bars of office in their hands.

Taken into custody, Phoebe turned hyper-regal. Her consort murdered? What blather. He had been tried *in absentia* by his Satanic peers and found guilty of attempted desertion. The man had been *executed*. As High Priestess, she was authorised to carry out such legal executions.

Judge and jury did not quite see it that way. Phoebe, Verren, and Michael Harmsworth, found guilty of murder, were all sentenced to life in July, 1980. Devilish bad luck, you could say.

The Poisoned Kettle

Whichever way you looked at it, the night of Friday, December 31, 1965, was not a happy Hogmanay for those having business, legitimate or otherwise, at the Chelsea College of Science and Technology, housed in the former Chelsea Public Library Building, in Manresa Road, right in the heart of London's artistic and bohemian quarter.

For the thieves, trundling away the safe, it was disastrous. It contained only £2. For respectable, 60-year-old Mr Frederick Whittle, who, in the course of the illicit proceedings, was coshed, it was even more disastrous. And for Mr William Barnett, aged 57, it was the ultimate disaster. He was murdered.

Hear ye, then, the passing strange tale of three men and a kettle – full of lethal hot water.

The story, no ordinary thud-and-blunder one of robbery with violence, begins, as all good New Year's Eve stories should, with a party, and glasses – not coshes – raised. Albeit a very modest party. Scarcely more than a few token mouthfuls of grog in glasses lifted to 1966 by three old men – the college caretaker, Herbert Weighall, and two night-watchmen, Whittle and Barnett – working unsociable hours in the dark, empty, shuttered and locked college building.

At first, all was, as it should have been, dead quiet in the deserted building, with its untenanted laboratories and lecture rooms and long, silent corridors. Just the occasional muffled echo of distant revelry borne in upon a restless night breeze. The likes of the Chelsea Arts Ball could have been held on another planet. The old men swallowed the lees of 1965. Big Ben boomed on a million radios and TV sets.

Then, suddenly, Fred Whittle's ear caught a different kind of sound. Nearer. Noises from somewhere inside the building. His first thought was that it was probably students. Young devils. Climbed in, perhaps. Up to New Year's Eve pranks. He shuffled off to investigate. And in one of those dim, sinister corridors, came face to face with a gang of raiders, wheeling a safe away on a trolley. One of them, a slim, dark-haired young man, dealt him a swingeing blow to the head. The intruders then took to their heels, leaving the safe, and the £2 it contained, behind.

Head still ringing, stars still dancing before his eyes, dazed and dazzled, poor old Fred staggered off to Casualty at St Stephen's Hospital, in nearby Fulham Road. Just to make sure. Better that than be sorry. No bones broken, they told him. Injuries not serious, they said, and packed him off back to work.

Returned to the college, he joined the other two for that universal British remedy for disasters of all dimensions – a nice cup of tea. He downed only half his mugful before, good, conscientious fellow that he was, trotting off to make a further security check. It was now just after 5 am on New Year's Day.

Arriving back from his rounds, the previously "wounded soldier" found Bill and Bert in a state of collapse. Now he, too, was beginning to feel very sick. Soon, all three were feeling so diabolical that Barnett said he would drive them to St Stephen's. Dr Satyabrata Banerjee, the night casualty officer, wasn't too well himself when woken up. He said that, because of his head injuries, Whittle could be admitted. But the other two were sent off, and told to see their GPs.

Barnett shakily drove himself and Weighall back to the college. Weighall decided to go home – and subsequently recovered. Barnett was found later, moaning and twisting on the floor of one of the corridors. He died on his way back to St Stephen's.

His death was at first assumed to have been from natural causes. Then – a dramatic development. A check of the college's poisons' cabinet revealed that a bottle of arsenic was missing. Near where it had stood, was a jar containing a barbiturate. This led to a theory that arsenic had been administered in a bungled attempt by the raiders to dope the watchmen's tea. A post-mortem yielded evidence of arsenical poisoning.

It was originally thought that the poison had been mixed into the sugar. This was later shown to be incorrect. The coroner, Gavin Thurston, said it was clear that the arsenic had been put in the kettle. Whittle stated that he had previously made tea *in the same kettle* at 8 pm. So, the poison must have been introduced after that.

Police interrogated 1,800 students, collected 4,000 statements, recorded fingerprints of everybody connected with the college, to compare with sets found on the poisons' cabinet. All to no avail.

Had the arsenic been taken from the cabinet while Barnett, Weighall and Whittle were enjoying their little New Year party? Or while Whittle was away at the hospital for treatment? Or had it been removed much earlier in the evening – though after 8 pm? Was the poisoning connected with the burglary attempt that failed? Or was it a simple coincidence that both events occurred that same night?

There is, too, the possibility of a malicious prankster; an itinerant venenator, possessed of laudable curiosity and the happy psychopath's no-conscience syndrome, whose idea of letting the New Year in was letting a fellow-human out; not so much a first-footing as a last footing! It could have been a lethal grotesque of the kind later – 1972 – typified by the thallium freak, Graham Young.

In October, 1966, Barnett's widow sued the hospital for turning her husband away. Dr Banerjee was found negligent, but the judge ruled that the hospital was not liable, because it would have been impossible to have diagnosed arsenical poisoning in time to have saved William Barnett's life.

The Case of the Deadly Manchurian Partridges

If ever there was a case for Mr Sherlock Holmes it was that of the mysterious death of Lieutenant Chevis after eating a dish of Manchurian partridge at his own dinner-table, and the extraordinary telegram delivered on the day of his funeral bearing the three words, "Hooray. Hooray. Hooray."

How eagerly Holmes would have set forth on one of those rare forays of his into the Home Counties, to, in this case, Deepcut, in that military south-west corner of the Surrey of dense bracken, sandy soil, and the sad sound of bugles coming through the pine-trees in the evening.

On Saturday, June 20, 1931, Lieutenant Hubert George ("Hugh") Chevis, regular artillery officer, aged 28, sat down to dinner with his wife, Frances Howard, in D Hut, Aisne Bungalows, Blackdown Camp. Batman, Nicholas Bulger, served the main course – roast partridge. One each.

Chevis took a single bite. "It tastes horrible!" He handed his wife a piece of the larger bird on his plate. She just touched it with her tongue. Her verdict: "Simply ghastly."

"Take this bird away and destroy it," Chevis ordered Bulger. He did not want his Alsatian to get at it. Frances apparently ate her partridge, merely observing that it tasted "fusty".

After a final course of cheese and salad, they went into the drawing-room for coffee, but within minutes Chevis collapsed. His legs became paralysed. He developed terrible convulsions. Frances telephoned their doctor.

Dr E. F. Bindloss found Chevis stretched rigid on a couch, body arched, heels touching the floor. The classic opisthotonos spasm of strychnine poisoning. Then Frances began to shiver. She went into convulsions. Stiffened.

The doctor drove both patients to Frimley and Camberley College

Hospital. Frances slowly recovered, but, at about 9.40 am on Sunday, June 21, Hugh Chevis died.

Tests carried out by Home Office analyst, Dr J. H. Ryffel, confirmed death by strychnine. The bird carcasses had been burned in the kitchen range, but strychnine was found in a piece of partridge from Chevis' stomach. It was present also in the dripping and gravy. Ryffel calculated that the bird must have contained at least 2 grains. A fatal dose is ½ grain.

Mrs Chevis had telephoned the order for a brace of partridges to a highly reputable Farnborough poulterer's on Friday, June 19. Their partridges came, frozen, from Manchuria. The brace was delivered to the Chevises' cook, Mrs Yeomans, at 1.30 pm on Saturday, by Frank Noyes, who swore on oath that his van was never left unlocked. She placed them in the meat-safe – an unlocked wood and mesh box on the *outside* wall at the back of the bungalow-hut. There the partridges remained, easily accessible to anyone, for 4½ hours. It would only have taken seconds for someone with a hypodermic syringe to inject one or both with strychnine.

And that, Ryffel believed, is what must have happened, for not only did a random sampling of other birds from the poulterer's cold storage disclose no poison, but Ryffel said that no living bird could have picked up and absorbed the quantity of poison shown by his analysis.

On Wednesday, June 24, Lieutenant Chevis was buried. At 4.30 that afternoon a man walked into the Merion Row Post Office, St Stephen's Green, Dublin, and sent a telegram to Chevis, 14 Argyle Road, Boscombe, Hants. He filled in the back of the form. Sender: J. Hartigan. Address: Hibernian. The Hibernian was a hotel in nearby Dawson Street. The identity of J. Hartigan remains to this day a mystery.

The telegram arrived at 5 pm while Sir William and Lady Chevis were on their way back from their son's funeral. It bore a cruel message: "Hooray. Hooray. Hooray."

Hugh Chevis had been born in India in 1903. His father was a judge of the Punjab, and the boy had been heir to the life of privilege and comfort accorded to the "Heaven born" in the days of the British Raj. After 30 years on the Bench, Sir William had, in 1923, come to live in retirement near Bournemouth. Was the murder of the old judge's son perhaps the revenge of a criminal who nurtured a savage grudge against Sir William, and, cloaked behind the *nomme de meutre*

"J. Hartigan", triumphantly mocked his grief? Or was there a man who might have had his own more particular reason to hate Lieutenant Chevis?

The inquest, opened at Camberley Police Court House on June 23, was twice adjourned. On August 11, the jury, instructed by Mr W. J. Francis, Deputy-Coroner for West Sussex, returned an open verdict. Two years later, Mrs Chevis remarried. Her third husband was a Hampstead businessman.

What, then, of the other candidate for being the harsh reality behind the shadowy persona of the elusive Mr Hartigan? Well . . . in the summer of 1926, Chevis, a tall, good-looking subaltern of 23, had met the wife of a fellow-officer, Major Jackson, of the Royal Army Veterinary Corps. Jackson was 49. His wife, Frances, half his age, was not only a rich woman in her own right who drove a big open Bentley, but also a strikingly attractive one. She and Hugh fell in love. She divorced the Major, and when, in December 1930, Chevis returned from a tour of duty in Quetta, married him, parking her three children with a nurse and maid in a flat she owned behind Harrods in Knightsbridge, and spending most of her time with her new husband at Blackdown Camp.

It was Major Jackson, who had also served in India, who first suggested the native vengeance theory. Oddly enough, the Irish post office clerk's description of J. Hartigan *could* have applied to Major Jackson. Questioned, he claimed an alibi. He had been staying in Northamptonshire – 70 miles away. Major Jackson died in the 1930s.

On June 30, 1931, a postcard was delivered to Sir William Chevis' home. It bore a Belfast postmark and read: "It is a mystery they will never solve. J. Hartigan. Hooray."

The Secret of Bredon Hill

The shock of non-recognition of plain murder by medical men at GP level, and its alarmingly wide incidence, brought a shock of recognition to the readers of J. D. J. Harvard's Cambridge monograph, *The Detection of Secret Homicide*.

For the doctor who, failing to lift the bed sheet, certifies as due to natural causes the death of a patient whose throat is cut from ear to ear, there is small exoneration, but consider the perplexing case of the death in summertime on Bredon . . .

Not quite summertime, actually, for it was at 5.30 pm on May 9, 1939, that Harry Francis Dean, a solicitor's clerk, aged 49, recently promoted Borough Accountant in the Town Clerk's Department at Tewkesbury, Gloucestershire, laid down his pen, got up from his desk, and strode happily out into the old Tudor-timbered town.

Instead of going home, he boarded a bus. It put him down at the long, straggling village of Kemerton, Worcestershire. The silence and the dusk closing in about him, he made his way through the ever-deepening lanes, up a rough cart-track leading to the 1,000-foot summit of Bredon Hill.

For many years Dean had been weirdly fascinated by the looming hill, a kind of mini Ayers Rock – scene of the Australian dingo baby case – and, like it, surrounded by a menacing aura of ancient mysteries. In fact, he and his wife, Janet, were planning to put up a tent on the slopes of lonely Bredon and spend their next summer holiday there.

Oblivious of time and the shadows moving swiftly over the foot-lands, Harry Dean slogged his way up over a treacherous terrain of loose screes, towards where, on the hill's brow, stood the old Iron Age camp.

He was never seen alive again.

When, by midnight, her husband had not returned home, Janet Dean, frantic with worry, called the police. No, she did not know where her husband was – but she suspected. "He'll be somewhere on Bredon," she told them.

At 10.30 am on the following morning – Wednesday, May 10, 1939 – the village constable, PC Maund, of Bredon, accompanied by a search-party of Dean's friends, found his body. It was lying huddled at the foot of a boulder in an eerie hill-top quarry. They thought he must have fallen to his death off the boulder. But it was only 2 feet 6 inches high. *And Harry Dean had been strangled.*

There was an inquest in Bredon Village Hall. Dr Margaret Wilkinson, of Kemerton, who had examined the body *in situ* and later conducted a post-mortem, came up with a very odd finding. She said that in her opinion Dean had climbed on to the boulder to look around him in the quarry, slipped off it, and, in the course of falling – *less than three feet* – had been choked to death by his own collar and tie!

It was a theory as full of holes as a colander. To start with, the quarry floor, where medicinal herbs and wild flowers grew in profusion, was dead-flat, and the quarry was bounded on all sides by stone cliffs from 30 to 60 feet high. Dean had no reason to clamber on to a boulder. There was nothing to see.

Mr H. J. H. Saunders, coroner for South Worcestershire, recorded a verdict of death by misadventure. It was a finding that begged too many questions. The accidental death solution assumed the validity of suggestions which seem so very far-fetched.

Suicide? There was no evidence to support it. Dean was in good health, had no financial or other anxieties and no known enemies.

Murder? Again, no evidence. But . . . All of this area around Bredon has a long history of magic and witchcraft. Until quite recently corn-dollies – symbols of human sacrifice fertility rites – were carried on the harvest wains in the Vale of Bredon. And the strange hill forms one side of a four-sided figure of magical significance. Due East, 13 miles away, is Long Compton Hill, with its sinister circle of Rollright Stones, the centre of black magic in the sixteenth and seventeenth centuries. Away in another angle is Meon Hill, where, on St Valentine's night, 1945, an old hedger and ditcher, Charles Walton, of Lower Quinton, was found murdered. To this day there are those who will swear that it was a ritual killing – a cross cut on his chest, a pitchfork through his throat, his blood fertilising the earth. And they tell of the black dog, the hound of death, said to be encountered by those marked down by the dark forces. Charles Walton saw it as a boy.

The entrance to the quarry where Harry Dean's body was found is flanked by an ancient, grass-banked causeway, the sides and top of which are hummocked with still unopened barrows of the Stone Age. Not many yards away, across turf deep and immemorial, there stand, close to a copse of tall trees, two "magic" sentinels, the King and Queen Stones. Prehistoric in origin, they are said to have been the focus of ritual for thousands of years – and they still are. On the floor of the quarry of death, four lesser sentinels mark the cardinal points of the compass. It was at the base of the south-guarding one of these, a curiously sculpted, weathered and fissured boulder, that Dean's corpse was found.

The whisper – and, remember, it is only a primitive, rural whisper, coming on wings of superstition down the long flight of centuries –

is that by pure misfortunate chance Harry Dean strayed into the age-old magic killing ground on a very special night in the black calendar Walpurgis month of May.

Or would you be happier with the coroner's more conventional collar and tie solution?

With a parodist's apology to A. E. Housman:

> *The bells they sound on Bredon,*
> *Tolling his passing knell,*
> *Whose modus moribundi*
> *No living man can tell.*

Edmund Galley and the Burden of Innocence

If, in the best of all possible worlds, the sincere affirmations of all defendants could be believed, then, irrespective of the burden of proof, an additional burden – of guilt – would crook the back of the professionally cynical, doubting-Thomas prosecutor: the guilt of having contributed to a wrongful conviction.

Even in an imperfect world, there are exceptional cases – Beck, Slater, Meehan, and, less certainly, Edalji – where this has been so. But none carried the burden of innocence longer, and to more triumphant vindication, than Edmund Galley.

It is an epic which could have come straight from the Wessex of Hardy, set in its beginning at the Lammas-tide fair, held on two July days in 1835, at Moreton Hampstead, in the cream-thick depths of Devonshire, moving among the stalls and booths of pedlars, gypsies, petty chapmen and showmen, woven about such Hardyesque characters as "Buckingham Joe", "Dick Turpin", George Avery, the fair-booth wrestler, and his fancy woman, Elizabeth Harris.

The long shadows of the first day of the fair had fallen. Now, shortly after ten o'clock on the night of Thursday, July 16, full-fed after a good dinner at the White Hart, Moreton Hampstead, Jonathan May, prosperous farmer, aged 48, unmarried, but courting a lady near Tiverton, was riding his small bay nag homeward along the Exeter Road to his farm at Sowton Barton, nestling in a fold of hills near Dunsford.

The night was peaceful and starlit. A plump yellow cheese-slice moon shone. Just as he came abreast the first milestone, hard by the spring of Jacob's Well, Jonathan May was pounced upon. Two ruffian shadows came out of a high hedge, clubbed him from his horse, seized pocket-book and gold watch, and left him dying on the lonely highway.

Found there, pooled in his own life's blood, by a family party returning from the gaiety of the fair-lit town, he was carried back to the White Hart, where, next day, he died from his terrible head injuries. They buried him in Dunsford churchyard.

A hue and cry was raised. Out of a netful of vagrants and dubious itinerant strangers, suspicion fastened upon George Avery and Elizabeth Harris. They were arrested and later cleared of complicity in the murder. Then, in February, 1836, the woman swore that, hiding in a hedge, she had seen two men, nicknamed "Buckingham Joe" and "Dick Turpin", actually commit the crime.

"Buckingham Joe" *alias* Thomas Oliver was found in Dorchester Gaol, lying under charge of committing highway robberies. "Dick Turpin" was in London, lodged in Coldbath Fields House of Correction (a site now covered by Mount Pleasant sorting office), whither he had been committed for begging. He, too, was a travelling man, but nothing so bold as a toby, high or low. Unmarried, homeless, chronically peripatetic, wandering from fair to fair – mainly in Essex and Sussex, Surrey and Kent – he earned a shoddy living minding stalls at fairs, trading in broken-down horses, working the pea-and-thimble scam, and cheating at cards. No beauty, a fat little man with a tangled hedge of beard about a gap-toothed mouth, he totally lacked charisma, knew not brio, and was conspicuously short on "dash". For all of which reasons he was derisively dubbed "Dick Turpin". His real name was Edmund Galley.

Put up with Oliver at Exeter Assizes, 32-year-old Galley was found guilty along with Oliver, and sentenced to death by Baron John Williams. It mattered not that Galley, in a myriad agonised little speeches, protested innocence. Even the unparalleled interruption by Oliver of the actual pronouncement of sentence – "My Lord, this man had nothing to do with it. He is innocent" – did not stay the doom.

Before he hanged, Oliver named his accomplice, John Longley, a native of Biddenden, known variously as "The Kentish Youth", "Young Hero", and "Dick Turpin."

Edmund Galley did not hang. Reprieved, he was sent to the hulks at Woolwich, to await the discovery of Longley. But the alternative Dick Turpin was never run to earth, and, in 1839, Galley was transported, a convict in irons, to New South Wales.

Thirty-eight years now pass. In that time Galley laboured hard in a chain-gang, behaved well and docilely, qualified for his ticket of leave, earned his good-conduct sheet, and, freed, established himself as a shepherd.

Then, in May, 1877, 73-year-old Edmund Galley took up his pen and wrote a letter to a dead man – Moses Harvey, the solicitor who had prosecuted him. Harvey's son, also a solicitor, showed the letter, in which Galley not only still affirmed his innocence, but added the extraordinary intelligence that "The Kentish Youth", known now as John French, was living out there in the colony, having subsequently been transported for another offence.

Made public, Galley's letter caused a fluttering in high places. A young barrister; Alexander Cockburn, who had been in court at Exeter and heard and believed Galley's avowals, was now Lord Chief Justice. Thomas Latimer, editor and proprietor of the *Western Times*, gave Galley wide publicity. His cause was taken up in London. On July 25, 1879, the House of Commons unconditionally granted him a free pardon. Two years later, he was awarded £1,000 compensation as "the means of returning to this country at public expense."

He did not take a passage home. He had completed the only journey he wanted to . . . the journey to justice . . . to establish the innocence of Edmund Galley.

A Death in Broadmoor

Murderers come frequently to Broadmoor. Murder is a rarer visitant. Not always identifiable. Never doubt it, though, it has arrived, mysteriously, behind those high, red-brick Berkshire walls, beyond the bland, flat face of the main gate's "timeless" clock. So, too, has death at its most enigmatic.

It was a quiet night, insofar as any night is ever quiet in the crowded and tormented fastness of Broadmoor's cells and wards. Suddenly, just after 11 pm on Thursday, August 8, 1963, the clangour of the alarm-bell fragmented the uneasy stillness in Block 4. Medical staff, rushing into ward 3, found a young patient, John Berridge, lying unconscious on his bed. A fellow-inmate, Gordon Gylby, was crouching anxiously over him.

"I thought he was having a fit," he explained. "He came over sort of queer. When I turned him on to his side to ease him a bit, he took a few deep breaths and then went all quiet. I think he's dead."

Gylby was right. And within hours, the Broadmoor authorities were to be faced with what may well have been one of the most baffling mysteries in the long and bizarre history of their institution.

The bombshell came in a buff envelope. It was a pathologist's report. Berridge had died of cyanide poisoning. How could such a thing be possible in what was unquestionably one of the most carefully monitored special hospitals in Britain? To begin with, how could Berridge have got hold of cyanide? As was, indeed, later stated at the inquest, they did not even keep cyanide in the Broadmoor dispensary. Nevertheless, a lethal dose of the substance was subsequently recovered from the body of John Berridge.

Did someone smuggle it in to him from the outside? A possibility – for visitors were not searched. But who would willingly provide him with the means to destroy himself? That is if it *was* suicide – and the official view was that it most likely was, since the dead man was a known suicide risk, and was under close and constant supervision.

But there was one man, Berridge's closest friend and fellow-patient, Sidney Henry, who believed he knew the true answer to the riddle. Henry, 38 at the time, was himself an interesting character. For one thing, he claimed – and was supported in his claim by a former male nurse who knew him well – that he was sane. He had, he said, faked insanity for purposes of his own, rather overplayed his hand, and ended up in Broadmoor. He was, however, eventually discharged with a clean bill of health in February, 1964.

Naïve Henry was not. No *ingénu*, he had heard plenty of crazy tales during the long, lonely nights in Broadmoor. Talk, talk, talk. There isn't much else to do but talk when the day has died and the raucour of the rooks in the tall dark trees has faded away until another dawn. Most of the talk is the rambling maunderings of disordered minds, but Henry, listening at first with half an ear, became gradually, unwillingly, both ears cocked, convinced that Berridge was telling the truth.

Serving in the RAF, Berridge had been posted to Butzweilerhof

Airfield, West Germany. He had been approached there by a tall man of about 45, who, speaking perfect English, said he was a Communist agent and would buy any information. "He wanted to know things like squadron strengths, the kind of bombs we stocked at Butzweilerhof and anything I could find out about a secret radio-fuse for detonating H-bombs at predetermined heights. He also wanted to know about a bombing test we'd carried out involving smaller nuclear weapons.

"Well, I did what he asked. It was easy money. I also gave him impressions of all the keys to the bomb dump. Then one night, back in South Wales on leave, I did the most stupid thing I've ever done. I confided in my father, and he threatened to expose me."

Back to the world of extremely concrete fact. At 6 am on April 25, 1959, John Berridge took a 12-bore shotgun, went into his father and mother's bedroom and shot them as they slept. Found guilty but insane at Pembrokeshire Assizes, he was sentenced to be detained during Her Majesty's pleasure, and sent to Broadmoor. Like many an insane killer before him – Ronald True and Christiana Edmunds spring to mind – Berridge might have ended his days at a ripe old age in Broadmoor. But he was only 23 when he died – by cyanide.

Sidney Henry told me: "A few days before his death, John got a parcel, the first I'd ever known him to receive. And later he said: 'I've got a phial of cyanide in a bag of sugar that came in that parcel.' I tried to persuade him to throw the stuff away, even pretended I'd grassed him, but before I'd worked out what to do, he'd taken it and died."

Henry was adamant that it was the Russian Secret Service, who, knowing Berridge's suicidal tendencies, had posted to him the poison which would seal his lips for ever. "I remember, too, he'd had two or three letters. Usually we shared our letters, but he'd hidden them away. I think they told him to expect the parcel with the cyanide and what to do when he got it."

There is not, of course, and probably never can be now, any sure solution to this enigmatic death in Broadmoor. Very likely it was suicide. But, a nice point, does suicide shade into murder if someone knowingly slips the easy means into the ready hand?

Remember, Broadmoor is full to the gunnels with killers for pleasure. Some of them – such as Master Graham Frederick Young, despatched in July 1962, at the age of 14, for his own and everybody else's good (under s 66 Mental Health Act 1959), from the Bailey to Broadmoor, by Melford Stevenson J., who tried him in respect of the murder by poison of his stepmother, and took into the reckoning three other alleged poisoning attempts, and who, released prematurely in 1971, was to become the celebrated thallium poisoner – are absolute masters of the art of venenation.

Remember, too, the lush bushes of Broadmoor – and how richly the bruised leaves of the laurel furnish the lepidopterist's killing-bottle.

The Man from the Clay-pits

Arsenic was in the air. There are, it has been criminologically observed, fashions, modes, or epidemics in crime. Liverpool, for instance, in the mid-1880s endured a fashionable wave of garrotting, until Mr Justice Day, setting the cat (o'-nine-tails) among the thievish pigeons, suppressed the outbreak of Victorian muggings. Day J believed that the only appeal to muggers' reason lay "through their epidermis".

Arsenic, then, was in vogue, the modish style of despatch, in 1921, which was when, sandwiched between the cases of two allegedly arsenious solicitors – Harold Greenwood, of Kidwelly, who walked from the dock a free man in 1920, and Herbert Rowse Armstrong, of Hay, who, less fortunate, became in 1922 the only solicitor ever to be hanged for legal malpractice, *videlicet* diverting doses of weed-killer from the dandelions to, as he saw it, an equally deserving pest, Mrs Armstrong – death by arsenic came to Tregonnisey, in Cornwall.

The tale of Edward and Annie Black is one copied by life from what could well have been a D. H. Lawrence story – the ill-fated love of the man from the clay-pits and the older woman.

When, in August, 1914, 29-year-old Edward Ernest Black married the widow with the village sweet shop, he did all right for himself. The only impost he had to pay on the transaction was that his wife was 18 years his senior. In every other way the benefits were most satisfactory. The marriage gave him the get up and go to clamber out of the clay-pit, made him part-owner of the confectionary business, and encouraged him to set up on his own account – like Frederick Seddon – as an insurance agent. It also brought him a ten-year-old stepdaughter; Marion, to whom he became deeply attached.

Life in the home above the shop seems to have been as cosy and secure as it could be for any family during the anxious years of the First World War. So far as anybody knew – and hamlet gossip makes no secret of a thing if it suspects any different – Ted and Annie got on well enough. He seemed a considerate husband. A good man. Regular churchgoer with wife and daughter. Sang in the choir. Liked to go dancing – on his own. Well, Annie *was* a bit old, wasn't she?

There were, stepdaughter Marion later revealed, fairly frequent quarrels; always about money, which was tight in the Black household. And there were, according to Ted, Annie's painful bouts of indigestion. But on the heaped-up horizon of a seven years' marriage, these were all very small clouds.

It was on the morning of Saturday, October 31, 1921, that that chronic indigestion took a grotesque turn for the worse. After Ted had prepared for her a breakfast of cake, bread and butter and tea – shades of the disgusting Borden breakfast of warmed-up mutton broth and bananas and Edwin Bartlett's invalid menu of jugged hare, oyster and cake, large haddock – Annie was taken ill with gastritis.

Then . . . all of a sudden . . . the measured saraband of Cornish village life was sped dramatically into a tarantella of disasters . . .

November 3: Black dismissed by the insurance company. He has been fiddling.
November 8: Black vanishes from Tregonnisey.
November 11: Annie dies.

Dr Edwin Andrew, the Blacks' GP, doubtless with the recent Greenwood case in mind, suspected poisoning and refused to sign a death certificate. Post-mortem, followed by organ analysis, revealed arsenic in Annie's corpse. Only about ⅛th grain in the whole body – considerably less than a fatal 2 grains – but it could have been the residuum of a much larger dose. The kidneys, however, exhibited signs of long-standing disease, and Sir William Willcox, Home Office Medical Advisers's expert opinion postulated death as a consequence of debility from defective kidney function aggravated by poisoning.

Friends and neighbours began to remember . . . How Black, the very soul of attentiveness in his wife's illness, had always insisted on administering Dr Andrew's bismuth mixture to her himself . . . How she had complained that it was "peppery" and burned her throat, and soon after would start to vomit and have diarrhoea. Yet several doses given by friends caused no ill effects.

A 14-day police hunt ended on November 21 in Liverpool. At midnight a detective burst into a third-floor bedroom in Cashin's Temperance Hotel, Bell Street. The room was in darkness. Black was sitting, fully clothed, on the bed, both hands to his cut throat, blood pouring down through his fingers, an open pocket-knife lying on the floor.

Rushed to hospital, he recovered from his suicide act to stand trial at Bodmin Assizes in February, 1922. He was defended by John Lhind Pratt, brother of actor Boris Karloff.

A St Austell chemist testified to selling Black 2 ozs of arsenic "to kill rats" on October 29. He had duly signed the poison book. Black denied everything. Repudiated the signature as a forgery. His policy of bland denial extended, too, to a Red Cross instruction manual discovered by police in a search of his house. The corner of a page dealing with arsenic and other poisons was turned down. He denied all knowledge of its existence in his home since the war's end.

The defence was a difficult one to run: counsel did his best, emphasising absence of motive – no other woman; no question of gain (Annie left £61 2s 10d) – and suggested death due to gastritis, an epidemic of which had been sweeping Cornwall at the time. The Cornish jury took 40 minutes to find Black, the "foreigner" – born in Lancashire beyond the Tamar – guilty. He hanged at Exeter.

It was not, of course, incumbent upon the prosecution to establish motive, and the crime does indeed seem, as in the celebrated Wallace case, to be totally lacking in one obvious to the normal mind. But therein lies a whole universe of psychopathological possibility.

For whatever reason, or crazy lack of one, the likelihood is that Black did bring about his wife's demise. Poor Annie. Her idol from the pit had feet of clay.

A Cornish Tea

Penny-plain, middle-aged, country mouse ordinary – that is how, falling into the easy trap of assessment by appearance, one might have underrated the enigmatic Mrs Sarah Ann Hearn, dark sphinx at the heart of what Lord Birkett described as "the dramatic happenings in the peaceful village of Lewannick."

It was to this haven, 4½ miles south-west of the Cornish market-town of Launceston, that, in the autumn of 1925, Mrs Hearn brought her invalid sister, Lydia Mary ("Minnie") Everard.

Actually, it had been four years earlier that, for the sake of Minnie's health, she, Mrs Hearn, and their aunt, Mary Ann Everard, had come from Harrogate to North Hill, Cornwall. Aunt Mary had died and the sisters had moved into Trenhorne House, Lewannick.

Mrs Hearn's devotion to Minnie, a martyr to gastric troubles, was a local byword – the loving solicitude with which she nursed her, the way she spent hours reading heartening passages of scripture to her. But Minnie's condition deteriorated. She complained that the medicine Mrs Hearn was giving her was "too strong", that it was "going into her hands and legs". She told the doctor she thought she was being poisoned by it.

On July 21, 1930, she died of what Dr Charles Gibson certified as "chronic gastric catarrh and colitis." She was laid to rest in Lewannick churchyard alongside Aunt Mary.

Since their arrival, Sarah, usually called Annie, and Minnie had become very friendly with their neighbours, farmer William Thomas and his 47-year-old wife, Alice, who lived at Trenhorne Farm, "a couple of gunshots away". The Thomases knew the sisters were poor and showed them great kindness. Alice would make junkets and custards for Minnie, and William made a point of taking them out on car rides and picnics.

After Minnie's death, the Thomases kept in closer touch than ever with Sarah. On Saturday, October 18, they invited her to drive to Bude with them. At five o'clock they went to Littlejohn's Café, on Bellevue Hill, and ordered a pot of tea, bread and butter and cakes. Mrs Hearn produced some tinned salmon sandwishes and chocolate cake which she had brought as her contribution to the outing.

On the way home, Alice was dreadfully sick. William had also felt queasy and had a whisky at the Globe Hotel before leaving Bude. Back at the farm, Alice had to be helped up to bed. Dr Eric Saunders was called. He diagnosed food poisoning. Mrs Hearn agreed to stay at the farm to do the cooking and nurse Alice.

Gradually, Alice improved. Then, after lunch on November 2, she had a bad relapse. A consultant from Plymouth, Dr William Lister, pronounced it a case of arsenical poisoning. Admitted to Plymouth City Hospital, Alice died there on November 4. A post-mortem was performed and certain specimens were sent to the city analyst. Didn't that set village tongues a'wag. Arsenic . . . sandwiches . . . organs from the corpse being analysed . . . the way farmer Thomas hung around *her*.

There was a nasty scene at the funeral feast. Alice's brother, Roy Parsons, who'd never liked his brother-in-law and said outright that his sister and her husband had never got on together from the first, questioned Mrs Hearn sharply about those salmon sandwiches. In loud, hostile tones he told her: "This looks serious and will have to be seen into." It was after this that Mrs Hearn disappeared.

She wrote a note to William Thomas – "Goodbye. I'm going *out* if I can. I cannot forget that awful man and the things he said. I am *innocent*, *innocent*, but she is dead and it was my lunch she eat (*sic*). I cannot bear it. When I'm dead they will be sure I am guilty and you at least will be cleared."

Her black and white check coat was found on the cliffs at Looe. A shoe was washed up on the beach. But Mrs Hearn had not done away with herself. She was found in Torquay, calling herself Mrs Faithful, working as a cook-general.

Arsenic had been found in Alice Thomas; also in the exhumed bodies of Minnie and Aunt Mary. Mrs Hearn was arrested and brought to trial at Bodmin. She was defended by Mr Norman Birkett, KC, Mr Herbert du Parc, KC, with Mr (later Lord) Patrick Devlin as his junior, prosecuting.

The only arsenic traceable to Mrs Hearn was a weed-killer, mixed with blue dye, purchased in 1926. Birkett told the jury that if it had been used in the sandwiches the bread would have been stained a bright, mottled blue. On the other hand, at the Thomases' farm there was arsenic in sheep-dip and some Cooper's sheep worm tablets. They also contained copper, and traces of copper had been found in Alice's body.

But Birkett's trump-card was that in tin-mining Cornwall arsenic was an admitted heavy ingredient of the churchyard soil.

In the box, a small, smart figure, Mrs Hearn made a good but puzzling showing. She did not know her age. She had lost her marriage lines, but said she had wed Leonard Wilmot Hearn, a medical student, at a London register officer near Bedford Square. The marriage lasted two days. Four days after that, she read of

Hearn's death in a Harrogate paper. Investigation revealed no trace of this marriage at Somerset House. A photo of her husband proved to be one she had bought of Lieutenant Charles Stewart Vane-Tempest, great-grandson of the 3rd Marquess of Londonderry, killed in the Great War.

The Crown offered as motive, Mrs Hearn's desire to marry farmer Thomas. It was sheer speculation unsupported by an iota of evidence.

"I do not suppose," said Mr Justice Roche in his summing-up, "you have any doubt in your minds that the issue is now down to two people – Mrs Hearn and Mr Thomas. It lies between them. If, at the end of this case, you cannot say which it is, you ought to acquit Mrs Hearn." The jury could not. The jury did.

The Crown offered no evidence on the remaining indictment for the murder of Minnie.

Supported by a wardress and a nurse, Mrs Hearn stumbled out of the dock and back into the shadowed life from which she had so briefly and mysteriously emerged.

William Thomas died on December 14, 1949, on the remote Cornish farm at Broadoak, where he had led a lonely life ever since Alice's murder 19 years before.

The Elephant Man Murder Case

A sultry August night. A bright moon riding the clouds above London's Regent's Park. At 12.20 am Police-Constable Maynard Evans was treading his soft-footed beat around the Outer Circle. All was quiet. Just the distant rumble of the West End traffic; the occasional sharp night-cry of some caged beast in the nearby London Zoo.

Suddenly the constable stopped dead,. A different noise. Unmistakable. The sound of a human groaning. Constable Evans clambered over the fence separating the zoo from the park, and there, lying in a small, scooped-out hole at the back of the Tapir House, was a man. Dressed only in pyjama-jacket, vest and underpants, he seemed excited and hysterical as he pointed wildly to his foot. Evans saw that it was injured, and carried him to the office building at the main entrance. There, the man gabbled out a strange story – the story of a savage killing that was to make headlines as the Zoo Murder.

The man's name was San Dwe. He was Burmese and had come over to England the previous November as the mahout in charge of the sacred white elephant named Pa Wa. He shared living quarters – a couple of rooms above the Tapir House – with another elephant keeper, an Indian, Said Ali. That night – Saturday, August 25, 1928 – four men had, he said, burst into the room and attacked Said and himself with a pickaxe. He had managed to get out of the window, 30 feet up, injuring his foot as he hit the ground. He feared for Said. He was right to.

San Dwe was removed in an ambulance to the infirmary at St Pancras, where, after his foot, which was only very slightly injured, had been dressed, he was, as a temporary precautionary measure, placed in a mental ward.

PC Evans, accompanied by another policeman, PC Buzzy, Dr Geoffrey Vevers, the Zoo Superintendent, and his assistant, Mr C. H. Hicks, ran to the Tapir House. The door leading to the elephant men's apartment had been smashed in from the outside. In the dark and silent upstairs room a dreadful scene awaited them. The whole place was a shambles. The viciously battered body of Said Ali lay pooled in blood upon the bed. On the floor beside it, a bespattered pickaxe. And in the living-room was a bloodstained sledge-hammer. Between the sheet and mattress of Said's bed was a wallet containing £36, and a Post Office Savings book showing £60 deposit. There was, too, a wooden box of Said's, which had been broken open, and on top of it two bags of copper coins.

It hardly looked, as Detective Inspector Arthur Askew – the Yard officer called in – was quick to note, like robbery.

Said Ali's body was taken off to St Pancras mortuary, where a post-mortem would be carried out later by Sir Bernard Spilsbury. On the face of it, there was no reason to suspect San Dwe's story. But Askew, an old hand, was aware of a pulse of unease ticking away like a metronome at the back of his mind.

As he inched over the murder scene, the Inspector spotted the clue of the blood-stained door. There were deep indentations on the outside of the door. They fitted exactly the head of the sledge-hammer. BUT there were bloodstains in the marks. If the sledge-hammer had been used to burst the door open *before* the murder, how could there be blood in the indentations?

Conclusion: San Dwe faked the burst-in. Askew made a decision.

At Albany Street police station he charged 22-year-old San Dwe with the murder of 31-year-old Said Ali. Then he began to dig for a motive.

Askew, a shrewd man, and, after long years in the force no stranger to rule-of-thumb psychology, reckoned that the clue to the whole tragedy lay in the conflicting personalities of the two mahouts. He guessed – and it was an inspired guess – that jealousy and rivalry had flared up into murder.

Slowly, the facts came to light. Said had first come to England in 1922. He used to go home to Calcutta every winter, returning to the zoo each year for the June to September season. As Chief Elephant Keeper, Said Ali held supreme sway. He was paid £2 10s. (£2.50) a week, but, giving elephant rides to the children and showing off tricks he had taught his charges, he was able to earn as much as 30s. (£1.50) a week extra in tips.

Then, in November 1927, another mahout – San Dwe – arrived at the zoo. Said Ali was home in Calcutta at the time, so Dwe took charge of the elephants. He was soon giving elephant rides, pocketing the tips, and becoming a great favourite with the children, who nicknamed him 'Sandy Wee'.

Said Ali returned, as usual, in June, 1928. He took over the elephant rides – and the tips – and "Sandy Wee" was relegated to the sanatorium, to look after two baby elephants. That meant no tips. His wages were only £2 a week. San Dwe felt hard done by. He had a grievance. He began to brood. If Said Ali were out of the way . . . if he were to die . . . then he, San Dwe, would be back giving the joy-rides, piling up the pennies.

And so he hatched his plot. The plot that was to land him in the dock at the Old Bailey. Defended by Sir Henry Curtis-Bennett, Dwe came up before Swift J, who was angered by the fact that the police had detained San Dwe at the police station while making inquiries. The jury did not believe the story of the four mysterious assailants. San Dwe was found guilty and sentenced to death.

As he lay in the condemned cell at Pentonville, strange news came out of India. Pa Wa, the sacred white elephant, had died from an unknown malady in Calcutta just *two hours* before the slaying of Said Ali. The wise old Buddhist monks nodded their heads. Hadn't they said that the taking of Pa Wa out of his native land would bring a curse upon those responsible for the sacrilege? Well, now it had happened. Pa Wa's mahout was doomed.

In fact, San Dwe did not hang. His sentence was commuted to life imprisonment. The first document signed by Queen Mary as a Member of the Council of State during the illness of King George V, was the reprieve of San Dwe. When, in 1932, his sentence came up for revision, a special board released him, and San Dwe returned to Burma . . . and disappeared back into the elephant forest from which he had come.

The Maybrick Affair

All my life I have been haunted by the frail ghost of a celebrated Victorian murderess, or, more accurately, by what those great pioneers of psychical research, Gurney and Myers, called a "phantasm of the living", for Florence Elizabeth Maybrick did not die until 1941, 52 years after the murder of which she was judged guilty.

I apologise for, but cannot avoid, this personal gloss, for not only was my native city, Liverpool, the scene of the poisoning, and Battlecrease House, where Mrs Maybrick lived, a familiar place of my childhood, but the Maybricks themselves were frequent guests at my grandfather's dinner-table. He was, moreover, in their company at the Grand National on the day of the quarrel which is alleged to have precipitated the murder. My grandfather was convinced of Mrs Maybrick's innocence.

On July 27, 1881, Florrie Chandler, an 18-year-old Southern belle from Mobile, Alabama, married 42-year-old James Maybrick, a well-fleeced Liverpool cotton broker, chance-met on an Atlantic liner the previous year. In March, 1882, a son was born; a daughter in 1886. But 1887 brought shock. Florrie discovered that her loving husband had fathered five children to a mistress – two of them post-nuptially. An uneasy truce was struck, but Maybrick was banished forthwith from the matrimonial bed.

Frustrated, stalwartly refusing to pay hip service to Victorian sexual dualism, the young wife frolicked off to seek consolation in the ultimately unsatisfactory person of Alfred Brierley, a Cotton Exchange colleague of Jim's. The romantic apotheosis of their hole-and-corner relationship was a three-night dalliance at Flatman's Hotel in London, in March, 1889.

Florrie returned to Liverpool in time for the Grand National on March 29. The excursion was a fiasco. She and Jim had a bad quarrel on the course. It escalated after they got home. No gentleman, he blacked her eye. She was all set to walk out there and then, but was persuaded, for the sake of the children, to stay, and with the aid of the family doctor a sort of peace was patched up. End of domestic fracas. Or was it?

The calendar leaves tell the rest of the tale. In April, James Maybrick fell ill. For 15 days, from April 27 to May 11, he rode a sort of switch-back of sickness – now better, now worse, then better again, then worse than worse, finally . . . dead. Between these peaks and troughs, Florrie goes shopping for fly-papers – by the dozen. While Florrie soaks the fly-papers to extract the arsenic for, she will later say, a face lotion, James is drawing up a new will excluding his wife.

It was the children's nursemaid, Alice, well named Yapp, who reported to Florence's Judas friend, Mrs Briggs, seeing a dish of water-logged fly-papers in the mistress' bedroom. Matilda Briggs promptly wired to James' brother, Michael, in London: "Come at once. Strange things going on here."

Yapp's second contribution was a letter, entrusted to her by her mistress to post, and for which she had contrived an excuse for opening. Addressed to Brierley, it contained the ominous words, 'He is sick unto death,' which was not precisely how the doctors would have put it at that stage of James' illness.

Now Battlecrease House became a house of hate. Its air was stiff with unease. The brothers Maybrick – Michael and Edwin – entered in.

Doctors came and went. Nurses came and stayed. Diagnoses flickered between dyspepsia and gastro-enteritis. The flame of suspicion burned steadily. The flame of James Maybrick's life burnt low. On May 11, it went out.

Like hawks, the watchers pounced. As Florrie – isolated, confined, a prisoner of suspicion, to her room – lay in a swoon, they searched the house and came up with a packet labelled: "Arsenic: Poison for Cats." And, at a post-mortem, performed on James Maybrick on May 13, traces of arsenic were found.

The following day Mrs Maybrick was arrested, and, on July 31, put to her trial.

Under scrutiny in court, appearances crumbled about the edges, definitions merged, realities came into hard focus. James Maybrick lay revealed as a life-long hypochondriac dependent upon the solaces of patent nostrums, and a womaniser in permanent need of the sexual reassurement of arsenical aphrodisiac "pick-me-ups". "Stomach like a druggist's waste-pipe." He might or might not, according to differing medical expert witnesses, have succumbed to arsenic. Disregarding reasonable doubt, the jury found the adulterous wife guilty. Stephen J., who, contrary to a widely canvassed canard, conducted the trial with care and fairness, sentenced her to death. But Home Secretary Henry Matthews, who had previously bungled the case of Israel Lipski (1887), announced that "although the evidence leads clearly to the conclusion that the prisoner administered and attempted to administer arsenic to her husband, yet it does not wholly exclude a reasonable doubt whether his death was in fact caused by the administration of arsenic."

So Mrs Maybrick, judged guilty by Matthews of a crime with which she had never been charged, and found guilty by a jury of a murder which may never have been committed, went to prison, where, despite her counsel Sir Charles Russell's protests, she remained for 15 years. This anomaly is revealed now to have been the result of Queen Victoria's inflexible conviction of her guilt. The Queen's only regret, she wrote, was that "so wicked a woman should escape by a mere legal quibble . . . her sentence must never be further commuted." And as long as the old Queen lived it never was.

In 1904, Florence Maybrick was released and returned to America. For a while she received hand-outs and hospitality from relatives, friends, and sympathetic well-wishers, but, as the shadows lengthened and memories shortened, life became harsh, and she was forced to all manner of shifts for a living. She sold books door-to-door, worked as a domestic servant, cast herself upon the charity of the Salvation Army, and, interestingly, proved, like Lizzie Borden, light-fingered. At last, she secured a small state pension and ended up an eccentric recluse living, surrounded by cats, in a shack in the woods in Connecticut.

Undoubtedly Florence Maybrick was wrongfully convicted – but did she do it? Some months after her reprieve, a Liverpool chemist, Richard H. Aspinall, admitted that she had come to his shop in Leece Street and he had sold her two packets of poison labelled "Arsenic . . . For Cats".

The Glasgow Go-Cart Murder

The crime of Susan Newell is a puzzle – a complete, baffling puzzle. There is even a point of view which regards it as that criminous *rara avis*, murder *acte gratuite*. Permit me to place the circumstances before you for your consideration.

First, the murderess. Susan Newell. A tall, gaunt, but not unattractive woman, aged 30, described as being "of the tinker class". Previously married to a man named Macleod, she has an 8-year-old daughter, Janet, by him. She is married now to 33-year-old John Newell. The marriage is not going well. They quarrel incessantly. The Newells live in a single room in the flat occupied by a Mrs Young, at No 2 Newlands Street, Coatbridge. For this wretched and restricted living – existing – qualities they pay a rent of nine shillings a week.

The year is 1923. Coatbridge, in Lanarkshire, the industrial town once known as the Land of Fire, because of the red glow staining the sky from its countless iron and steel furnaces, is in the cold grip of the start of the Depression of the 'twenties. On the night of Monday, June 18, John and Susan Newell had yet another of their monumental quarrels. Twice she hit him on the head. The next day John Newell attended his brother's funeral. That evening when he returned, she started up a row with him again, and, having had just about all that he could take, he walked out on her. The following day – Wednesday – Mrs Young, who, after the Newells' three-week occupancy had also had just about all that she could take of her tenants' noisy mutual disenchantment, gave Susan notice to quit.

So much for the beguiling persona of the murderess. Now, let us take a look at the victim. Thirteen-year-old John Johnston was a good boy. He was a well thought of member of the Boys' Brigade and the Good Templars, a catch-'em-young temperance society. The eldest son in the family of five children of Robert Johnston, who was employed as a tube worker, he lived at No 23 Whifflet Street, Coatbridge.

Shortly after six o'clock on the evening of Wednesday, June 20, 1923, young John Johnston went out. He had had his tea and his sister said afterwards that she thought that he was going to the pictures. In fact, he met one of his school friends, who gave him some newspapers to sell. Perhaps this was how he was hoping to raise his picture money. It was between half past six and 7 pm when young John came up to No 2 Newlands Street with his bundle of newspapers. Mrs

Young, the landlady, heard Susan Newell invite the boy into her room; heard the door click tight-shut.

When, by 10.30 pm, there was no sign of young John at Whifflet Street, his father was angry. As the hours passed, anger turned to anxiety. Eventually, worried sick, Robert Johnston went to the police. All night the search went on.

Early on the morning of June 21 – the first day of summer – a lorry driver, Robert Dickson, saw a woman pushing an old-fashioned go-cart with a little girl sitting on top of a large bundle on it, trudging along Dundyvan Road, heading for Glasgow. He stopped and gave them a lift.

A Glasgow housewife looking out of her kitchen window saw a lorry pull up at Parkhead Cross, hard by Duke Street, and watched a woman and child alighting from it. She also saw a bundle fall on to the road from the go-cart as it was being lowered from the back of the lorry, and, to her horror, spotted a small booted foot protruding from one end of the bundle and saw a head topple from the other. The housewife and her sister followed the woman and child, and while one of them went off in search of a policeman, the other kept watch. The woman sneaked up a court, carrying the bundle on her back, deposited it at the foot of a tenement stair – precursive shades of the Jeannie Donald case of 1934 – then scaled a six-foot wall. On the far, hidden, side, she dropped straight into the arms of a waiting constable.

The woman was Susan Newell. The bundle contained the body of little Johnnie Johnston, trussed up like a chicken.

Susan Newell tried to blame the murder on her husband. Fortunately, he had an indisputable defence of alibi, and, early in the trial, was, on the Lord Justice-Clerk's direction, discharged.

What really happened within the four walls of that nightmarish little room we shall never know. We do know from the medical evidence that John Johnston was first hit on the head, probably with a poker, and then throttled. And we know that Mrs Newell tried to bury his body under the floorboards – and failed. In the High Court of Justiciary at Glasgow, Mrs Newell's little daughter told, in the piping child's voice of innocence, the story of the murder which she had witnessed, but, mercifully, not understood. Susan Newell's defence of insanity – one very rarely pleaded in Scotland – was dismissed, and on October 10, 1923, she became the first woman to be hanged in

Scotland since 1889, when the Stockbridge baby-farmer, Jessie King, was judicially terminated. Susan Newell was also the last.

Several notions of what constituted the motive for the murder have been floated. One is that Mrs Newell killed the boy for the sake of the ninepence that he *may* have had in his pocket, so that she could buy drink with it to alleviate the horror of her situation: penniless, deserted by her husband, being thrown out on the street by her landlady. Of course ninepence would not purchase much in the way of alleviation, but it would – and indeed did – buy a gill of cheap wine and a pint of beer for her. Another suggestion is that Susan Newell did it in order to "set up" her husband. A more charitable interpretation of the circumstances postulates accident and concealment. And, inevitably, a sexual motive was canvassed.

Certainly, there was nothing to support the plea of insanity. Professor John Glaister, widely experienced in lunacy, was specific: "I do not think the prisoner a person of unsound mind or that she is not perfectly competent to plead to the offence of which she is charged."

The prison doctor reported finding Mrs Newell "bright, ready to talk, respectful and well conducted." She did not strike him as being callous.

She never confessed her guilt. She went bravely to her death. She had always treated her child well and her last desire was that the little girl should be brought up in a convent.

It is a sad, inexplicable case, and one to which, one cannot help feeling, Mr Hangman Ellis' running knot was an ill-suited and ill-advised corrective.

A Pellet for the Preacher

As came still evening on, an assassins' quorum of six met in the June twilight to determine the disposal of an exceedingly tiresome man of the cloth.

Even as the bogey shadow of "Boney" was falling darkly over all England – for it was 1806 and across St George's Channel Napoleon was rampant – so was the fell shadow of the Reverend "Bonaparte" Parker, as the villagers of Oddingley spitefully nicknamed their hated parson, bringing anguish to the homely cottages, lanes, fields and farmsteads in the deep heart of rural Worcestershire.

It was all a matter of tithes. The demands and collecting methods of the Reverend George Parker were more akin to those of a mafioso enforcer than a homespun, beneficed cleric, meek and mild, of the early nineteenth century Church of England. The reverend gentleman's begging-bowl had become too razor-edged for comfort. Things had indeed come to so unpretty a pass that the local yokelry – farmers, tenants, smallholders, husbandmen, and Old Uncle Tom Cobbleigh and all – were rakes and hoes at ready red alert in bucolic revolt. Who, as their precursing regal better had once demanded, would free them from this turbulent priest?

A consortium of the principal debtors – i.e. the most successful farmers, of this grasping parson, so unashamedly intent upon laying up for himself treasure on earth, was formed. The six conspirators in chief, the action men of the parish – Captain Samuel Evans, the brothers John and William Barnett, Thomas Clewes, John Marshall, and George Bankes – had met at The Plough, Tibberton, and passing a unanimous vote against his animus, had raised their glasses and drunk a left-handed toast: "Death to the Bonaparte of Oddingley." Pursuing the Mafia metaphor, a hit man was sought, found and hired.

At five o'clock on Tuesday evening, June 24, Midsummer day, 1806, a shot scattered rising flocks of birds and laid flat the black target-bird in parson's plumage. The Reverend George Parker, gone up to tend his cows, lay dying, murdered upon the meadow-grass of his own field, a gunshot wound on the right side, his coat still smouldering from the gun wadding, three wounds to the head, his life leaking away, red on green, through main arteries pierced by myriad small shot.

The identity of the gunman who had murdered the 43-year-old clergyman did not remain long a secret. Sharp country eyes had glimpsed the contract killer as he fled the scene of the shooting. His name was Richard Hemming. He was 34. A small jobbing carpenter and wheelwright by trade, he lived in Droitwich.

Men were despatched to apprehend him. He was nowhere to be found. Luck, they decided, had been on his side. Before they closed the cordon he had escaped, probably to America.

The years passed. Quaffing their mugs of ale and cider in the taprooms of old country inns and public-houses the locals would mull over the Oddingley murder, wonder aloud whatever became of Dick

Hemming. It was his brother-in-law, Charles Burton – Hemming had married his sister, Elizabeth Burton – who was destined to find the answer to the pastoral conundrum . . . at 4 pm on Thursday, January 21, 1830, twenty-four years on. Burton was taking down a barn at Netherwood Farm, which had once belonged to Thomas Clewes, for the new owner, Mr Howard. Removing the foundations, he found a human skeleton. It was subsequently identified as that of Richard Hemming by his widow – now Mrs Newbury. She recognised a distinctively marked carpenter's rule which he had always carried in his breeches' pocket and also a pair of shoes. Even more interesting was the fact that the man had obviously been murdered.

So . . . one conundrum solved . . . only to raise another: who murdered the murderer? Who hit the hit man?

The truth emerged at Worcester Lent Assizes, March 11, 1830, where, before Mr Justice Littledale, Thomas Clewes, George Bankes and John Barnett, the surviving trio from the sextet of sinners who had conspired to the lethal unfrocking of Parson Parker, were put up. Thomas Clewes was the one who had confessed.

It was about seven o'clock in the morning of the day after the shooting of "Bonaparte" Parker that George Bankes had, said Clewes, called to tell him that they had the vanished Hemmings safely hidden away at Captain Evans' house. Later, Clewes met Captain Evans, who told him that he had ordered Hemming to take shelter in his (Clewes') barn. At 11 o'clock that night Clewes had met Evans, Bankes, a man named James Taylor, and Hemming in the barn, and witnessed the murder of Hemming by Taylor, who hit him two or three blows on the head "with a blood-stick". Taylor and the Captain then buried the body under the floor of the barn.

Mr Curwood, prosecuting, commented: "Gentlemen, the whole of this confession must be given to you, but you are not bound to believe the whole of it. You may believe the prisoner when he says he was present, but you are not compelled to credit his statement when he attempts to explain away his presence. Gentlemen, I may here remark to you that in the whole course of my practice I never knew an accessory who did not, according to his statement, fill a very insignificant part of the transaction. He never confesses to being the person who struck the blow or gave the poison."

Littledale J., however, took a different view. He told the jury: "You will observe that, in the evidence before you, the confession of

Clewes forms the leading feature. In this he confesses himself a criminal amenable to the law – he confesses himself an accessory after the fact; but it does not seem that he knew anything of the intention of murdering Hemming until the fatal blow was struck; and, Gentlemen, the rule of law is, that when you take a criminal's confession, you must take the whole of it as it stands, unless you have evidence to contradict any part of it, or evidence to supply its deficiencies. But here what have you to supply?"

The only thing which, in the circumstances, the jury had to supply was a verdict of not guilty, which they duly supplied.

Mr Greenacre's Unmerry Christmas

Mr James Greenacre, of Camberwell, south east London, spent Christmas Day, 1836, carving up not the turkey but the mortal remains of his late betrothed, Hannah Brown.

The aforesaid Mr Greenacre's premature New Year's resolution being to dispose of that lady piecemeal over as many distant points of the compass as he could conveniently contrive, forth he sallied with the absolute minimum of delay upon his macabre Yuletide odyssey. An innocuous plum-pudding-shaped bundle clasped on his lap, he rode the horse-bus to Gracechurch Street in the City, haphazardly changed omnibuses, and proceeded to the Regent's Canal, Mile End. And there, beside the Stepney Lock, dropped into the murky water the content of his silk-handkerchief-wrapped globular bundle – the severed head of Hannah Brown. A grim joke apocryphally reports that when Greenacre inquired of the bus conductor the fare, he replied "sixpence a head."

On his next perambulation Mr Greenacre disembarrassed himself of Hannah's lower limbs, planting them in an osier-bed in the vicinity of Cold Harbour Lane, Camberwell. Her torso, stuffed into a sack, he humped upon his back, and on the tail-board of an innocently obliging carrier's cart, as far as the Elephant and Castle public-house at Newington, whence he drove in a hackney-cab to the Pineapple Gate on the Edgware Road, there abandoning his encumbrance behind a large paving-stone which stood upright amidst the building materials being employed in the construction of some new dwellings called the Canterbury Villas.

These three gruesome deposits being within the course of the six weeks ensuing discovered by, respectively, an appalled lock-keeper, a startled osier, a badly shaken bricklayer, the police set to work to reassemble the cadaver and put a name to it. On March 20, 1837, there stepped forward a Mr Gay, a broker resident in Goodge Street, Tottenham Court Road, who, anxious about his sister, who had been missing from her lodgings at 45 Union Street, since Christmas, asked if he might see the head – which had been prudently preserved in spirits at the Paddington Workhouse – as it might prove to be the very personal property of his widowed sister, Hannah.

Indeed it was. Thus it came out that the Widow Brown had lost her head, in another sense, to the blandishments of a polished cabinet-maker by the name of Greenacre.

A strange one this Greenacre. Truly a ladies' man of parts. Taking his marital history would have gladdened the diagnostic heart of any self-respecting psychiatrist. Born: Norfolk, 1785. Aged 19, commenced business as a wholesale grocer and tea-dealer in London, and married the daughter of Charles Ware, keeper to the Crown and Anchor tavern, Woolwich. She died suddenly. Greenacre married again, the daughter of John Romford, an Essex farmer. She bore him two children and died of a brain fever. His third wife, the *ci-devant* Miss Simmonds of Bermondsey, presented him with seven children, then died of the cholera three weeks after Greenacre's departure for New York, where he planned to start a new business as a carpenter. This venture failed. He returned from America. And that was when he met Mrs Hannah Brown, a widowed washerwoman in her late forties. The couple had bruited it abroad that they were to be married at St Giles' Church, Camberwell, on Boxing Day, and on Christmas Eve, his intended, quitting her lodgings, had accompanied Greenacre to where he lodged, in Carpenter's Buildings, situated close to where Bethwin Road runs today, in Camberwell. There they celebrated the spirit of the festive season, quoffing immoderately, and inflammatorily as it transpired, tea laced with rum. Then she – and he – had vanished.

Sound police work tracked Greenacre down to No 1 St Alban's Place, Kennington Road, where he was currently sharing domestic bliss with the latest risen Venus on his horizon, Mrs Sarah Gale, *circa* 35, and her 4-year-old child. James and Sarah were in bed. Greenacre shouted out to the callers – Inspector Feltham and a police constable – to wait while he found the tinder-box, but, hearing Greenacre groping about. Feltham decided to run no risks and burst into the room. He found in Greenacre's pocket-book two pawnbroker's tickets for silk gowns. Discovered also were two pawn-tickets for shoes, Hannah Brown's earrings, and a bloodstained handkerchief. The pair were promptly whisked away to Paddington police office. Greenacre attempted to strangle himself with his pocket-handkerchief, but survived for Calcraft to make a much neater job of it.

James Greenacre claimed that Hannah Brown's death was an accident. He had taken a rolling-pin to her on learning that the three or four hundred pounds' worth of property of which she had boasted ownership was estate no more real than the rich personalty which *he* had confided to her would be his contribution to the prosperity of their union. A spirited tussle ensued. He had struck her, and to his horror, she fell dead. Surely an over harsh penalty for false pretences!

The trial of Greenacre and Gale opened before Tindal, LCJ (Common Pleas), Coleridge J and Coltman J at the Central Criminal Court on April 10, 1837. It lasted two days. Greenacre was sentenced to hang. Gale was ordered to be transported beyond the sea for the term of her natural life.

The English have always nurtured a very proper horror and loathing of murders in which the victim is mutilated *post-mortem*, and for this reason Greenacre's name became the universal synonym for contempt and detestation – a name, like that of "Boney" (Napoleon) a few years before, and Jack the Ripper, a few decades later, with which to scare the otherwise unbiddable. But there is an end to all things, even ignominy and the law's delays, and with the passage of the years Greenacre's name has ceased to raise echoes of ill-repute. Indeed, its last quaint usage was among stevedores in the London docks. When, by mischance of course, a packing case happened to fall and split open and the soft fruits rolled – like heads – each such object, a to be picked up and pocketed "perk", was referred to as "a Greenacre".

The Accusant Ghost of Cock Lane

A small, inexplicable scratching in the wainscotting of a house in Cock Lane, a narrow thoroughfare within the purlieus of Smithfield and the parish of the tolling of the hanging bell of Newgate Prison, was the modest herald of a curious case which was to blossom into a classic eighteenth-century enigma.

All London was set, literally, by the ears by the escalating furore of rappings, crashings, and scratchings perpetrated by an alleged spirit entity nicknamed "Scratching Fanny".

No less a personage than Dr Samuel Johnson, the Great Cham himself, was to set forth upon intrepid investigation, and, in due course, pronounce the prankish poltergeist a great sham, and the whole paradox was to culminate in court, with a man accused of murder by a ghost, defending his good repute by counter-charging criminal conspiracy.

To unfold the origami-complex pattern of this "Cock Lane Tale"* we must travel first to Norfolk. There, in 1758, dwelt one William Kent, innkeeper and owner of the post office at Stoke Ferry, who, the previous year, had wed Elizabeth Lynes, daughter of a prosperous Norfolk grocer. Within 12 months she died in childbirth. Her sister, Fanny, who had come to tend her during her confinement, stayed on to look after the child, who soon died, and she remained with the widower.

Predictably, they fell in love. Marriage was, however, out of the question. A deceased wife's sister came within the forbidden degrees of consanguinity. They decided to live together as man and wife, and, in October, 1759, took lodgings in the Cock Lane home of Richard Parsons, officiating clerk of the church of St Sepulchre without Newgate.

In November, Kent had to attend a wedding in the country. While he was away, Elizabeth, Richard Parson's ten-year-old daughter, kept Fanny company, sharing her bed. And that was when, for the first time, the eerie scratchings and knockings were heard.

Shortly after William's return, the Kents left Cock Lane. Not only was Fanny by now a good six months pregnant and needing a house of her own, but bad feelings had blown up between Kent, who had lent Parsons, a feckless drunkard, 12 guineas, and Parsons, who, having failed to make any effort at repayment, had been informed that the matter was in the hands of Kent's lawyer.

On February 2, 1760, Fanny died, at the new house in Bartlet's

---

*The term a "Cock Lane Tale" came to have the same meaning and usage as "cock and bull story" – a long, incredible yarn.

Court, Clerkenwell, of smallpox. She was buried in the vault of St John's, Clerkenwell. In the course of the ensuing year William Kent did his best to put his twice shattered life back together. He set up in business as a stockbroker. He married again.

Meanwhile, at the house in Cock Lane the noisy manifestations had, after a lull, broken out afresh, the unquiet spirit which seemed to focus on and around the bed of little Elizabeth Parsons proving more boisterous than ever. Parsons called in a carpenter to dismantle the wainscotting. No down-to-earth explanation there. Turning his eyelids heavenwards, he humbly prayed the Reverend John Moore, assistant preacher at St Sepulchre's, to bring his spiritual expertise to bear. A code of taps was introduced – one for yes, two for no, a scratching for displeasure. By a system of leading questions, the entity was induced to state that it was the spirit of Fanny, that her "husband" had poisoned her with red arsenic administered in purl (a popular restorative infusion of bitter herbs and ale or beer), and that she hoped he would hang! The spirit knocking while Fanny was yet alive was said to have been that of her sister, Elizabeth, warning her against Kent.

It was a scenario which did not entirely displease the grudge-nurturing Parsons, and one, moreover, which it was his pleasure to bruit abroad. Neither was it exactly anathema to Fanny's brothers and sisters, who were disputatious regarding her will, in which she had devised all – bar half-a-crown apiece to them – to William. A caveat was entered to prevent Kent from proving the will in Doctors' Commons, but it stood legally invulnerable.

It was not until January, 1762, that Kent saw an item in a newspaper, the *Public Ledger*, and became aware of the "phantastic" accusation being levelled against him. Horrified by the public scandal, he went promptly to attend a séance at Cock Lane, and hearing the accusations rapped out, shouted angrily: "Thou art a lying spirit!"

In February, 1762, the Reverend Stephen Aldrich, Rector of St John's, Clerkenwell, persuaded Parsons to allow his daughter, Elizabeth, to come to his vicarage to be tested by an ad hoc committee of learned investigators, including Dr Johnson. Fanny did not manifest. She had, however, previously promised to rap evidentially on her own coffin if, at 1 am, the investigators adjourned to St John's vault. They did. She didn't. Then . . . little Elizabeth was caught in the act of secreting a sounding-board of wood in her bed. The Cock Lane Ghost collapsed amid widely sounding charges of fraud.

To complete his already partial vindication, William Kent brought, on July 10, 1762, the affair to the Court of King's Bench at the Guildhall. On an information laid against them by William Kent, the Reverend John Moore, Richard Parsons, Mrs Parsons, Mary Frazer (who had acted as entrepreneurial "medium" at Cock Lane), and Richard James (responsible for the prejudicial insertions in the *Public Ledger*) were charged with a conspiracy to take away Kent's life by charging him with the murder of Frances Lynes. The trial judge, Lord Mansfield, summed up for 90 minutes. The jury took a quarter of an hour to find all the defendants guilty. Moore and James were ordered to pay £588 to Mr Kent. Richard Parsons was sentenced to two years imprisonment and three spells in the pillory. Mrs Parsons got one year, and Mary Frazer six months.

Parsons protested to the end that the knockings were genuine, and it must in all fairness be said that posterity has come to recognise that the Cock Lane manifestations did unquestionably bear the character-istic stigmata of similar outbreaks of poltergeistic infestation subse-quently held by serious investigators of psychic phenomena to display the diagnostic hall-marks of paranormality.

Lancaster Castle's Death Curse

Murder in Lancaster Castle. The phrase has a fine mediaeval ring to it, scattering about the mind images of the knife behind the arras, the poison chalice. In fact, the beefsteak of Old England did figure sinisterly in the mystery play, but it was fatally consumed in the Year of Our Lord One Thousand Nine Hundred and Eleven – the historic pageant of unnatural deaths, three in a period of eight months, afflicting the members of the Bingham family, occupants of the castle, but in a latter-day menial capacity.

Head of the clan, William Hodgson Bingham, a 73-year-old widower with several children, had, since the 1870s, been the official resident custodian, caretaker, and guide to the gaunt Norman castle on the hill. A healthy, spry septuagenarian, the suddenness of his collapse with vomiting and diarrhoea on Sunday, January 22, 1911, and death the following day came as a great shock. It was certified as being due to old age, gastric and intestinal catarrh, and heart failure.

For the second time in ten weeks the family put on mourning. Old William's daughter, Annie, aged 30, had passed away on November 12, 1910, of "hysteria and cerebral congestion".

Like an hereditary office, the position of keeper of the castle passed to old William's son, James. A bachelor, he invited his half-sister, Margaret, previously matron of a home for the subnormal in Hull, to come and keep house for him. She came – and within days was dead. Her death, on July 23, following a four-day illness similar in pattern to that of old William, was ascribed to a brain tumour.

Standing in dire need of a new housekeeper, James, not without some misgivings, asked his 29-year-old sister, Edith, if she would take on the job. She agreed. And brother James' worst fears were confirmed.

Edith made a real hash of it. That she was slightly mentally subnormal and only partially literate into the bargain did not help, but the real trouble was her attitude. She was very bolshy, constantly quarrelling with James and upsetting him by the late hours she kept with her boyfriend Charlie Emerson. Household affairs ran, in consequence, anything but smoothly.

A couple of weeks of it was about as much as James could stomach. Early in August, he engaged a Mrs Cox Walker to come and work for him as a paid housekeeper. She was to start on Monday, August 14.

On Saturday, August 12, two days before Mrs Cox Walker was due to take up her duties, James Bingham, while showing a group of visitors around the castle, suddenly doubled up in excruciating pain, followed by violent sickness and diarrhoea. His GP, Dr J. W. McIntosh, made a very shrewd tentative diagnosis of arsenical poisoning. James Henry Bingham died on August 15, 1911.

Four of them dead up at the castle in a ten-month! Superstitious Lancashire folk nudged and nodded. Looked like some ancient curse coming home to roost up there, didn't it?

More pragmatic folk were reaching more pragmatic conclusions. Analyses of vomited material, and of various organs, tissues and fluid samples taken at post-mortem, evidenced the presence of the residuum of an heroic dose of arsenic. The coroner was informed.

At the subsequent inquest it was disclosed that less than an hour before he was taken ill, James ate some beefsteak which he had bought in the town as a treat for himself. It was cooked for him by

Edith. No one else ate any of the meat. It was further disclosed that several tins of a powerful arsenical weed-killer, Acme, used in the castle grounds, had been found in one of the Bingham household cupboards. Clearly the notion entered the jury's heads that Edith – none too bright, was she? – might have poisoned her brother in a fit of crazy pique at her ousting as *châtelaine*.

The inquest was adjourned while a Home Office order for the exhumation of the three previous Bingham corpses was obtained and put into effect.

Only the body of Annie, the first-dead, was free of arsenic.

At the resumed inquest, another of Edith's brothers, William Edward Bingham, fuelled the jury's embryo suspicions – Edith had lived in Lancaster Castle all her life; she had been a source of trouble for some years, getting into debt, telling lies, leaving the house untidy.

That did it. Guilty. At the close of Coroner Neville Holden's inquest on August 30, Edith Agnes Bingham was arrested on the coroner's warrant.

Brought up before Mr Justice Avory at Lancaster Assizes in Lancaster Castle on October 27, 1911, she was charged with triple murder. The charge of murdering her brother, James, was proceeded with. There was circumstantial evidence. But there were also large, materially significant areas of doubt. A charwoman who had witnessed the cooking of James' beefsteak testified to seeing nothing in the least suspicious. Edith's boyfriend who, incidentally, denied that they had ever been actually engaged, told the Court that she had lied to him, saying that she owned three houses and had had a lot of property left to her by her father.

The prisoner's comportment in the dock displayed great distress. She was deathly pale. She moaned. She wept hysterically. She sank from her chair, collapsed, and had to be carried from the court.

Things could, unquestionably, be made to look black for her, but where was the motive? She stood – a good point to put to a practically-headed Lancastrian jury – only to lose by the deaths of her relatives.

Avory J., belying his reputation as the Acid Drop, summed up in the accused's favour. It was not easy to see how the prisoner could have introduced poison into Margaret Bingham's food, the same food eaten by others of the household, at breakfast on July 19. There was no evidence that her father had food prepared by her just before he was taken fatally ill. There was ample testimony that she was deeply distressed when the deaths took place.

Taking their cue from the judge, the jury, absent a mere 20 minutes, decided at the end of the three-day trial that Edith Agnes Bingham was innocent. The Crown offered no evidence on either of the two remaining indictments. Still weeping, the acquitted Miss Bingham was led from the court, to join the secret poisoner of Lancaster Castle in the long shade.

Murder in the Temple

Old-fashioned lawyers' London – North, South, East and just, West of Temple Bar. Rich in historic fact and what we may, in this context, call legal fictions. Pope's Court, lying once between Bell Yard and Chancery Lan, was the locus of the Sherlock Holmes adventure "The Red-Headed League". It was in Bell Yard itself that Mrs Lovett had her pie-shop, and by St Dunstan's round the corner that her supplier, Mr Sweeney Todd, cut hair and throats. It is even said that Jack the Ripper rested at No. 9 King's Bench Walk. More certainly, murder has been known within the precincts of the Temple itself.

The scene of the visitation – blasted by the bombs of the Second World War – was Tanfield Court, a brick and mortar monument to Sir Lawrence Tanfield, a somewhat tarnished judge of the days of James I. Put the clock back two centuries. It is the stormy night of February 3, 1733. No one is stirring abroad, save watchmen crying the hour. In her chambers in Tanfield Court sits Mrs Lydia Duncomb, attended by her two servants, Elizabeth Harrison, in her sixties, the cook, and 17-year-old Ann Price, the housemaid. Mrs Duncomb, some 80 years of age, had no connection with the law. It is true that the Temple and other Inns of Court were built to accommodate lawyers alone, but it was also true that, consequent upon the fashion of men of law to take private houses, wherein they could at one and the same time and place practise their vocation and raise their families, chambers came to be neglected; whereat, the landlords, men of practical practise, considering tenants of no legal standing preferable to no standing tenants at all, threw chambers' portals open to all stout purse owners. There was, however, upon each set of chambers a kind of entail. This was the laundress. She was to the Inns of Court what the scout is to Oxford and the gyp to Cambridge, serving perhaps, six, eight, or even ten, sets of chambers. She would daily attend each single gentleman, making his bed, and, from time to time, sweeping and generally tidying up the rooms.

One of these laundresses was a 22-year-old young woman, Sarah Malcolm. It is with her that we are concerned. The laundresses were necessarily a band of tried and trusty women, for they had always the keys of the chambers which, almost in the capacity of caretakers, they looked after, and must needs respect the law of private ownership. That is not to say that there were no small pilferings of inconsiderable and unconsidered trifles, but there were certainly no gross appropriations and permanent deprivals; nothing to imperil the security of tenure of a position which, with the comfortable additional profit of washing, mending, and so on, could, extending over, say, ten sets, yield a handsome yearly hundred pounds. Compare that with the average female servant's wage in London of ten pounds a year. Sarah Malcolm, coming from good stock, her father having been a man of some property in the county of Durham, might have been considered a suitable candidate for trust, but she was actually severely flawed. Circumstances conspiring in one way and another against her, she found herself cut off from her family and was obliged to go into service to earn a livelihood. These arrangements did not prosper, and from living and serving with reputable families, she sank to the abysmal level of servant at the notorious low public-house, the Black Horse, in Boswell Court, near Temple Bar. It was there, unfortunately for her, that she fell in with lethally bad company. These fatal companions were Mrs Mary Tracy, a woman of, in the quaint parlance of the 18th century, "light character", and the brothers Alexander – Thomas and James. With one of these young men Sarah fancied herself in love, and casting a nuptial eye upon him, began to scheme as to where she might acquire the purchase money that would tempt him into a gilded cage of matrimony. By malevolent happenstance it was at this precise "dangerous corner" that Sarah was recommended as a laundress.

Among her charges was old Mrs Duncomb. She was reputedly very rich. The wheels in Sarah Malcolm's lovesick brain began to turn. A plot was hatched. Mary Tracy and the Alexander brothers met with her at Cheapside and agreed to carry out a robbery.

Between 7 and 8 pm on the Saturday evening (February 3) Sarah called in at Tanfield Court to see Elizabeth Harrison, who was ill. She stayed with her, spying out the land, for a short time. Then, later, Sarah, Mary, Tom, and James all went round to Tanfield Court. Making their way up the stairs, they met Ann Price, going out to fetch a mug of milk to make a sack-posset.

Said Sarah: "I know the chambers door is left ajar because the old maid is ill and can't get up to let the young maid in when she comes back." James Alexander went in, and hid under the bed. Sarah and the others sat on Mrs Duncomb's stair . . . waiting . . . listening . . . still and silent as statues in the dark, as the watchman cried the hours. At 12 o'clock they heard another tenant, Mr Knight, come in, and shut his chambers door. About 2 am another gentleman came to light his candle from the watchman. Shortly after, came the stealthy sound of Mrs Duncomb's door inching open. James Alexander peered out. "Now is the time," he said. Time for the slaughter. Next afternoon, Mrs Duncomb and Betty Harrison were discovered strangled in their beds, and the girl Price with her throat cut from ear to ear.

The hue and cry went up. Suspicion fixed on Sarah Malcolm when a silver tankard, its handle covered with fresh blood, and a quantity of linen were found concealed in a close-stool in the chambers of Mr Kerril, one of Sarah's employers. She was arrested, and when taken to Newgate tried to bribe a turnkey, Roger Johnson, who, on searching her, had found a bag containing a large sum of money concealed under her hair At her trial, Sarah – whose portrait was painted by Hogarth – freely acknowledged that she and Mary Tracy had planned and contrived the robbery, but she insisted then, and to the very moment when Jack Ketch's necklace encircled her fair throat on the scaffold, at the Fleet Street end of Mitre Court on the morning of March 7, 1733, that hers was not one of the black shadows that slipped through Mrs Duncomb's door to emerge bloodied by murder in the red eye of the dawn.

The Golden Mile Murder

I remember Alfred Merrifield as a bemused old man in a somewhat overripe caravan at Peel Corner, by Blackpool. Bland, with the resigned bafflement of the non-coping deaf, he faced alone a dauntingly bleak future. His wife, a Salvation Army lass, Louisa May, had just been hanged for varying an old lady's invalid diet with off-the-menu helpings of phosphoric rat poison. He was about to step into the black limelight as the star attraction of a Golden Mile galanty show – "Roll up! Roll up! See the murderess' husband!"

"The old bugger would have had me next," he told me, with rather more candour than uxorial affection. Not a pretty pair.

It was an advertisement in the *Blackpool Evening Gazette* of March 10, 1953, that introduced the Merrifields to 79-year-old Sarah Ann Ricketts. She was seeking domestic help and offered in return accommodation in her attractive modern bungalow – The Homestead, 339 Devonshire Road, on Blackpool's North Shore. And, out of more than 50 applicants, it had to be Louisa Merrifield, aged 46, and her 70-year-old third husband, Alfred, whom it was her misfortune to choose. A rackety pair – they had had more than 20 domestic, caretaking, and miscellaneous odd jobs in Blackpool over the past year or so – they moved in, all their worldly goods in five cheap fibre suitcases, on March 12. Beware the Ides of March.

All was, at first, sweetness and light. So delighted, indeed, was Mrs Ricketts with her new housekeeper-companions that, after a mere 12 days, she unwisely confided her intent to devise her bungalow to them.

"I'm looking after them that look after me," she said.

The honeymoon period did not last long. Mrs Ricketts, her true colours revealed, proved a querulous, difficult mistress. Both her husbands had committed suicide, gassing themselves in the happy homestead where the widow still lived. Four feet eight inches of sheer vitriol when the turn took her, her sharp temper was not improved by a discomfort which was the legacy of several strokes, or the comfort she found in alcohol – therapy resorted to with greater gusto than good sense.

In consequence of her disagreeable demeanour, she had fallen out with her two daughters, and could boast few, if any, friends.

Abroad about the windy plazas of breezy Blackpool on March 26, a buoyant, bubbling Mrs Merrifield enthusiastically hailed a chance-met old friend, David Brindley. "I've had a bit of good luck," she told him. "Where I've been living an old lady has died and left me a bungalow worth about £3,000."

"Coming events cast their shadows before," observes Thomas Campbell, the Scottish poet. On March 26, however, Mrs Ricketts' innings still had 21 days to run. Continuing in prophetic vein, fortune's favourite wrote, on March 31, to a former employer, Mrs Lowe: "I got a nice job nursing an old lady and she left me a lovely little bungalow, and thank God for it. So you see, love, all comes right in the end." The end had not, of course, yet come for Mrs Ricketts. But it was drawing nigh.

By now the discord between the lady of the house and her ministering household angels were uncomfortably apparent. Not only seabreezes rattled the shutters.

Ever a chatty Lancashire body, Mrs Merrifield struck up a bus stop conversation with a total stranger, confiding that she had found her husband in bed with Mrs Ricketts. "If it goes on again I'll poison the old —— and him as well." That was on April 13. Did she, that night, suit the deed to the word? Mrs Ricketts' bedside table was ritually set out by the housekeeper companions – one small bottle of rum, one small bottle of brandy, a pint glass of water, a packet of Aspirins and a carton of stomach powders. Before dawn crept up over the water beyond the promenade, Sarah Ann Ricketts' doom had been pronounced. She was dying of a dose of Rodine rat poison. By 1.50 pm on April 14, she was dead. And, sure enough, in the last of many wills, the loyal housekeeper-companions found themselves joint beneficiaries. Louisa began to talk of raising a mortgage on the bungalow and buying a seaward-facing nursing home. In her handbag, unbeknown to her husband, nestled a sheaf of insurance policies secretly effected on his life. Louisa let it be known that she was arranging for the Salvation Army band to come and play *Abide With Me* outside the bungalow as a final tribute to Mrs Ricketts' memory.

But she had not been forgotten by the police either. They had been plying a metal detector in the bungalow's back garden, seeking a poison tin.

They were anxious that Mrs Merrifield should abide with them – in Strangeways Gaol. At Manchester in July, the Merrifields were put on trial. A short, dumpy woman in a dove-grey hat and coat, round-faced, thin-lipped, wearing large horn-rimmed glasses, Mrs Merrifield nurtured enormous faith in her ability to put up a convincing show. Each night her hair was curled by other prisoners. Each day in court she radiated a superficially pleasant, cheerful, homebody personality. But, in the witness-box, it soon became sadly plain that the eloquence that swayed the snugs of Blackpool and Wigan public-houses was compounded of coarse language, smutty jokes, and maudlin sentimentality. Gradually, her blithe optimism seeped away. The jury found her guilty.

Seeming to pass suddenly from spry middle age to a palsied senescence, she heard *her* doom pronounced. On September 18, 1953, Louisa May Merrifield was hanged at Strangeways. Alfred Edward Merrifield benefited from the Attorney-General's entering of a *nolle prosequi*. He went back to the Homestead. He had inherited his half-share of the bungalow, where he continued to live until 1956. He died, aged 80, in 1962, a fortunate man who had had two lucky escapes: from the hands of the hangman . . . and the clutches of his wife!

Mummy in the Cupboard

Until the day she went into hospital, a little shrivelled Welsh woman named Mrs Sarah Jane Harvey was just a very ordinary, colourless widow, leading, in the North Wales coastal resort of Rhyl, a life the most remarkable thing about which was its unremarkableness.

For 41 years she had lived in the same neat but drab, two-storey, red brick terrace house, 35 West Kinmel Street. There, in 1931, she had given birth to her son, Leslie. There, in 1938, her second husband, Alfred James Harvey, had died. There, in her long widowhood, she had eked things out, made ends meet, by taking in a succession of lodgers.

Then, in April, 1960, at the age of 65, worn down by the unremitting years, ailing, but presenting no firmly diagnosable frank symptoms, she was sent by her unable to diagnose GP into hospital "for observation".

It was while she was there, that Leslie, aged 29, married now and living in nearby Abergele, where he was running a taxi business, a good son, decided to decorate his mother's house. It was to be a nice surprise for her. It turned out to be a horrible shock for him. On the afternoon of May 5, 1960, Leslie and his wife went along to West Kinmel Street to make a start on the job. Up on the landing at the top of the stairs stood the massive wooden cupboard – bland and challenging, as Leslie remembered it of old. What a fuss his mother had always made about it. Kept it locked. Insisted it was never to be touched. Said something about its containing the sacrosanct belongings of a long since departed boarder, Mrs Knight.

Well, too bad. It was going to have to be opened now. That was, if the decorating was to be done properly.

He fetched a knife and, not without a resurgence of the old curiosity, prised open the big double doors. Then . . . what had he expected? Mildewed suitcases, moth-ravaged coats and dresses, mangy furs. The pointlessly conserved detritus of a lost existence. The left luggage of a burnt-out lifetime.

Instead, his horrified eyes fastened upon not the possessions but the late possessor.

Huddled on the cupboard floor – a body. Doubled up, hunched in the foetal position, as though gone back in death to life before birth. A woman. Mummified by freak accident of currents of warm breaths of air, blown across long years through the ligneous sarcophagus. Her flesh brick-hard, she was clothed in a nightdress, over which she wore a faded blue coat. The spiders had woven a delicate gossamer shroud for her. Leslie Harvey went to the police. The police went to Mrs Harvey.

They told her they had seen a body in the cupboard at her home. "Oh, goodness gracious!" was her reply. She said she knew nothing about it. What about Mrs Knight, they asked? Oh, yes, she remembered her. Had lodged with her until the end of the war. Went off to live in Llandudno then, she died.

Later, at Rhyl police station, Mrs Harvey's memory improved, became more circumstantially precise. Around the end of February, 1940, Mrs Frances Knight, a woman of 50 she'd be, took her first-floor front as a bed-sitter. Suffering from disseminated sclerosis, she was. A semi-invalid. Separated from her husband, a retired dentist, living in Hove, Sussex, she received £2 a week from him on a court maintenance order. Unable to walk properly, she had given her landlady written authority to collect the money for her each week.

One night, four or five weeks after Mrs Knight's arrival, Mrs Harvey had been getting ready for bed when she heard Mrs Knight screaming. "I went into her room and saw her lying on the floor. She said: 'I am in an awful lot of pain and I would rather be dead.'" Whereupon, Mrs Harvey hurried downstairs to make her the British universal panacea – a nice cup of tea. But when she got back, Mrs Knight was dead. This tale did not make the police happy. They were even less happy when the pathologist, Dr Gerald Evans, reported finding a lisle stocking tied tightly like a ligature in a deep groove around the corpse's neck. They arrested Mrs Harvey. She was put up at Denbighshire Assizes, at Ruthin. The prosecution libelled strangulation for the motive of acquisition of the maintenance money. In 20 years the accused had pocketed some £2099.

Mrs Harvey's story was that, scared stiff, she had panicked and decided to hide the body. Drawing and keeping Mrs Knight's weekly allowance was merely part of the concealment of the death. A hopeful defence suggested a possible reason for the stocking round the neck: Mrs Knight's faith in the old wives' tale that it is a sovereign cure for the common cold. Where was the proof that Mrs Knight had died of violence? What proof was there that she had not died of natural disease? The Solicitor-General had to admit that there was none, and, with the agreement of the judge, accordingly withdrew the prosecution. Acquitted of murder, Mrs Harvey was found guilty on her own admission of fraudulently obtaining money, and sent to prison for 15 months.

What are we to make of Sarah Jane Harvey? A liar – callous, cunning, cool and calculating? Or just a simple, foolish woman, who gave way to a moment's unreasoning panic? One would have thought, though, that death ought not to have so unbalanced her, for in the 16 years between 1926 and 1941, no less than seven other deaths had occurred among the occupants of No 35. Also, she had, in fact, a previous conviction for larceny in 1942. Lord Elwyn-Jones, who, led by Sir Jocelyn Simon, prosecuted, recounts how the accused, when asked from time to time at the magistrates' clerks' office, where she went to collect the maintenance, "How is the old lady?" would invariably reply: "Oh, she's keeping very well."

Sarah Jane Harvey did not, as it happens, survive long. Her mysterious ailment turned out to be cancer.

Nicotine Can Kill You

It was two oddly assorted Belgians, the Count Hippolyte Visart de Bocarmé, scion of one of the first families of Belgium, and Jean Servais Stas, a young professor of chemistry at the École Royale Militaire in Brussels, who – the aristocrat unwittingly, the scientist by exercise of acutest wit – made one of the great toxicological contributions to forensic medicine. The Count it was who presented the, as it were, raw material for the triumph. It came about thus.

In the year 1843, casting around for a means of repairing the de Bocarmé family fortune, which, hitherto, he had been engaged in most assiduously destroying, young Hippolyte's eye lighted upon Mademoiselle Lydie Fougnies, the obviously well-endowed daughter of a fiscally well-endowed retired grocer of Mons. A marriage was arranged, but the *nouvelle* comtesse's *dot* was grievously short in fall of the order of sum upon which Monsieur le Comte had been counting – a mere 2,000 francs a year.

All was surely not lost, however, for when the bourgeoise bartered bride's father died, there would be more. Alas, that sad event coming to pass in 1845, the even sadder actuarial fact was that Lydie's patrimony tipped the flagging financial scale no higher than another 5,000 francs income per annum. To her brother, Gustavus, had been devised the far tidier share.

Still all was surely not lost, for Gustavus, a cripple, having had a leg amputated at the thigh following a fall from a horse, was heateningly weak and sickly All prophecies were that he would make young bones. Then his lion's share would flow into his sister's – or, rather, her tigrish husband's – coffers.

Then, suddenly, all *was* surely lost. Gustavus announced his impending nuptials. Grave circumstances called for grave measures. On Wednesday, November 20, 1850, the bridegroom not-to-be was invited to dine with his sister and brother-in-law at their country place – the Château de Birtremont, near the village of Bury, between Tournai and Mons, in the province of Hainaut. And there, on that convenient day, did Gustavus Fougnies considerately fall dead of what was described by his grieving kinsfolk as an apoplectic fit.

The strength of ensuing rumour about the countryside brought the Examining Magistrate from Tournai, M. Heughebaert, to the Château Birtroment. Unwillingly, the Bocarmés acceded to his request to view the body. Gustavus lay naked on the bed in a servant's room. His corpse reeked of vinegar. Heughebaert saw that his cheeks bore contusions and scratch-like wounds, and his mouth presented a curious blackened and burnt appearance.

The magistrate ordered an on-the-spot medical examination by the three doctors he had brought with him. Heughebaert instructed them to remove all the significant organs and their contents, together with appropriate tissue specimens, and place them in alcohol in sealed jars. These he personally delivered into the hands of Professor Stas in Brussels for analysis.

After numerous washings, filterings; and distillings of the material, and the inspiration of a final floating-off with ether, Stas eventually managed to separate, by evaporation from the liquid distillate, the deadly poison, nicotine. Meanwhile, further investigations by Examining Magistrate Heughebaert and the police were bringing important supportive evidence to light.

The Count's gardener, a somewhat feeble-minded man named Deblicqui, told of having helped his master to prepare eau-de-Cologne from tobacco leaves in his laboratory in the château's wash-house. Professor Loppers, who taught chemistry at an industrial school in Ghent, said that Bocarmé, calling himself Bérant, had consulted him regarding the method of extracting nicotine from tobacco leaves. And two Brussels firms, Vandenberghe and Vanbeukelaer, were discovered to have supplied 120 different types of chemical apparatus and vessels to Château Birtremont.

Bit by bit, a picture emerged of what had undoubtedly taken place that fatal Wednesday behind the frowning stone walls of the moated château. After dinner, which was concluded by about 4.30 pm, Gustavus, lulled by food and wine and convivial conversation into a false sense of comfortable security, had been suddenly set upon by his host, thrown to the dining-room floor, and held fast by the Count while the Countess poured the poison into her brother's mouth. For all that he was a cripple, Gustavus had put up a spirited fight for his life, and strong-smelling nicotine had been splashed all around. This was why the Bocarmés had removed and washed the dead man's clothing, burnt his crutches, scraped the floorboards where there had been spillage, and flooded everything with vinegar to mask the potent odour of nicotine. Bocarmé had poured glass after glass of vinegar into Gustavus' mouth. That had been a bad mistake, for the vinegar had combined in chemical reaction with the nicotine to produce the burns which were to arouse official suspicion.

The Count and Countess de Bocarmé were placed on their trial at the Court of Assize in the Hall of Justice at Mons, on May 27, 1851. They presented an unedifying spectacle, each, in effect, attempting to lay the blame upon the other. The Countess said that the Count had killed her brother, and that he had forced her to assist at the murder. The Count, whose right hand bore the mark of a mysterious bite, sought defence in denial, but achieved only a confused and unconvincing performance. The jury found him guilty. The Countess was acquitted.

Hippolyte Visart de Bocarmé spent the last days of his 32 years on earth obsessively concerned as to the sharpness of the guillotine's knife. He had been put to fear by hearing a blunt tale of its recent inefficiency. But, on the night of July 19, 1851, by torchlight in the market-place of Mons, the 'widow's' blade bit sweet and swift, and the Count's head fell clean into the basket.

And the method of detecting vegetable poisons, on which he had inadvertently collaborated with Stas, became duly established toxicological routine. It is still in use today.

A Hardy Hanging in Agro Dorcestrensi

In the thin grey drizzle of that doleful August dawn a crowd of between three and four thousand souls had turned out to see another soul "turned off", as the harsh vernacular of the 19th century expressed it, by the none-too-steady hand of executioner Calcraft.

One among that congregation, gathered outside Dorchester Jail to see man's justice meted out to a jealous wife, who, nearly 40 years before her sister in sin, Miss Lizzie Borden, took an axe – in this case not unfilially but unuxorially – and despatched her errant husband, was to become in several senses imprinted by the experience. His name was Thomas Hardy.

On this Saturday, August 9, 1865, he was just 16 and starting his apprenticeship with John Hicks, architect, of South Street, Dorchester. That morning's spectacle was to mar him psychopathologically, and provide the emotional dynamic for his greatest work of literature, 35 years on, *Tess of the d'Urbervilles*. The fictional Tess and the woman who was to be hanged, Elizabeth Martha Brown, had this in common: both were driven to murder as unwilling participants in the eternal triangle.

Martha met John Anthony Brown when they were fellow servants in a Dorset farmer's house. Brown was some 20 years younger than she was. The cruel, unbridled tongue of local gossip averred that he married for her savings – at least £50. The couple settled in a cottage at Staples Barton, Birdsmoor Gate, near Beaminster. By all accounts Martha was a most handsome woman – dark complexion, beautiful dark curls and younger looking than her years. But she was in her late 30s, and by 19th-century standards that was not only well past the prime of youth, but quite a way into the territory of middle age.

The union produced one child, but in every other respect was not a happy one. John, who had become a carrier by trade, developed a wanderer's wandering eye. It came to rest on Mary Davies, the sportive wife of the village butcher. Caught by Martha being sportive, the fat was in the fire. At 9 am on Saturday, July 5, 1865, Brown and his friend and fellow carrier George Fooks, set off for Beaminster with loads of wooden poles on their horse-drawn wagons. They reached Beaminster about 1 pm, delivered the piles, and returned as far as Broadwindsor, about half-way home, where they stopped for beer and skittles until 11.30 pm. They parted. Except by his wife, Brown was never seen alive again. Around 5 am on the Sunday, Martha called on her husband's cousin, Richard Damon, who lived a mere 150 yards away, and asked him to come round as the horse had nearly killed John.

There was no nearly about it. John Brown was stone-dead. Martha's tale – told, as it were, straight from the horse's foot – was that she had found John crouched injured on the door-step at 2 am, muttering something about "the horse". She took it to mean that he had been kicked. She had dragged him in, but had been unable to get away to call Damon until now, because John had caught hold of her by her dress with an inescapable grip of iron. They searched for traces of blood to confirm her story. They found none. Clues outside on the road there were. Someone had knelt in the dust. Someone had vomited. A drunken homecoming, not a bloodied one, was betokened. Also, the dead man's head, duly examined, displayed a great many wounds, not just one shattering horse-kick.

An inquest was held at the Rose and Crown, Birdsmoor Gate, at which it was stated that quantities of blood and portions of brain were found adhering to the walls of the room in which Brown's body lay; that he and his wife had long been living on uncomfortable terms as a result of her jealousy and suspicion of his extra-marital concupiscence; that the medical men who examined the deceased declared it would have been impossible for him to have crawled or spoken after the first blow, which must have caused instantaneous death.

The inquest jury returned a verdict of wilful murder by person or persons unknown. Following examination by local magistrates, Martha was committed to Dorchester Jail. Visited by the Reverend Augustus Newland de la Foss, in his spiritual capacity, the accused woman put it directly to that inquisitory cleric: "What should make I kill him to lose my home and have to lie under the hedge?" Sent for trial at Dorset Midsummer Assize, she appeared at Dorchester Crown Court on July 21, 1865, and was found guilty.

She later confessed the true scenario. Her husband had arrived home drunk, as he often did. She charged him with infidelity. He charged her with his tranter's whip, laying into her bad and proper. Provoked beyond endurance, she responded to his advances with the wood-chopping hatchet, returning the compliment with fatal enthusiasm. Surely a classic domestic *crime passionel*?

In the latitude of Gaul, where they order these things, if not better, then differently, Martha might have found mercy. A sterner morality pervaded and prevailed in Victorian Grande Bretagne. The black cap was donned.

Hardy never forgot the rustle of Martha's thin black gown as she was led forth by the warders, and the white cap, soaked by the penetrating rain so that it clung, making her features come gradually visible through it, the noose seemingly put around the neck of a marble statue . . . Never forgot the hanged woman, dangling and gently twirling on the gallows high above the entrance to Dorchester Jail. It was an image that entered into the Pantheon of his sexual symbolism. In 1925, aged 85, he wrote: "I remember what a fine figure she showed against the sky as she hung in the misty rain, and how the tight black silk gown set off her shape as she wheeled half-round and back."

Martha Brown's body haunted Hardy right to the end of his life.

John Brown's body lies a'mouldering in the grave – in the churchyard at Blackdown – but on dark moonless nights his soul is said to go marching on, a ghost haunting the tiny hamlet of Birdsmoor Gate.

Christmas Killer

The no-man's land stretch of time that lies between Christmas and New Year's Day had fallen like a muffling blanket over workaday London. In the atmosphere of protracted seasonal celebration, the typewriters and the cash registers were silent, the buses and tubes and trains deserted, offices barely manned, shoppers' bustle reduced to a trickle.

One of the few people moving through the empty Sunday night streets on December 26, 1948 was Detective Superintendent Peter Beveridge, not best pleased at having had to abandon his suburban yuletide hearth, victim of the urgent call of duty.

Passing from relatively brisk Baker Street into the quieter residential purlieus of George Street, he could catch the echoes of discreet revelry coming from behind the bright, multicoloured squares and oblongs of curtained windows. The police car purring smoothly towards the Edgware Road end where, bounded by Nutford Place and Brown Street, the huge block of flats called Fursecroft rose within the shadow of equally bulky Bryanston Court to meet the sky, he could see the Christmas trees twinkling with fairy lights, hear the sound of music, singing, laughter and, faintly, the clink of glasses.

But down in the cold, black basement flat at Fursecroft, was only silence – the silence that remains after death has passed by. For it was here that murder had been done.

Strangely enough, Beveridge had known the victim. Only days before, he had been invited to a pre-Christmas party at Elliott House, the local police section house in Paddington. Star of the evening's variety show was Harry Saul Michaelson, "One Minute Michaelson", a 50-year-old commercial artist and lightning cartoonist, famous for his stage and television performances. They had been introduced and chatted briefly.

Chief Inspector Jock Jamieson was waiting at Fursecroft to fill his guv'nor in on the murder. In the early hours of Boxing Day the porter of the flats had heard screaming and found Michaelson standing at the door of his flat bleeding copiously from a ghastly wound in the temple. The injured man was borne swiftly off to St Mary's Hospital, Paddington.

The room where the attack had taken place was in a shambles – table up-ended, chairs overturned, lamps upset, carpets rucked up, ornaments smashed to smithereens, blood splashes broadcast. But it was a modernistic, tubular steel chair, lying on its side and slightly dented, that had caught Jamieson's eye. "I fancy that," he said. There were bloodstains on the legs. It could well have been the murder weapon.

To the practised eyes of the police officers it was easy to see what had happened. Michaelson had been alone in the three-room flat. His wife, a pianist, had been fulfilling a professional engagement in Bournemouth. There was an open window, easily accessible from the street. Someone had entered through it. Michaelson, in bed, had been awakened. He had turned on the light, challenged the intruder. A blow, blows, had been struck.

The motive for the crime was patently theft. Very petty theft as it turned out. The victim's trousers lay on the floor. His jacket was draped round an overturned chair. There was no money in the pockets.

Of all the many categories of murder, the most difficult solution is that in which there is no history of association of the killer with the victim and no witness to provide a description of the assailant. This was one of those cases in which the chance of an arrest being made was dishearteningly remote. But there was one ray of hope. Experts at the Yard had found a single fingerprint on the metal chair. In those pre-computerised days, though, single print impressions took a long, long time to search.

In the end, it was good old-fashioned police work, persistence and know-how that, against all the heavily stacked odds, ran the killer to ground. Beveridge had registered the fact that there had been several small cases of local flat breaking, and his policeman's instinct suggested to him that the man they were after might have been fool enough to stay in the district and carry on his burglaries there. If that were so, Beveridge felt that he was most unlikely to be a Londoner. Jamieson felt sure the thief had come into the Smoke from the country

– "So look twice at anyone with an accent," he told his young police officers.

On January 19, 1949, a little over three weeks after the murder, an alert young aide to the CID, Martin Walsh, spotted a man in the St John's Wood area acting suspiciously and arrested him. As was routine in all arrests, his fingerprints were sent to the Yard for checking – and one of them matched that found on the chair in the Boxing Day murder case.

The man's name was Harry Lewis. Slim, dark, roughly dressed, 21 years old, he was a Welshman and a complete stranger to London. He was a provincial professional with a record of burglary. He admitted stealing £5 8s 9d (£5.44), said he had been wandering on the streets penniless, saw the open window and was tempted.

It had been a spur of the miserable minute thing. He confirmed that the subsequent course of events had been pretty much as Beveridge and Jamieson had surmised.

Lewis was tried at the Old Bailey in March, 1949. His counsel put forward the suggestion that since Michaelson had at first seemed to be recovering from the brain surgery which he had undergone at St Mary's, he might still be alive had there been no operation. But that cock would not fight – -especially in Lord Goddard's cockpit. To be fair, Dr Donald Teare, the pathologist, did testify that Michaelson would have died anyway, operation or no operation.

Goddard summed up characteristically. Applying the letter of the law, he told the jury that if they found it to be a case of a burglar killing a householder to escape being apprehended, they must find the prisoner guilty of murder.

They duly found thus – but with an added recommendation to mercy. It was not adopted. On April 21, 1949, Harry Lewis was hanged at Pentonville.

When the Body is Missing

Scratching desperately as a couple of starveling hens at the thin soil of Cefn Hendre Farm in the Dark Valley (Cwm Du), the two old soldiers were failing to scrape a living from the sour land. Neither man was a stranger to adversity. Both were displaced Poles. Michial

Onufrejczyk (pronounced Ono-free-shic), at 58 the elder – just – had
served with gallantry; nine medals as a sergeant-major in the Polish
Army. At war's end he had remained with the Polish Resettlement
Corps in South Wales, and, in 1949, had purchased the lonely
Carmarthenshire farm, ten miles from Llandilo.

On March, 1953, Stanislaw Sykut arrived at Cefn Hendre.
Previously employed as a nurse at Whitchurch Hospital, Shropshire,
he was the third in a succession of partners who had hitched their
hopeful farm wagons to Onufrejczyk's 120-acre holding. He handed
over £600. Things did not go well. Onufrejczyk's violent temper was
provoked by Sykut's sheer physical inability to cope with his back-
breaking share of the farm work. Onufrejczyk, arrogant, forward-
jutting, patriarchal white beard bristling with fury – he was known
among the local hill farmers as "Mr Whiskers" – laid into his small,
frailish partner. Sykut complained to the police. Onufrejczyk was
warned. Sykut made a trip to a solicitor, Mr Vaughan Roberts, in
Llandilo, and six months' notice to terminate the partnership on
November 14, 1953, was served on Onufrejczyk. Unless, said
Roberts' letter, Onufrejczyk, or some other potential partner, paid
Sykut for his share, the farm would be put up for public auction.

November 14 came – and went.

Sykut was last seen alive by the local blacksmith on December 14,
when he took a cob to be shod.

When, on December 30, Sergeant Phillips, the local police officer,
was making his routine monthly check on aliens, Onufrejczyk told
him that Sykut had gone to London for a fortnight.

T'ime passed. Still no Sykut.

Now Onufrejczyk had a tale to tell. Around 8 pm on December 18,
three Polish men had arrived at the farm by car. Sykut had then said
that he would sell his share of Cefn Hendre for £600, a down payment
of £450 and a promissory note for £150 falling due in May, 1954. A
document had been prepared – Onufrejczyk produced it – and duly
signed by Sykut and witnessed by one of the men, Jablonski. Sykut
was then driven off into the darkness.

From where had Onufrejczyk got the £450? Borrowed it from a
Mrs Pokora, who lived in Holloway, North London, he said. She
denied it. Suspicion against the surly Onufrejczyk mounted. Sykut's
mail, which he used to collect daily, lay piling up at Cwm Du post
office. His Post Office savings account, in credit £290, lay untouched.

His ration card remained unused at the village store. What had Onufrejczyk to say? That his ex-partner had gone to join his wife behind the Iron Curtain of Communist Poland.

The police decided to take a closer look. An examination of the bleak farmhouse kitchen proved rewarding. More than 2,000 tiny blood specks were discovered on the walls and ceilings. Glued into one was a spicule of bone. On the Welsh dresser was an ominous hand-sized bloodstain. It was plain that murder had been done. But of a body there was not then – or ever – any sign. No matter. On August 19, 1954, Onufrejczyk was arrested and charged.

Defended by Elwyn-Jones, QC, prosecuted by Edmund Davies, QC, Onufrejczyk's trial opened before Oliver J at Swansea in November. And the case made legal history, because, for the first time in English criminal law, an accused was convicted of murder – *on land* – without a body having been found.

James Camb had been similarly convicted in 1948, but that was for a murder committed on the high seas. And Edward Ball, found guilty of matricide without benefit of body in 1936, was an Eire case.

At the Onufrejczyk trial, Oliver J., quoting from a judgment given in the New Zealand Court of Appeal in *Horry* 1952, declared: "In the trial of a person charged with murder the fact of death is provable by circumstantial evidence, notwithstanding that neither the body nor any trace of the body has been found and that the accused has made no confession of any participation in the crime. Before he can be convicted the fact of death must be proved by such circumstances as render the commission of the crime morally certain and leave no ground for reasonable doubt. The circumstantial evidence should be so cogent and compelling as to convince a jury that upon no rational hypothesis other than murder can the fact be accounted for." The jury found Onufrejczyk guilty.

He appealed. In dismissing the appeal, Goddard LCJ laid down the guideline for all future cases in which no body can be produced: "The fact of death can be proved, like any other fact can be proved, by circumstantial evidence, that is to say, by evidence of facts which lead to one conclusion, provided that the jury are satisfied and are warned that the evidence must lead to one conclusion only."

Onufrejczyk did not hang. The Home Secretary, Gwilym Lloyd George, commuted the sentence to life imprisonment. He confided to Elwyn-Jones that he was afraid that if Onufrejczyk had hanged and someone beyond the Iron Curtain were put forward on the radio claiming to be Sykut there could be trouble. Onufrejczyk was released in 1965. In 1966 he moved to Bradford, and it was there that, later that year, he was killed in a road accident. He took with him to the grave the answer to the overwhelming question. What became of Sykut's body? The widely held belief is that Onufrejczyk fed his partner's cadaver to the pigs. But Elwyn-Jones, the prosecutor, has pointed out: "In fact there were no pigs on the farm".

Woolmington and the Golden Thread

A shot in a Somerset cottage kitchen on a cold December morning 72 years ago was to overturn completely a fundamental concept of the criminal law relating to murder which had prevailed unchallenged for close on 200 years. There seemed nothing exceptional about the constellation of circumstances which set all this in train. It appeared a commonplace enough story of a man who had murdered his wife, intending then to kill himself, but had lost his nerve. Reginald Woolmington, a farm labourer of 21, married 17-year-old Violet Smith at the Parish Church of Milborne Port, Somerset, on August 24, 1934. For the first six weeks of their married life the young couple lived with Reg's parents. Then they moved to a tiny cottage of their own, provided, at a rent of three shillings per week, by Mr Cheeseman, the farmer for whom Reg worked. His weekly wage was 33 shillings.

Seven weeks after the marriage, a baby son was born. Then things began to go wrong; to get on Vi's nerves. The baby cried too much. Reg was out at work too long. She felt lonely. Became edgy and bad-tempered. Before her marriage, Vi and her mother, with whom she lived, had boosted the family money by making up gloves, at piece-rates, in their own home for local manufacturers. Doubtless, Mrs Smith felt the pinch losing V's contribution. Anyway, she began visiting her daughter, bringing bundles of piecemeal gloves for them to assemble. Reg got it into his head that his mother-in-law was deliberately trying to induce Vi to leave him and go back home. Her visits caused increasingly bitter quarrels between husband and wife. Things came to a head on November 22, when Vi told Reg that she and her mother were going to Sherborne that afternoon and taking the baby with them. It was, he objected, far too cold for such a young baby to be out-of-doors. "We're going whether you like it or not," his wife told him. When he returned from work that evening, Reg found the cottage dark and empty. On the mantelshelf was propped a note: "I've gone home. Don't come up. I've asked my mother to have me. I've made up my mind to go into service." On the evening of Sunday, December 9, Reg, lonely and disconsolate, mooning about Sherborne, the nearest sizable town, bumped into Vi's brother, who, tactlessly, let it slip that the previous night Vi had been seen at the cinema with another man. All that night Reg tossed sleeplessly. Red-eyed, he rose early on Monday morning and made his way to Cheeseman's farm. There, he went to the barn, where he knew there was an old double-barrelled shotgun. He sawed down the barrels, loaded it with two cartridges, tucked it under his overcoat, and cycled to his mother-in-law's – 24 Newtown, Milborne Port. He found Vi washing some clothes in the back kitchen. The baby was asleep in his cot. Mrs Smith was out. Reg pleaded with Vi to come back to him. She would not budge. He produced the gun from beneath his coat.

Next-door, Vi's aunt, Mrs Daisy Brine, heard Reg's voice. "Are you coming home or not?" The sound of a shot. A glimpse of Reg running out . . . cycling frantically away. On the floor, in front of the fire, beside the washtub, Vi, shot through the heart, seeping blood. Reg was arrested. In the pocket of his coat was found a letter. "Goodbye all. It is agonies to carry on any longer. I have kept true hoping she would return. This is the only way out . . . Have no more cartridges, only two, one for her and one for me." He also wrote to his employer "I shall not be coming to work today. I have shot my wife." Woolmington was put up for trial before Finlay J at Taunton Assizes in January, 1935. The jury failed to agree. His second trial opened at Bristol Assizes on St Valentine's Day, before Swift J. Summing up, Swift quoted *Archbold*: "All homicide is presumed to be malicious, and murder, unless the contrary appears from circumstances of alleviation, excuse or justification. In every charge of murder, the fact of killing being first proved, all the circumstances of accident, necessity, or infirmity, are to be satisfactorily proved by the prisoner unless they arise out of the evidence produced against him, for the law presumeth the fact to have been founded in malice until the contrary appeareth."

These words had been taken by Archbold from Sir Michael Foster's *Crown Law*, published in 1762.

Swift, obviously aware that the defence were looking for manslaughter, told the jury: "If once you find that a person has been guilty of killing another, it is for the person who has been guilty of the killing to satisfy you that the crime is something less than the murder with which he is charged."

The Bristol jury found Woolmington guilty. But his counsel, Mr J. D. Casswell, appealed on the grounds of misdirection. Whatever Foster or Archbold or Swift J said, he was utterly convinced that the burden of proof lay upon the Crown. In Hewart LCJ's absence due to illness, the appeal was presided over by the senior King's Bench Judge, Avory J., with Lawrence J and Greaves Lord J. Following precedent, the Court of Criminal Appeal confirmed the conviction. Undeterred, Mr Casswell sought, and obtained, the Attorney-General's *fiat* to take the case to the House of Lords. On April 4, 1935, the point was argued afresh before the Lord Chancellor (Lord Sankey), Hewart LCJ, and Lords Atkin, Tomlin and Wright. And on April 5, Lord Sankey announced that Woolmington's conviction would be quashed.

Later, delivering his judgment, Lord Sankey went back to first principles: "Throughout the web of the English Criminal Law one golden thread is always to be seen, that it is the duty of the prosecution to prove the prisoner's guilt . . . No matter what the charge or where the trial, the principle that the prosecution must prove the guilt of the prisoner is part of the Common Law of England and no attempt to whittle it down can be entertained." Thus Reginald Woolmington, after 81 days in the condemned cell, walked a free man out of the Palace of Westminster, and into the pages of legal history.

Beard's Close Shave

Arthur Beard was a night-watchman. From 6 pm to 6 am it was his responsibility to oversee the safety and security of the extensive premises of the Carfield Cotton Mills, at Hyde in Cheshire. On the evening of July 25, 1919, a Friday, Ivy Lydia Wood, 13 years old, was sent on an errand for her father, a respectable and respected tradesman of Hyde. He wanted some ferrules for umbrellas and walking sticks. She was to fetch them from the shop of Francis Booth: she never came back home. The last person to clap innocent eyes on her was a youth named Ernest Gosling. That was at around 6 pm, when she was by the gates of Carfield Mill, talking to Beard.

Between 6.30 and 7 that evening, Charles Jones, a friend of Beard's, popped into the otherwise deserted Carfield Mills to pick him up. They had been drinking together earlier at the Great War Comrades Club in Hyde; had had quite a few, and when they parted Beard carried a newly purchased bottle of whisky away with him. Although, officially, Beard should have remained at his watchman's post, he was playing truant that evening, going with Jones to the Navigation Hotel, where there was to be a meeting of the Engine and Fireman's Union, which it had long been Beard's ambition to join. That night he was duly elected, and, after a celebratory glass or two, rolled back to the mill a seemingly happy man.

At 1.30 am, Samuel Bower, nightwatchman of a neighbouring mill, was startled by the sudden apparition of a gesticulating and mumbling Beard, distinctly the worse for drink. "I'm in a mess. I've found a girl pegged out. I was in the grounds near the dining-room. I carried her on my back to the lodge." Mr Bower's advice was blunt. "Call the police at once." At 2 am PC Vernon arrived. He viewed the child's body. Sharp-eyed, he noted clay soiling around the knees of Beard's trousers. Later, the watchman showed Vernon and the chief constable, who had arrived on the scene, the spot on the waste land behind the mill where, he said, he had found the dead girl. Something about Beard did not seem to ring true. He was taken into custody and detained.

The following day, Scotland Yard, responding to a request for help, sent Chief Inspector Arthur Fowler Neil and his sergeant, Eveleigh, up to Cheshire. They arrived in the early hours of Sunday, July 27. Neil found signs of a fierce struggle in the basement of the mill. Chipped tiles bore bloodstains and hairs of the same colour as Ivy Wood's. A post-mortem showed that the little girl had been raped and suffocated. There was no evidence, however, to justify the continued holding of Beard.

Then, unexpectedly and unbelievably, the watchman sent for Neil and said he wanted to tell the truth. He had been drinking. He knew

Ivy and had often spoken to her before. He had invited her into the mill. He didn't know what came over him. There was a struggle. He had put his hands across her mouth. When he "came to" she was dead. The pressure of his thumb on her throat had caused suffocation. Beard, aged 31, tried at Chester Assizes before Bailhache J., was sentenced to death on October 6, 1919. His counsel appealed on the ground of the judge's misdirection. Beard's defence had been that he was drunk and his mind so affected as to reduce the crime from murder to manslaughter, in accordance with the rule laid down in *R* v. *Meade* [1909] 1 KB 895. In that case the prisoner had brutally ill-treated the deceased woman, breaking a broomstick over her and causing her death by rupture with a blow of his fist. It was decided that where the evidence shows that the killer is too drunk to form the intention, the killing is not murder but manslaughter, and the Court so reduced the charge because it held that intoxication had rendered the man incapable of the required *mens rea*. The Court of Criminal Appeal, finding that Beard was drunk at the time of the assault and incapable of acting with malice aforethought, quashed the conviction and substituted a sentence of 20 years' penal servitude for manslaughter.

The DPP appealed to the House of Lords, and for the first time on record an appeal in connection with a charge of murder by a commoner – albeit a Crown plea – was taken to the Upper House. The Lord Chancellor at the time was Birkenhead. At the very outset of the proceedings he announced that whatever the outcome of the appeal the Home Secretary would advise His Majesty that the capital sentence should not be carried out. On March 5, 1920, Lord Birkenhead, uttering his reserved judgment from the Woolsack, stated: "I doubt, without reaching a conclusion, whether there was any sufficient evidence to go to the jury that the prisoner was, in the only relevant sense, drunk at all. There was certainly no evidence that he was too drunk to form intent of committing rape. Under these circumstances, it was proved that death was caused by an act of violence done in furtherance of the felony of rape. Such a killing is by the law of England murder."

In other words, because, by the doctrine of constructive malice, killing in the course of committing a felony was legally murder, Beard was guilty. All seven other learned Lords concurred, including, rather oddly, Reading LCJ who, instead of dissenting as might reasonably have been expected by the man on the Clapham omnibus, meekly acquiesced in the reversal of his own judgment in the court below. Thus Arthur Beard came to be branded a murderer and *R* v. *Beard* to represent an important legal landmark, defining the relationship between drunkenness and criminal responsibility, and drawing the dividing line between murder and manslaughter in case of intoxication. Since, however, the doctrine of constructive malice was abolished by the Homicide Act 1957, the chances are that the CCA's decision, were it given in similar circumstances today, would stand – and Arthur Beard would be guilty of killing, not murder. One of life – and death's – little ironies.

Urban Napoleon Stanger

The case of the vanishing baker is cast perfectly in the mould of a story from the casebook of Sherlock Holmes: the very style and title, *Urban Napoleon Stanger*, bears the veritable *imprimatur* of the late John H. Watson MD's Holmesian saga.

The owner of that curious and evocative name was a German. Born about 1843 in the Prussian spa town of Bad Kreuznach, in the Rhine province of Germany, Stanger was 25, and a master baker, when he married Elizabeth, an 18-year-old girl from his native town. In 1870, or perhaps 1871, they came to England to seek their fortune. After a short period of intensive work and a dedicated spell of scrimping and saving, Stanger was able to set up his own business at 136 Lever Street, City Road, in the East End district of St Luke's. Lever Street was in the centre of a densely populated area of London favoured by a community of expatriate and inward-turning Germans. Stanger's bakery prospered. Working in nearby St John Street, was Stanger's compatriot, Franz Felix Stumm. He, too, was a baker. He, too, hailed from Kreuznach. But he had not done so well for himself and was glad to be invited to lend a hand – and earn an extra crust – at his friend's bakehouse.

So the trio is completed . . . Urban Napoleon Stanger. Age 38. By all accounts dull, unimaginative, mild-mannered, amiable, and hardworking. His sole apparent interest: making and amassing money. Elizabeth Stanger, age 31, superior in education to her husband.

Described as a hard-faced, coarse-looking, rough-tongued woman, with a fondness for bedecking her stout, massively built person with showy dresses and cheap jewellery. A creature of moods, said to have alternated between slaving over a hot (baker's) oven from morn till eve in the shop and sitting sullen upstairs, sipping brandy, until she would take to petulant pelting of the baker with his own loaves. Franz Felix Stumm, age 34. A black-bearded, hook-nosed, corpulent and powerful-bodied, mercenary Lothario. Dark, deep-set eyes. Exuding a definite air of cunning; a possible aura of malice. On the edge of the circle, or rather, triangle, was Stumm's wife.

November 12, 1881, was a Saturday, traditionally a night for going out for a drink. Honouring tradition, Stanger went out with his friend, Stumm, and his employee, Christian Zentler. It was ten minutes to midnight when Stanger said goodnight to Stumm and Zentler. They, and two passers-by of his acquaintance – Mr Kramer and Mr Lang – saw him enter his home. He was never seen again.

When, at eight o'clock on Sunday morning, Zentler presented himself at the bakery, he was promptly despatched by an agitated Madame Stanger to fetch Franz Stumm. Her husband, she explained, had gone away, and she wanted Stumm to run the business in his absence. Stumm arrived – and stayed. Indeed, he seemed to have found the entire arrangement so much to his taste that after ten days he ceased to go home in the evening and gave every sign of having abandoned his own business.

Weeks passed. Tongues wagged. Enquirers after Stanger's health and well-being were told that his private affairs had necessitated a hurried trip to Germany. Two pressing creditors, Simon Moll and Thomas Letch, both in the flour trade, managed to wrest cheques from Stumm – ostensibly signed by Stanger.

For Stumm and Mrs Stanger to allow themselves to be seen walking out arm-in-arm was tactless, but for Stumm to paint out Stanger's name and substitute his own over the bakery was positively asking for trouble. The ugly word "murder" might now occasionally be heard among the susurrant observations of alive-to-suspicion neighbours. Thin gossip waxed fat. Talk of a dreadful scream, whose scimitar had pierced the silence of Lever Street in the small hours of November 13 . . . of Stumm staggering along the City Road beneath the weight of a bulging sack . . . of certain meat-pies akin in composition to Mrs Lovett's confections.

Then, in October, 1882, Stumm and Stanger *femme* were arrested. The police had first shown interest when, in April, Wendel Scherer, private inquiry agent, offered a £50 reward for information. The money had been put up by John Geisal, a friend and business colleague of Stanger's who, along with William Evans, a solicitor's clerk, was Stanger's executor. These two had applied for warrants against Stumm and Mrs Stanger on charges of forging and uttering a cheque with intent to defraud and with conspiring together to cheat and defraud the executors.

The case against Mrs Stanger, who was found to be pregnant, was subsequently withdrawn, but in December, Stumm was put up at the Old Bailey before Hawkins J., the much-feared 'Anging 'Awkins. At the end of a three-day trial, the jury convicted on both charges. Stumm, white with fury, roundly cursed his legal representatives.

Hawkins J., casting a cold eye, told him in a voice of parchment that he had been convicted of a very wicked forgery and had not improved his position by throwing unmerited abuse on his legal advisers, and sentenced him to penal servitude for ten years. The stout German, staggering beneath the impact of this hefty sentence, said: ""Thank you. I am very much obliged to you." Defiant insolence giving place to cold fury he added with heavy contempt, "This is English justice, is it not?" And Franz Felix Stumm vanished into the permanent blackness of an oblivion as complete as that which had encompassed Urban Napoleon Stanger.

Some people said that Stumm had murdered Stanger, some that Elizabeth had made away with him so that she could be with Stumm, and that he had helped her to get rid of the body. How? By destroying it in the ready-to-hand incinerator of the baker's oven; or, hazarded the more gruesome (with a folk memory of the legend of Sweeney Todd, the Demon Barber of Fleet Street), by making pie-filling mincemeat of it.

Who knows? Whatever, the vanishment of Urban Napoleon Stanger remains a deep mystery, unenlightened by 125 years' sunrises.

Unnatural Lore: the Burning Question

Edith Middleton was a widow, living alone in a small terrace house in Passmore Street, Pimlico, South-West London, leading a lonely life and never feeling anything other than rather poorly. Thin, frail, 70 years old, she was tottery on her legs, and her doctor was treating her for blood pressure and mild Parkinson's disease. She had a fretful appetite, did not drink any alcohol, and took, by prescription, half a grain of phenobarbitone at bedtime each night.

On the afternoon of January 29, 1958, at about 3 pm, a friendly neighbour, Mrs Annie Law, visited Mrs Middleton, made up her coal fire for her, and left her sitting on her bed. Between 5 and 6 that evening, standing out on her doorstep, Mrs Law saw an unusual amount of smoke and sparks pouring from the widow's chimney, but thought no more about it.

Next day, however, not seeing Mrs Middleton around as usual, Mrs Law became worried and got her grandson to climb in through a window to make sure that all was well. It was not. He found Edith Middleton's charred body lying in the hearth. And, the horror of it apart, there was something very odd about the discovery. Although only an inferno-like blaze of great intensity could have caused the charring and almost complete destruction of the body, there was no fire damage whatsoever to the surrounding furniture or fabrics. It was only a small, tight-packed room. Chairs, curtains, cushions, cloths and a made-up bed were all very close to the narrow fireplace, yet nothing was so much as singed. The sole sign of great heat was a hole, 1 ft. 5 in. by 7 in. burnt in the floorboards in front of the hearth. The pathologist, Dr Donald Teare, examining the body, recognised the presence of advanced hardening of the coronary arteries. He noted, too, the absence of soot in the air passages and lack of carbon monoxide in the blood. This showed that she was dead before the fire touched her.

At the inquest, held by Dr Gavin Thurston, at West London Coroner's Court, Hammersmith, on February 7, 1958, the official finding was of death due to coronary occlusion from atheroma.

Thurston duly recorded that verdict of death from natural causes. But it was his additional and private opinion that this was an instance of the rare phenomenon of preternatural combustibility (PN), which, together with the allied phenomenon of spontaneous human combustion (SHC), has been sporadically recorded for centuries. PN is defined as a condition in which the body becomes super-combustible, but the source of ignition is some *external* factor. SHC is where the source of the consuming conflagration arises from *within* the substance of the body itself

Up to the mid-19th century the belief in SHC, the Burning Death, the weird blue flames that came from nowhere and reduced a human being to a small pile of ashes, was widespread and entrenched.

Charles Dickens fanned the flames of credulity in *Bleak House* (1853), describing in Chapter 32 the death by spontaneous combustion of Mr Krook, the old miser addicted to drink, who vanished amid "smouldering suffocating vapour" and left only "a dark greasy coating on the walls and ceiling" and something small and charred, sprinkled with white ashes.

Captain Marryatt's *Jacob Faithful* (1834) also provided a vivid vignette of SHC: "Nothing was burning – not even the curtains to my mother's bed appeared to be singed . . . there appeared to be a black mass in the middle of the bed . . . a sort of unctuous pitchy cinder . . ."

Zola, too, in *Doctor Pascal* (1893), has Macquart "igniting like a sponge soaked in brandy".

But no matter how susceptible literary men may have proved, the medical profession as a whole seems to have regarded the entire question with profound scepticism. And yet, in countries all over the world, there are individual doctors, firemen, policemen, and special investigators who are convinced that they have come face to face with the indubitable evidence of the mysterious flickering blue flame which is only *intensified* by water.

Most burning deaths seem to have involved elderly people, and women are more frequent victims than men. Curiously, the process does not appear to cause any pain, the fire seems to anaesthetise as it burns. It used to be thought that fat people were more liable to SHC than thin ones, and that spirit drinkers, their body tissues saturated with alcohol, were more likely to go up in smoke, but both these theories have been abandoned. How, ask scientists, can human tissue, made up of over 90 per cent. water, become so critically combustible that it bursts into spontaneous fire, or can be touched off by an outside spark? How can the heat, which must top 3,000 degrees F in order to do the damage that it does, be so selective that it burns only living tissue, and leaves untouched eminently flammable objects in close proximity?

Although putative cases have been reported over a substantial period of time, the consensus of modern forensic opinion tends to the view that SHC and PC do not occur, and practically every medico-legal textbook and manual of forensic pathology refuses to give credence to the possibility of these phenomena, treating both as mythical entities, mere legacies from a more naïve past. Physically, the problems which such eruptions postulate are enormous, and it is admittedly difficult to see how, in line with the established laws of natural science, they could take place. In the present climate of scientific thinking it is customary to ascribe these unyielding propositions to mal-observation, exaggeration, a cover story for crime, or plain factual distortion. The genesis of the notion is commonly held to have derived its initial impulse from fiction.

The awkward thing is that if you keep an alert and informed eye upon your newspaper, cases of what *could* be PC or SHC will keep disconcertingly cropping up. Is it all smoke without fire? Surely the legal, as opposed to the medical, mind ought to bring in upon this burning question an open verdict.

A Hanging in the Balance

Among the comparatively few – albeit bulking rightly large when they occur – question-marks standing against the administrative record of British law, the perhaps less widely cited – but on that account scarcely less important – case of Robert William Hoolhouse, a 20-year-old Durham farm-labourer hanged for murder, should not go unremarked.

Wolviston, County Durham, was a remote rural area where feudalism lingered on. Farm-labourers were called hinds, as they had been for a thousand years, and were expected to touch their caps to Mrs Margaret Jane Dobson, 67-year-old wife of Henry Dobson, who had farmed High Grange for 30 years.

In the thickening dusk of a mid-January afternoon, Mrs Dobson set off down the 520-yard cinder track, leading between ploughed fields from the farmhouse to the highway, to walk to the village. She was not seen alive again. Next morning her husband found her lying beside the track, 50 yards from the road. She had been struck down, ravished and stabbed to death.

Within 36 hours, the police had a suspect under lock and key. At 1.15 am on January 20, 1938, they had knocked at the door of the Hoolhouse family in nearby Haverton Hill. Long rustic memories had recalled that "five year back" bad blood had flowed between the Hoolhouses and the Dobsons. Frederick and Florence Hoolhouse and their 15-year-old son, Robert, were then occupying the hind's cottage on the farm. There was talk of milk being tampered with. The Hoolhouses were turned out and told never to come on to High Grange Farm again. Robert, now rising 21, might have harboured a grudge.

The police made inquiries. Young Hoolhouse had been seen, between 1.45 and 2.45 pm on the afternoon of the murder – January 18 – drinking in the Blue Bell, Newton Bewley. At 3.10, Ronald Baldry met Hoolhouse on the road to Wolviston and they rode there together on their bicycles. They parted at 3.35 pm, Hoolhouse going to visit a girlfriend, Dorothy Lax, who lived with her aunt, Miss Beatrice Husband. Both women said that he remained until between 4.30 and 4.40 pm.

At what time had Margaret Dobson been killed? The evidence was not clear. Henry Dobson said that at 3.15 pm they had tea together. She ate a boiled beef sandwich. It was at about 4.30 that she left. But Bertram Smith and his men, who brought a threshing-machine, departed at 4.30, and did not see Mrs Dobson on the track.

Then, at 5.30, Percy Swales and Thomas Nelson delivered some pigs. As their lorry's lights swept across the track they picked out the figure of a man. He was standing some 50 yards away, with his hands above his head. As the lights hit him he dropped instantly to the ground. Swales described him: aged about 30, wearing a cap, a sort of bluish coloured smock on a farm-labourer's brown-coloured coat and what looked like leggings.

Lying on the track was a bicycle. A racing type with dropped handlebars. The man was now lying flat on the ploughed field. Swales called out: "Hullo, what's the game here?" Back came the answer in a gruff voice with a local accent: "I'm all right. I've had one over the nine. Drive on." They did. Unloaded the pigs. On the way back – around 5.45pm – both man and bicycle had gone.

Apart from the notional motive of revenge against his family's evictors, the principal evidential points telling against Hoolhouse were: (1) That he was in Wolviston and less than two minutes' bicycle ride from High Grange farm that afternoon. (2) His correspondence in general appearance with the man seen by Swales and Nelson, although they made no mention of glasses, which Hoolhouse habitually wore. (3) That he was the owner of a racing type bicycle with dropped handlebars. (4) That he had scratches on his face typical of those sustained from a rape or murder victim. These he accounted for as the result of a fall from his bicycle. Also noteworthy is the circumstance that Mrs Dobson was still wearing knitted woollen gloves when found. (5) That he had Group II (Moss) blood, the same group as Mrs Dobson and 42 per cent of the population, on his clothing – in consequence of cutting himself shaving, he said. (6) Alien hairs were found on his shirt flap and elsewhere. As regards the first point, reasonable doubt was imported by official uncertainty as to the time of death. Undigested food in the stomach suggested to the pathologist that death had taken place before 4 pm.

However, the time of her departure testified to by Mrs Dobson's husband would put the time of death as between 4.30 and 5 pm. And Swales and Nelson's sighting of the man on the track at 5.30 pm suggested an even later time. Hoolhouse was with Miss Lax and Miss Husband until between 4.30 pm and 4.40 pm. He claimed that immediately after leaving them he cycled home to Haverton Hill, where he washed, changed, and had his tea and, indisputably, caught the six o'clock bus back to Wolviston to take Miss Lax to the pictures.

Despite expert examination it was impossible to assign the foreign hairs to any particular individual. In Hoolhouse's favour was the absence of any seminal staining. Also in his favour was the discovery of a footprint which was not his beside the body. It was the only print other than those of the rubber boots of Mr Dobson. It was locked under a Dobson heel print, proving its priority. Telling against Hoolhouse was his refusal to submit to a blood test.

He came up at Leeds Assizes, March 28–30, 1938. Defence counsel submitted that there was no case to go to the jury. Wrottesley J disagreed. The defence called no witnesses. The prosecution admitted: "It is a case of very much less evidence than one usually finds." The judge summing up: "They (the prosecution) have got a number of things in regard to each one of which, when you test it, it amounts to no more than this, that it is quite consistent with this man having committed the murder; but it is consistent with him not having committed it."

A not guilty verdict was expected. The jury were out for four hours. Hoolhouse's parents had a taxi waiting to take him home. The guilty verdict was a shock. An appeal failed. The Home Secretary – Sir Samuel Hoare – refused a reprieve. Hoolhouse hanged at Durham on May 26, 1938. There are those who still believe that the rope of evidence was one of uncomfortably slender texture.

Abraham Throws Down the Gauntlet

Gross of body, greasy of face, graceless of movement, 24-year-old Abraham Thornton made an unprepossessing Don Juan. Nevertheless, despite his short, squat, round-shouldered, bull-necked physique, his bullet head, deep-set piggy eyes and "swollen shining face", this son of a prosperous Castle Bromwich, Warwickshire, builder fulfilled the rôle of local Lothario with signal success so far as the lusty country wenches of those parts were concerned.

Long before, in 1871, Sir John Lubbock "invented" the British Bank Holiday, Whit Monday – May 26 – was traditionally a rubric day of rustic frivolity in the villages and hamlets strewn about the more tightly held-in skirted edges of Birmingham. And on Whit Monday, 1817, 20-year-old Mary Ashford, who kept house for her uncle, John Coleman, a small yeoman farmer at Langley Heath, was excited. That evening she would be going with her friend Hannah Cox, to the big Friendly Society dance, held annually at the Three Tuns Inn, kept by Daniel Clarke, in the hamlet of Tyburn.

About 6 pm Mary arrived at the cottage in Erdington where Hannah lived with her widowed mother, Mrs Mary Butler. Already, Mary, who had had to go to Birmingham Market for her uncle – a seven-mile walk each way – had, at eight o'clock that morning, left at the Widow Butler's a bundle containing her dancing finery – white spencer coat, white muslin dress, a dimity petticoat, and white silk stockings. To provide the finishing touch, Hannah had that day purchased for her at the Erdington village shop, a pair of white shoes. Bedecked now, the two young girls set off to walk the couple of country miles to Tyburn House, as the Three Tuns was invariably called locally. They reached it at 7.40 pm. The dancing had already begun.

From the very start, Abe Thornton's wandering eye had leeched on to – and leched after – Mary. To a fellow clodhopper, the coarse-mouthed Thornton boasted his intention to have his will with Mary, "or I'll die for it". That evening he monopolised and mesmerised her.

Eleven o'clock struck. Hannah, the more prudent of the two, a rath Cinderella, decided it was time to leave before the rapidly rising tide of rough beer and rude spirits frothed into too heady a brew of bucolic merrymaking. Together with a young neighbour, Benjamin Carter, who had undertaken to see her home, she waited on the bridge outside the inn for Mary, who, accompanied by Thornton, presently appeared. All four then set off walking the Chester road to Erdington.

Not far into the trudge, Carter, reneging on his promise, loped guiltily off to the still-flaring moth-flame dance. The remaining trio forged on until they struck the by-road turning off to Erdington. There, Hannah left them; Mary announcing her intention to spend the night with her grandfather, William Coleman, whose cottage was situated at the nearby corner of Chester Road and Bell Lane, and Thornton fulsomely assuring that he would escort her safely there.

It was by now midnight. Four blank hours of blackness and silence ensue.

At 3.59 am Mary knocks at Hannah's door. She has, she says, and it is untrue, spent the night at her grandfather's. She must now return to her uncle's. She changes into her everyday clothes, rolls the finery into a bundle, except for the white shoes, which she keeps on. At 4.15 am she takes her leave of Hannah. She heads for home.

At approximately 6.30 am, George Jackson, a road-mender on his way to work, clambered over a stile out of Bell Lane (now Orphanage Road) and followed a footpath to a gate leading into Penn's Mill Lane (now Penns Lane). Close to the gate was a deep pit filled with water. At the top of the sloping bank beside the pit he saw lying a woman's straw bonnet, a bundle and a pair of bloodstained white shoes.

The news of Jackson's discovery spread fast. A small group assembled. A makeshift drag of rake and long reins was put to work. At the third casting it brought out of the dark waters Mary Ashford's body. She had been a virgin, was no longer, and, as duckweed in her stomach showed, had been flung live into the pit to drown.

Abraham Thornton was arrested and charged with her murder and rape, "moved and seduced by the instigation of the Devil."

His defence was alibi. It was unassailable. He admitted carnal knowledge of the girl, but with her full consent. He had left her alive and well – and called seven witnesses who testified to his having been at locations miles from the scene of the tragedy at the time of its occurrence. The jury took six minutes to acquit.

Outraged by the verdict, those convinced of Thornton's guilt sought a means to bring him again before a court. Recourse was had to the ancient, seldom invoked law of "Appeal of Murder", enacted in the reign of Henry VII, whereby, *autrefois acquit* and double jeopardy notwithstanding, the heir-at-law of the decedent may set on foot a prosecution. Mary's elder brother, William Ashford, labourer, of Hints, Staffordshire, duly appealed.

The second trial of Abraham Thornton took place at Westminster Hall on November 16, 1817. Called to plead, Thornton's response made history. "Not guilty. And I am ready to defend the same by my body." At this, he threw a gauntlet down upon the floor of the court. Words and action imparted the archaic Wager of Battel. A privilege last exercised in the time of Charles 1. Two attorneys could play the Ancient Laws game.

"Our poor little Knight", as prosecuting counsel dubbed his appellant client, Ashford, underfed, undersized, unfit for such ordeal of combat, did not take up the challenge, and, as prescribed by law in that event, Thornton, on April 20, 1818, walked free. Perhaps that was just. Perhaps there never was a murder. Perhaps Mary Ashford committed suicide, or fell accidentally into the pit. Certainly in Thornton's case, the *corpus delecti* was assumed. It was never proved.

In consequence, Parliament smartly abolished both ""appeal of murder" and "trial by combat" by statute 1819 (59 Geo III C46). Thornton emigrated to America. After a reportedly prosperous career, he, it is said, died in Baltimore, in 1860. William Ashford followed in later years the trade of a fish hawker. He died in Birmingham in 1867. Mary has lain these last 189 cherry blossom springs, a fallen bloom, in the mouldering ground, close to the South porch of Holy Trinity Parish church, Sutton Coldfield.

Little Girl Lost

Christmas was just ten days away. The little girl stood peering entranced into the bright-lit Aladdin's cave of the chemist's shop window, her wide-eyed gaze fixed on a box of soap dominoes. Mentally she was counting, fingering the saved pennies in her money-box. She wanted so much to buy those dominoes for a present.

But Christmas never came for ten-year-old Vera Page.

It was just on half-past four on Monday, December 14, 1931, when Vera came skipping merrily home from her North Kensington school. An only child, she lived with her parents, Charles and Isobel Page, at 22 Blenheim Crescent, in London's Notting Hill district. She was, she told her mother, feeling hungry, and would hurry back for tea, which would be at half-past five. But first, she wanted to run round to Aunt Minnie's to collect the couple of school swimming certificates which she had won and proudly taken to show her. Mrs Minnie Maria Essex lived just a few doors up the Crescent, at No 70.

Vera duly called there, picked up her certificates, which were in a large envelope, and left again at 4.45 pm. A young girl who knew Vera reported seeing her looking in the window of the chemist on the corner of Blenheim Crescent, just a few yards beyond her home. She had tapped her on the back and Vera had smiled at her.

Vera was seen again, still looking in the same chemist's window, by a young sailor, a friend of the Page family, who knew her by name. He gave the time of the sighting as about 6.30 pm, but this could have been slightly out.

Next, a Mr Ritches, also a friend of the Pages and who knew Vera, walking at about 6.45 pm along Montpelier Road (now Lansdowne Rise), which led from Clarendon Road to Lansdowne Crescent, saw Vera. She clutched some papers – her envelope of certificates – in her hand. Swinging her red beret in her other hand, she turned into Lansdowne Road and walked cheerily off into the December darkness, into oblivion. He was the last person, her murderer apart, to see little Vera alive.

When his daughter failed to come home, her father, a painter employed by the Great Western Railway Company at Paddington, went to the police. The child's description was circulated. Particulars of her disappearance and pictures of her appeared in the newspapers of December 15. An SOS was broadcast for her.

Still . . . nothing . . . not a sign.

Then, at about ten minutes to ten on Wednesday morning, December 16, a milkman doing his second round made a terrible discovery. Entering by the tradesmen's entrance at No 89 Addison Road, Holland Park, he saw the fully clothed body of a child lying there among the shrubs by the driveway.

Vera Page had been found.

Medical examinations disclosed that she had been strangled and maltreated. Nothing so distresses the police as the brutal murder of a little child. Most of them, family men themselves, can share the anguish of the parents. So, in the few, short, dark December days before Christmas they worked with a will. They had only one real clue to help them. In the crook of Vera's right elbow they had found trapped a finger-stall bandage. It was stained with soot or coal-dust and smelt of ammonia.

Now they began the mammoth task of interviewing everybody who might have known, or been known, by the dead girl, looking especially for anyone with a wounded finger. And from all the thousand or more people from whom the police took statements, there was only one who knew Vera, and was known to her, who had been wearing a finger-stall – and he worked with ammonia.

His name was Percy Orlando Rush. Married, aged 41, a short thickset man with bushy black eyebrows, horn-rimmed spectacles, and a heavy moustache, he lived with his wife at 128 Talbot Road, just a few minutes away from Vera's home, and his parents occupied the upper part of the self-same house as that in which Vera and her parents lived. He was employed as a flannel washer at Whiteley's Laundry, near Olympia; work which involved contact with ammonia. He had cut the little finger of his left hand in two places while at work on Wednesday, December 9, and had been wearing a finger-stall up to the following Saturday. Meanwhile, further clues had turned up. Mrs Kathleen Short, living at 23 Stanley Crescent, Ladbroke Grove, had found a red beret, reeking of paraffin, a candle-end and some torn fragments of cardboard – perhaps swimming certificates – in the basement area in front of her house. Down there also was an outside empty coal-cellar with an open door. Indeed, spots of candle grease on Vera's coat and the presence of coal-dust had suggested that she might have been kept in a coal-cellar before being deposited in the shrubbery. There was a similar coal-cellar at Rush's house. A rag soaked in paraffin was found in his home. There were traces of coal-dust in his clothes.

There was the evidence of the tell-tale ammoniated finger-stall. A pyjama-cord, such as might have been used in moving the body, was tucked in his pocket. He could produce no solid alibi. Everyone who knew Vera said that she was a shy, retiring child who would not speak to, let alone go off with, a stranger. He knew Vera. She would have trusted him. Margaret Key, of Goldhawk Road, on her way to work at 7 am on December 16, saw a man wheeling a barrow towards Addison Road. There was a bundle covered with a red table-cloth on it. An almost, but not quite similar red table-cloth was uncovered at the Rush home. Rush became the prime suspect. But the circum-stantial evidence lacked the necessary weight and cohesion. The death of little Vera Page became just one more tragic count in the statistics of unsolved murder.

I can now reveal that Percy Orlando Rush survived to see 31 more Christmases. Before his retirement he had worked as a road orderly for Acton Borough Council. He died, aged 70, in Acton Hospital, London, on November 17, 1961, of peritonitis associated with cancer of the bladder. Only then did certain old members of the Met feel with an undeniable glow of satisfaction that the Vera Page murder file could be closed.

A Dentist's Fatal Extraction

At about a quarter to eleven one January night, sundry witnesses observed a portly, middle-aged man with a shawl around his shoulders walk casually along Bond Street, New York, ascend the steps of No 31, open the door with a latchkey and step inside. Shortly thereafter a cry was heard. "Mur . . . !" – cut off, like its maker's life, approximately midway.

The gentleman whose earthly tenancy had been thus summarily foreclosed was Dr Harvey Burdell, a 46-year-old surgeon dentist. (Dentists are accorded the title "Doctor" in the United States.) If *post mortem* character references are anything to go by, Dr Burdell was somewhat less than a charmer. Mercenary, selfish, bullying, cowardly, quarrelsome, litigious, were the epithets attached to his wreaths. His loss seems to have been as much regretted as that of an aching molar. The household over which he had presided at No 31 was an odd one. It included Mrs Emma Augusta Cunningham, a handsome putative widow at the distal end of her thirties, and her two daughters – Augusta (18) and Helen (16) – and two sons, William (10) and George (9). Her position was that of main tenant of the doctor, and provider of board and lodging for three sub-tenants of her own.

The first of these – for we must take stock of all the strange tenantry of this curious ménage – was the Dickensianly named George Vail Snodgrass, a poetaster of nineteen, fanatically addicted to playing the banjo. Then there was the Honourable Daniel Ullman, a lawyer of some moment who had only recently missed, by a very few voting papers' breadth, becoming Governor of the State of New York. Finally, there was John J. Eckel, a minor politician, seriously bestricken by an intemperate love of canaries, embowered amid chirrupy cages of them, and reputedly far from immune to the plumage of Mrs C. Bringing the full household strength up to eleven, there were additionally Hannah Conlan, the cook, and another servant, Mary Donahue, both in the employ of Mrs Cunningham. It was Dr Burdell's office-boy, John Burchell, arriving at 8.30 the following morning, Saturday, January 31, 1857, who discovered the corpse of the dentist. He was lying on his face close to the front-door. He had been stabbed ferociously at least 15 times. One stab wound was in the heart and his carotid artery had been severed.

There were no signs of any break-in: no indications of robbery. The obvious conclusion was that one of the occupants of the house must have been the murderer. It was a conclusion reinforced by the, possibly, suspicious fact that although the strangled cry of "Murder!" which the doctor gave had been sufficiently loud for three people outside the house to hear it, not one of the ten indwellers would admit to having heard anything. But wait . . . it was at this point that the stately Mrs Cunningham stepped forward. Loud with grief where, witnesses could later say, she had been previously loud with anger, she now claimed that she and the defunct dentist had been secretly married. Observing the wailing widow, the wondering witnesses recalled the stormy passages at arms between that copiously weeping lady and the angry doctor, when the air about had been filled with the flying hailstones of accusation and counter-accusation. Where and when did this peace-making match take place? A good three months ago, said Mrs Cunningham; at the Dutch Reformed Church in nearby Bleeker Street, on October 28, 1856. The minister had been the Reverend Uriah Marvine. That gentleman testified that he had indeed performed a marriage ceremony upon that date between a man who called himself Harvey Burdell and a woman, but he proved unable to recognise either Mrs Cunningham as the previous blushing bride or the wan corpse of the late doctor as one of the happy couple. He did, however, recognise Augusta Cunningham, who had been a witness. All that that proved was that Mrs Cunningham had married someone.

That someone, it came to be thought, was John J. Eckel, the canary man, posing as Dr Burdell. Eckel, bald as a coot, had a known fancy for the donning of borrowed plumes in the form of wigs of different colours. Surely the heavily hirsute groom recalled by the Reverend Marvine was Eckel in nuptial fancy dress. Theories of a black collusion between the couple to get their claws into the dentist's money-bags began to take shape. The medical examiner opined the death stabs were dealt by a left-handed person. Mrs Cunningham was sinistral as well as sinister. She and Eckel were arrested and deposited in the Tombs Prison. Calling herself now Mrs Cunningham-Burdell, milady Emma was put up before Supreme Court Judge, the Honourable Henry E. Davies. The trial lasted three days. The jury took three minutes to find her not guilty. Eckel, who had been awaiting in custody the outcome of Mrs Cunningham's arraignment, was duly released. What joyous canary twittering and celebratory twangings of banjo strings must have ensued in Bond Street that merry month of May, 1857.

But Madame Cunningham-Burdell was not yet done. She now introduced the culminating grotesquerie of a thoroughly grotesque affair. Flushed with victory, profit motive revived and refreshed, she announced that the arrival of a little Cunningham-Burdell was imminent. He or she would, of course, be heir to the considerable Burdell property. Art and artifice aided the determined mother in the early stages of the immaculate deception. But nature will out – and in this case it couldn't!

And this was where this terrifying woman made her fatal mistake. She offered her GP, Dr David Uhl, a thousand dollars to provide a bogus infant for her. He communicated with the authorities. Playing along, they produced the new-born daughter of a poor woman from the Bellevue Hospital lying-in ward. And Mrs Cunningham's sham confinement was exchanged for real confinement, back in the Tombs.

But once more the She-Devil's own luck held. At the preliminary hearing, Judge Peabody ruled that the act of producing the baby as her own did not in itself constitute a criminal fraud within the section of the statute upon which the new criminal accusation was founded, and she was set free.

The one person to emerge from the whole disreputable charade with a profit was Mrs Elizabeth Ann Anderson, whose baby, appropriately christened Justitia, was used in the attempted hoax. Mother and baby were exhibited live by Phineas T. Barnum – to the handsome profit of all.

Sweeney Todd and Bell Yard

"Easy Shaving for a Penny
As good as you will find any"

Thus ran the rough poetry of the secret invitation to death – the sign winking and twinkling beside the red and white, bandage and blood, barber's pole outside the little shop amid the vital turmoil of London's Fleet Street.

Having succumbed to its temptation, entered into the somewhat cramped and shabby premises, the alert eye would be given pause by the odd position of the barber's chair, standing, hypnotically, right in the centre of the shop.

Nor was the aspect of the proprietor himself calculated to promote ease of feeling. Hulking, thick-necked, coarse-visaged, beetle-browed, with great hams of hands, Mr Sweeney Todd's physique seemed to fit him better for the trade of butcher than the fine art of *perruquier*. Looming over one with what we would call today his catch-phrase, "Oh, I'll soon polish you off," brandishing lather brush and open cut-throat razor, he was a fearsome spectacle, apt herald of the undreamt horror to come.

Warm and beguiling, the lather was expertly swept about the stubbly chin. Lulled, one watched the barber glide swiftly and silently to the back of his shop, to fetch, one thought, a freshly sweet-edged razor. In fact, he went to operate the crank activating the mechanism of the diabolical apparatus of the revolving trap which sent his barber's chair somersaulting backwards. And as, in a great flurry and whirl, chair and circambient floor up-ended, the half-shaved man hurtled into a cellar 15 feet deep, paved with sharp edges of stone, set perpendicularly to cause the greatest damage. And if the fall did not kill outright, the barber would pad down into the dark pit to "polish off" his victim with a well-honed blade. Crouched with the dead man in this secret underground kingdom of night, the demon barber would, at his leisure, relieve the body of all its money and valuables before the corpse was meticulously butchered, cut-up into handy-sized portions and delivered piecemeal to his evil accomplice, Mrs Lovett's pie-shop, just round the corner in Bell Yard. This outwardly respectable establishment was famed throughout Fleet Street and the legal purlieus of the Temple for the fine flavour and sweet succulence of its meat-pies. Exquisite irony indeed that lawyers shoul have been the principal consumers of the materia of *Grand Guignol* multicide!

But – and the question has to be asked – this demon barber, was he just another Sawney Beane, flesh or phantasm, man or myth? Where precisely in Bell Yard was Mrs Lovett's pie-shop, with its bakehouse which communicated with the vaults of St Dunstan's?

Sweeney Agonistes! A couple of hundred years later the argument still goes on: the die-hard pro-Sweeneyans poring over ancient records and anti-Toddites peering at faded and friable newspapers in quest of a clue.

Perhaps the strongest card in the hand of the anti-Todd lobby is his glaring absence from the archive of the Newgate calendar.

Cut-throat competition among the cynics ensures finger-pointing to a variety of characters to whom Sweeney and his alleged activities bear persuasive resemblance.

For instance: a tale has been told in Italy these two centuries past of a pastrycook of Venice the superlative tenderness of whose meat-pies turned out to be not unconnected with the disappearance of a large number of children from the city.

There is, too, the butcher of Magdeburg, Ressel, who, in the Germany of the 1750s, despatched the occasional customer with a meat-cleaver and sold him on, dismembered, wih the rest of his stock-in-flesh.

While France, not to be outdone by the old foe, the Bosche, can pipe up a Parisian barber of the rue de la Harpe, convicted of killing a client and, after robbing him, donating what remained to his female accomplice, a *pâtissière*. Police, making a subsequent search, are said to have found the remains of another 200 bodies in the cellar of his shop.

For the defence, that notorious *presbyter vagans* and expert on all matters Gothic, the Reverend Montague Summers, wrote in his classic, *A Gothic Bibliography*: "The old watchman outside the gate of St Bartholemew's Hospital about 1798 used to aver that his father had been murdered for his coin by 'Sweeney Todd'."

And in 1913, workmen demolishing 186 Fleet Street – traditionally the location of Sweeney Todd's shop – found a large number of human bones in the cellar. "From the ancient burial crypt of St Dunstan's adjoining," chorused the anti-Sweeney brigade.

In terms of fiction – or is it factión? – the name and story of Sweeney Todd indisputably first appeared in a frankly spinal serial, "The String of Pearls", in the *People's Periodical*, published from Salisbury Square, off Fleet Street, in the winter of 1846–7.

The author, Thomas Peckett Prest (1810–1859), the wayward virtuoso of Salisbury Square, was a sub-Dickensian hack or penny-a-liner, one of Edward Lloyd's (founder of *Lloyd's Newspaper*) young men of penny-dreadful imagination and prodigious output; the pioneer Grub Streeters. The story was very precisely set in the year 1785. Did Prest invent Todd? Or was he the chronicler of a true history buried beneath the curlicued crockets and finials of his melodramatic account?

Here, written in the key of the time, is a slice of Prest's confection:

"The youths who visited Lovett's pie-shop and there luxuriated upon those delicacies are youths no longer. Indeed, the grave has closed over all but one, and he is very, very old, but even now as he thinks of how many pies he ate, and how he enjoyed the flavour of the 'veal', he shudders and has to take a drop of brandy.

"Beneath the old church of St Dunstan's were found the heads and bones of Todd's victims. As little as possible was said by the authorities about it, but it was supposed that some hundreds of persons must have perished in the frightful manner we have detailed."

To the riddle of Bell Yard the answer must be the Scottish one – not proven.

Under the Greenwood Family Tree

A curious taut atmosphere, like that brooding about one of those French villages in a Simenon novel, pervaded the small, deep Welsh town of Kidwelly. When Harold Greenwood, a Yorkshire man from Ingleton, recently admitted solicitor, arrived there in 1898, his name was his misfortune. It should have been Jones or Jenkins, Evans or Pugh. The Cymric mafia ruled. To the end of his days there, Greenwood remained a foreigner.

His practice in Llanelly, nine miles away, a busy industrial town with legal business enough to sustain a fair number of solicitors, was always a marginal, threadbare one; mostly modest land transactions, together with a small garnishing of money-lender clients. For sure, it was in odd contrast to the prosperity of his home, Rumsey House, a three-storey mansion standing in its own extensive gardener-tended grounds at Kidwelly – upkept, so it was said, by the private money of his well-to-do wife, Mabel, a Bowater of the ilk which begat a Lord Mayor of London, her brother, Sir Vanisittart Bowater.

Kidwelly was not a happy place. It was a small town in the worst sense: enlivened by vicious scandal-mongering and poisonous gossip over the teacups. Envy, spite, malice and mischief tripped arm-in-arm vindictively through the dull streets and gathered viper's tongue-wagging in the open marts. No one's sorrows were secret – or sacred. All fears and misfortunes were public, not private, affairs. It is against this perpetual backcloth that the tragedy of Rumsey House must be assayed.

The *huis clos* of Kidwelly was extended and intensified in the great mansion where, apart from Harold, Mabel and two of their children – Irene, 21, and Kenneth, 10, (the other two, Eileen, 17, and Ivor, 15, were at boarding-school) – lived three women servants and, an oppressive presence, Mabel's spinster sister, Miss Edith Bowater, who occupied a single room, furnished by herself, and paid a fixed contribution to the household expenses.

Among the townspeople of Kidwelly, Mrs Greenwood was liked. She was thought of – and thought of herself – as "delicate", suffering from a weak heart. She also suffered from carcinophobia. The *post mortem* facts are that she had no valvular heart disease, and only a small, non-malignant uterine fibroid tumour. Her doctor – the family doctor since 1903 – was Dr Thomas Griffiths. He was soon to retire.

Mabel's closest friend was Miss Florence Phillips. Harold did not like her. She was a gossipy spreader of rumours. He called her the "Kidwelly Postman".

Greenwood himself was not liked: too much of a ladies' man was the Welsh choral verdict. His name was romantically entwined with, among others, that of Mary, Dr Griffiths' sister, who, it was reported by whisper, had been seen sitting on his knee in a railway carriage. He was friendly, too, wasn't he, with young Gladys Jones, one of the daughters of his great friend and remote kinsman, W. B. Jones, proprietor of the *Llanelly Mercury*.

Strangely, with the exception of Mary Griffiths and Gladys Jones, all who knew the Greenwoods – including their servants, who knew them best – spoke to the happiness and harmony of their union.

That is . . . until the aftermath of June 15, 1919. It was a Sunday. A day of lovely summer's weather. Mabel spent the morning writing letters and reading on the lawn. Harold was fussing around his motor-car, cleaning and overhauling it. Lunch, served at one o'clock, consisted of a joint, vegetables, gooseberry tart and custard. A bottle of Burgundy was on the table. Mabel had a glass of wine. After lunch she retired to her bedroom for a brief rest, before going to sit in a deck-chair on the lawn.

It was at about 6.30 pm that she complained of a pain in the region of her heart. Harold gave her some brandy. She was very sick. Dr Griffiths was summoned. Mabel told him that the gooseberry tart had disagreed with her. He prescribed sips of brandy and soda and, later, sent over a bottle of bismuth mixture.

At 7.30, Florence Phillips arrived for supper. Told by Harold that Mabel was "very ill", she took it upon herself to go and ask District Nurse Elizabeth Jones to come. Nurse Jones arrived at about 8 pm, and did not like what she saw. But Dr Griffiths, paying repeated visits, found nothing inconsistent with a gastric upset.

Shortly after 3 am, Mabel Greenwood died. The Kidwelly tongues really got busy then. And when, four months later, Greenwood married Gladys Jones, 18 years younger than himself, they wagged so vigorously and effectively that an exhumation was ordered. A quarter of a grain of arsenic was found in the first Mrs Greenwood's body, and Greenwood was put on trial for her murder.

He appeared at the Camarthen Assizes in November, 1920, defended by Marshall Hall, who did his best to muddy the medical waters, in the process accusing Dr Griffiths of criminal negligence, which led to one of many passages of arms between Sir Edward and Shearman J. In the event, the medical battling proved meaningless. The prosecution was relying heavily upon the suggestion that the arsenic – in the form of weed-killer – had been administered in the bottle of Burgundy served at Sunday lunch. However, daughter Irene declared that she, too, had had a glass of wine from that same bottle at lunch – and two more glasses besides from it at supper. And that was an end to the affair.

Rumsey House was sold. Greenwood changed his name to Pilkington, and with his wife and son Kenneth, moved to the tiny Herefordshire village of Walford, near Ross-on-Wye. In March, 1922, taking a leaf out of A. J. Monson's book, he won himself £150 damages from a waxworks showman at Cardiff, who had exhibited his effigy in his Chamber of Horrors. In April, he earned an honest crust attending, and writing for *John Bull* a subjective account of the trial for murder of his fellow, and less fortunate, solicitor, Major Herbert Armstrong, the Hay Poisoner. His financial state became precarious. He applied for the position of Clerk to Ross Urban Council. They turned him down. His health broke, and he died at his house, The Paddock, on January 17, 1929. The wagging tongues revived, and the word on the lips of that fickle jade, Gossip, was "retribution".

The Sydney Double-death Riddle

The expectation that a post-mortem will disclose the cause of death is rarely disappointed. When, moreover, two corpses are found side by side, neither of them presenting traumata or a recognisable pathology, then the mystery is indeed deep.

It was two teenage boys, out on an early morning hunt for lost golf-balls, who first saw the man. He was lying face down amid the scrub on the bank of Sydney's Lane Cove River, partially covered by a "blanket" of grimy carpet. They thought he was a hobo sleeping off the previous night's celebration, for this was 8 am on New Year's Day.

However, when returning an hour later from their fossicking in the hem of boscage around nearby Chatswood Golf Course, they saw the man stretched in identical pose and position, they investigated. The man was dead. They called the police.

This was no tramp. Papers on the body identified Dr Gilbert Stanley Bogle, top-flight, solid state physicist, Rhodes Scholar and important official at the Commonwealth Scientific and Industrial Research Organisation. Investigating police officers also discovered that, below his carpet coverlet, Bogle was only partly dressed.

A constable searching for clues came upon a second body. It lay some 150 feet away, covered by flattened beer cartons. It was that of a young woman, lying on her back. Her dress had been bunched up, exposing the lower part of her body. There was nothing to identify her.

This was the beginning of one of the most extraordinary mysteries of modern times, for although both of them had as it turned out died unnatural deaths, the manner and cause of those deaths remain as obscure today as on that January morning in 1963. The woman was subsequently identified as Margaret Chandler, aged 29, wife of Geoffrey Chandler – a CSIRO experimental officer – and mother of two young sons.

Margaret and Bogle had come together at a New Year's Eve party. Leaving his wife, Vivienne, at home with her four children in their fine house behind the copse of tall, straight, slender gum trees, Gib, as intimates called him, leapt into his 1948 green Ford Prefect, and sped unencumbered to the revelry. Away from the laboratory Gib was an excessively free-ranging character. He played a mean clarinet. He was a dab foot at Spanish dancing. He loved Bach and beer. But best of all he loved women. And he had had strings of them.

So it was that this New Year's Eve, sleek, smart, sweet-smelling of after-shave, Lothario Gil, "liberated" in that era before the bonds of AIDS would bind the would-be sexual voyager to a cringing chastity, adventured forth, resolved upon a little fetter-free romance. Margaret Chandler, similarly oriented, liberated by her and Geoffrey's "modern marriage" agreement, willingly partnered the magnetic Gib.

They drive, these two, through the star-hung, promissory night to the solitudes of Lane Cove River Park, and cruise down secluded Lovers' Lane to where the fates await them.

There was, so far as is evidenced, none to witness their agonies. The privacy they sought for their joys isolated them in their suffering.

Their purgatory amid the litter of broken bottles, old cans and rotting newspapers, mouldering among the rank weeds and the slime of the circumambient marshland, is attested to only by the bodily traces which marked their anguish as they crawled in crazy circles, going nowhere.

The two poor vessels were borne to the old Sydney morgue. And there the surprise exploded upon the battalions of medical and forensic scientists who sought to label their mortality. All forms of violence, all kinds of disease, were excluded as causes of death. The cadavers were inspected for such injuries as ruptured eardrums, resultant upon high-frequency sound-waves or supersonic waves – nothing. Checks were run for radiation and residual radio-activity – nothing.

The next logical step: toxicological investigation. The couple's brain, heart, liver and spleen tissues were examined; also their blood. Hair was tested for arsenic. Traces of henbane, mercury, nicotine, opium, phenol, phosphorus, strychnine, and those of scores of other poisons, including even the venom of the Queensland cone fish, were sought. Nothing was found.

Tests were conducted for the use of fluorides. Ionising influences were scanned for, with rays, ultra-violet and infra-red, and radiation monitors. Signs of food poisoning, the presence of alcohol, sedatives and carbon monoxide were canvassed – again, nothing. The bodies were scrutinised for the marks of hypodermic needles, pin-pricks, or animal bites. Blood tests eliminated snake or spider venoms.

Thus, the entire causal spectrum seemingly exhausted, the pathologists had, reluctantly, to ascribe both deaths to acute circulatory failure. That was a description; not a diagnosis.

Two years after the mysterious Bogle-Chandler deaths, Dr Pang Teng Cheung, Director of forensic medicine for the Hong Kong police, reported two deaths which showed precisely the same symptom pattern. They occurred after the taking of yohimbine. Sometimes called "Japanese chocolate", yohimbine is an illegal Asian sex-drug.

Now there was a certain intimate friend of Gib's – Margaret Fowler. Young, vivacious, eye-catchingly well-dressed, ear-captivatingly intelligent, holding degrees in physics and mathematics, she was married to a Sydney chemical engineer. She and Gib became lovers. He, after his usual fashion, tired of her. But for her he became an obsession. She would not accept that the affair was over. When the police got round to her she had an alibi for them – attendance at another New Year's Eve party. There were those who were convinced that, in a frenzy of jealousy, she had somehow contrived to spike the drinks of Gib and her favoured rival with the fatal sex-drug.

Graham Carlton, a colleague of hers, testified that at the time of the double death she was in a state of great distress and kept repeating "It's all going to come out." Asked what she meant, she would only reply, "You'll soon know." And later remarked of Gib and Margaret, "They were going to cop it." She gave Carlton the strong impression that she was somehow involved in the deaths.

Like the song the sirens sang, we shall never now know, for on June 18, 1977, Margaret Fowler died in a London hospital.

The Midnight Gardener

Like everything else about the neat suburban villa in Erith Road, Belvedere, on the London lip of north west Kent, the garden was immaculate. House and garden reflected the obsessional personality of their owner, Charles Frederick Lewis, aged 60, education officer of Erith, who lived there with his wife, Maude, two years younger, and 20-year-old Freda, whom they had adopted after her father perished in the *Titanic* disaster.

But, to the uncompromisingly critical eye of Charles Lewis, that perfect garden lacked one vital feature – a lily pond; for, like Monet, Mr Lewis found in the vision of their still, shining surfaces and the curling green platelets of the lilies, beneath which goldfish swam, an especial delight.

So it was that for nearly a month now he had been hard at work in his spare time, helped by Maude and Freda, preparing the foundations for the kidney-shaped lily pond of his dreams, which this Whit weekend of 1931 should see completed.

The stone nymphs lay prone in waiting on the lawn. All that was needed now was a final thick layer of cement.

Whit Monday came – and went.

Of Mr Lewis, upon whose creative activities the neighbours were inclined to keep an interested – not to say envious – eye, there was no sign. What should have been the great celebratory day of the pool had passed dully. The fact of the matter was that Mr Lewis, whose neurotic energy permitted him no single moment's luxury of idleness, had already embarked upon the next job-in-waiting on his do-it-yourself list; re-papering the dining-room.

However, had his inquisitive neighbours extended their curtain-peeping vigil into the dark hours of Monday night, their persistence would have been rewarded. For it was then, when all was still, and only the blank and empty windows of the music school on the one side, and those of the adjoining villa on the other, stared blindly, that the furtive, burdened figure of the midnight gardener appeared, shambling along the 50 yards leading from the house to the the half-finished lily pond.

The following morning – Tuesday, June 2 – a Mr John Davidson walked into a shipping office in Cannon Street and booked a passage to Leith aboard the London & Edinburgh Shipping Company's steamer, the *Royal Scott*, sailing from Wapping on June 5.

That Tuesday morning also, Mr Lewis telephoned the principal of the college at Stockwell, where Freda was training to become a teacher. "Freda will not return tonight," he told her curtly. "I will write to you about it." And abruptly rang off. The letter which arrived next day said that Freda had met with an accident and might not be back for some time.

Letters from Charles Lewis began to arrive, too, at the homes of various relatives. They said that both Maude and Freda had had accidents and that he would be sending details later.

Then . . . nothing . . . absolute silence.

On Friday, June 5, one worried relative arrived from Wales to find the house in Erith Road locked and deserted. Thoroughly uneasy, he went to Blackheath Road Police Station. The police telephoned Erith Education Authority. Mr Lewis had not been back to his office since the holiday He had rung up saying that his wife was dead.

Hearing this, the police went round to Erith Road. They forced a window and entered the house. There was no sign of any mischief. The furniture piled in the centre, and the dining-room's stripped walls indicated that the energetic Mr Lewis had already set about his next DIY task. The three beds in the house had been slept in, but were unmade. Also – and it was something that alerted suspicion – one sheet from each bed was missing. A search revealed no soiled sheets anywhere in the place.

Neighbours were questioned. No one had seen Mr Lewis, Mrs Lewis, Freda or, come to think of it, their little terrier, for days. Glancing out of the window, Superintendent William Brown's eye was caught by the flapping tarpaulin half-covering the unfinished lily pond.

> "When I look into the fish ponds in my garden,
> Methinks I see a thing arm'd with a rake,
> That seems to strike at me."
> – Webster, *The Duchess of Malfi*

With pickaxes, the police it was who struck, and raked aside the iron-set concrete . . . and there the "things" were – the two women, the dog, and the three missing sheets.

Sir Bernard Spilsbury's post-mortems attributed all three deaths to cyanide. A chemist in Eardley Road, Belvedere, reported selling two and a half ounces of cyanide – for use as an insecticide – to Mr Lewis, who had duly signed the poisons book, six weeks before.

Lewis' description was circulated. Height: six feet, slim build, grizzled grey hair, grey eyes, gold rimmed spectacles, walks with a limp, suggestive of a withered leg.

The *Royal Scott* was 14 miles north of Whitby when one of his six fellow-passengers asked Mr Davidson sympathetically about his injured leg. Davidson reacted oddly; rose without a word and limped out of the smoking-room.

A steward, just passing Mr Davidson's cabin, heard a splash. He caught a glimpse of the man in the water. Mr Davidson had jumped overboard.

The ship stopped. Boats were lowered. They searched in vain.

Mr Davidson was, of course, Charles Frederick Lewis.

When the dead man's affairs were looked into it was revealed that, a few years before, there had been a discrepancy of some hundreds of pounds in the Erith Education Committee's accounts, of which he had charge. Colleagues recalled an angry discussion between Lewis and his chief, Mr Flux. Flux had so worked himself up that he had a seizure, lost the power of speech, and died soon afterwards.

Now, an auditor's investigation showed irregularities amounting to between £500 and £600 which, beginning before the death of Mr Flux, continued right up to the time of the disappearance of Mr Lewis.

Haunted by guilt and fear of exposure, and having issued, as it were, an irrefusable Tennysonian invitation to his wife – that to include daughter and dog – Charles Frederick Lewis elected to write with his own hand a Strindbergian end to the affair: to balance the books by total erasure.

Jewels in the Irish Crown

The heraldic dovecot –the Office of Arms in Dublin Castle –was in a state of unparalleled flutter. His Majesty the King was due to arrive within a matter of days, and the Irish Crown jewels had disappeared; vanished as utterly as if the cluricaunes had made off with them.

The jewels, a diamond star and diamond badge, both enhanced with emeralds and rubies – actually the insignia of the Order of St Patrick – had been presented by William IV in 1830, and were worn on formal occasions by the Lord Lieutenant of Ireland, as Grand Master. The custodianship of the jewels was the responsibility of Ulster King of Arms, the Chief Herald of Ireland, Sir Arthur Vicars.

Vicars, 43 years of age, an effete, scholarly, fussy man, had been appointed to office, *quamdiu se bene gesserit*, by the King himself in 1893, and had since gathered around him a curious *cénacle*, centred upon the Heraldic Office in the Bedford Tower of the castle. This included his nephew, Peirce Gun Mahony, aged 27, upon whom he bestowed the post of Cork Herald. Another young friend, Francis Richard Shackleton, brother of the Antarctic explorer Ernest Shackleton, was created Dublin Herald. And, completing the trinity of favourites, Francis Bennett-Goldney, young kinsman of Sir Arthur Evans, explorer and exponent of ancient Crete, was appointed Athlone Pursuivant.

The first, albeit veiled, intimation of trouble to come was when, arriving between seven and eight o'clock on the morning of Wednesday, July 3, 1907, the cleaning woman, Mrs Mary Farrell, found the front-door of the Office of Arms unlocked. This was duly reported by her to William Stivey, the office messenger. He informed

Sir Arthur, whose oddly unconcerned reaction was simply, "Is that so?" Never another word about it.

Three days later – Saturday, July 6, Mrs Farrell made another disquieting discovery. This time she saw that the door of the strong-room, leading off the library in the Bedford Tower, was open, although the inner grille was locked, *its key in the lock*. Again, Sir Arthur received the news from Stivey with an extraordinary *sang-froid*. But this was soon to be shattered. Before Sir Arthur's arrival that morning, Peirce Mahony had received a parcel from Messrs West & Son, the Dublin jewellers. It contained a gold collar of the Order of St Patrick which had been sent to have the name of the recently deceased Lord de Ros, who had previously ceremonially worn it, inscribed memorially upon one of its links.

Finding it on his table, a temporarily harassed Sir Arthur had handed it and the key of the safe, which was located *not*, as might be expected, in the strong-room, but in the open library, to Stivey, telling him to put it away. Minutes later, a worried Stivey reported that he had found the safe unlocked . . . and, to his horror, Sir Arthur discovered that the star, the badge, and five ceremonial gold collars worn by the Knights of the Order – as well as a case of diamonds belonging to the Vicars family which he kept in the safe – were missing. The viceregal world was stunned by the news. Rumours began to circulate. It was whispered that Vicars had been associating with a circle of highly-placed homosexuals.

Unsavoury tales were bartered of scandalous stag-parties and unspeakable orgies of unnameable vices. It is certainly true that Shackleton practised homosexuality, and there are circumstances that strongly indicate that Vicars was of like persuasion, but that does not justify suspicion of either as regards the robbery. On the other hand, Shackleton admitted to being in severely turbulent financial waters, owing large sums to money-lenders. Sir Arthur displayed every indication of baffled innocence, even to the credulous extent of holding a séance at his St James' Terrace house and, in consequence of clairvoyant spirit tidings threat relayed, went scampering off post-haste to scrabble among the tombstones of disused churchyards at Clonsilla and Mulhuddert – alas! to no avail.

There were only two keys to the safe. Both were in the possession of Vicars. It was thought that Shackleton, who shared Vicars' house with him, might have abstracted the safe key and made a wax impression of it. But nothing was ever proved: nor did the jewels ever come to light. "*Quis Separabit*"? was the motto which, significantly, decorated them. A special Commission of Inquiry was set up, not to discover the thief, but to consider whether Sir Arthur had exercised due vigilance and proper care as the custodian of the regalia. It was decided that he had not, and at the express wish of Edward VII, who had knighted him in 1905, Vicars was dismissed.

An appalling Tutankhamen-like nemesis overtook the three heraldic bachelors connected with the Irish Crown jewels mystery. It struck down Vicars' nephew, too. Peirce Mahony died in 1914, victim of a very peculiar shooting accident. Armed with a double-barrelled gun, he had set off to shoot water-fowl at Grange Con, County Wicklow, and, climbing a fence, had somehow tripped the trigger and shot himself through the heart.

Four years later, Francis Bennett-Goldney died as the delayed result of a motor accident. Francis Shackleton did not for many years die, but his life wound slowly down to a seedy end. Adjudged bankrupt in 1910, he was imprisoned for fraud in 1913. After his release, he lived under a pseudonym, dying obscurely a forgotten death in the twilight of the years between the wars.

And Sir Andrew Vicars? He folded his sumptuously emblazoned tabard and retired to Kilmorna House, County Kerry, where, doubt-less, dabbling still with quarterings, co-heirs, escutcheons of honour and bars of bastardy, cultivating the more esoteric parterres of Irish genealogy, he continued to wander in the enchanted mediaeval world of his imaginings. He also contracted, in 1917, a marriage – *blanc*? – to propitiate, perhaps, the homoerotic furies. But fate was not to be propitiated. Surviving the invasion of his house in 1920, by 100 armed men, he was murdered on April 14, 1921; shot at the foot of the terrace steps at Kilmorna, a label hung about his neck: "Spy. Informers beware. IRA never forgets." Behind him the house perished in flames. The IRA denied responsibility.

From beyond the barriers, Sir Arthur made one last valiant attempt. In his will he named Shackleton as the thief, and denounced the Irish government and Edward VII. But higher powers bested him once again. The law had long been quite clear that the text of a will cannot be used to publish libels.

Beast of the Fields: or Pure Sadism

What manner of freak is it that comes reeking out of the pages of Krafft-Ebing to lope under the quilt of darkness across the slumbering fields to where, soft and warm, a horse stands gently grazing, or lies folded in sleep, whip out a slick knife and slit half-open the trusting, nuzzling creature's cord-veined under-belly?

The folk of the primitive colliery village of Great Wyrley, Staffordshire, thought they knew the answer. Sly rustic looks sidled towards the alien figure of George Ernest Thompson Edalji, a 27-year-old solicitor. An expert on railway law, and author of a widely appreciated handbook on the subject, he practised with Osborne & Company in Birmingham, travelling there daily fiom his parents' home in Great Wyrley.

Ever since, in December, 1875, the Edalji family had come to the scattered village set in a forbidding landscape of dismal fields, stunted trees, and smoke-darkened hedgerows, scarred by pit workings, traversed by railway lines, intersected by dreary expanses of leaden canals, and moved into Great Wyrley Vicarage, it seemed to have become, like Wesley's Epworth or Latter-day Borley, an epicentre of unease.

Scuds of storm clouds massed about it. Ill-luck and elfish pranks plagued it, like an infestation of poltergeist. Showers of poison-pen letters drenched it. Scurrilous scrawlings appeared upon the garden wall. Like an apport, a massive key – it proved to have been taken from Walsall Grammar School – -materialised upon the door-step. Malice was in the air – the Edalji family its afflicted nexus.

That was no surprise in the village. Where you find queer events look for queer people, went the stolid bucolic whisper. And, incontrovertibly, the Edaljis were queer ones; an odd tenantry for the rectory of a parish in the rudely rural heart of nineteenth-century England. For the Reverend Shapurji Edalji was a Parsee from Bombay, who had seen the Anglican light, married a genteel Englishwoman, Charlotte Elizabeth Stuart Stoneham, and, through the beneficent influence of his bride's uncle, received the living of Great Wyrley. The sheep, black and white, of this remote flock of 5,000 souls viewed the advent of a black shepherd – white wife and three half-caste children – with a not always hedge-hidden hostility. For nearly three decades the Reverend Shapurji had been parson in residence, when, in February, 1903, the first terrible maiming occurred. Between then and August, much blameless animal blood stained the pasturage. The toll of pathetic beasts was five horses, three cows, and several sheep. We will not dilate upon the savagery of the onslaughts.

Suspicion, fanned by a spate of letters naming him the culprit, fastened upon the vicar's dark-skinned, peculiarly bulging-eyed son, George.

On the night of August 17, devil's work was afoot. A pony was dreadfully gashed and bled so near to death that it had to be destroyed. The police, who had been called in in force in the wake of previous incidents – and the immense anxiety engendered by a letter promising "There will be merry times at Wyrley in November", when, said the writer, the mutilations would start on little girls, doing "20 wenches like the horses before next March," – had been watching the vicarage, lair of the suspect designate. But they had seen no one leave it. Later, discovering footprints the size of Edalji's boots at the scene of the outrage, they called at the vicarage, where they found mud on his boots and trouser ends, and blood and, they claimed, horse hairs, on his coat.

Despite an alibi – for in that curious household George slept with his father in a locked bedroom, the vicar's wife and daughter sleeping together in another room – Edalji was arrested on suspicion.

Probably to Edalji's disadvantage, he was not tried at the Assizes, but came up at the Staffordshire Quarter Sessions before the Assistant Chairman, Sir Reginald Hardy, JP, a local landowner. He was sentenced to seven years' penal servitude and, of course, struck off the roll of solicitors.

However, with Edalji locked securely away the cattle-maiming did not cease. Neither did the anonymous letters, which they had believed to be in his handwriting. Following growing public concern about his conviction, Edalji was released on ticket-of-leave on October 19, 1906. It was at this point that that great paladin of lost causes, Sir Arthur Conan Doyle, responding to Edalji's appeal for help to clear his name, determined to play the rôle of a real-life Sherlock Holmes. Meeting Edalji, he took one look at him, and, in clipped, Holmes-like tones told him, "You suffer from astigmatic myopia." And to such a severe degree that, in his medical opinion, Edalji was half-blind by day and totally incapable of seeing enough at night to be able to pick his way over pitch-black country fields to locate and mutilate the victims of a quirky sadism.

Doyle investigated further. To his professional eye the type of slashing perpetrated suggested that it was the work of someone who had been a butcher. He analysed the anonymous letters. From three ecstatic references to the ocean he deduced that the writer had been to sea. Scandalous remarks written about a master at Walsall Grammar School provided yet another clue. Searching around, he eventually found a local man who was known to have slashed railway seats, had been expelled from Walsall Grammar School, and had both nautical and butchering experience. His name was Royden Sharp. Meanwhile, a Committee was appointed by the Home Secretary to assess the Edalji case, and he was exonerated and granted a free pardon. He did not, however, receive any compensation.

As a result of the case, there was renewed agitation for the establishment of a Criminal Appeal Court. This had to wait until 1907, when it was constituted in the wake of the Beck case of 1904. Edalji's name was restored to the roll of solicitors, and he returned to practice in London. From 1907 to 1941 he had an office in Borough High Street. Thereafter, from 1941 until 1953, he practised in and around Argyle Square, off Gray's Inn Road.

He died on June 17, 1953, aged 77, at Welwyn Garden City, Hertfordshire, preserving as a mystery to the end what Conan Doyle called in his most characteristically Watsonian manner, "One of the most singular cases in the chronicles of crime."

Doctor Donnall's Tea-party

It was what, according to my learned attorney father, was the purest of all motives, money, which drove young Dr Donnall to murder – the need which many a practical-minded beneficiary has impellingly felt to hasten the deliverance of a life-saving legacy. It was in pursuance of this objective that Robert Sawle Donnall made, like his Caledonian medical *confrère*, the illustrious Dr Pritchard, many a more timorous man's dream to murder his mother-in-law a reality. And the Falmouth physician got away with it, whereas Pritchard, quite properly, paid for his parricide pendant on Glasgow Green.

Here, then, are the whole circumstances whereby the delightful old

Cornish seaport town of Falmouth became the scene of a most weasily and pitiless poisoning.

Robert Donnall, surgeon and apothecary, recently qualified and smart as new paint, moved, complete with neatly-caparisoned house-maid and liveried man-servant to usher the patients in and out, into the house next door to the well-respected, well-to-do Downings. This substantial local family consisted of Mrs Elizabeth Downing, widow, aged 60, her four sons – Samuel, John, William and Edward – and two daughters, Betsy, married, and Harriet, single and available.

Diagnostic ear professionally attuned to the *rhonchi* and *râles* of the well-filled Downing family cash register, young Dr Donnall began assiduously to pay his best bedside manner address to Harriet. Prognosis: a wife entitled on the death of her mother to a future share in her not inconsiderable property.

On July 15, 1816, after two years' impeccable courtship, the doctor claimed his bride, upon whom a sum in the vicinity of £3,000 had been pre-nuptially secured and settled.

A circumstance to which some mystery attaches is that before his marriage Donnall had borrowed, in dribs and drabs, a total of £125 from a Falmouth money-lender, Gabriel Abrahams. The mystery is what Donnall needed the money for. There is no evidence that his practice was anything other than modestly flourishing, yielding an annual £300–£400. When borrowing the money, Donnall made a point of informing Abrahams that he was about to be married to the well-provided-for Downing girl, and in two or three weeks' time would be in a position to repay the loan.

July, August, and September slipped by. No sign of any repayment. The money-lender began to press. Dr Donnall's constant off-putting excuses grew progressively thinner, at which Mr Abrahams' menace increased. At last, Dr Donnall produced a firm assurance. His mother-in-law, he said, was a sick woman. She would not live long. Would not, indeed, be likely to see Christmas. Then, of course, money would flow.

The position in truth was this: although his newly-ringed wife was possessed of a handsome fortune, it was settled firmly upon herself, and in the future. Here and now, at his purse's, and wits', end, the doctor turned his diagnostic eye to the property belonging to his mother-in-law, and reached the professional conclusion that the specific therapy for his acute shortage was a tincturing of self-help.

And to quicken access to that source of fiscal healing, he decided upon a prescription of *liquor arsenicalis*, or it may be, as the ever more subtle French periphrasise it, *poudre de succession*.

The first step in the therapeutic process would be to invite his mother-in-law to take "a dish of tay" with them. This, on Saturday, October 19, 1816, a fortnight before her tea-drinking days ended for ever, she did. The result, for her, was not auspicious. A sickness and heat in the stomach. Retching, vomiting, purging, cramps and thirst – four exceedingly discommodious days, attended by her solicitous son-in-law. Despite this, she recovered.

Foolishly – but how should the poor woman know – she went again to tea with her daughter and son-in-law, on Sunday, November 3. This time she took cocoa. The tea-table stood in the centre of the room. On it was placed the tea-urn and plates of bread and butter. The maid fetched in a jug of cocoa. The doctor's behaviour at the tea-party was an odd mixture of officiousness and attentiveness. He fussed about his mother-in-law, contriving, like a conjurer with his mis-directions, to steer Mrs Downing towards her appointed portion. The poison, it is thought, was slipped into the first cup of cocoa, borne to Mrs Downing by the doctor, who took a circuitous route which, the place being illuminated only by the flickering light of a single candle, and himself dodging around and behind the other guests and in and out of the plenitude of patches of shadow, gave him good opportunity to doctor the cocoa.

Taken again violently ill, Mrs Downing returned home – that is, next door. Her son-in-law took medical charge of her. As the night wore on her symptoms became more and more frightful. He sent for another physician, Dr Richard Edwards. At 8 am Mrs Downing died. Dr Donnall proposed that with Solomon Grundy-like celerity, Elizabeth Downing, who died on Monday, should be buried on Wednesday. But the Mayor of Falmouth intervened. He had received an anonymous letter. He ordered an inquest and post-mortem.

Dr Donnall turned up all set to do the post-mortem. But his scalpel was stayed by the hands of Dr Edwards and Mr John Street, surgeon. Dr Donnall's contribution was to do some juggling with the jug into which had been poured the stomach contents of the deceased. He poured them into a chamber utensil, but failed to make away with them. His tricks availed him nothing. Even an attempted escape up the chimney proved vain. He was arrested and put up at the Launceston Spring Assize.

The body of evidence advanced on behalf of the prisoner was calculated to show that the post-mortem appearances might just as easily be the result of natural disease – cholera morbus – as of arsenical poisoning, and despite a distinctly hostile charge by Abbott J, the jury thought so, and acquitted.

As the late William Roughend drily commented:

"The court then rose; and the prisoner, being duly discharged, was free to resume practice. It is unlikely, despite the local feeling in his favour which unquestionably influenced the finding, that any future tea-party he might give would be attended by other than members of the jury."

Death and the Dancing Waiter

According to the calendar, the man sitting across the table from Edgar Lustgarten and me in that upper room of Stone's Chop-House in London's Panton Street, was old. But, with his raven-black, marcel-waved, brilliantined hair and neat, black, Ronald Colman moustache, he looked not only anachronistically young, but also extraordinarily like a film star of the Hollywood heyday. And, indeed, his name had once, like that of one of those now forgotten celluloid shadows, blazed famously the length and breadth of Britain. Not for acting ability – although perhaps it should have been – but as the notorious Brighton Trunk Murderer

For this supper table-fellow of ours was none other than Toni Mancini aka Hyman Gold aka Jack Notyre.

Nor was Mancini his name. The son of a Deptford, South London, shipping clerk, he was really Cecil Lois England, but bedazzled by the lives and styles of the Italo-American gangsters of Chicago, he became Toni Mancini, unsuccessful *ersatz* hood.

Fresh out, in August, 1933, from a spell inside following his latest disastrous enterprise in petty theft, he got a menial bread-and-margarine job at an eating-house in the Leicester Square hinterland. It was here that he met Violette Kaye, aka Mrs Violet Saunders, *ci-devant* vaudeville toe-dancer, now, at 42, playing the streets.

He, with his dark Italianate façade and carefully projected Valentino-Novarro aura, caught her fancy. He was 25. She invited him to share a new life.

So they set out, the erstwhile *soubrette* and the fledgling *souteneur*, to set up shop together in the shoddy underworld Greeneland of Pinkie and *Brighton Rock*. She established her seedy clientele. Things settled into a flyblown pattern. She paid the rent, bought the food, doled out pocket-money to Mancini. He danced attendance upon her. Did the household chores, including the cooking, warmed her bed, made himself scarce when she brought gentlemen home to occupy it. On free evenings he, an expert dancer, too, escorted her to the dance-halls.

Then Mancini got himself a job. Nothing spectacular. Just as a waiter-cum-washer-up at the Skylark Café, underneath the arches, at shingle level, just below the point where West Street meets the promenade. And the trouble started. Violette grew jealous. There were rows. A final crescendo public row in the Skylark, over a waitress. That was on Thursday, May 10, 1934. Next morning Mancini announced that Violette had left him. Which was true. But she had not gone to Paris.

Tidings of the basement drama enacted at 44 Park Crescent came about as the result of Brighton Trunk Murder No 1. A light-brown canvas trunk containing a headless and legless female torso, discovered in the left luggage at Brighton Station, set off a massive investigation into all cases of missing women. This led to the finding of a big, black, evil-smelling trunk abandoned by Mancini in his last lodgings, in Kemp Street. Police opened it. Inside was the body of Violette Kaye. Mancini, arrested as he trudged aimlessly along the Sidcup bypass, near Blackheath, was put to his trial in December, as Jack Notyre, at Lewes Assizes. His defence was handled magnificently by Norman Birkett. According to Sir Bernard Spilsbury, a depressed fracture of the skull was the cause of death. Produced by a blow delivered by Mancini, said the Crown. The result of a drunken fall down the steep area steps, said the defence.

In the witness-box the man the press nicknamed the "Dancing Waiter" made a very plausible showing. The jury, told by Birkett to "stand firm", took two hours weighing the pros and cons. When they delivered their finding, Mancini appeared, in the elegant parlance of posterity, to be 'gobsmacked'. "Not guilty, Mr Birkett, not guilty" was all that, in startled amazement, he could say.

There is an epilogue. Forty-two years went by. Hugging his secret to himself, Mancini worked for a time in a sideshow, touring fairgrounds. Then he went to sea. He settled ashore in Liverpool. It was in November, 1976, that he stepped back into the black limelight with a confession in the *News of the World*: "Before I die I want to set the record straight. The verdict was wrong. I did kill Violette Kaye."

And, over the supper table that April night in 1977, Lustgarten and I heard the tale from Mancini's own lips.

"After the scene Violette made in the Skylark, I came home filled with an awful anger. I found her lying on the bed drunk and under the influence of morphine. She glared at me and shouted: 'Come here, you. You belong to me, d'you hear?' Suddenly I hated her. I was disgusted by her. I turned to go to the kitchen, felt a blow on the shoulder. She'd launched herself at me like a wild cat, clawing and scratching at my face and eyes. I struck out at her. She reeled backwards into the fireplace. I went to pick her up and she spat full in my face. That's when things went blank. Next I knew, she was limp in my arms, head lolling back, blood coming from her nose and mouth. I realised she was dead. I had thought that I was banging her head on the floor. I'd been banging it on the knob of the fender.

"I crouched there for some time, nursing her head in my arms. I was in a daze. Couldn't think straight. And I knew the police wouldn't believe I hadn't intended to kill her. I lifted her on to the bed. Suddenly I had to get out of that room. I walked down to the sea. And that was when I decided the only thing to do, the only way out, was to hide the body. I put her in the corner cupboard we used as a wardrobe. I spent the night cleaning up the flat. A few days later I bought that big black trunk, and . . ."

At that moment, most timeously, the waiter set down three large brandies beside our coffees.

The Waterloo Bridge Bag of Bones

The received image of Sacheverell Sitwell is as the poet and esoteric essayist of *Canons of Giant Art*, the aesthete of *The Gothick North* and *Southern Baroque Art*, the biographic singer of Liszt and Paganini and, more marginally, as the apologist of the poltergeist. His interest in matters criminous comes, therefore, as something of a surprise. Yet, scattered between pages dealing with such abstrusities as the Oracle of Dodona and Cupid and the Jacaranda, you will find evocations of what his generation called *causes célèbres*.

He unfolds dreads and drolls. The mystery of the murdered actor in the empty Battersea flat, where in true Sherlock Holmes style, a brown paper parcel containing his carpet-slippers was found lying on the mantelshelf; the lady poisoner, *âme damné*, who frisked in the woods at Rowaleyn and passed the cup of bitter-sweet cocoa through the basement stanchions in Glasgow's Blythswood Square; the pathetic little Italian boy, with a cage of white mice round his neck, a waif of the London streets, slain for the anatomists.

Of like Victorian vintage is the strange tale of the bag of bones on old Waterloo Bridge. It comes to us out of the yellow gaslight and peasoupers which alternately shone and swirled about Rennie's old bridge.

In the early morning grey of October 9, 1857, two boys rowing up the Thames saw, lodged upon an abutment at the foot of one of the bridge's Doric columns, a large parcel bound with several coils of rope. On closer inspection it proved to be a carpet-bag. On closer inspection still, at Bow Street Police Station, it was found to contain twenty pieces of a human body – but no head. The bones had been sawn through. The flesh, cleanly cut, had been boiled and pickled in brine. Also in the bag were a man's coat, waistcoat, trousers, vest, drawers, socks, shirt, and surtout. The clothes, without labels, seemed of foreign make. Short lengths of black hair marked the body that of an adult.

Mr Paynter, divisional surgeon of police, noted a wound between the third and fourth ribs on the left side. Caused by a very sharp-pointed weapon, such as a stiletto, it indicated a violent death. Long black hairs belonging to a woman were found on the coat and waistcoat.

The police cast forth a wide net of enquiry and trawled up an odd incident which account was rehearsed at the inquest. Henry Errington, toll-keeper at the north end of the bridge, said that at about 11.30 pm on October 8, he saw a solitary woman carrying a heavy-looking

Murder Files

carpet-bag. She came from the direction of the Strand. He spoke to her, but she just grunted something in a guttural voice. She was about 5 feet 3 inches tall, stout, with hair that looked as if it had been powdered and plastered thickly down. She seemed very agitated and, walking quickly on to the bridge, vanished into the darkness.

A Mr Samuel Bell testified to seeing Errington talking to a woman – if it *was* a woman and not a man in disguise. She had a sallow complexion, rather sunken eyes, a mole on her left cheek, near her nose, and his attention was particularly arrested by her hair. It was startlingly white – and did not look natural.

The famous nineteenth-century naturalist, Frank Buckland, wrote in his *Curiosities of Natural History*, Second Series, of how he had personally inspected the Waterloo Bridge bones. Himself a doctor, he was able to conclude that the cuts had been made by someone accustomed to handling a saw, but who had no knowledge of anatomy. He also held that a woman and a black cat were somehow mixed up in the affair, for he and the great microscopist, Professor Quekett, found the hairs of both sticking to the remains.

Two years after the discovery of the tell-tale "rag and a bone and a hank of hair", the following curious item appeared in the *News of the World*, May, 1859.

For some time prior to 1857, an old Irishwoman, Biddy, had had a fruit stall by Barking Road railway station bridge. In April, 1859, she was taken seriously ill, and, thinking she was dying, sent for a Roman Catholic priest. The woman who was nursing Biddy suspected she had something to confess and listened outside the door. She could not hear properly but gathered that one October night a couple of years back, Biddy had been employed by two men to carry a bag on to Waterloo Bridge. And that, tantalisingly, was all she heard.

The case created a tremendous sensation, but, despite their best efforts, the police, goaded unmercifully by the press, made no arrests and, indeed, seemed just about as baffled as they were to be 30 years later when Jack the Ripper stalked their patch.

They did, however, painfully contrive what they held to be a likely theory. They said that, judging by his clothes, his dark skin and hair, the victim was, they strongly suspected, a foreign sailor. There were at the time a number of foreign vessels lying at anchorage in the Thames.

The man might have been struck down in a scuffle over a game of cards, or in the course of a drunken brawl. He might have died as the result of a quick flare-up over a woman. Or his murder could, perhaps, have been a long-planned act of vengeance. The seamen of those times were notoriously badly treated, and it might be that the recipient of some act of bullying or injustice had nursed his grievance, bided his time, and struck when opportunity offered.

If, then, the police suspected that this was some murdered voyager from a distant land, why did they not search every ship in the river, demand to see a list of the crew? Perhaps they did. Perhaps they discovered some crewman missing, but were fobbed off by plausible explanation of his absence – and defeated by time and tides. It was like searching for a splinter in a yard-arm. Hopeless from the start.

Or may it not have been that, as we know so often happens, the police were pretty certain in their own minds who had committed the crime, but had no means of bringing it home to that person? One hundred and fifty years on, the mystery remains . . .

The Ghost of the Murdered Cheesemonger

Getting on for a century ago, there stood at the corner of Leinster Terrace and Craven Hill Gardens, in the Bayswater district of London, the old-fashioned shop of Philip Lowry & Co, cheesemongers and high class provisioners, which was to be the scene of a terrible murder and a terrifying haunting.

The man who investigated the murder was "The Weasel", that celebrated policeman from Jack the Ripper's East End, Chief Constable Fred Wensley. The man who investigated the subsequent alleged haunting was Elliott O'Donnell (1872–1965), for 60 years Britain's best known psychic writer and researcher. What was not so widely known was O'Donnell's interest in criminal matters. In fact, he edited the *Notable British Trials* volume on Kate Webster, and scattered throughout his 60-odd books are many tales of the criminous. Bridging the gap between these two interests is the case of Edwin Creed, the murdered cheesemonger.

At 7.10 pm on July 28, 1926, Alfred Leonard, the last of the assistants to leave, called goodnight to Edwin Creed, the manager of Lowry's, and went off home. Creed, left alone, was in the basement, washing his hands in the bowl of warm water customarily left down there for him by Leonard.

At 10.15 pm, Mr Andrews, the chemist at number 34, next door, worried by the strong smell of gas coming from Lowry's, collared the policeman on the beat, PC Watts. Between them they forced an entry. Blood was all over the place: on a box-bicycle used for deliveries; up the walls; in a pool by the door leading to the basement. And, halfway down the cellar stairs, hunched like a thrown sack, was the battered corpse of the late Mr Creed.

Powerfully built, 46 years old, recently a sergeant in the special police, Creed, a married man with two schoolgirl daughters, had died following repeated blows to the head with some heavy instrument – perhaps a jemmy.

Three gas-jets in the cellar were turned on full, but unlighted. Between £70 and £80 was missing from the safe – opened with Mr Creed's keys.

The police thought that Creed had answered a knock at the shop-door and been attacked immediately. Marks in the sawdust suggested that he had been killed in the shop, dragged along the ground, and tossed down the cellar stairs. The only clues were two bloodstained chamois leather gloves, both for the left hand, one slightly larger, and footprints of a type which proved impossible to match. There were indications that two men had been involved, but the assailants were never found.

It was three years later to the day that O'Donnell arrived to keep an all-night vigil at the murder scene. At closing time he was locked in the shop, his only company the cat that had been there on the night of the murder.

He recorded: "Though it was light outside, the drawn down door-blinds and the closed shutters made the interior of the shop rather dark . . . a curious sense of solitude seemed to hang about the place. I was glad the little cat was there." He searched the cellars, making sure no one was hiding down there; then sat at the cashier's desk, commanding a full view of the shop.

The evening wore on. Voices and footsteps from outside grew fewer; the gloom inside increased. The stillness of night became perceptible. 11 pm. Only the sonorous ticking of the clock high up on the wall. "Suddenly there was a loud clanging noise in the nearest of the two cellars. I descended and searched around. No one and nothing to explain the noise. But a strong uncanny feeling in the first cellar. Resuming my seat at the desk, I noticed a sudden lowering of the temperature."

It was raining now. The wind moaned and howled around the shop, beating the rain with great violence against the shuttered windows. O'Donnell sat in the darkness. About 1 am the handle of the shop-door was tried. Then, another cautious turning, He listened. No footsteps.

"I felt, however, that something had entered the premises. I was conscious of it moving past me in the darkness and heading for the cellar steps. Again and again I heard curious noises in the nearest cellar, then whisperings at the bottom of the staircase, and footsteps shuffling stealthily up the stairs towards me." O'Donnell turned on the light. Instantly, the whispering and footsteps ceased. Once more he searched the cellars. Nothing. Again he turned off the light. "Suddenly I saw a man standing on the floor of the shop directly in front of me. His profile was turned towards me. He was talking to someone. I switched on my torch fully prepared for him to vanish. He did not. I turned on the lamp. He had gone. It was just 2 am." Sitting once more in darkness, O'Donnell heard another clanging sound in the cellar, more whisperings, steps on the stairs, and the noise of something being dragged across the floor of the shop right past him. Shortly afterwards, he became conscious of a presence "leaning on the desk and peering stealthily at me . . . a wiry, pale-faced man, intensely vicious . . . There was a noise as of a hand on the desk moving about, searching for something." The scrabbling of "a rather dirty, coarse hand, muscular fingers, ugly spatulate nails . . . a young hand, of someone in his twenties or early thirties."

A feeling that he must go down into the cellar overcame O'Donnell. "I felt, as I stood peering around me, that it was in the cellar that Creed was taken unawares. It was there that the first blow was struck. I saw, mentally, the victim bending over a basin of water in the act of washing his face. Then the murderer, slim, of medium height, stole up behind and hit him on the head with an iron bar. Dazed, Creed staggered up the staircase to the shop, almost gaining the door before his relentless assailant overtook him, rained more blows, and dragged his battered corpse to the staircase." And there O'Donnell's picture ended.

It is an empirical fact that conditions alter perceptions. Did some sixth sense of O'Donnell's receive impressions of electric horror staining the air of the locus of past violence? Did he experience something beyond the dreams of our philosophy?

The Case of the Green-tailed Mare

It belongs to the Alice in Wonderland world of googly Carbolic Smoke Balls, peripatetic snails in ginger-beer bottles, and runaway reservoirs; it is the law-changing case of the green-tailed mare.

The event which was to produce such revolutionary repercussions took place on April 27, 1938.

Like so many other 14-year-olds, the young girl in the case was horse-struck, and when that evening three friendly Lifeguards coming off duty at Horse Guards Parade, in Whitehall, approached, smiling, to ask her if she had ever seen a green-tailed mare, she was instantly captivated. And when she replied that indeed she never had, they told her that, lucky girl, her chance to do so had come. Happily, she skipped along with the troopers to the horse-box and was raped. Not just raped, but made pregnant.

The Guardsmen were not to get away with it. There was an identity parade. The girl was able to pick them out. The three soldiers went to trial at the Old Bailey, charged respectively, with rape, aiding and abetting rape, and attempted rape.

"This girl went through a terrible experience," du Parcq J told the jury. "I am bound to add this: I have seldom heard of a more horrible case of this horrible offence."

The jury heard – and heeded. They brought in a guilty verdict in all three cases. Two of the men were sentenced to four years' penal servitude. The third man was given 22 months' hard labour on the attempted rape charge.

All of which was very satisfactory so far as it went, but that was not very far so far as the pathetic 14-year-old mother-to-be was concerned.

It was a woman doctor – Dr Joan Malleson – who, moved to a great pity by the predicament of this appallingly wronged child, took a bold step on her behalf. She sat down and wrote a letter. It was the sort of letter which, at that time, not one in a thousand doctors would have written.

The letter was duly delivered to the fashionable consulting rooms of another doctor at 12 Wimpole Street.

"Dear Mr Bourne," it began, "I am afraid I may be wasting your time by approaching you in this matter, but will you give consideration to it, if possible . . ." He read on.

In 1938, Aleck Bourne, had, at the age of 51, reached the top of his profession – obstetric surgeon to St Mary's, Paddington, consultant obstetric surgeon to Queen Charlotte's, consulting gynaecologist to the Samaritan Hospital. The letter asked him to perform an illegal operation. "Unless someone of your standing is prepared to undertake the operation . . ."

He was being politely requested, albeit on common humanitarian grounds, to commit a crime; a crime, moreover, carrying the maximum penalty to penal servitude for life. All who "unlawfully use an instrument with intent to procure a miscarriage" contravene Section 58 of the Offences Against the Person Act 1861. According to the generally accepted interpretation of the Act at that time, the only lawful abortion was one which was held to be necessary in order to save the life of a pregnant woman. In the case of the 14-year-old girl about whom Dr Malleson had written to him, there was no reason to suppose that there was any danger to her life. Well, not physically, anyway.

But the plight of this girl with child – herself no more than a child – touched the heart of Aleck Bourne, perhaps because he himself was the father of three young daughters.

Whatever . . . he took a brave decision.

On June 6, 1938, he admitted the girl to St Mary's Hospital, Paddington. At the same time he informed the Attorney-General's Department of what he intended to do.

A week went by. Every day Bourne anticipated some action by the police. Nothing happened. At 10 o'clock on the morning of June 14, he carried out a successful operation on the girl.

That same Tuesday evening two detectives arrived at St Mary's asking to see Mr Bourne. He had just finished his evening operating list. "You had better arrest me," he told them. They did not there and then, but on July 1, at Marylebone Police Court the ordeal of Aleck Bourne began.

He was committed for trial.

Preaching at Westminster Cathedral, the celebrated Roman Catholic priest, Father Bernard Delany OP, told the congregation: "People have been so moved by the terrible hurt inflicted on a child, so swayed by the emotional character of the circumstances, that they have been blinded to the real facts, and the moral issues involved."

On July 19, Aleck Bourne stood in the dock at the Old Bailey. His counsel, Roland Oliver, took the line that the operation had been vital for the girl's mental health. Prosecuting, the Attorney-General, Sir Donald Somervell, argued the pragmatic legalistic view that there was a clear distinction between danger to life and danger to health. Crown evidence was limited to the establishment of the basic facts of the case, which were not in dispute anyway.

For the defence a number of exceedingly eminent medical men-including Lord Horder, Dr J. A. Rees, a much respected psychiatrist, and Mr William Gilliatt, senior gynaecologist at King's College Hospital – came forward to speak in support of their colleague's action.

In his address at the close of the trial, on its second day, Mr Oliver told the jury: "I do not suppose that ever before has a man stood in this dock who has acted from a motive of purest charity. He has pilloried himself for what he believes to be right." The jury filed out impassive.

A long, long forty minutes ticked by.

The jury returned.

"Not guilty."

Within minutes the news swept across the country. A BMA Conference was in progress at Plymouth. Suddenly the doctors were standing on their chairs, cheering and cheering. "Not guilty, not guilty," someone was shouting.

The ambiguities in the law had been resolved. A suitable operation in fenestration adeptly effected. Henceforth lawful abortion would include not only life and death cases, but also life cases, which is to say those in which it is genuinely felt that either the physical or mental health of the patient is endangered by having a haby.

And what became of the girl? Aleck Bourne never knew. Neither she nor her parents ever communicated with him again.

The Harley Street Cellar Mystery

Of all the thoroughfares of London – what the late Patrick Hamilton called, for his London trilogy, "Twenty Thousand Streets Under the Sky" – there is surely none where more frequently the mysteries of life and death meet, mingle, and are, one way or another, resolved, than Harley Street.

Behind the chaste façades of its tall houses, in finely proportioned, luxuriously appointed rooms, men and women sit in well-bred isolation, turning the leaves of old copies of *Tatler*, temporary prisoners of, in HV Morton's memorable phrase, "the Bastille of a specialist's waiting room."

The strange episode in the many-hued history of the Street of Doctors which concerns us here has nothing to do with the drama of medicine – except in the broadest medico-legal sense. The house upon which this life and death mystery centred was Number 139. It had for many years before the gruesome find was made, been in the possession of the eminently respectable and appropriately well-to-do Henriques family.

It was on Thursday, June 3, 1880, that all London was excited by a startling discovery in one of the cellars of this house. Apparently, the first somewhat insubstantial clue that something was amiss had been the sudden presence, about 18 months before, of a very unpleasant smell, to which Mr Henriques' butler had drawn the master's attention.

The smell seemed to be coming from the three inter-linking vaults, built in under the street pavement contingent to the basement area fronting the house. Mr Henriques arranged for workmen to re-lay suspect drains. But the odour persisted. Intensified. The footman, Tinapp, whose job it was to clean the boots in the cellar, complained to Mr Spendlove, the butler, that the smell was back and worse than ever.

In a recess of the middle vault was a big galvanised iron cistern, supported on a brick staging. In the space beneath the cistern was a large, lidless barrel, the upper part of which was filled with old bottles, gallipots, and the like. These were assiduously removed. Then – horror of horrors – the butler cried out, "There's somebody in here."

Indeed there was. Thrust in with power, doubled up, nether extremities uppermost, was a human body.

Police Inspector Lucas arrived. So, about noon, did the Divisional Surgeon of Police, Dr Spurgin. The body proved to be that of a woman. Age between 40 and 45. Height about 4ft 9in. Of moderate build. Hair dark brown interspersed with grey. The coarse quality of surviving bits of clothing indicated that she came from what was then designated "a lowly station in life". Cause of death was a stab wound in the left breast. The body had been where it was found for about two years, and prior to being forced into the cask had been either buried in, or covered with, chloride of lime.

There was an inquest. Evidence was given by a young man in the army. His name was Henry Smith. He was the Henriques' previous butler, discharged in November, 1878, for being found the worse for drink. Married then, he stated now: "My wife is alive, but I do not live with her." He knew of no one being brought into the house clandestinely at night, although the area gate, which was supposed to be locked after dark, was frequently left open. Smith admitted that in August, 1878, about three months before his dismissal, he had asked an old man named Green to dig a hole in one of the cellars, because "I had a great accumulation of stale bread, and I thought I should get into trouble, so I would bury it."

John Green, 73-year-old jobbing man or coachman, of Weymouth Mews, told the coroner, Dr Hardwicke, "Mr Smith asked me if I was a paviour, and I went to the house. I saw bricks in the middle cellar, all being taken up, the hole being about a yard across. I did not dig any hole. I relaid the bricks. Smith never said he wanted to bury bread."

And Mrs Jewry, cook at No 139 from 1874 to 1879, denied that there was ever any waste bread. Mr Spendlove, the present butler, confirmed that there was never such waste of bread in the house as to render it necessary to bury it under the bricks in the cellar. George Campbell, a servant who had lived five months in the house in 1876–7, said there was no barrel and no smell at that time. Both facts confirmed by John Bertham, a butler, and George Minton, a footman, who were in service there in 1877. But another footman, William Tinapp, a German, deponed that the barrel was in the cellar in August, 1878, and there was then a bad smell.

Finally, Mr Woodroffe, a caretaker, testified: "For the last six summers I have taken care of the house in the autumn. In the autumn of 1878, I went into the cellar to hunt out a rat, and saw the barrel, for I knocked a stick against it. Bottles were on it. Smith was butler at the time, but was with the family in the country."

So what did it all add up to? Murder? For sure. That was as far as the inquest jury would – -indeed, could – go. The murder of an unknown woman by person or persons unknown. And, in spite of prolonged police inquiries, no further light was ever shed on the mystery.

Looking back across the chasm of 126 years, the blown dust seems to leave the perspective a little sharper. Henry Smith arrived at Mr Henriques' house in June, 1877. Before that, there was no barrel in the cellar, no bad smell. By August, 1878, there is a barrel in the cellar and, at Mr Smith's behest, bricks are being replaced by Mr Green over an area of exposed earth. Traces of chloride of lime were, as we have seen, found on the body. Had it first been buried, with a view to rapid destruction, mistakenly in chloride of lime instead of quick-lime – which would have acted as a preservative anyway? It will come as small surprise that Mr Smith told the coroner, "I do not remember seeing the cask in the cellar at all."

Officially, the mystery must, of course, remain – like many another that lies in shadow behind the gas-lamps' flicker on Harley Street's glimmering brass plates. But, between ourselves, I think that the solution may well lie in a time-honoured Agatha Christie-style cliché – the butler did it!

Who Put Bella Down the Wych Elm?

Stark white and grinning, the skull reminded the boy of an illustration from a pirate island adventure story. But this one was not lying between the pages of a book, on the golden sand of a tropic isle; it was staring bleakly back at him from the darkness deep in the bole of the old wych elm.

It was a Sunday evening – April 18, 1943 – and the three lads had been out bird's-nesting in Hagley Wood, a couple of miles from Stourbridge, in Worcestershire. Now, as the light was failing, creeping towards the shadow of the Clent Hills, they came upon the immense black bulk of the venerable old elm. Massive, squat, gnarled, it seemed to crouch in the waning light like some vast prehistoric animal. The tree's top long ago broken off some five feet above the ground, the ancient stump had compensated by sprouting a lion's mane of thick clusters of spindly branchlets, which seemed to them to make it a likely place to look for the last find of the day.

The boy clambered a few feet up, gazed hopefully into the large cavity at the elm's core . . . then started back, gasping with fright.

Through the falling gloom, the trio scampered home to tell their parents what they had seen in the wood.

The local sergeant of police, Skerratt by name, having been told of the boys' discovery over the telephone, lost no time in making his way to Hagley Wood, just to satisfy himself that the lads were not playing a joke. He came, he saw, he placed an overnight guard on the tree.

Next morning the men from Worcester CID arrived. The skull, the spinal column, a scattering of rib-bones and a shoulder-blade were fetched out of the tree's dark maw. They found, too, some wisps of rotted clothing and a single shoe. The search was extended. A shin-bone was found tangled in the roots of a nearby sapling. Buried separately, yet further away, were the finger-bones of the victim's severed hand. By the end of the search, the police had an almost complete skeleton.

Professor J. M. Webster, the pathologist, was called in.

Sorting his pile of bones, Webster contrived the reconstruction of a woman, aged about 35, five feet tall, mousy brown hair, and with quite noticeably irregular teeth in the lower jaw. And from the adherent rags and tatters, he clothed her in a dark blue and mustard striped knitted woollen cardigan, a mustard, or possibly pale khaki, skirt with a light-blue belt, a peach-coloured taffeta underskirt, and blue crêpe-soled shoes. There was also a cheap, rolled gold, enamelled wedding-ring, showing some four years' wear.

Webster calculated that the woman had been dead about 18 months. Cause of death: impossible to be sure, but part of an outer garment pressed tightly into the mouth cavity strongly indicated suffocation.

Then came the local nose-tappings and the nudges. This, they said, was no ordinary murder, but part of a black magic ritual killing. Daubed on walls in Halesowen, Old Hill, and Wolverhampton, chalked on the outsides of buildings throughout the West Midlands, was the cryptic question: "Who put Bella down the wych elm – Hagley Wood?" Sometimes the name was given as "Luebella".

Years later, a theory was formulated by the author, Donald McCormick, who studied this case closely, and that of the murder of Charles Walton at Lower Quinton, that the victim was a Dutch woman, an enemy agent code-named "Clara", who was known to have been parachuted into the Kidderminster area in March or April, 1941, and who subsequently vanished. She was a relative of Johannes

Marius Dronkers, who spied for the Germans and was executed by the British in 1942.

Another suggestion was that the victim was a Gypsy woman who had offended against the law of the Rommanies and had been tried and condemned by her tribe. And it is certainly true that about the estimated time of the murder, Gypsies were camping in the vicinity of the tree, and a man reported hearing a violent altercation followed by screams. Screams were also reported in July, 1941, when an executive of an industrial company and a schoolmaster heard them coming from Hagley Wood. The two men telephoned the police, and they, together with a police-sergeant. made a search in the wood – but found nothing.

There was, however, one more possibility.

Hagley Wood is situated well within the Witch Crescent which cuts across the heart of England – Warwickshire, Oxfordshire, Worcestershire, Herefordshire, Gloucestershire. Across the patchwork of these counties little rucks or pockets of the "Old Religion" remain; deep, ancient, rural, starting to life again suddenly like the spurtings of small Beltane fires, sinister fairy lights moving like Will-o'-the-Wisps, on the slopes of places such as Bredon Hill.

There are those – and they include Dr Margaret Murray, author of *The Witch Cult in Western Europe* and late Assistant Professor of Egyptology, University College, London, a formidable academic – who are convinced that witchcraft was at the root of both the entombment of the woman in the wych elm and the crop fertility ritual murder of Charles Walton in the shadow of Meon Hill. They point out that Bella and Luebella, especially, are known witch names. They refer to the odd fact that the elm tree victim's hand was cut off and buried separately. A severed dead man's hand has long been believed to hold strong mystical powers; one recalls the "Hand of Glory" in Barham's *Ingoldsby Legends*.

My own feelings, and I did actually discuss the Hagley Wood case with hundred-year-old Dr Murray, and the Charles Walton murder with the late Superintendent Robert Fabian, who conducted the official police investigation, and with Chalres Walton's niece tend to a more mundane explanation. Charles Walton, Fabian thought, died at the hands of a local farmer to whom he had lent considerable sums of money, repayment of which was long, long overdue.

The old wych elm was situated in a popular spot for ramblers, picnickers and courting couples, and it must have been earmarked as a convenient hideaway for a corpse by someone who was no stranger to the locality. Perhaps not. But my guess is that spies and witches had nothing to do with it. It was something even older than witchcraft that was at the bottom of it – that most lethal of all emotions, "love to hatred turn'd".

The Vanishings

Victorian London was a city of unsolved mysteries. Classic, and most widely remembered of these, is the series of Jack the Ripper murders which, in the "Autumn of Terror" of 1888, sent a *frisson* of fear crackling the length of the country. Wrote a contemporary chronicler: "Horror ran through the land. Men spoke of it with bated breath, and pale-lipped women shuddered as they read the dreadful details. People afar off smelled blood, and the superstitious said that the skies were of a deeper red that autumn."

But there were other mysteries . . . just as horrifying . . . just as inexplicable. Perhaps the strangest of all was the fearful epidemic of disappearances which became known as "The Vanishings". They centred on East London and came in two waves: the first in 1881–2 and the second in 1890.

In those sparsely documented days it was all too easy to melt into one of those swirling, saffron-yellow, pea-souper fogs which plagued London – and blow still out of the pages of Conan Doyle – never to be seen again. Easy to slip off some slimy quayside steps into a reeking cut or from the parapet of a canal. Or to plunge without taking thought down some narrow alley where a footpad or garrotter lay like an Angler-Fish in waiting in the enshrouding darkness. And, speaking of garrotters, it may be recalled how Day J, a strong judge in a fearsome Victorian tradition, put down single-handed a severe outbreak of garrotting which was terrorising the good citizens of Liverpool in the 1880s, by the judicial, and judicious, use of the cat. The enterprising stranglehold of the High Rip and Logwood gangs was most effectively stamped out.

But the Vanishings presented an additional, to many people's way of thinking almost supernatural, dimension.

On Saturday, January 28, 1882, 12-year-old Eliza Carter set out at 10 o'clock in the morning from her elder sister's home in West Road, West Ham, to go to her parents, who lived in nearby Church Street. On her way she dropped some clothes in at a laundry. She was not seen after that until around 5 pm, when she stopped one of her school-friends in Portway, opposite West Ham Park, and told her some garbled story about being afraid to go home because of "that man". What she meant has never been clarified. However, it was later reported that Eliza had been seen at about 11 o'clock that Saturday night. She was then with a middle-aged woman of unprepossessing appearance, dressed in a long ulster and a black frock. The following day, a blue dress, identified as "the one with buttons all down the front", which Eliza had been wearing, was found on the local football field – shorn of all its buttons. Rewards were offered for news that would lead to the discovery of Eliza Carter, but from that day to this nothing more has ever been heard of her.

The child's mysterious disappearance set folk remembering how, around Easter 1881, a small girl named Seward had also disappeared from her home in West Ham, and how, despite a wide and careful search and the offer of a reward, nothing was ever seen or heard of her again, either.

The next to vanish – on April 1, 1882 – was a young boy, Charles Wagner, the son of a West Ham butcher. In this case his body was found at the foot of a cliff in Ramsgate, 74 miles from his home. There was, however, a simple explanation in his case. He had left his father's home with a bag containing £150 in gold. He was stabbed in the head with a screwdriver. A James Walters was arrested for his murder.

Barely a fortnight later, there was another genuine vanishing in West Ham. This time it was a well-to-do lady, 67 years of age, who disappeared from her home in Keogh Road. On the evening of April 12, 1882, she left her house, went to the shops in Stratford, and bought some soap and candles. The next morning the postman, the milkman, and various other tradesmen called at the house in Keogh Road as usual, but received no answer to their knocks. Eventually, the police forced an entry, fearing that some accident had befallen her, and that the woman might be in need of help. What they found was a kind of land-locked *Mary Celeste* mystery. The grandfather-clock was ticking peaceably away in the hall. The soap and candles had been stowed carefully in the kitchen cupboard. The washing-up had been done. The bed was made. Everything in the house was in apple-pie order. The only thing that was not in its accustomed state and place was – the lady of the house. Of her there was not a sign. She was never seen again.

The second wave of "Vanishings" broke over West Ham in January, 1890, when three girls, all living in the same neighbourhood, disappeared one after the other. The fate of only one of them was ever ascertained. Several weeks after she had gone missing from her home, the body of Amelia Jeffs, aged 15, was found in an empty house in Portway, opposite West Ham Park – the same thoroughfare where Eliza Carter had been encountered by her school-friend. Amelia had been strangled. If the other two missing girls had been similarly attacked, it might have been reasonably expected that, in the fulness of time, their bodies, too, would have been discovered. They never were. A medical examination established that Amelia Jeffs had put up a desperate fight for her life, and it was generally supposed that she – and the others – had fallen victim to some wandering sexual marauder.

In January, 1890, the terrible Ripper murders of little more than a year before were still very much in the forefront of people's minds, and more than once the question was anxiously asked: has Jack the Ripper come back? Happily, as things turned out, there were no more Vanishings after January, 1890. The dreadful epidemic – as some truly believed it to be – had finally run its course. But such "illnesses" of humanity are sadly recurrent. Throughout the decades of our own twentieth century there were periodic "rashes" of vanishings – inexplicable, irreversible disappearances, April Fabb, Genette Tate, Suzy Lamplugh.

But the "Vanishings" of the 1880s and 90s were, and remain, one of the most disturbing and provocative mysteries of the Victorian Age.

Murder of a Manhattan Midas

Unaccustomed as he was to being bested in matters crumenical, Midas touch multi-millionaire William Marsh Rice was currently finding his dearest desire frustrated by a woman. A dead woman. His late wife.

The bottom line of the trouble was the community property law of Texas. Before her death, Elizabeth, his second spouse, availing herself of that law's decree that, she and her husband being citizens of the Lone Star State, were equal part-owners of the Rice millions, she had willed her half of the money away to her relatives. And this, her – as he saw it – final defection from beyond the grave, was bitterly resented by her 84-year-old, childless widower, for, like Martin Luther King, he was a man who had a dream. His dream . . . to found and endow at Houston a seat of learning, a citadel of science, letters, and art, which would gloriously perpetuate his name as the Rice Institute.

In a fury of novel bafflement, his best ploy, he decided, was to resist most strenuously the suggestion that he was a citizen of the state of Texas. Betaking himself to a drab and dismal fifth-floor apartment in a towering red brick edifice on the north-west corner of Manhattan's Madison and Fifty-second, he proclaimed himself a New Yorker. Known as the Berkshire, the building was actually No 500 Madison Avenue. Here, in the heart of Manhattan, Mr Rice lived the life of a virtual recluse – a sort of modern Simon Stylites on a high-rise pillar – tended in his isolation by a young man in his early twenties, Charles F. Jones, former storekeeper in one of the Rice chain hotels.

They shared no life of luxury. Their staple diet was bouillon and bread sent up from the local Woman's Exchange. Another engaging eccentricity was Mr Jones' parsimonious master's bedtime ritual; his scrawny body wrapped naked in a blanket, the octogenarian would woo Morpheus by rolling vigorously about his bedroom floor for an exact two and a half hours.

The twilight days of the stubborn old self-made Croesus were being rendered vexatious by the law suit he had brought in the Federal Court at Galveston against Mr O. T. Holt, lawyer and executor, to set aside Mrs Rice's will. Holt, in retaliatory vein, sought to establish that Rice was a true-flag, yellow-rosaceous Texan, and to this end enlisted the services of a sharp and non-aromatic New York attorney, one Albert T. Patrick.

Thus it came about that the lone wolf was brought down upon the fold; in the delicate phrase of Mr Rice, "Hired by Holt to do the dirty work" – i.e. secure depositions confirming Rice's Texan citizenship.

The plot began, as the cliché has it, to thicken.

By devious flatteries and divers promises, Patrick contrived to corrupt the amanuensical Jones. Entering into, as it were, a deed of partnership, the one covenanting to undertake and execute on behalf of the other, consideration being the promise of a share in the ensuant emoluments, an exercise in leisurely homicide. Messrs Patrick & Jones fashioned their web. First, a will was forged, naming Patrick residuary legatee to millions. Meanwhile, ante-mortem cheques were forged, made out to Patrick, totalling $250,000. Anticipatory petty cash. Lastly, an assignment of all Rice's property was made to Patrick.

All was now set and waiting for the bizarre evening of Sunday, September 23,1900.

Twilight comes creeping like twin winding-sheets up the Hudson and the East River. In the duskening apartment an old man lies stretched upon the bed. Over his face a cone of twisted towel and chloroform-saturated sponge are silently stealing away his life. In the room next door, listening to the heavy ticking of the clock, terror's sweat of guilt and fear on scalp and brow, sits the murderer, Jones. Waiting. Suddenly, obscenely ripping the almost holy silence apart, rings the shrill and insistent door-bell. Outside in the shining mahogany lobby are two old ladies, rare friends, bearing their little gifts of cake and wine for the man who is almost no more. They do not get in. Mr Rice has travelled beyond the reach of dreams.

A doctor. innocently obliging, certified *causa mortis* "Old age and weak heart . . . indigestion followed by colicqotue diarrhoea".

It was a banker, less obliging, refusing to certify one of the dubious cheques, who precipitated the lawyer's disaster. Patrick's alarmed reaction was less than judicious. Attempting to flush away the evidence of too many awkward Rice papers, he blocked-up and caused the overflow of the water closet pipes at his Broadway office, creating an "incident" at one o'clock in the moming.

This led to Patrick and Jones' arrest on charges of forgery. The pair were lodged in the Tombs Prison. The charge escalated to murder. Bland as ever, Mr Rice's heir apparent laid the blame for his benefactor's demise fair and square on an overdose of bananas. Rice, he explained, consumed five baked and four raw as a cure for indigestion. This time the indigestion had gone – but so had Mr Rice.

Patrick's next stratagem was to urge Jones to commit suicide, even providing him with a nice sharp penknife. The ineffectual Jones made a hash of it. He did not, however, make a hash of giving evidence against Patrick, and that wily gentleman was duly found guilty of murder and, in March, 1902, sentenced to death.

He was still alive in January, 1906, and, having exhausted all legal resources of deferment, was within a week of extinction, when his sentence was commuted to life.

On November 28, 1912, to the mighty astonishment of practically everybody, and not without whispers of circumambient graft, Governor John A. Dix, as a last gesture before leaving office, granted Patrick an unconditional pardon, and, with a song in his heart, he walked out of Sing Sing.

But Patrick's efforts to divert the golden stream from Houston to his own backyard had failed and, at litigation's end, some $10 million burst over the dam and flooded into the coffers of the Rice Institute. Rice's ashes rest today, it is sentimentally reported, in the base of an heroic statue of the old man sited at the centre of the Academic Court, gazing out on his long-ago dream made figuratively marmoreal.

The Breaking of a "Red Indian's" will

The case before Anderson J in the Saskatchewan Court of King's Bench seemed typical enough. A widow sought a portion of her husband's estate. Existing beneficiaries resisted, claiming that she had committed adultery while her husband was still alive. But before the Court could reach a decision, it had to unravel the escapades of one of the most colourful characters in Canadian history.

It is, unbelievably, 69 years now since, as a boy, I beheld the dead man in question, then vibrantly alive in all the splendour of his non-aggressive war-paint. Only the eyes did not look right: blazing blue in the lined brown face. I see him now, the tall Red Indian in fringed buckskins, beads, moccasins, sheathed knife and wampum belt, a single feather rising from his braided black hair. I see him brandishing the tomahawk which, turned over on its side, became a pipe of peace. I hear his greeting in a full, deep voice that seemed to carry echoes of the land of big lakes and tall pines, "Wa-Sha-Quon-Asin. I am Grey Owl."

And so fleet-footed a thief is time, that it is, as of this coming

September 18, one hundred and eighteen years since he was, in the veritable autumn of Jack the Ripper, born – not in the wild woods of Canada's Frozen North, but in a tame street of a Sussex town. For Wa-Sha-Quon-Asin was truly Archie Belaney of Hastings.

But it was in his dishonest Injun persona that, in 1937, 1 heard him lecture at Harrods about his adventures looking after the beavers in the Northern Territories. He gave that same lecture under the sparkling crystal chandeliers of the great drawing-room at Buckingham Palace. The entire royal family was present, including a fascinated little girl of eleven named Elizabeth. And as he left, Grey Owl clasped the King's shoulder and said, "Goodbye, brother. I'll be seeing you." He never did see the King, again. Four months later, on April 13, 1938, aged 50, Grey Owl went to the Silent Land Beyond the Pines whence no Redskin ever returns, widely mourned as a noble savage.

Then the gossipy tom-toms and wisping smoke-signals began to spell out their tidings of doubt.

Grey Owl was a fake, a fraud, an impostor.

Cables flashed to and fro across the Atlantic. One, to Mr Hamilton, undertaker, Prince Albert, Saskatchewan, read: "Count Grey Owl's toes." Mr Hamilton wired back: "Nine. Fourth toe, right foot, missing."

That settled it.

It was in 1906 that 17-year-old Archibald Stansfield Belaney set sail alone for Canada, where he was to become a farm pupil. But as he waved goodbye to Aunt Ada, seeing him off from the Liverpool landing-stage, he nursed a very different plan. Obsessed all through his boyhood by tales of Redskin derring-do, he had dreamt of actually meeting them. He found his Indians – the Ojibway tribe of Bear Island. He made friends. Picked up the language. Grew his dark hair long. Plaited it. And, on August 23, 1910, married a 20-year-old Ojibway maiden, Angel Aguena. The pair scraped a living, trapping. She was to bear him three children.

On the outbreak of the First World War, Archibald Belaney enlisted. He served in France, was gassed, and invalided out when he had the fourth toe of his right foot shot off. Recuperating in Hastings, he "married" a childhood sweetheart. She did not want to leave England. In 1919 he returned alone to Canada – and Angel – and his English "wife" divorced him.

Angel found him a changed man. Now he drank "plenty fire-water" and, subject to fits of wanderlust – and woman lust – would leave her for long periods. In May, 1925, on one of these walkabouts, he met a splendid, full-blooded Iroquois girl, Anahareo. Angel last saw him in September, 1925. With pathetic faithfulness, she waited in vain for his return. She never heard from him again. He "married" Anahareo in an Indian ceremony in 1927. She gave him a daughter, Shirley Dawn, born 1932.

It was now that he started his literary career, writing about his beavers in newspapers and magazines, and then best-selling books.

On a visit to Ottawa, Grey Owl, as he was now calling himself, met Yvonne Perrier. They were ""married" in Montreal.

And that was how it came about that by the time of his sudden death of pneumonia, Grey Owl had four "wives" – and the wisdom of Solomon was required of Mr Justice Anderson.

Grey Owl's will bequeathed half of his $14,600 estate, plus future royalties on his books, to Shirley Dawn, and the other half to Yvonne.

For Angel there was nothing. She applied for a modest third share- under the Widows Relief Act 1930 – claiming that Archie Belaney was married legally only to her. The one possible stumbling-block was the section of the Act declaring that a widow was entitled to a share of her husband's money unless her conduct had been such that, if she had sued for alimony when he was alive, a judge would have felt it unnecessary to award it.

Awaiting her errant husband's return, Angel had been responsible for feeding and clothing their children. She had earned a living of sorts scrubbing floors, trapping, hunting, and felling trees in the bush. By 1939 she was, she testified, too old to do that any more. It was she who had made the Indian buckskin costume in which Archie lectured, met royalty and dined in stately English and American homes.

The trickiest point was in regard to a boy child to which, long after Archie's desertion, Angel had given birth. The father, she said, was Charlie Potts, an Indian who had raped her. He, naturally, denied it.

Anderson J in his judgment chose to believe Angel. He considered the plaintiff to have had a moral code and to have remained faithful to her faithless husband. He allowed the claim. *Obiter* he observed that there was nothing in law to prevent it, even if she had committed adultery once or twice, Grey Owl's wilful desertion and neglect would have been the effective cause of such erring conduct.

The Little Tailor of Marylebone

One of the bonuses derived from the reading of the "psychological" novels of Georges Simenon is the insight which they impart. It matters not that their settings are practically all French or Belgian – the situations, the emotions, which they portray are universal. Their transformation scenes could, and no doubt do, take place behind any bland front-door face or lace-curtained window anywhere. Indeed, one comes after a time to experience sudden flashes of a "Simenon atmosphere", which is to say that, at unexpected moments, perhaps catching a line of poplars in a certain slant of sunlight, perhaps driving down an unfamiliar street on a dull day awash with a particular pattern of rain glints, or perhaps just traversing ribbons of spick-and-span painted suburban villas, hedge-boxed in their regimented pales of bright gardens, Simenonesque fantasies of the hidden stories which they may enfold begin to tease one's imaginings.

On one such day, making my way along Park Road, just past the top of Baker Street, I encountered an overwhelming "epiphany" – as James Joyce would call it – of Simenon atmosphere. It centred upon the premises above a shop. It arose, however, out of memory, not imagination.

If ever there was a Simenon character, it was Cecil Maltby, the little tailor of Marylebone . . . shades of *The Watchmaker of Everton*! He lived over the shop which his father, James, had worn his busy sewing fingers raw building to a prosperity which reached its apogee in taking the sartorial measure of Edward VII, when he was Prince of Wales.

By 1922, however, James was long dead, neatly pressed and laid away like an old mourning cloak, and the business, in the idle fingers of his son, was sadly coming apart at the seams. Moreover, beyond the still-splendid Victorian frontage of the shop, extremely strange things were going on.

It is not possible to put a precise date to the beginning of the disintegration of Cecil Maltby. It was a gradual, insidious process, but the Simenonesque point at which his story becomes ripe, as it were, for the gathering in and recounting, is the time in the heady, alcoholic summer of 1922, when he invited Alice Hilda Middleton – or Pat, as he called her – to move in above the shop with him. Maltby was then 46, a well-matured psychopath, who had from his early youth clearly signalled laziness, self-indulgence, and an assortment of less than admirable traits labelling him a "wrong 'un". Provided by a fond father with every possible life-enhancer, Master Cecil received good schooling and proud and assiduous grooming to take over his birthright of the thriving business.

But Cecil preferred cutting a dash to cutting cloth. He made the circuit of the racecourses, the smart bars and restaurants, and matching women. And they loved him. He was the prototype "Man with power over women". He married early, a woman who worshipped him – as, indeed, all women seemed to do – but the fabric of their relationship grew threadbare as he vaunted his female conquests before his wife. In the end, she felt compelled to take herself and their five children away to seek quiet and decency elsewhere.

One September day in 1922, Jack Middleton, a chief officer in the Mercantile Service, presented a worried face at Marylebone Police Station. Mrs Middleton had disappeared. He had last seen her in July, before sailing for the Far East. During his blue days at sea, she led, like her husband, something of a floating life, putting up at various boarding-houses. This time she had given him an address at 24 Park Road, Regent's Park. He wrote to her. Received no reply to any of his letters. A telegram from Cherbourg went undelivered. Moreover, recently she had not been drawing her money.

Back in London, he had made his way to the Park Road house. Persistent knockings and ringings went unanswered.

Time passed.

New discoveries began to surface about Maltby. He had gone bankrupt some 18 months before, but still went on living above his shop. How he lived was a mystery. He did not seem to have any money. He had paid no rates or taxes for several years. The gas, electricity and water had all been cut off. It was this insanitary state of affairs that gave the police their chance. Under the Public Health (London) Act 1891, the Medical Officer of Health obtained a warrant, and at 1.15 pm on January 10, 1923, police and sanitary authorities forced Maltby's front-door with a crowbar. Mingling with the noise of the splintering door wood came the sharp crack of a shot.

Inside the dirty, cobweb-festooned and musty-smelling house, all was gloom and heavy silence. It seemed to spawn its own especial *huis clos*, which distanced it dramatically from the sunlit outside world of chattering voices and ringing footsteps. It *felt* like an abode of the dead. Starting from the cellar, the searchers moved soft-footedly up, passing through room after filthy, dishevelled room.

It was in the top-floor-front, behind another locked door, that they found him. The blinds were drawn. The room was dim. It smelt of gunpowder. On a double bed lay Maltby, dressed in pyjamas; not quite dead. Clutched in his right hand, a heavy service revolver. Of Alice Middleton there was no sign.

The other room on this top floor was a kitchen-bathroom. The bath, covered by a board, had been used as a table. On it were the remains of that day's breakfast. Beneath the board, in the bath, wrapped in sheets, was a body. They had found Mrs Middleton. Lying on the body was a note saying that she had committed a suicide on the evening of August 24, 1922. And, a Simenonesque touch indeed, all over the house, nailed to doors, propped on mantelshelves, were notes and letters in Maltby's handwriting, scrawled with weird messages and references to Pat's suicide; patent outpourings from an unhinged mind.

When the post-mortem was conducted it was obvious that Alice Middleton had been murdered – probably in a drunken quarrel. A suicide cannot shoot herself three times in the back of the head.

Oddly enough, as a boy, I knew that house of tragedy well. It was only a few doors away from the shop of Mr Pollard the taxidermist, who once sold me a naked platypus!

The Uneasy Conscience of William Sheward

At half-past ten on New Year's Night, a stranger – a slight man in his sixties, with a lugubrious face and more than a whiff of alcohol about him – was ushered into Walworth Police Station, in south east London, on the arm of a police constable.

Having asked to see the officer in charge, and, addressing somewhat unsteadily Inspector Davis, of P Division of the Metropolitan Police, he announced: "I have a charge I wish to make against myself, for the wilful murder of my first wife at Norwich."

Thus did William Sheward, sorely troubled by his conscience, disabuse himself of the terrible secret which he had carried within him for 18 years.

But Inspector Davis' initial reaction was scepticism. He suggested that the stranger might "sleep it off". He told him: "I daresay you will find it all a delusion." And with that the man was lodged safely away in a cell for the night.

Early the following morning, having passed a restless and uneasy night, the man, whose name was now known to be William Sheward, soberly reaffirmed his blood guilt, supplying the date June 15th, 1851, as that of his despatch of the first Mrs. Sheward.

Inquiries were set in train. The Norwich constabular authorities confirmed the basic fact of Mrs. Sheward's mysterious disappearance. They also gave information concerning a number of disquieting discoveries that had been made in and around Norwich at the material time.

A severed human hand had been found by a dog in Lakenham Lane in the suburbs of Norwich. Another dog brought home a human foot it had found lying by a fence. A second foot turned up in the churchyard, and a second hand lay in the long grass of a local garden. Sundry bones and pieces of human flesh had been discovered in a number of locations in and around Norwich. Gathered together, they had been handed over to the doctors, who, after due examination, had pronounced them to constitute the remains of an adult human female of between sixteen and twenty-six years of age. Mrs Sheward, twelve or thirteen years older than her husband, had, however, at the time that she vanished been about fifty-four.

William Sheward, a tailor, described by all who knew him as a quiet, inoffensive and respectable man, had met his first wife, Martha Francis, who was actually a native of the Norfolk town of Wymondham, in London, where they had resided at St Giles. In 1840, the couple moved to Norwich. Eleven years later, Martha vanished from the scene. Her husband told the neighbours that she had left home on a long journey. Even though she never returned, curiously enough, no suspicion seems to have been aroused.

It was around this time that several changes came about in his life. First of all, he gave up tailoring and went into pawnbroking, he was observed to be drinking, and he installed a woman in his home in the place of his still absent wife. In the course of the next twelve or thirteen years, she presented him with two or three children, and on February 13th, 1862, he finally married her.

The pawnbroking business was not prospering, and in August,

1868, Sheward disposed of his stock to a rival pawnbroker, a Mr Boston, and took over as landlord of the King and Castle Inn, at St Martin's-at-Oak.

On December 28th, 1868, he left home saying that he was going to London to pay a visit to his sister. For some while before his departure he had appeared to be in very low spirits, and from the time of his leaving Norwich to the time that he walked into Walworth Police Station nothing was known of his movements.

But Sheward told Inspector Davis: "I went to a house in Richmond Street, here in Walworth last night. That's where I first saw my first wife, and it brought it all so forcibly to my mind that I was obliged to come to you and give myself up."

He said that he had left home in Norwich intending to destroy himself with a razor that he had in his pocket. Extremely smartly Davis insisted that he hand that razor over to him right away, which, like a lamb, he did. Continuing his narrative he said that he had been to Chelsea by steamboat, intending to take his life, but "the Almighty would not let me do it."

It was not long before Inspector Davis had collected sufficient evidence to convince him that Sheward had been speaking the truth, and he was accordingly charged with murder. He was committed for trial at the Norfolk Spring Assizes.

By that time he had decided to withdraw his confession, which, he said, had been made under the influence of drink. He pleaded not guilty.

The three Norwich medical men – Peter William Nicholls, surgeon, Dr Dalrymple, and Mr Norgate – who had examined the various human remains that had surfaced in 1851, revised their conclusions as to the age of the woman from whom they came, saying now that she could well have been a person of 54 or 56 years of age.

Sheward was found guilty and was hanged by Calcraft in Norwich Castle on April 20th, 1869.

He left behind a confession. There had been a quarrel with his wife over money on Sunday morning, June 15th.

"I ran the razor into her throat. She never spoke after. I then covered an apron over her head and went to Yarmouth. I came home at night and slept on the sofa downstairs.

"On the Monday I went to work. I left off at four o'clock and went home. The house began to smell very faint; with that I made a fire in the bedroom and commenced to mutilate the body. Kept on until half-past nine pm. I then took some portions of the body and threw them away, arriving home at half-past ten. That night slept on the sofa again. Went to work again the next day; went home about four o'clock and did the same. The same next night.

"Thursday – work same, and returned early. The head had been previously put in a saucepan and put on the fire, to keep the stench away. I then broke it up and distributed it about Thorpe; came home and emptied the pail in the "cockey" in Bishopsgate Street, with the entrails, etc.

I then put the hands and feet in the same saucepan, in the hope that they might boil to pieces.

"On Friday I went to work, and went home early and disposed of all the remains of the body, hands and feet included, that night, because I knew I should not be able to be home on Saturday until late.

"On the Sunday morning I burnt all the sheets, nightgown, pillow-cases, and bed-tick, and all that had any blood about them. The blankets, where there was any blood, I cut in small pieces, and distributed them about the city, and made away with anything that had the appearance of blood about it. The long hair, on my return from Thorpe, I cut with a pair of scissors into small pieces and they blew away as I walked along."

As the Sage of Stratford has Hamlet observe: "Thus conscience doth make cowards of us all." And mark well Congreve's apophthegm: "Love and murder will out."

Murder Among the Mummy-cases

That area of London which lies behind the Strand, embracing Maiden Lane and continuing through St Martin's Lane and Cecil Court to the happy book-hunting acres of the Charing Cross Road, has always been of especial significance to me. Here it was that my father and mother would regularly attend Mass at the Catholic Church of Corpus Christi, Maiden Lane, (celebrated by Graham Green in *The End of the Affair*), their names to this day commemorated in brass on pew-plates beside those of Radclyffe Hall and Una, Lady Troubridge, who, in the 1930s, occupied seats next to my parents.

It was in Maiden Lane, too, that my father and I found, in addition to Sunday's spiritual sustenance, incomparable weekday physical fare amid the brass and mahogany splendour of Rule's.

And it was just over the other side of St Martin's Lane, in dusky Cecil Court, that, the very day before her murder, I last spoke to my friend, Elsie Batten.

Elsie May Batten was 59 years old, and as the wife of a recent president of the Royal Society of British Sculptors, she had no financial need to work, but, she told me, her part-time job in Louis Meier's – he was actually the co-owner – little shop at No 23 Cecil Court gave her an outside interest. She enjoyed meeting and chatting with people.

Meier's curio shop was a strange place. I knew it well. My acquaintance with it coincided with the time when I was battling to learn how to read Egyptian hieroglyphs. A deep, dark cave, it was literally bulging at the brick seams with wonderful antiquities – a glorious jumble of temporally disparate, cheek by jowl Georgian snuffboxes, opalescent Roman lachrymals, ancient Boeotian Tanagra figurines, shrunken human heads, exotic jades and ivories, voodoo devil sticks, miscellaneous pictures and prints, fearsome native masks, vases and stone jars, swords ancient and modern, ferocious Oriental daggers, miniatures, and human skulls, and, I especially recall, wonderful Ancient Egyptian antiquities, including brilliantly coloured sarcophagi – mummy-cases.

It was on Thursday, March 2, 1961, during Mrs Batten's lunch-break, that a young Eurasian man came, in company with a teenage blonde girl, into the shop, and asked Mr Meier about antique swords, saying that he wanted to give his girlfriend a present of one. Shown a dress sword, he had found it too expensive at £15, but expressed interest in a Saxon sword, price £6. He departed, however, without transaction.

Friday morning, March 3, 1961, dawned bright and springlike. At about 9.15 am my friend Elsie – seen by a hairdresser opposite – arrived and opened the shop. Thereafter, no one had observed any comings or goings. It was Louis Meier, who, just after midday, found the body.

As a matter of fact, a 15-year-old apprentice sign-writer had gone into Meier's shop at about 11.30 that morning to buy a billiard cue. He saw what he thought was a dummy lying on the floor. Looking more closely, he realised that it was a woman. Assuming that she had fainted, he promptly left the shop. Clearly a chivalrous lad!

Mrs Batten lay supine in an alcove at the rear of the dark, Dickensian old curiosity shop. The white handle of a long-bladed antique dagger which had stabbed her through the heart protruded from her chest. Another dagger had been stuck deep into her neck. Both were clearly impromptu weapons seized from the shop's stock. The price tickets still dangled from them. No reason, then, to suppose this to be the premeditated attack of a personal enemy. When, later, Dr Keith Simpson examined the corpse, he found a third dagger driven into her back, and he said that she had also been struck on the head with a heavy stone object. Death had been made quadruply sure. She had not been sexually assaulted. Robbery seemed the likeliest motive, although Mrs Batten's handbag and the box used as the shop's till were both untouched. Meier was, hardly surprisingly, unable to say if anything had been stolen from his plethoric stock.

But then he remembered something – the young Eurasian who had come into the shop, looked at the antique daggers, and left without buying anything, and then, shortly afterwards, had returned to ask the price of a dress sword.

At a nearby gunsmith's shop police inquiries elicited a vital clue. Paul Roberts, 19-year-old son of the proprietor, told them that soon after ten o'clock on the morning of the murder a young Indian had tried to sell him a dress sword. "I paid £15 for it, but I'll take ten," he said. He wanted the money to buy his girlfriend an engagement ring. Roberts asked him to come back at 11.15, when his father who did the buying would be there. The would-be vendor had left the sword, wrapped in a sheet of brown paper, but never returned.

Meier and Roberts were able to supply good descriptions of the young Indian. Now, by an accident of time, it so happened that that very day one of the detectives who was to play a major part in the investigation, Sergeant Ray Dagg, had just completed a course on a new American crime-busting invention, the Identikit, and he was able to produce with it what proved to be a remarkable likeness of the wanted man. So remarkable indeed that, on March 8, PC John Cole, on duty in Old Compton Street, Soho, spotted and arrested a 21-year-old half-caste Indian and his blonde girlfriend.

Interestingly, Mr Meier had been mistaken in thinking that the girl he saw with the man in his shop was a blonde. Actually, she was the killer's sister, and she was as dark as he was. But the man did have a blonde fiancée, and Meier's mistake had in fact helped Constable Cole to catch the murderer.

At Bow Street, Edwin Albert Bush, of Forest Hill, admitted his guilt. But put up at the Bailey the following May he tried a slippery move. He told the Court: "I started haggling about the price. She [Mrs Batten] let off about my colour and said, 'You niggers are all the same. You come in and never buy anything.' I lost my head and hit her with my fist. She fell down and started screaming. I lost my nerve and then I hit her with a stone jar." Then came the predictable: "I cannot remember much after that."

I knew Elsie Batten. I knew her views on racism. I knew that she would never have made that disparaging remark. I didn't believe Bush. Neither did the jury. Had they done so, it would have put a different complexion on his trial for capital murder in the furtherance of theft.

I admit that I shed few tears when Bush was duly hanged at Pentonville the following July.

Corpus Delictus or No Body Worries

There is a persistent belief among non-lawyers that, such cases as those of *R* v *Ball* (1936), *R* v *Camb* (1948), *R* v *Onufrejczyk* (1954), *R* v *Hosein and Hosein* (1970), and the celebrated antipodean so-called Shark Arm Case, *R* v *Brady* (1935) notwithstanding, in any case of alleged murder where there is no body – which they mistakenly refer to as the *corpus delicti* – there can be no conviction.

They are not, of course, right; although one sometimes wonders if, for safety's sake, they perhaps should be.

The cautionary tale dubbed the Campden Wonder, like that known as the Canning Wonder, which took place 96 years later, is that of a mysterious disappearance and the telling of what Ben Jonson called a tale of a tub to account for it.

As Lord Denning might have told it ... The market-town of Chipping Campden in Gloucestershire, lies on the verge of the Cotswold Hills. On an August afternoon in the year 1660, William Harrison, 70 years old, steward to the Dowager Lady Campden, set out on foot to collect rents from outlying tenants. But he did not return. Between eight and nine o'clock that evening, his wife sent Mr Harrison's servant, John Perry, to meet his master on his way back from the village of Charringworth. Neither Mr Harrison nor his servant returned that night. The following morning William Harrison's son, Edward, went out to enquire after his father. Making his way to Charringworth, he met John Perry coming thence. Told by Perry that his father was not at Charringworth, the pair searched for him in the villages of Ebrington and Paxford, but without success. Wending their way back to Campden, they were told of a hat, neck-band and comb, found by a woman gleaner beside a great furze-brake on the Ebrington-Campden Road. They were shown these objects and recognised them as belonging to Mr Harrison. The hat and comb being hacked and cut, and the neck-band bloody, they feared the worst.

Those were disturbed, unsafe times, with Cavaliers and Roundheads alike liable to prove unpredictable. Murder, robbery, and kidnap were current coin. However, suspicion came to rest on John Perry. He was brought before a Justice of the Peace, generally believed to have been Sir Thomas Overbury, the nephew of Sir Thomas Overbury the elder, who was murdered in the Tower of London in 1613. Perry was kept in custody.

Coming a second time before the magistrate, Perry now said that his master was murdered – not by him, but by his mother and brother. He confessed also that a robbery which had taken place at Mr Harrison's one Campden market-day the previous year, had been carried out by his mother and brother, with his assistance.

Brought up at the Autumn Assize, Joan and Richard Perry, ill advised, pleaded guilty to the robbery, knowing that the Act of Oblivion – the Act of Indemnity (1660) for crimes committed before the Restoration of King Charles II – would pardon them. On the charge of murder, the judge, Sir Christopher Turnor, would not try them because the body had not been found. Put up again at the Spring Assize, before Sir Robert Hyde, Joan, Richard, and John Perry were all adjudged guilty of the murder of William Harrison. The three were brought to Broadway Hill and there hanged – first the mother, who rumour had it was a witch; then Richard, professing his innocence from the ladder rung; finally, John, the architect of all their disaster, of dogged and surly carriage, but telling at the last that he knew nothing of his master's death, nor of what had become of him. But, he added cryptically, they might hereafter possibly hear.

Two years had gone by when, bright and breathing, who should come walking back into Chipping Campden but William Harrison. He brought with him a strange tale to tell . . . of being robbed, kidnapped, and sold into slavery. He had, he said, been taken by three horsemen to Deal, in Kent, and there put aboard a ship. He found himself in Turkey, where, at a town near Smyrna, he was sold into the service of an 87-year-old physician. He remained in that employment, keeping the still-house where distillations were carried out, about a year and three-quarters. Then his master fell sick and died. Taking with him the silver drinking-bowl which the old physician had given him, he made his way to a port, where, bribing some sailors with his silver bowl, he was helped to stow away on a vessel bound for Lisbon. From there he took ship for England, arrived at Dover, and travelled, via London, home to Campden.

The strange affair known down the centuries as the riddle of the Campden Wonder is really compounded of two mysteries. What possessed John Perry to accuse himself, his mother and his brother of a murder that never was? And where, in truth, had old William Harrison spent those two lost years? Historians have been wondering and theorising for centuries.

It seems obvious that John Perry must have been suffering from some kind of mental sickness. Indeed, we encounter such delusional self-accusation among the disturbed today.

Lord Maugham LC, who studied the *corpus delicti* of the case, considered Perry "subject to chronic mental derangement (a paranoiac)". Harrison, he decided, was a rascal. The particular rascality envisaged was the misapplication of money belonging to Lady Campden. He absconded at the time when he believed the defalcations were about to be discovered – ergo, he did a Stonehouse! He returned when he had spent all the money he had taken with him, and when, anyway, he thought that the post-Interregnum Act of Indemnity would protect him.

Andrew Lang's sagacious suggestion was that for some reason Harrison's presence at Campden was inconvenient to somebody of substance. He knew some perilous secret of the troubled times, was a witness better out of the way until the revenges of the Restoration were accomplished. He was, therefore, with his agreement, spirited away, a false trail laid. By sheer bad chance, John Perry went more or less mad. It was made worth Harrison's while to spin his picaresque yarn. An interesting coda: upon Harrison's return, John Perry's body, still hanging in chains, was cut down from the gallows and buried. And, shortly thereafter Mrs Harrison hanged herself.

The Little Italian Boy: a Memorial

Barely three years have gone by since the old North British firm of Messrs Burke & Hare, purveyors by appointment of choice wares for the tables of the surgeons of Edinburgh, went into involuntary liquidation. Now, in London, under new management, has emerged a fresh enterprise in the old trade, the Bethnal Green firm of Messrs Bishop & Williams, at the appropriate-seeming address of Nova Scotia Gardens, to offer their services as suppliers of select merchandise to the profession.

It is 1831. The paint upon the stucco of the curves and colonnades of Nash's Regent Street is scarcely dry. It is here, and in the actor-haunted purlieus of Drury Lane, that the little Italian boy is to be discovered. A waif of the streets, one of legion, he is a quaint, pathetic figure, with his worn blue smock, shabby fur cap, and, slung around his neck, the revolving squirrel-cage, containing his pet tortoise and the pair of tame white mice which he exhibits to make a living. Then, as suddenly as out of the bright Italian sun he had appeared, mysteriously he vanishes into the mists and damps of London, never to be seen again.

It was at about 11.45 on the morning of Saturday, November 5, 1831, that the bell of the dissecting room at King's College, in the Strand, rang. Answering its summons, the porter, William Hill, found two men whom he well knew, John Bishop and James May of the metropolitan body-snatching brotherhood, seeking to sell him what was euphemistically described as a "subject". This, he was assured, was a good one; nice and fresh, a boy about 14 years old. And they wanted 12 guineas for it. There followed an interlude of haggling. Mr Richard Partridge, the anatomical demonstrator, would not budge beyond nine guineas. They accepted. At 2.15pm Bishop and May returned. With them came Thomas Williams and a porter, James

Shields, carrying a hamper, from which they tipped out the young boy's body.

Accustomed as he was to the sight of corpses, Hill observed certain signs about this one which alerted him. He noted that it had not been buried, noted that it seemed too rigid, that the fingers of the left hand were tightly clenched, that there was bruising, and a cut on the forehead – all of which he interpreted as indications of violence. He communicated his suspicion to Mr Partridge, who took a close look at the body and did not like what he saw. Explaining that the vendors would have to wait while he got change of a £50 note to pay them, Hill delayed matters until the arrival of Police Inspector Rogers and several constables. All four men were arrested.

Shields, who was not involved, was released. Bishop, Williams and May were put on trial at the Old Bailey. They appeared before Chief Justice Tindal, Mr Justice Littledale and Mr Baron Vaughan. On Friday, December 2, they were found guilty and sentenced to death. Present at the trial, making a shorthand note of the proceedings for an East End publisher, was a 19-yearold youth, Charles Dickens.

In the course of their last weekend on earth, Williams – or to give him his real name, Head – and Bishop both made confessions. Williams was the first to crack. Then Bishop, under the duress of spiritual blackmail by the Reverend Theodore Williams, admitted three murders: that of the boy, that of a young woman, Frances Pigburn, and that of another boy named Cunningham.

The procedure in all cases was the same. The victim was plied with rum spiked with laudanum, then, stupefied, was taken out and, a rope tied to his or her legs, lowered into a well in the back garden of Nova Scotia Gardens, to drown.

Both Bishop and Williams exonerated May. He played no part in, and had no knowledge of the murders. He was consequently reprieved and transported to Australia. Bishop and Williams were hanged on Monday, December 5, and, poetic justice, their bodies delivered up for dissection. Bishop went to King's College. To the end they denied that the little Italian boy, Carlo Ferrari was his name, had been their victim. The nameless boy they drowned had, they maintained, been a Lincolnshire lad, a drover, whom they had carried off from Smithfield; a boy who apparently looked extraordinarily like the little Italian boy.

Those who had known Carlo Ferrari, a Quaker stockbroker who had given him money, Augustus Bruin who had brought him over from Genoa, and Mr and Mrs Pellagrini with whom he had lodged for several months, all came to view the body. All agreed upon the matching build, colouring and general appearance. But, so distorted was it, that none was able to speak positively as to identity.

Time has ticked on. Nowadays it is the cardboard-box folk who have taken the vagrant's place upon our streets, once the province of the Italian hurdy-gurdy man, the children with performing monkeys on sticks, the gypsies with the dancing bears, the sellers of the plaster statuettes of gaudy saints. But, for those with tutored eyes to see, spectres arise out of the wet pavements to pass between the cardboard-boxes and the buildings ancient and modern. Metropolitan ghosts! As Sacheverell Sitwell puts it: "It is not otherwise than round the pools of Malebolge. We hear again that little sound of scratching. Were one half asleep, one would say it is a mouse nibbling in the wainscoting . . . but is it scratching on wood, or is it metal? For it makes a little ringing sound. And now in the fog, but it is near Drury Lane or Covent Garden . . . we see him sitting on a door-step. The cage is on his lap. The door is open, and he is feeding his white mice. Talking to them in mountain *patois*, the speech of cretins and goitres in the high valleys. The tune in the distance is a little Savoyard air. He is on his way in the rainy night to Nova Scotia Gardens."

Poison in the Asylum

Those old sanctuaries for the mentally sick are now, not by medical advice but by political edict, being torn down, their bewildered and disorientated inmates emptied out into the "care" of a not especially caring community.

Misadventurers, though, must take things as they find them,
And look for pickings where the pickings are,
The drives of love and hunger are behind them,
They can't afford to be particular.
To almost quote Auden and MacNeice *(Letters from Iceland).*

Sanctuaries were havens compared with the rough-and-tumble world outside, but they were places where strange things happened;

their flaking archives bristle with curious tales. Such a one is that which I want to recount here. It is the story – just one sad little story out of the heaped up misery of the world – of Mary Ann Ansell, aged 22, who died because she "baked an indigestible cake in a London basement, where she was living in the sad frontier country of the feeble-minded."

Leavesden, the large asylum built for chronic patients at Watford, Hertfordshire, was, in the year 1899, cram-full with two thousand inmates, sheltering and sheltered from the demands of normalcy. Among them was 26-year-old Caroline Ansell. A small parcel, addressed to her in Ward 7, arrived on March 9. It contained a sandwich cake, spread with a seductive, very bright yellow filling. Next day the cake was cut and shared with several fellow-patients. All were taken ill; Caroline seriously so. In fact, on March 14, she died.

When, two days later, the dead girl's mother and sister, Mary, came to Leavesden, the doctors, who thought her death due to peritonitis, asked permission to conduct a post-mortem. This was given and then later withdrawn. Even so, an examination was made, and evidence of phosphorus poisoning was found.

It was then that someone remembered a previous parcel – of tea and sugar – sent to Caroline on February 2. The tea had brewed so bitter that it was all thrown away.

The police were now called in. The investigations of Superintendent Wood and Constable Piggot soon led them to Caroline's sister Mary, who, on the death, had immediately applied for the life insurance money which she had staked. Raking through the asylum's refuse, Piggot came up with the brown paper wrapping of Caroline's parcel. It bore a WC1 postmark. For the past five years Mary had been employed as a domestic servant – wages £13 a year – by Mrs Maloney, of Great Coram Street, London, WC1.

It was in September, 1898, that Mary had insured Caroline's life, paying a premium of three pence a week to John Cooper, agent of the Royal London Friendly Society. She told him that her sister was a maid-servant, not an inmate, at Leavesden. The policy had been for £22 10s, but since the claim had been submitted within six months, the company agreed to pay only £11.5s.

The discovery was then made that Mary had, in February and March, 1899, purchased four or five penny-jars of phosphorus paste at a hardware shop in nearby Marchmont Street. She said she wanted to rid the kitchen where she slept of rats.

Mary Ansell was arrested and put up at Hertfordshire Assizes on June 29, 1899. Taking advantage of the recently passed Criminal Evidence Act 1898, she gave evidence in her own defence. She denied sending any parcel to her sister. She denied authorship of a letter addressed to Caroline on February 24, purportedly signed by the girl's cousin, Harriet Parker, falsely stating "your father and mother is dead". A handwriting expert had testified that Mary had written that letter and the address on the paper of the cake parcel. Mary said that she had insured Caroline so as to be able to give her a good funeral. Under cross-examination, she was confused and unconvincing. And Mary's father had told the court that it was she who had insisted on his refusing permission for a post-mortem. Mrs Maloney testified that she knew nothing about poison being purchased to kill rats.

The jury took over two hours to find a verdict of guilty, and added no recommendations to mercy. Matthew J sentenced the girl to death. She listened without the slightest sign of emotion – while her poor mother had hysterics outside.

But why should Mary have wished to kill her sister? The motive was alleged to have been her desire to get married at Easter. Her boyfriend said that he had not even proposed to her, although he admitted she had been pressuring him. Moreover, she had bought a number of items of furniture for their future home.

So . . . the motive was that purest of all motives – money. Albeit £11 5s seemed a pitifully paltry sum for the agonising sacrifice of a human life. Any doubts as to her guilt were dispelled by her confession shortly afterwards.

Dr Forbes Winslow, the most eminent alienist of his day, declared Mary to be a woman of very weak mind. Her appearance was that of an imbecile. Two of her sisters were insane. There was inherited insanity on both sides of her family. All of her mother's sisters died in asylums. She had frequent attacks of mental vacancy, talked to herself incoherently, had strange hallucinations, and would burst into loud fits of reasonless laughter. He wrote: "I came to the conclusion that she was a mental degenerate and ought not to be held responsible in the eyes of the law".

The prison chaplain at St Albans, the Reverend H. Fowler, said that the prisoner "did not seem to comprehend the serious nature of the crime". Miss Ellen Hayes, a woman inspector of prisons, wrote in her memoirs twenty years later: "Mary Ansell had all the marks of imbecility about her." It is surprising that no defence of insanity was offered.

The case of Mary Ann Ansell was the first in which serious doubt regarding the sanity of a woman about to be executed aroused wide public concern. There were petitions, letters to the press – including one of protest from the foreman of the jury, Mr Frank Cusworth – questions in the House. An unmoved and immovable Home Secretary, Sir Matthew White Ridley, simply stated that under the provisions of the Criminal Lunatic Act 1884 the condemned woman had been examined by two doctors and found not wanting in sanity.

At 8am on July 19, 1899, at St Albans prison, "Simple" Mary kept a bemused appointment with Mr James Billington.

Mercifully, to the last she was too simple-minded to realise her position: that is, until the procession to the scaffold was formed. Then she collapsed. Thirty-one years later, upon the partial demolition of the prison, her remains were exhumed and reinterred in St Albans Cemetery, where they still lie. It is said, but I cannot vouch upon the authority, that Mary's brother confessed to the murder – for which she was hanged – on his deathbed some years later.

The Birmingham YWCA killing

One of the loneliest places on earth – particularly two days before Christmas – is the corridor of a YWCA hostel, with its tight-shut anonymous brown doors. Back in the 1950s, these hostels provided a safe haven for girls from out of town; often those too timid to live in a bed-sitter. Such a one was Sidney Stephanie Baird. Aged 19, shy, retiring, a confirmed spinster with an aversion to men, she was a lonely creature with a none too happy history. Her home was at Bishop's Cleeve, near Cheltenham. A well-qualified shorthand typist, she had worked in Gloucestershire until 1957, when she had a mental breakdown. Seemingly recovered, she got a job in Birmingham, but after being made redundant she attempted suicide. Still unemployed, she took a room at the YWCA, a converted Victorian family house, Edencroft, at 64 Wheeleys Road, Edgbaston, and was undergoing psychiatric treatment at the time of her murder.

Living, also in lodgings, at 97 Islington Row, barely 400 yards from the YWCA, was Patrick Joseph Byrne. A couple of years younger than Stephanie, he was a builder's labourer, working for Tarmacs. A roaring Irish bhoy in the direct Brendan Behan bar line, he both looked and behaved like his compatriot Dubliner, especially when drink taken. Yet Acky – so nicknamed by his work-mates ("boot fellows" as Gerard Manley Hopkins called them) – was, however, where women were concerned, a shy, shrinking wallflower, like Stephanie.

Fate was to bring these two tragically together on December 23, 1959. At 1 o'clock that Wednesday, Acky Byrne and several of his bootfellows left the Hagley Road building site facing St Chad's Hospital, and sloped off for a lunch-time session in the Ivy Bush, Hagley Road. They staggered back to the site at 3 pm. Byrne was so drunk that the foreman would not let him up the scaffolding. He just hung about until knocking-off time, around 4.30 pm.

It was as he was crossing Wheeleys Road from St James Road that Byrne spotted the pretty girl in the red pullover going into the YWCA. He watched and followed and saw a window light up in the annex in the weedy garden at the back of the main building. Its yellow radiance in the wet, black night drew him like a moth. A death's-head moth.

It had been just about 5.30 pm when Stephanie had arrived back at the YWCA. She had been out having a hairdo, preparatory to going off home to Gloucester next day to spend Christmas with her mother and stepfather. She did not see the lurking Acky; the wall-creeper. He saw her – through a chink in the pulled curtains – red pullover, pink underskirt, combing her hair. He liked what he saw. Wanted a better view. Stealthily climbed into the building, then stood on a chair peering through the frosted glass fanlight above her door.

But there was all the difference in the perverted world between this big bumbling Behan lookalike and Bundy, the lithe and whippy American serial killer, who went into the Chi Omega sorority house dorms at Tallahassee, Florida, with the fully-formed intent to kill. Byrne was a mere peeping Tom, self-indulgently padding around the YWCA, as he had done quite a few times before, looking for stimulating revelations.

Suddenly the door below opened. Stephanie came out. Ran straight into him. He tried to kiss her. There was a struggle. Once, piercingly, she screamed. He wrapped fat sausage fingers round her windpipe. Then . . . alone with her corpse in the little back sleeping cubicle, he let the pent-up sadistic fantasies of all the long years of his frustrations and resentments literally rip. The least of his atrocities was the beheading of Stephanie Baird. His blood lust up, he prowled for another victim. Margaret Brown, 21, was alone in the ironing-room. He fell upon her, hitting her on the head with a chunk of rock, picked up in the garden. Her searing screams sent him scorching off in a panic.

The police were called. Searching the place for an intruder they found Stephanie's naked and desecrated body on the floor in Room No 4. Her severed head was lying on the bed. The rest of her body had been sexually abused and maimed. They found, too, a cryptic message scribbled in biro on an old envelope: "This was the thing I Tought (*sic*) would never come." He later explained that he had thought that he might perhaps one day be found guilty of rape, but never murder.

A massive, seven-week manhunt ended suddenly and unexpectedly at a small house in cobbled, gas-lit Birchall Street, in Warrington, Cheshire. No 80 was the home of Acky's widowed mother, Mrs Elizabeth Byrne. He had spent Christmas there with her and his three sisters – singing jolly songs and attending Mass. He had found himself a good £10-a-week job on the buildings in Warrington. But he now told Detective Sergeant George Welborn that the butchery in the Birmingham YWCA had left its hall-mark of horror upon him. "I cannot sleep. It's been on my mind. I was coming down to see the police."

He was tried at Birmingham Assizes in March, 1960. He made no attempt to dispute the facts alleged against him. The defence set out to avail itself of the provisions of the Homicide Act 1957. But after an absence of 45 minutes an all male jury brought in a verdict of guilty.

At the time, seven years before the abolition of capital punishment, there existed transitional exceptions from the temporary suspension of the death sentence: such as guilt of the murder of more than one person; the use of a gun; theft in the course of the killing; the killing of a policeman or prison officer. Since none of these applied in the case of Byrne, he was not guilty of capital murder, and could therefore be sentenced only to life imprisonment.

The judge, Stable J, had told the jury that s 2 of the new Homicide Act 1957 did not apply to uncontrollable lust such as this, but on appeal, after a thorough ventilation of the constituents of the defence of diminished responsibility, the trial judge, who was clearly wrong, was overturned. For the verdict of wilful murder was substituted, that of manslaughter by reason of diminished responsibility, but the sentence, of course, remained unaffected. Patrick Joseph Byrne was stowed safely out of temptation's way – for a while.

A Grimm Christmas Tale of New York

It is a fairy-tale (Grimm) of old New York. It invokes a city, a milieu, a way of life as vanished as *les neiges d'antan*, under which, that long-ago December, the stately West Side streets and avenues beside Central Park lay gleaming bluish in the winter twilight.

There stood at that time, on the corner of Madison Avenue and 45th Street, a great Gothic palace of a place – the Knickerbocker Athletic Club. It was to this splendidly named slab of towering monumental masonry – a sort of Manhattan Doge's Palace – that two intertwined riddles of love and death were to bring immortality as the legendary setting for one of America's truly classic mysteries of murder.

Christmas, 1898. Seasonable snow fell. The bells and carols rang out across white-muffled Broadway, Fifth, Madison, and Park. To sentimentally festive Manhattan came red-robed Santa, mock reindeer sleigh – and a slaying. For that Yuletide brought – carried by Christmas Eve mail, unheralded by any token of its donor – a silver gift of death. Addressed to Harry S. Cornish, Athletic Director of the Knickerbocker Club, there arrived, nestling in tissue-paper in a discreet, delicate blue Tiffany's box, a bottle of Bromo-seltzer and an elegant silver vessel, clearly intended as a sort of *de luxe* Bromo-seltzer-bottle-holder! Season of japes and jolly jestings: this unexpected gift, with its sly connotation of Christmas-tide hangovers, provoked considerable mirth among Mr Cornish's acquaintance.

It was not, however, Cornish – the obviously intended – but his aunt, Katherine Adams, with whom he lodged, who fell victim to the cyanide with which the bogus healing draught had been thoughtfully laced.

Minds at the athletic club were exercised. Memories flexed. They recalled the strange death at the club, where he had taken rooms last autumn, of a notably sexually athletic member, man-about-the-avenues, Henry Barnet. What, muscularity and and fine pectorals aside, had Barnet in common with Cornish? Both were linked, as friend and enemy, respectively, with Roland Molineux. Tall, handsome, 31 years old, reigning national champion amateur horizontal bar performer no less, and ex-member of the Knickerbocker Club, Molineux was by profession a chemist. Henry Barnet, fat and jovial, aged 33, was a wealthy broker. Molineux and Barnet had both fallen for the same girl – 24-year-old Blanche Chesebrough. She seemed to favour Barnet's suit. They were planning to marry when, in October, 1898, Barnet received by mail an unsolicited and anonymously despatched package of Kutnow powders. They proved veritable *poudres de succession*. He fell ill and died in his room at the Club of what was certified at the time as diphtheria. Nineteen days after Barnet's demise, his place as bridegroom at the side of Blanche before the altar of the Church of Heavenly Rest, at Fifth Avenue and 45th, was usurped by Molineux.

It was now that the mills of God began to grind. Cornish, who, at his late Aunt Kate's behest, had taken a probative sip of her nasty, bitter-tasting Bromo-seltzer, was feeling very ill. Dr Wendell C. Phillips, sent for to examine Cornish at the Club, shrewdly observed that his symptoms were very like those exhibited by the late Henry Barnet, to whom he had been similarly summoned at the Club some seven or eight weeks before. The doctor also recalled that prior to his illness Barnet had received a sample of a patent medicine through the post.

Fortunately, someone, suspecting that Mr Cornish's anonymous Christmas present was a leg-pull, had suggested keeping the paper in which the box had been wrapped, upon which the reticent donor had written the donee's name and address – it might be possible to identify the unknown's handwriting, to set for the jester a retaliative trap. Now that holographic clue became of far more sinister importance. Thumbing through the Knickerbocker correspondence files, club secretary John D. Adams drew forth in triumph letters written by Molineux. The writing matched exactly that on the Cornish poison packet.

In February, 1899, Barnet's body was exhumed. It was found to be riddled with cyanide of mercury. Molineux was arrested.

After some to-ing and fro-ing between indicting and non-indicting grand juries, he was finally indicted for murder. His trial took place on November 14, 1899. Fourteen experts testified that his handwriting matched that of the sender of the lethal package to Cornish. The sale of the silver Bromo-seltzer-bottle-holder – it was actually designed as a toothpick or match holder – was traced to a shop hard by the Newark factory where Molineux worked. He was found guilty and sentenced to die in the electric chair at Sing Sing.

However, in October, 1901, the Appeal Court reversed the trial verdict, because of the improper admission of evidence relating to Barnet's death, and a new trial was ordered. The second jury took just 25 minutes to find Molineux not guilty. On November 11, 1902, he stepped out into freedom.

He was to achieve some success as an author and as a playwright. He married again in 1905, but as time wore on he grew increasingly odd in his conduct, and in 1914 he was committed to the Kings Park State Hospital for the Insane. He died there on November 2, 1917, of GPI – the cerebral type due to syphilitic infection.

There died in Minneapolis in 1954, a stooped, eighty-year-old woman with hennaed hair, a painted face, and outlandish garments. She had lived in a tattered room, with perpetually drawn curtains and rose-coloured cloths covering the shades of lighted lamps, in an old house on Kenwood Parkway. There, like a ghost, frail, insubstantial, she sat by the fireplace, setting down the past on paper sometimes wet with tears. A ghost indeed; the wrinkled shade of the dashing young seductress of the nineties – she who, after Barnet's demise, had so casually exchanged a Roland for, not an Oliver, but a Henry. Blanche Molineux, the last of those ill-starred players whose shame, compounded of pride, ambition, and old green-eye, brought about New York's unmerry Christmas, vintage 1898.

A Selective Silence

It was a shepherd driving his flock through the ruins of the Emperor Hadrian's villa in the *campagna* between Rome and Tivoli who heard the groaning. It came from a narrow opening in the double stone wall surrounding Hadrian's Temple of Serapis. Lying within was the body of a man dying of poison. His coat was drawn over his head. In its pockets was nothing to identify him.

At the mortuary, Rome police took the dead man's fingerprints.

They were identified in the criminal archives at Berlin as those of a one-time American attorney, Karl Hau. Apparently, Hau had himself executed the death sentence which had been passed on him nineteen years before in Karlsruhe.

It had been around the turn of the century that Hau, then aged 19, while staying in Corsica, had made the acquaintance of Frau Molitor, the wealthy widow of a public health official, holidaying there with her 25-year-old daughter, Lina. The young couple fell in love. Frau Molitor refused to consent to their marriage, and Lina eloped, Hau having drawn 2,000 marks from her savings bank account to finance their flight. An attempt by Lina to commit suicide induced her mother to agree to the marriage, which took place in 1901.

Then, supported by his father and mother-in-law, Hau spent three years studying law in America. Passing his examinations with distinction, he was called to the Washington Bar. Never, as an attorney, did he conduct a case in court. After a period of lecturing on Roman and German law at the University of Washington, he took the post of private secretary to the Turkish Consul-General in Washington, and began a series of trade mission travels to Bucharest, Paris, and Constantinople.

At the end of October, 1906, Hau and Lina, on their way to Constantinople, paid a visit to Frau Molitor at her Baden-Baden home. Thence they went on to Paris, taking with them Lina's sister, Olga.

A few days later, Frau Molitor received a telegram: "Expect you by next train. Olga ill. Come immediately. Lina." In a state of great agitation, Frau Molitor, 62 years of age and afflicted with heart disease, hurried to Paris. She found both her daughters perfectly well. No one could explain the telegram. Frau Molitor and Olga returned forthwith to Baden-Baden. Hau and his wife departed for London, where they were to stay before going home to Washington.

At about 5.45 pm on November 6, 1906, Frau Molitor's telephone rang. The caller was, he said, an official at her local post office. Would she please come round at once. The manager had some important information regarding the mysterious Paris telegram. Accompanied by Olga, she set out immediately. As they made their way along Kaiser Wilhelm Strasse, there was a sudden flash, a loud report, a glimpse of a running man, and Frau Molitor fell to the pavement. She had been shot dead. The telephone message luring her from her home proved as bogus as the telegram summoning her to Paris.

Suspicion came to centre upon Hau – the one person who would crucially benefit from his mother-in-law's death. Investigations disclosed that he had ruined himself by catastrophic business transactions. He had only 10,000 marks left, and had secretly lost his wife's 65,000-mark dowry as well. However, on her mother's death, Lina would inherit 75,000 marks.

There was a motive. But what opportunity? Had he not been in London with his wife and child at the time of the tragedy? It turned out that he had not. A telegram had suddenly summoned him to the Continent on an important secret business matter.

At the request of the German authorities Hau was arrested in London. His trial took place at Karlsruhe. The tactics he employed for his defence were remarkable. He elected silence. He was forced to admit that he had sent the Paris telegram to Frau Molitor. Why? He refused to say. He was forced to admit that on the day of her murder he had been standing, in disguise, waiting outside the Villa Molitor in Baden-Baden.

Why? He refused to say. As a lawyer, Hau knew full well that the prosecution must prove the crime against him. What was proved by evidence he would admit. Beyond that, he would say nothing. A former attorney, a fellow-prisoner on remand, declared that Hau had confided his reason for being in Baden-Baden, and said that Hau was an innocent man. But since Hau himself was refusing to give any information to the court regarding the purpose of his journey, he too felt himself morally bound to silence. Proceedings to compel this man to give evidence were about to be taken when Hau intimated that he would speak. Now, under the duress of circumstance, he would break silence. "I made the journey back from London to the Continent in order that I might once more see my sister-in-law, Olga, before leaving for America."

He went on to confess his secret passion for Olga. He had struggled to master it. Concealed it even from her. He had sent the Paris telegram to bring Frau Molitor there in order to shorten Ogla's stay, which was proving too painful to bear. Then, in London, his love proved too strong, and he escaped to Baden-Baden, where he had waited vainly outside her home for just one more sight of her face. When she did not appear, he had telephoned the Villa to get her mother out of the house. But mother and daughter had emerged together – and he had left the town thwarted.

It was a very clever ploy. Until his fellow-prisoner had come forward as a witness he had, it seemed, risked everything gallantly to keep his sisterin-law's name out of it. Now he had sown a seed of doubt. Unwillingly! True, he had been near when Frau Molitor was murdered . . . but Olga, too, had been there. Had he, perhaps, kept silence to shield the murderess, the woman he loved? It was, of course, preposterous. And so the jury thought, condemning him to death. But Hau escaped the axe. In September, 1924, having served 17 years, he was released from Bruchsal prison . . . into a changed and lonely world where a postponed death brought to him the only true release.

Death of a Showman

When a person suspected of murder commits suicide immediately after the event, and there are no surviving dependable witnesses, the true sequence of events can only be articulated in a circumstantial manner. The more so if there is an intention to cover up scandalous connections. And where the apparent murderer leaves a suicide note which is ambiguous and not an explicit confession, but hints strongly at a motive, there would appear to be no good reason to rearrange the pattern.

In the case of the killing of "Lord" George Sanger whilom proprietor of the "Greatest Circus on Earth", one version of the circumstances culminating in his death on November 28, 1911 prevailed for close on half a century – until his grandson, George Sanger Coleman, felt compelled to "put the record straight". By his interpretation, there was no murder at all, merely a bizarre accident; but murder was certainly in the air.

Sanger, widowed, in his 85th year, and showing some signs of confusion, had retired from his circus ring of swirling rosin-backs and shabby tigers to Park Farm, East Finchley, a property on the then rural outskirts of London which he had purchased some time previously with an eye to his narrowing future. Here he presided over a curious set-up, employing a succession of young male favourites, euphemistically described as valets, but whose true function seemed to be to assuage the loneliness which he had felt since his wife's death in 1900. A great fuss would be made of the young man of the moment, but he would be subject to erratic dethronement. The last such deposed person was Herbert Cooper, actually the son of Sanger's bailiff, Thomas Cooper, accused – probably wrongly – of having stolen £50 from "The Governor". In his distress, cast out not only from the Governor's bedroom, where he normally slept, but forbidden also the house, he slunk off and made himself a secret den in an outbuilding.

According to the evidence at the inquest – Dr Bernard Spilsbury, incidentally, had examined Sanger's body at Finchley mortuary – Cooper invaded the farmhouse at about 5.40 that Tuesday evening, and entered the kitchen armed with a cut-throat razor. Jackson, his usurper in the Governor's favour, was sitting smugly there. Cooper, saying that he wanted to get his gramophone which was in the cupboard behind Jackson's chair, leant across to the cupboard, suddenly clamped his hand over Jackson's mouth and slashed at his throat with the razor.

In the sitting-room at the far end of the passage were Sanger and his grandson-in-law, Harry Austin. Hearing the noise, Austin opened the door and saw Cooper with an axe in his hand rushing towards him. Austin tried to shut the sitting-room door, but Cooper burst in and hurled himself on Austin, splitting his head open with the axe. He then turned on Sanger, despatching him with the axe and a heavy brass vase, and vanished out into the night. Sanger managed to crawl to the door before lapsing into unconsciousness. Five hours later he died. Jackson was not seriously injured. Austin was taken to hospital and made a good recovery.

Shortly after 7 am on November 30, Cooper's decapitated body was found on the Great Northern Railway line, between Crouch End and Highgate stations. The suicide note discovered in his pocket was unsatisfactory, but good enough for the coroner's jury to return a verdict of wilful murder and suicide while of unsound mind.

"Dear Dad," he wrote, "Something at the farm has happened. I don't remember doing it. I can only call to mind someone speaking. I seemed to have come to my senses and no one knows what I have gone through. The Governor turned against me – what for I don't know – and blamed me for things I know nothing about . . . All my brain has turned. Hope you will forgive me for some great wrong. Your broken-hearted son, Herb."

And there the matter rested, a part of circus history, until Sanger's grandson revealed what was, he said, the truth, hushed up to burke pain and scandal. This is the story behind the story. There was an adulterous and banned love affair. Cooper, in his misery, had turned to Harry Austin's wife, Topsy, who was Sanger's granddaughter, for solace. She had been sympathetic. It was Jennie Beasley, the general servant at the farm, who saw them together and told Austin. And that is why Austin had told Cooper not to come into the farmhouse again.

Out of his mind indeed, Cooper did not enter with intent, but, verbally provoked by Jackson, he seized one of the razors – with their blades open and tied back ready for instant use in the lancing of abscesses or swellings on any of the animals – which Sanger kept in the cupboard where the gramophone was stored. Dashing out into the passage, Cooper snatched up a felling-axe which was leaning against the wall, and attacked the husband of the woman he loved. Lord George Sanger, brave as a tiger, jumped up from his chair and sought to intervene. He grabbed a stout brass candelabrum from the mantelshelf and aimed a blow at Cooper, but the young man saw it coming and knocked it aside with his arm. By a freak, the candelabrum struck the old man behind the ear, and he fell back into his chair. Cooper was horrified. He dropped the axe – and jumped clean through the big window on the opposite side of the room. At this time Sanger was apparently simply dazed. He seemed to recover and behaved quite normally for the remainder of the evening. He duly retired to his bedroom. Refusing the offer of help, he undressed himself, drank a glass of water and got into bed. A short while later, he died.

In spite of the physical evidence which must have been brought at the inquest, a female family member, who saw Sanger's body, said that she had seen only a small bruise behind his ear. Even so, Herbert Cooper had, in fact, already manifested a full murderous intent towards another person – and before the Homicide Act 1957 provocation had, in general, to consist of something *done*, not said.

The Money Mysteries

In the long-shadowed cool of a September evening – Sunday 24, – in the Year of Our Lord one thousand nine hundred and five, a fresh-faced young woman set out from Lavender Hill, in the Clapham district of London, to take a one-way train journey and keep, all unknowingly, an appointment in Samarra.

Her name was Mary Sophia Money. She was 22 years old, and about, thus prematurely, to reach the terminus of her life.

Mary worked as a live-in bookkeeper for Messrs Arthur Bridger, dairymen, at 245 Lavender Hill, Clapham Junction. At 7 o'clock that evening, Mary told her friend, Emma Hone, with whom she worked, that she was going out for a little walk. In fact, she took a little walk as far as Clapham Junction Station, where she bought six pennyworth of chocolates from the sweetshop at 2 Station Approach, whose proprietress, Miss Frances Golding, knew her well as a regular sweet-toothed customer, and whom she told that she was going to Victoria.

The house-door at the dairy was rigorously closed at 11 pm. Emma Hone waited up faithfully until 1 am to let Mary in. She never came back.

Monday morning's newspapers were full of the previous night's terrible discovery in Merstham Tunnel, on the London, Brighton and South Coast Railway line, a couple of miles north of Redhill. At around 11 pm, Sub Inspector William Peacock and his gang of railway maintenance workers had found the badly mutilated body of a woman lying between the down track and the tunnel wall. The body was conveyed to the Feathers Hotel, Merstham. It yielded no clues to identity: no papers, no money, no railway ticket. But on her under-wear were the figures "245". This turned out to be the 245 of her Lavender Hill address – a laundry mark. The likelihoods of suicide or misadventure were contra-indicated by a circumstance which cast a much more sinister light on the matter. More than a foot of the thin white scarf which the woman was wearing had been crammed down her throat – like a gag. The mystery woman's identity was revealed when her brother, Robert Henry Money, recognised her.

But the mystery of how Mary Money came to be in Merstham Tunnel remained – and to this day remains. *Cherchez l'homme* was in the constabulary's view the short-cut to a resolution. Nets were cast wide, but no suspicious man came to light. A theory was constructed. The girl had kept a clandestine appointment at Victoria. She and her escort had a meal (at the post-mortem food eaten *circa* 8 pm was found in her stomach), then got aboard a train, perhaps to enjoy the privacy of a first-class compartment for a spot of hectic love-play. He tried to go further than she was prepared to. Horse-play escalated to serious violence, and culminated in a hush-up murder.

There were two possible trains from which Mary could have been flung – the 9.33 pm from London Bridge or the 9.33 from Charing Cross. Both stopped at East Croydon, whither a train from Victoria would have brought the couple. Actually, the London Bridge train guard had noticed a young man and a girl in first-class compartment No 508 at East Croydon. At South Croydon halt he saw them sitting huddled together, the arm-rest pulled up. At Redhill, the station beyond Merstham Tunnel, the guard found compartment 508 empty, the door swinging open. No sign of the girl. The man was walking towards the station exit – alone. He had "a long face and thin chin" and was "of slim build, fairly tall and powerful, moustached and wearing a bowler hat."

Signalman Yarnley, at Purley Oaks, north of Merstham, subsequently reported seeing a man and woman struggling in a first-class compartment of the London Bridge train as it passed his signal-box.

Suspicion flickered back and forth. Mary's employer, Arthur Bridger, was said to have given her presents and to have been seen on a day trip to Bognor with her. Charles Bellchambers admitted giving her the gold ring found on her finger and also that they had met on the Monday preceding her death. For the night of the 24th, he could account satisfactorily. As long as three years later, fingers were still being pointed. Albert Cooper accused William Wakeman, who had refused to lend him his walking stick as he was "going to meet a very special tart". After Mary Money's death, Wakeman had some minor injuries and for six weeks would only go out after dark. When Cooper had said: "I know something which could hang you," Wakeman had turned pale. That was it!

There was a curious – perhaps significant – coda to the case.

About 1907, two sisters, Florence and Edith, were living with their parents in Clapham. Florence met Robert Hicks Murray, who said he was a captain in the Gordon Highlanders, and persuaded her to set up house with him. She bore him two children. In the summer of 1910, Florence's younger sister, 24-year-old Edith, came to see them, and she and the "Captain" fell in love. He *married* Edith and she gave birth to a child. Incredibly, Murray hid all from his mistress, Florence, and successfully ran two establishments. Two years on, though, the strain began to show financially, and in July, 1912, he settled Florence and her children into some rather poor lodgings in Eastbourne. Himself, Edith, and her child, he quartered in a stylish villa in Enys Road, Eastbourne, which he had rented posing as an American, Charles Richard Mackie.

On Saturday night, August 17, Murray shot his wife and child and locked their bodies in a first-floor room. On Sunday afternoon, he collected Florence and her children and, telling her that a brother officer had lent him a nice house, took them to Enys Road, and shot them. He poured petrol over the children's bodies, set it alight, then turned his revolver on himself. But he had failed to kill Florence. With two bullets in her neck, she staggered out of the flames into the safety of the street. He left a note saying that he was ruined and had killed everyone dependent on him. "Please bury us altogether (*sic*) – CR Mackie". Published in facsimile in the press, that note blew Captain Murray's cover. The handwriting was recognised.

He and Charles Richard Mackie were . . . Robert Henry Money. Did brother and sister share some strange genetic bias for tragedy?

A Coincidence of Corpses

On an ink-black, moonless night in July, 1912, a young woman was strangled with a shoe-lace on a lonely stretch of Great Yarmouth's South Beach.

On just such another dark and moonless night 12 years before, the corpse of a young woman with a boot-lace round her neck had lain murdered on that same South Beach.

The victim of the September, 1900, murder was 23-year-old Mary Jane Bennett. Three years before her death she had married 17-year-old Herbert John Bennett. It was a classic case of assortative mating. He was a petty thief and small-time con man; she was a superior confidence trickster. Her speciality was selling cheap violins to the kind-hearted and the gullible, with a sob-story sales pitch of being forced, after the death of her young musician husband to sell his "old master" violin for food for her baby and herself.

The couple's progression through a series of seedy South London furnished rooms was milestoned with bitter quarrelling. In June, 1900, they parted, Mary Jane taking their two-year-old daughter, Ruby, with her to live in Freta Road, Bexley Heath, Bennett moving into digs in Calderwood Street, Woolwich.

It was not long before Bennett had fixed himself up with another woman, Alice Meadows, a respectable young parlour-maid at a house in Bayswater, to whom, on August 28, 1900, he proposed marriage. Clearly, Mrs Bennett presented a substantive impediment. It was alleged by the DPP, in the person of Mr C. F. Gill KC, that Bennett had eliminated this problem by the simple expedient of strangulation.

On September 14, Mary Jane had delightedly told a neighbour: "My husband is taking me and the baby for a holiday." The following day, giving the name of Mrs Hood, Mary Jane took a room at Mrs Eliza Rudrum's lodging-house in Great Yarmouth. And it was from there that, on the evening of Saturday, September 22, 1900, Mary Jane set forth at 8.30 pm to keep, all unknowingly, an appointment with her killer.

Bennett denied that he had ever been to Yarmouth, but William Borking testified that between 9.30 and 10.00 pm Mary Jane and Bennett came into the "snug" of the South Quay Distillery, of which he was manager, and had drinks. Bennett was also seen at the Crown and Anchor, where he stayed the night. Moreover, William Reade, a waiter there, remembered Bennett and a young woman (presumably Alice Meadows) staying at the hotel – in separate bedrooms – one August Bank Holiday. Bennett, he said, had stayed again, alone, on September 16 and 22.

For all Marshall Hall's forensic eloquence, the jury found themselves unable to accept the proposition of his client's innocence. The trial judge, Alverstone LCJ, concurred. Bennett, protesting his asparagus-green youth and innocence to the trap-door's final thud, was "despatched" in a coach-house at Norwich Prison by the Billingtons, *père et fils*, who sprung the trap on the first day of spring, 1901.

What had most especially militated against Bennett was the fact that the prosecution had been able to produce a photograph of Mrs Bennett – taken on the beach that holiday – wearing a gold chain, which same chain was subsequently recovered by the police from Bennett's lodgings.

It is recorded that the hanging was somewhat less than a success: when the drop fell, Bennett's body twisted violently for more than two minutes. Further, when the mandatory black flag was raised the flagpole snapped, which the superstitious eagerly grasped as a "sign" that Bennett had indeed been innocent!

Herbert John Bennett had lain securely in his "burning winding-sheet . . . eaten by teeth of flame" a dozen years when a strangler came again to Yarmouth's South Beach. It must have been with a chilling stab or jolt of *déjà-vu* that they discovered, on the morning of July 15, 1912, ominously close to the site of the Bennett tragedy, the body of the young woman with the shoe-lace biting deep into her neck. She had been strangled in the identical way that Mary Jane Bennett had. What did it mean? Coincidence? Copy-cat killing? Or that Bennett had been, as he claimed, an innocent man – and that the real Yarmouth strangler was still at large and had struck again? The dead girl was 18-year-old Dora May Gray. The lace with which she had been strangled had been taken from one of her own shoes. There was no sign of a struggle. It was as if she had simply fallen into eternal sleep upon the sand. As well as the shoe-lace – tied with a reef-knot followed by a granny – her stockings had been wound tightly round her neck.

Dora Gray had been living with her "aunts", Mrs Brooks and Miss Eastwick, in Yarmouth. She was illegitimate, a "love child" as we say today, and they had adopted her when she was five. Recently, she had been working from 7.00 am to 8.00 pm as a daily help at a boarding-house in Manby Road, kept by a Mrs Newman.

On the day before her death she had been seen in the company of various men. One of them, who was thought to have some connection with yachts and yachting, was in his 40s; old enough, that is, to have been responsible for the earlier murder. Actually, Dora was known to have had three or four friends who were yachtsmen, and shortly before her murder she had confided to Hubert Baldry, the son of the master of the yachting station, that she had spent a week at Lowestoft with one of the yachtsmen.

On the Sunday (14) morning, she had gone aboard the yacht, *Medix*, where she had lunch and came ashore again at about 5.00 pm. As she was leaving the yacht station, she told Baldry that she was going for a walk on the Marine Drive with the gentleman with whom she had been to Lowestoft.

And, at about 8.45 pm, she was seen by her friend, Emily Blyth, going towards South Beach with a young man. There were those, however, who thought that it was another and older man, whom she met later that night, who murdered her. But the police, whatever their private convictions, most signally lacked the evidence to take on a prosecution leading to the conviction of their choice – a local man upon whom local suspicion bulldoggishly attached, and still attaches, itself.

A Chinese Puzzle in Lakeland

It was a typical June holiday day in the English Lake District. One minute sunlight, Wordsworthian daffodil-yellow, dappling lake, tarn, and fell; the next, the brisk patter of sharp showers of raindrops on earth and leaf and water, the sunshine vanished behind the blinds of fast-blown clouds.

Not, you might think, the appropriate setting for a Chinese puzzle.

The story, which ended so tragically in the quiet Cumbrian village of Grange-in-Borrowdale, opens in New York. It was there, in October, 1927, that Chung Yi Miao met Wai Sheung Siu. He, aged 28, was a young Chinese lawyer. She, the wealthy, 29-year-old daughter of a merchant prince from the island of Macao, was a graduate of Boston University. Chung and Wai were both of the Mandarin class. They fell swiftly in love and married in New York, in May, 1928. Then they set out on a honeymoon trip, travelling, via Albany and Buffalo, to Montreal, where they embarked on the *Letitia* for Glasgow, which they reached on June 11. After a week spent there and in Edinburgh, they decided that before continuing south to the Rubens Hotel in London, they would visit the Lakes.

They arrived at the Borrowdale Gates private hotel at Grange, on Monday, June 18, 1928. Before a second day's dawn the shyly smiling bride would be lying cold and strangled . . . and her polite attentive husband sitting pale and inscrutable in a police cell.

For the moment though, in this idyllic spot, close by Derwentwater, and three and a half miles from Keswick, where few Chinese couples visited, they were a conspicuous pair. He, tall for a Chinese male, seemed to tower over his diminutive, doll-like wife, barely 4 ft. 11in. in height. She, moreover, had a penchant for displaying items of the three or four thousand pounds' worth of exquisite, eye-catching jewellery which she carried with her.

After lunch on their first full day – Tuesday 19 – Miao and his wife went out for a walk together. Around 4 pm, Miao returned to the hotel alone. Asked if he would wait for his wife before having tea, he said no: she had gone to Keswick to do some shopping and would not be back until 6 pm.

Six came and went. No sign of Wai. At 7 pm, he dined, alone. At 9 pm, approached by the proprietress, Miss Crossley, he explained: he had caught a slight cold in Glasgow and his wife had told him to go to bed while she went into Keswick to buy medicine for him and some warmer underclothes for herself. At 10.30 pm, Miao asked a maid: "What do you think we ought to do? Should we inform the police?" He did nothing. He went to bed.

Meanwhile . . .

At about 7.30 pm, a local farmer, Thomas Wilson, had seen at a place close to the river on the edge of Cummacatta Wood, about a mile from the village, a woman wearing a fur coat lying, as he thought, asleep, under an open umbrella. When, later, he mentioned this rather odd encounter to some friends, one of them, William Pendlebury, a detective-constable from Southport holidaying with his wife at Grange, decided to investigate, and found the missing bride, dead. Round her neck were a piece of white string and two lengths of green window-blind cord. An attempt had been made to make it look as if she had been robbed and sexually assaulted. The police were not convinced. At 11 pm that night, Miao was arrested at the hotel.

The case unfolded at Carlisle Assizes was circumstantially sufficiently strong to persuade the jury of Miao's guilt. What weighed most significantly against him was the discovery of two valuable rings, allegedly torn from the dead woman's fingers by the insubstantial thief, concealed in the carton of one of Miao's Kodak camera films.

Miao hanged at Strangeways, Manchester, on December 6, 1928.

The Chinese puzzle is not one as to who committed the murder, but why Miao did it. Motive was, as the learned judge, Humphreys J, pointed out, a matter of small concern. "It is never necessary," he told the jury, "for the prosecution to establish the motive for a crime."

So be it. But, psychologically, one is bound to feel curious as to what possible reason could have exercised such a destructive power. Miao and Wai were surely two golden people – young, wealthy, socially and intellectually superior. The notion that Miao had killed in order to accede to his wife's property will not hold water. By Chinese law that property was already his.

The circumstance that, some ten days after her marriage, the petite

Wai consulted a woman doctor in Albany because marital intercourse was proving impossible, has led to the suggestion that Miao killed out of sexual frustration. The absurdity of this is testified to by the fact that a minor operation would immediately correct such a physical condition. It was actually performed on May 25.

On the dubious authority of a single Sunday newspaper article, published after Miao's execution and purporting to be in his own words, it has been thought that Miao discovered that his wife was unable to bear children. He was horror-struck, for the Chinese believe in ancestor-worship, and the thought of having no children to honour his memory made it necessary for him to replace Wai with a fertile wife.

A final tendered solution is that it was the malign influence of a Chinese tong that brought about the killing of Wai Sheung. There is a tong – the Chapa tong – of which Miao may have been a member. Its avowed purpose was to raise money. Young male members were expected to persuade young women of means to fall in love with them and, having married them, to obtain their property for the benefit of the tong.

More plausibly, perhaps, could Miao have been recruited under orders to carry out a secret tong revenge killing? Wai was the daughter of an important business man who might have antagonised the tong. Or was Miao totally innocent? Did he, as he claimed, see strange oriental figures shadowing him and his bride in Glasgow, Edinburgh, and Grange? Was it the tong's assassins who killed them both? Does charity allow room for such postulation?

A Rowland for an Olive?

One does not need to be long-toothed in the law to have encountered that hoary old and hopeful defence ploy of mistaken identity. Usually it is just that, but sometimes – and one thinks of Adolf Beck and Oscar Slater – it enfolds within it disquieting doubts. The murder we are about to consider is a case in point.

The crime was cruelly commonplace and crude. A sad 40-year-old prostitute lately arrived from Birmingham was brutally done to death with a hammer on a Manchester blitzed site. An equally sad and drab hostel habitué, Walter Graham Rowland, was arrested and charged.

It was two children homeward bound from church and risking, as children will, their Sunday-best shoes to adventure across the beckoning rough ground of the patch of waste land at the corner of Deansgate and Cumberland Street, who, at 11 am on Sunday, October 20, 1946, found Olive Balchin. She lay shrouded by clumps of dark blood-dappled willow-herb. Steps away, snared between weed-stalks by sticky skeins of blood, nestled a wicked-looking hammer.

A photograph of that hammer in the local newspapers brought forward a witness, Edward McDonald, owner of a second-hand bric-a-brac shop in Ardwick. He recalled selling it at 5.40 pm on Saturday, October 19. He described the purchaser: "A man aged 28–32. 5 ft 7 or 8 ins tall. Medium build. Very pale face, thin features, clean-shaven. Quiet spoken. No hat, white soft collar shirt, dark tie, dark suit, and a dark fawn cotton raincoat."

A second witness surfaced. Norman Mercer, licensee of the Dog and Partridge Inn, 298 Deansgate. He said that walking his dog, about midnight, he had seen a couple quarrelling near the murder site. He described the man as being "of proportionate build", having dark hair and wearing a dark suit. At the mortuary, he recognised Olive Balchin.

The third witness was Mrs Elizabeth Copley, waitress at the Queen's Café, just off Deansgate. Between 10.30 and 11 pm on October 19, a woman whom she identified as Olive Balchin came in with another, much older, woman and a man, whom she described as having dark hair, a fresh complexion, wearing a dark suit, and carrying a long, thin, brown paper parcel.

Combing the hostels and lodging-houses of the area, looking for anything vaguely out of the ordinary, the police pricked up their ears when they heard of a raincoat having been lent to a man named Rowland and never returned. Rowland was checked in the files, found to have a record of violence, and to correspond, roughly, with the descriptions given by the three witnesses.

Arrested, Rowland admitted knowing Olive Balchin. He also admitted that he had suspected that she might have given him the syphilis with which he was infected. (She had not. He had picked it up during wartime service as a soldier in Italy). He vehemently protested his innocence and put up an alibi defence strongly supported by the lodging-house keeper of the house where he claimed to have been staying on the night of the murder. The jury were unimpressed.

While awaiting execution at Strangeways – his second term of residence in the condemned cell there, for he had been sentenced for strangling his baby daughter in 1934, and reprieved – news came that David John Ware, serving a sentence for theft in Walton Gaol, Liverpool, had confessed to the Balchin murder.

There were already a number of irreconcilable discrepancies in the evidence – MacDonald's man had a pale, thin face, and was "on the dark side"; Mercer's man had a round, full face, and dark hair; Copley's man had black hair. Rowland's hair and complexion were fair. There was, moreover, virtually no forensic evidence to link him with the murder. Ware's confession, together with new evidence by Mrs Coppock, landlady of the Wellington, in Stockport, where Rowland had been drinking, seemed to augur well for the success of his appeal.

Heard before Goddard LCJ, Humphreys J and Lewis J, on February 10, 1947, by candlelight (due to power cuts) – which led to the view in some quarters that the judges seemed hopelessly in the dark! – the Court refused to allow the new witness on the grounds that she had been available for the original trial, but was not called.

It also refused to hear Ware's evidence. Had it done so, Humphrey J, explained, the Court would have been compelled to form some conclusion as to Ware's guilt or innocence and to express that opinion in open court: in effect trying both Rowland and Ware, usurping the functions of a jury. The appeal was dismissed.

On February 21, the Home Secretary asked Mr John Catterall Jolly, KC to investigate Ware's confession and any other material which had become available since Rowland's conviction. Ware withdrew his confession. Jolly rejected Rowland's innocence. Rowland was hanged at Strangeways on February 27, 1947.

There is, however, a somewhat disturbing sequel. Does it possibly suggest that a more proper conclusion in this case might have been that it was unsafe to convict? Walter Graham Rowland had lain four years in his nameless prison-yard grave, when, on August 2, 1951, David John Ware walked into a police station in Bristol and announced, "I have killed a woman. I don't know what is the matter with me, I keep having an urge to hit women on the head."

As a matter of fact, he had not killed anyone. But it was not for want of trying! He had most seriously attempted to murder Mrs Adelaine Fuidge, attacking her with a hammer in precisely the same way that Olive Balchin had been bludgeoned. He was sent to Broadmoor. He hanged himself there in 1954.

But what, one wonders, does that signify? Nothing more, perhaps, than that Ware, a long-standing case of mental impairment, had developed a powerful delusion in relation to the killing of Olive Balchin? Or does it lend a terrifying authenticity to Rowland's claim in his speech in reply to the Clerk of Assize's "Have you anything to say why sentence of death should not be passed according to law?" He said "The day will come when this case will be quoted in the courts of this country to show what can happen to a man in a case of mistaken identity." Is it? Was it?

A Christmas Death on the Dunes

The love-letters were supremely important exhibits at the trial. The court was stilled. Several members of the jury unashamedly wept, and tears welled even in the judge's eyes, as counsel read them out. One was, in the circumstances, especially poignant. He wrote: "My dear, darling Kathleen, I long for Christmas . . . I feel you will never leave me after Christmas. I long for some good Christmases with you in times to come."

He was Frederick Rothwell Holt, 31 years old, shell-shocked ex-officer, 4th Loyal North Lancashire Territorial Regiment.

She was 25-year-old, really outstandingly beautiful, Kathleen Harriet Elsie Breaks. Neither of them was to see another merry Christmas after that of 1919. She would spend it in the mortuary. He in a prison cell.

She called him Eric. He called her Kitty. They had met in Blackpool in 1918. Eric came from a moderately well-off family, who lived at Fairhaven, adjoining St Annes-on-Sea, on the Fylde coast of Lancashire, five miles south of Blackpool. After seeing action as a lieutenant during the terrible bombardment of Festubert, he was invalided out in 1916, and, following a brief interlude in Malaya, returned in 1918. Unmarried, having inherited from his mother an income of £300 a year, he had no need to work, and whiled his days happily away, drinking and chatting of sport and women in the bars and lounges of the best local hotels.

Kitty lived with her mother and sisters, Eva and Daisy, in a cottage at Ryecroft Farm, Dudley Hill, Bradford. She had worked as a shop assistant, but in 1913, at the age of 19, had married John Breaks. The couple had not lived together until 1917; and then for only six months. Kitty, who liked to wear expensive clothes and stay at the best seaside hotels, capitalised on her main asset, her beauty, to make this life-style possible – became, in short, a gentleman's high-class, *complaisante* companion.

Then . . . she had the misfortune to meet and fall in love with handsome Eric Holt. Her love was reciprocated. She became his mistress. They enjoyed frequent rendezvous – in Bradford, Manchester, Blackpool, and suchlike romantic trysting-places!

On December 23, 1919, after nights of love in a boarding-house in Bradford, this slightly seedy Romeo and his somewhat soiled Juliet travelled south, catching the 5.55 pm train from Manchester to Blackpool. Eric alighted at Ansdell and Fairhaven station, near his home. Kitty travelled on to Blackpool Central.

And that, according to Holt, was the last time that he saw her.

The desolate stretch of coast-line between Lytham and Blackpool, where islands of low, windswept dunes seem anchored by tufts of coarse tussocky grass in a never-ending sea of sand, is a bleak enough place at the best of times. On the pouring wet, blustery, dark night of December 23, it must have seemed forbidding indeed to the lone woman who ventured there. But she had an assignation to keep.

It was Edward Gillett, a local farmer with a penchant for beach-combing, who found her there in the early morning of Christmas Eve. She lay hidden, dead and bloody, in a hollow in the sand-hills, about 150 yards from the tram track which runs, the main route into Blackpool, along Clifton Drive North. Four shots had been fired into her body. Gillett telephoned the police. They identified the woman from letters in her handbag. It was Kitty Breaks. Footprints in the sand told their plain story. Footprints of a man and a woman who had walked abreast. Footprints which converged, then separated. And only one set of footprints travelled on.

The names of three men figured in the letters in the handbag. Two of them, Kitty's husband and a former lover, Tom Thornton, provided steel-strong alibis. The third man was Eric Holt.

Police investigations went apace. On the fatal evening Kitty had been seen walking towards the sand-hills. Holt had been spotted, too – in a tram travelling along Clifton Drive North. Vital clues surfaced. A pair of bloodstained gauntlets, traced to Holt's possession. A pair of his shoes, newly soled, the imprints precisely matching the footprints in the sand. A Webley revolver, the murder weapon, buried in the sand, revealed as Holt's property. Then – a clincher. Holt had persuaded Kitty, of whom there was evidence that he was growing tired, to insure her life for £5,000, and make a will leaving £4,800 to him. At 7.30 am on Christmas morning Eric Holt was arrested.

He came to trial before Greer J at Manchester Assizes, February 23, 1920. He was defended by Marshall Hall, who, having first had a stab at "unfit to plead" – which was rejected out of hand, Attorney-General Hewart for the Crown having pointed out that, asked if he objected to a medical examination, Holt had replied that he would like to see his solicitor first – put up a rather shaky defence of alibi. Namely, that after leaving the train at Ansdell, he had gone for a drink at the Fairhaven Hotel, then walked around, alone, before returning home for supper at about 10.15 pm.

The motive suggested was a frenzy of jealousy – that it was hot-blooded *crime passionel* rather than the cold-blooded insurance killing argued by Hewart.

Always tending to eccentricity, Holt had taken to behaving exceptionally weirdly latterly, claiming that the police had set dogs on him in his cell, and had sent in malaria – and typhoid – carrying mosquitoes, trained to bite him. Hewart believed that Holt exhibited Ganser syndrome – showing inappropriate responses to feign insanity and escape punishment. However, to the end of his life, Marshall Hall maintained that the State had hanged a madman.

Standing to attention in the dock, military-moustached, spruce in brown tweed suit, cream shirt and regimental tie, Holt made an initially good impression. But, as the trial wore on, this diminished. There was something rebarbative about the patent callousness of the man. He sat throughout with arms folded, giving the impression of brutal indifference. He was cramming an evening paper into his pocket when he was brought up to hear the verdict of the Court. Asked if he had anything to say why sentence of death should not be passed upon him, he shrugged. And when it had been passed, showing no concern, he put his hands into his pockets and walked away.

When he returned to Strangeways and was visited in the condemned cell by the governor, he said: "Well, and that is that! I hope they won't be late with my tea!" It was on time. So was Mr Hangman Ellis, on April 13, 1920.

Murder: the Browning Version

A mad dog Englishman out in the midday sun, braving the furnace of a Florentine noon-tide, found offered for sale on a market stall in the Piazza San Lorenzo a "square old yellow book". It proved to be a bundle of ancient documents, scribed for the most part in a stilted, clipped and barbarous form of seventeenth-century legal Latin, put together by one Monsignore Francesco Cancini of Florence, a lawyer "curious in the dry sophistries of his calling", and bound-up in vellum. Its subject was an extraordinary Roman murder case of 1698. But it was more than that: an absorbing chronicle of dateless human misery. The Englishman, a poet, fascinated, bought it that day in June, 1860, for one *lira* – a mere eight pence in old English money.

In the year 1693, Count Guido Franceschini, an impoverished Tuscan nobleman of Arezzo, having failed to find a lucrative sinecure in Rome, was seeking now, at the age of 35, an advantageous marriage to repair the dilapidations of a Palazzo Franceschini flapping with decay like an Italian Gormenghast. Lolling one day in the *salone* of a *parruchiere di qualità* on the Piazza Colonna, where he was wont to loaf when he was without a *scudo* in his purse, he confided that his mind had turned to the sacrament of matrimony and boasted of his fine Tuscan estates.

Now it so chanced that there lived in a quiet street, the Via Vittoria, in Rome, 64-year-old Pietro Comparini, his 61-year-old wife, Violante, and their sole child, a daughter, Pompilia. And it further chanced that about this time Violante had been whispering into the ear of the *coiffeuse* of the Piazza Colonna of the availability of Pompilia, and especially of the young girl's roseate fiscal prospects. The tidings were passed on. The floundering Guido took the bait.

Alas, things proved not quite as reported. The entire property of the Comparini family amounted to £2,400. A settlement was arrived at. A dowry of £520 was bestowed upon Pompilia. The balance of the

Comparini possessions were to be handed over on the condition that the Count maintained Pietro and Violante for the remainder of their days at his ancestral home in Arezzo. Guido and his child-bride – Pompilia was just 13 – were married on September 6, 1693.

It required no scryer to predict that the Arezzo "arrangement" would collapse. It did. The Comparini were happy to shake the brown dust of Tuscana from their heels. Bitter, disillusioned, Violante made then a revelation and took an action that was to place Pompilia in a truly terrible plight. The child was not her daughter. She had been purchased a day or two before her birth from a pregnant Roman prostitute. Why? For a very ignoble reason: an item in a covenant. A large portion of the Comparini family income arose out of a trust fund in which they held a reversionary interest, and which, failing an heir, would pass into the hands of strangers. Animated by a smouldering revenge, the Comparini brought a writ against Guido Franceschini for the recovery of Pompilia's dowry. An action for nullification came before the Court of Rome in the summer of 1694. It failed, the Court holding that the contract between the parties had been made in good faith. But the reversionary property, it was ruled, could not devolve upon Pompilia.

All this unleashed a demon which had, in fact, long nestled in the breast of Franceschini. His helpless, deserted child-wife became the focus of his frustrations, was subjected to a dreadful catalogue of brutalities as he vented upon her a spleen that had to ferocious hatred turned. Terrified for her life, the little Countess implored the aid of the Governor of Arezzo and of Arezzo's Bishop. Both failed her. It was a young priest, Canon Giuseppe Caponsacchi, who came to her rescue.

In the early days of April, 1697, Pompilia found that she was pregnant, and determined to run away to her parents. Canon Caponsacchi agreed to escort her to Rome. The pair had got as far as Castelnuovo, 15 miles from Rome, when Guido caught up with them. He had known all along of Pompilia's plan and had secretly abetted it, for *his* plan was first to place her in an ambivalent situation, and then bring accusation of adultery against her. This would make him free to kill her – for it had in those times been held that, in certain circumstances, killing an adulterous wife was no murder.

Pompilia and Caponsacchi were brought to trial. Adultery was not proved. The canon was banished for three years to *Civita Vecchia*, and Pompilia sent to a nunnery. After a few weeks she was released into the care of her parents, and on December 18, 1697, gave birth to a son, Gaetano. Some sixth sense must have warned her, for the child was almost immediately sent away to a secret destination.

Meantimes the savage Franceschini had not been idle. He had contrived to have Pompilia pronounced guilty of adultery by a court presided over by his friend the Commissioner of Arezzo. And this had placed the weapon in his hand for Pompilia's killing-no-murder slaying

On Christmas Eve, Guido arrived in Rome with a band of four cutthroat bravoes. Nine days they lay hidden in the *Campagna Romana*. On the night of January 2, 1698, they arrived at the quiet house in the Via Vittoria. Pietro and Violante Comparini were hacked to death by Guido. Hadn't they passed off a prostitute's brat on him? Then he went in search of Pompilia, dragged her from beneath the bed where she hid, and stabbed her in more than a score of places.

The murderers fled, but the police captured them at the tavern of Merluzza, a mere 14½ miles outside the walls of Rome. Of Franceschini's guilt there could be no doubt. Pompilia lived long enough to testify to it. She died four days after the attack . . . on January 6. Franceschini and his ruffians were all found guilty.

The Count, having taken minor orders, claimed benefit of clergy. Pope Innocent XII would have none of it. In the Piazza del Popolo, on the afternoon of February 22, 1698, all five were executed. The four bravoes were hanged. The Count, permitted aristocratic privilege, bent his neck to the headsman's axe.

Out of this sad tale of a notable Roman trial, the genius of Robert Browning fashioned one of the finest poems in the English language – "The Ring and the Book". And Lawyer Cencini's old yellow book may still be seen, three hundred years on, preserved in Balliol College library.

The Rector and the Daniel Syndrome

The vicar lay in his glass coffin surrounded by blocks of ice. Beside him lay a young woman named Pamela. They were both starving – and hundreds of people were paying sixpence a time to come and gawp at them.

It was Blackpool in the high summer of 1935. He was the Reverend Harold Davidson, the notorious Rector of Stiffkey (pronounced "Stewky"). Pamela was his extremely attractive daughter. And I was a short-trousered, eleven-year-old on holiday, exploring the Golden Mile. I was – it *is* a very long time ago – an innocent. I understood nothing of the somewhat tacky constellation of circumstances which had brought the diminutive clerk, with, I remember, the exceptionally beautiful speaking voice, to this unpretty pass. All that I knew was that he seemed a very pleasant person, who appeared to enjoy my daily visit for a chat.

The Reverend Harold Francis Davidson, MA (Oxon), was a man of two worlds. His Sunday world was the pulpit of the Norfolk village church of Stiffkey. It was Dean Swift's observation that "Monday is parson's holiday", but Mr Davidson's was all the rest of the week as well. The instant the last hymn book had snapped shut, the last candle been extinguished, the Rector would peck his wife on the cheek, wave cheerily to his children, and scamper off to catch the London train from Wells-next-the-Sea in time to greet the dawn's break in the metropolis. And there he would remain until the very last Liverpool Street train back to far-flung Norfolk on the following Saturday night.

It was how the Rector filled those long hours in the wicked city of the 1920s that was to come disastrously under the ecclesiastical quizzing-glass. Styling himself the Prostitutes' Padre, he pricked about London like a gadfly, whirling in a cloud of taxis, tubes, and buses; pausing briefly in pubs, cafés, restaurants, and teashops; escorting young girls to the theatre; popping into the Charing Cross Hotel to write letters; puffing away at innumerable cigars the while. Innocent gleaning in God's field . . . a gathering to safety of the threatened flowers of youth. That was how the Rector professed to see his activities. Always *female* flowers, observed sundry cynical onlookers. And it was true, the reverend gentleman did display a distinct partiality for effecting the salvation of nubile waitresses and waifs. Those presiding Hebes of Lyons' teashops of the inter-war years, the Nippies, were his especial cup of tea. He liked their smoothed-down black dresses, embellished with a double row of red-thread-sewn little pearl buttons, their crisp white caps, thigh-riding, stiff-starched aprons, black stockings, and highly polished, black ankle-strap shoes. So keen was his pursuit of their souls that he would even chase them to their behind-the-scenes cloakrooms. The waifs were, typically, sixteen-year-old, singed and sinning "mothettes", snared by the West-End candle flame, whom God's trawling man would pick up at places like Marble Arch tube station and Piccadilly Circus, befriend, certainly kiss and fondle, and, allegedly, seduce.

Then, in 1931, a Judas nymphet by the name of Rose Ellis despatched a billet to the Bishop of Norwich. His Lordship, pained and puzzled, set private detectives on the track of the Rector to find out how upright he was. Rose recanted. Plied with port by the inquiry agent she had obligingly lied. Then Barbara Harris, aged 18, pushed herself forward. The epistle according to Barbara was to prove lethal. It was decided to convene Norwich Consistory Court.

The Rector defended himself in "Tell All" articles in the press. The law and the Bishop made legal history prosecuting the *Empire News*, the *Daily Herald*, and the Reverend Davidson for contempt of a consistory court.

The trial opened at Church House, Westminster, on March 29th, 1932 – the year of the yo-yo. President of the Consistory Court was the Chancellor of the Diocese of Norwich, F. Keppel North. Representing the Bishop were Roland Oliver, KC, Walter Monckton, KC, and Humphrey King. For Davidson was Richard Levy. The point to be decided was: were Davidson's friendships innocent? No, came the verdict on July 8th. On hearing it, the Rector snatched up his silk hat, ran full speed down the entire length of the Great Hall . . . and out to proclaim henceforth *urbi et orbi* his entire blame-lessness.

His selection of forums was bizarre. He made himself the centre of a succession of raree side-shows. Ostensibly to raise money for an appeal, he sat like Diogenes in a barrel on the promenade at Blackpool. In fact, his appeal to the Privy Council had been dismissed. He had presented a private bill. That, too, the Council had dismissed. He was unfrocked.

He emerged from the Diogenic barrel to recline in the ice-coffin, wherein I made, as already related, his acquaintance. He was there-after roasted in a glass oven, an automated demon prodding the rectorial posterior the while with a pitchfork!

The years wound down; the Rector's exculpatory enthusiasm did not. His billing continued unabated in increasingly *outré* circum-stances and environs. He came at length, in the summer of 1937, at the age of sixty-two, to his final and most desperate act of misplaced courage. The previous winter had been truly his winter of discontent, eked out in a small house at South Harrow, bought by his wife, Molly, with money realised on life insurance policies, and a small currency for food, heat, light, bare necessities, garnered by pawnshop visits and the begging of hand-outs from a handful of compassionate old friends. Now, he who had always nurtured a deadly fear of animals – a phobia virtually – signed a contract to appear in a lion's cage at Skegness Amusement Park.

The date was July 28th. The time 8 pm. The lion's name was Freddie. He had his mate, Toto, in there with him, too. To Davidson, never renowned for sound judgment, the lion and lioness seemed too docile. He cracked his whip. Freddie pounced, seized the Rector by his still dog-collared neck and carried him round the cage as a cat would carry a mouse. The lion-tamer dashed in to the rescue, fought Freddie off, dragged the Rector out. Her name was Irene Somner. She was sixteen years old.

Harold Davidson died on July 30th, 1937, in Skegness Cottage Hospital. They buried him at Stiffkey. In a way, he had been playing the part of Daniel in the lions' den all his life. In the end, reality echoed in a strange way the classic deaths of the old Christian martyrs . . . and in an equally strange way the whilom Rector of Stiffkey died for *his*, albeit unconventional, cherished beliefs.

The Cardiff Carpet Murder

If, that December afternoon in 1989, the builders had not decided to dig down an extra six inches . . . if the BBC TV programme *Crimewatch* had not given air space to Detective Chief Superintendent John Williams' appeal for public help . . . if it had not been for the expertise of forensic entomologist Dr Zakaria Erzinçlioğlu, and that of Richard Neave, the uniquely talented "face maker" of Manchester University's Medical School, the killing of Karen Price would surely have gone undetected and unavenged.

This is the astonishing medico-legal story of how a series of cast-iron scientific links were forged between a handful of bones, their identity, a murder, and the capture, ten years later, of two killers.

It was in the gathering dusk of a winter's afternoon end on Thursday, December 7,1989, that what proved to be the evidence of murder came to light. Wide-ranging alterations were under way at Nos 27–29 Fitzhamon Embankment, a terrace of decaying Victorian houses beside the River Taff, not all that far from Cardiff's "Tiger Bay". A new landlord was renovating the houses in preparation for upgraded lettings. Workmen were digging a trench for a new soil-pipe when their eye was caught by a piece of orangey-reddish-brown material poking out of the earth. Scraping the soil carefully away, they exposed a long roll of carpet, bound sinisterly around with black electric flex. Opening the bundle – they found in it, polythene wrapped, the trussed-up remains of a human body. They downed tools and called the police.

Upon closer examination, the remains proved to be a skeleton. Obviously, the body had been buried there in the garden a long time ago. How long? There were clues: tattered remnants of clothing which, it transpired, would have been on sale in the Cardiff area in the early 1980s. Unlikely, then, that the body was buried much before 1981 – a first date to work with. The carpeting was an off-cut of a relatively common make, a Shaw's beige-brown Kaleidoscope, retailed by the South Wales Carpets shop in Clifton Street, and sold locally in considerable quantity. However, the workmen usefully remembered that the colour and texture of the buried carpet seemed identical with those of one which they had taken up from the floor of the basement flat at No 29.

The skeleton was removed to Cardiff Infirmary. Professor Bernard Knight reported the bones to be those of a girl, aged about 15, with long fair hair and prominent front teeth. Her height: 5 ft. 3–4 in. He could assign no cause of death. But a forensic odontologist, Dr David Whittaker, subsequently noted a pink discoloration of the teeth, often seen in cases of strangulation. A post-mortem dental chart was constructed and circulated – a kind of buccal "fingerprint" – to all dental surgeries in the region.

Meanwhile, Dr Erzinçlioğlu, the entomologist from Cambridge University Department of Zoology, was studying the insects found in and about the carpet shroud and makeshift grave, and was able to state that the body had been in the ground for at least five years.

So the police had now to look for a girl who had gone missing around 1984.

Then came a flash of inspiration which was to light up – and ultimately solve – the whole mystery. An approach was made to Richard Neave, the Manchester medical artist. Working with the skull, he sculpted a clay model of the dead girl's face, and by the beginning of 1990, photographs and posters of the teenager's portrait in clay were being widely distributed. It was recognised. A Cardiff social worker identified Karen Wendy Price, a 15-year-old who had absconded on July 2, 1981, from Maes-Yr-Eglwys Assessment Centre, at Church Village, near Pontypridd.

The police had now put a face and a name to the bones. But how, and at whose hands, she had met her death remained unanswered questions. The Karen Price story seemed to have come to an abrupt end. Grasping, some might think, at straws, Superintendent Williams appeared on *Crimewatch* on January 15, 1990, recounted the investigation so far into what the press had, inevitably, christened "The Case of Little Miss Nobody", and showed yet again Karen's clay-fashioned likeness. The telephone rang. It was a viewer, Meic Corcoran, of Birchgrove Road, in a northern Cardiff suburb. "There's a bloke in the house that knew Karen Price," he said.

The "bloke" was Idris Ali. Watching the TV programme had brought all the horror of it back to him, and he had felt that he just had to contact the police.

The tale he had to tell was a sordid one of how, on an August night in 1981, he, then fifteen years old, and Alan Charlton (21), a bouncer at one of Cardiff's tough night spots, had invited a couple of young girls – Karen, for whom Ali had been pimping, and Mandy (13) – to a party in Charlton's basement flat at 29 Fitzhamon Embankment. In a confused welter of glue-sniffing, dope-smoking, and lager-drinking, things had taken a nasty turn, and Karen had been killed – beaten to death with his fists by Charlton, according to one version; strangled by Ali, according to another account. The precise details never emerged. But one thing was certain: both men had buried her corpse in the shabby little riverside back garden of No 29.

And both men – having spent a year on remand in Cardiff Prison, were put up at Cardiff Crown Court on January 21, 1991. Charlton, whose response to the accusation was that it was "well out of order", denied everything. He did not know Karen Price. He did not know

Idris Ali. But that cock wouldn't fight with the jury, who found both men guilty. The judge, Rose J, told the prisoners that they had been convicted on overwhelming evidence. He sentenced Charlton to life, Ali to be detained during Her Majesty's pleasure.

The police, understandably, congratulated themselves on obtaining what, ten years after the commission of the crime, could fairly be described as a good "result".

The Legend of Ireland's Eye

High in the ordinal of family legend reposes the story of how my great-grandfather was killed by the corpse in the Ireland's Eye murder case. Dr Richard Whittington-Egan was, my Irish great-aunts used to tell me, Crown Pathologist in the Ireland of the middle years of the nineteenth century, and it was in this capacity that he came into lethal contact with Mrs Kirwan.

Sarah Maria Louisa Kirwan, an exceptionally handsome, as they were wont to say, woman of some twenty-nine summers, was married – and had, in 1852, been for twelve years – to William Burke Kirwan, a 35-year-old professional artist, anatomical draughtsman, and map colourist. The couple resided, when in Dublin, at No 11 fashionable Upper Merrion Street, just round the corner from where, in 1854, Oscar Wilde and his parents went to live. The one thing, apart from her husband one hopes, about which Mrs Kirwan was passionate, was sea-bathing, and from long addiction had developed into a most powerful and venturesome swimmer.

It was in mid-June, 1852, that the Kirwans took lodgings with a Mrs Margaret Campbell in the small fishing village of Howth, some ten miles north east of Dublin. They had decided there each to indulge individual holiday preferences; he for sketching, his mermaidenish wife for disportment amid the waves. And both found themselves, for the aforesaid different reasons, attracted to Ireland's Eye, the rocky islet set in the bay of the Irish Sea, an Irish mile north of the Hill of Howth. There were thereon the picturesque ruins of the old chapel of St Nessan for him to paint, and there were thereabouts multitudes of beckoning watery delights for her to wallow in.

Monday, September 6, was a day selected for such an expedition;

the last, in fact, before their scheduled return to Dublin. At ten o'clock that morning, well provisioned – a crammed carpet-bag, a basket of picnic fare, two bottles of water, bathing-dress and art materials – the couple set off in a hired boat for Ireland's Eye.

The boatman was instructed to rescue them from their voluntary marooning at eight o'clock that evening.

At around half-past seven, shortly before the boat left Howth to collect the Kirwans, Hugh Campbell, leaning against the harbour wall, heard, more than once repeated, loud banshee wailings coming from the island. Similar keenings were reported by Alicia Abernethey, Catherine Flood, and John Bennett – Thomas Larkin, aboard a boat returning from fishing, also heard the cries as it passed close to Ireland's Eye.

From his position, half-way between the Martello Tower and the bay, they seemed to him to be coming from a rocky inlet known as Long Hole.

When the chartered boat arrived to take the Kirwans back, its owner, Patrick Nangle, found William Kirwan standing alone in the gathering darkness on the shores. He had not, he said, seen sight nor sound of his wife for the last two hours. She had left him to go off and have a bathe on the other side of the island.

A search disclosed Mrs Kirwan's body splayed upon a rock in the middle of Long Hole. She was lying face upwards on a wet bathing sheet. William rushed forward and flung himself upon his spouse's lifeless form, calling out "Oh! Maria! Maria!" Wrapped in a sail, the corpse was brought back to Howth around 11 o'clock that night.

And this is where great-grandfather is supposed to have come in. He, I was solemnly informed, had performed a post-mortem, and in the process contrived to cut his hand upon a jagged angle of the woman's pelvis, contracted consequent septicaemia, and died thereof.

However, investigation has revealed that the examination of the cadaver is recorded as having been carried out, albeit most unusually, by a medical student, Mr James Alexander Hamilton. This does seem passing strange. Nevertheless, following an inquisitional verdict of "Found drowned", the late Mrs Kirwan was stowed safely away below ground in Dublin's Glasnevin Cemetery

Or so it seemed. But that was to reckon without the celebrated capacity for malice and mischief-making proclivities of the genial fellow-members of my race. There was joyful, calumnious talk of foul play; lip-smacking rumour of another woman – Theresa Mary Frances Kenny – mother of his seven children, for whom he provided a home, and part-time spousage, in Spafield Avenue, Sandymount.

Maria Kirwan was exhumed. A second post-mortem was conducted. By great grandfather, surely? No. By George Hatchell, MD, who was unable to report anything conclusively suspicious; a fact not entirely unconnected, perhaps, with the circumstance that the body had been lying for a month in some two feet of water in the grave.

In finest Hibernian tradition, so small a matter as the autopsy's hesitant clean bill of health was not permitted to interfere with public conviction. An unauthorised paragraph, written in invisible ink, adumbrating burking with a wet bathing-sheet as the possible agency of demise, appears to have inserted itself into the collective unconscience.

Kirwan was arrested, charged with murder, tried, found guilty, and sentenced to death. But it was a narrow case. Unease was voiced in influential quarters. No less a medical grandee than Dr Alfred Swaine Taylor, the father of forensic medicine, was to express grievous doubts as to Mrs Kirwan's death having resulted from "violence at the hands of another". What was more, his view was ratified by an assemblage of nine of Ireland's leading medicine men, who jointly certified that "the appearances were compatible with death caused by simple drowning, or by the seizure of a fit in the water".

Life was substituted for death, and Kirwan served 27 years on Spike Island, in Cork Harbour. Islands do not seem to have figured in the constellation of his lucky stars. Released on March 3, 1879, he sailed from Liverpool to America, where, Irish sentiment asserts, he was to join and marry the mother of his children.

Perhaps great-grandfather could have observed, like the old hermit who, dying, whispered to the acolytes clustered around his deathbed, counselling them not to worry, "I've lived through some terrible things – and half of them never happened." Or perhaps, it occurs to me, since Irish records were destroyed in the "troubles", the story could have slipped a generation, and it was great-great-grandfather Dr Richard Whittington-Egan who fell victim to the *post mortem* wiles of the fatally seductive Maria Kirwan.

It Was the Butler Who Did It

Suave, deferential, imperturbable and inscrutable behind a mask of dignified servitude stands the traditional image of the British butler, and the simulation of every one of those desirable qualities came easily to Archibald Thomson Hall aka Roy Fontaine, the master con man and monster butler.

Whatever the whodunit buffs may say, it is never – well, hardly ever – the butler who did it, but, in December, 1977, Hall was the exception that proved the rule. The Glasgow-born jewel thief, fresh out of prison – where he had spent 19 of the last 26 years, furnishing himself with glowing testimonials that made him seem to have stepped straight out of the pages of Jeeves and Wooster – had found himself a position with the wealthy, 82-year-old, ex-Labour MP, Walter Travers Scott-Elliot, and his wife, Dorothy – and murdered them both.

The Scott-Elliots' London flat, in Richmond Court, Sloane Street, was a treasure trove of priceless paintings and antiques, and Hall planned to plunder it. Mercilessly pursuing that glistering objective, he enlisted two most unwholesome accomplices, a hitherto markedly unsuccessful petty villain, Michael Kitto (39) and a strange underworld woman, Mary Coggle, ex-prostitute, ex-mistress of both the 53-year-old Hall and Kitto.

Entering Mrs Scott-Elliot's bedroom, they smothered her with a pillow. Her aged and ailing husband they kept under control by drugging him incessantly with overdoses of his prescribed sleeping tablets. Bundling the bemused old man into a hired car, with Mrs Scott-Elliot's body in the boot, and Mary Coggle, in blonde wig and Dorothy Scott Elliot's mink coat, fooling Scott-Elliot into believing that she was his wife, the party of five – four alive, one dead – set off for Scotland. There, the dead woman was buried in a roadside ditch, and her husband was subsequently battered to death with the same spade that had been used to dig his wife's grave. He, too, was buried by the Scottish roadside.

There was a falling out over the late Mrs Scott-Elliot's mink coat – and Hall, aided and abetted by Kitto, killed Coggle. Then there were two.

Hall and Kitto were arrested when a hotelier at North Berwick became suspicious that the two guests with such light luggage were potential baulkers, and contacted the police. The body of Hall's young brother, Donald, whom they had also murdered for fear of his loose tongue, but not yet buried, was found in the boot of their car. The evil butler's murder spree was over. Kitto was sentenced to 15 years. Hall went back to the best place for him – prison, for life.

We have to go back more than 150 years to find another murderous man-servant. This was Francois Benjamin Courvoisier, a 23-year-old Swiss, who was actually described as a valet. But no matter. The office of butler derives from the mediaeval position of Yeoman of the Buttery, the servant who in the royal and noble households had charge of the beer-brewing. By the mid-eighteenth century, butlers of expansionist inclination had taken over additionally as Yeoman of the Cellar and Yeoman of the Pantry. It was thence a small step forward to becoming major-domo of the servants' hall; and he would not infrequently double as very special valet to his master.

Courvoiser, for what precise reason it is not altogether clear, but most likely with robbery in mind, lethally wounded his employer, Lord William Russell. On May 5, 1840, the 73-year-old nobleman was found at his fashionable London home in Norfolk Street, lying in bed, a gaping wound in his throat. Courvoisier had tried to make it look like the work of a burglar, but missing Russell valuables were traced to his possession. And, although rumour had it that he had committed the murder naked, bloodstained clothing was found in his room. He was hanged at Newgate.

It was not the butler – actually it was the butler who was killed – but trainee footman 19-year-old Harold Winstanley who sprayed death from the muzzle of a Schmeiser at Knowsley Hall, near Liverpool, the stately home of the Earls of Derby. At 7 o'clock one October evening in 1952, Lady Derby was dining alone at a small table in the smoke-room. Suddenly, without a knock, the door opened, and in walked Winstanley, a cigarette dangling from his mouth. He pointed the gun at her ladyship, told her to turn round, and shot her. Bleeding from a neck wound, she crashed to the carpet and lay still, feigning death. Alarmed by the commotion, the butler, Walter Stannard, and the under-butler, Douglas Stuart, came bustling on the scene. Winstanley fired. Both died.

Impassively, Winstanley walked briskly away from Knowsley and had a pint and some crisps at the nearby Coppull House Inn. Later that night of October 9, he gave himself up. He was sent to Broadmoor.

Less fortunate was Henry Jacoby, an 18-year-old pantry boy, who, in March, 1922, murdered Lady White, a guest at the Spencer Hotel, Portman Street, London. The 65-year-old widow had awoken when Jocoby, intent on stealing from guests' rooms, had entered her bedroom. In panic, he battered her to death with a hammer. Jacoby was hanged at Pentonville.

How different from the fate of another youngster, John Lee, aged 19. Lee was a footman in the employ of an elderly and wealthy spinster, Miss Emma Keyse, at her fine old house, The Glen, at Babbacombe, in Devonshire. On November 15, 1884, Miss Keyse was found dead in her dining-room. Her throat had been cut and her head battered in, and the room had been set on fire. It was discovered that young Lee had been quarrelling with his mistress, and bore a grudge against her. She had been finding fault with his work and had reduced his wages from half-a-crown to two shillings a week.

Arrested, he was tried and found guilty of her murder. Then something incredible happened. Three times Mr. Hangman Berry tried to hang him. Three times the scaffold's trap failed to open. Returned to his cell, he was reprieved. Christened "The Man They Could Not Hang", Lee spent 22 years in gaol. Released from Portland Prison in 1907, he married Jessie Bulled, a mental nurse at Newton Abbot Workhouse, in 1909. Thereafter, he settled in America, where his deferred death caught up with him at Milwaukee on 19 March, 1945.

Demise of a Welsh Wizardess

Kate Jackson, although she had married and lived and died in Wales, was not really Welsh. But she *was* a wizardess, a woman of mystery, the culminating mystery of whose life was . . . her death. It was about ten o'clock on a February night when she and her friend and neighbour, Mrs Dimmock, arrived back at Limeslade Bungalow Colony, Mumbles, some five miles from Swansea, after a trip to the pictures. They said goodnight, Mrs Jackson walking off towards the bungalow, "Kenilworth", where she and her husband lived.

Mrs Dimmock had barely closed the door behind her when she heard the scream. Bravely, she rushed out to see what had happened.

There, lying, unconscious and bleeding on the ground just outside her back-door was Mrs Jackson. Joined seconds later by a distraught Mr Jackson, she and the stricken woman's husband looked in vain for any sign of Kate Jackson's attacker. Then, in the silence of the night, they heard the sound of a car starting up. Mrs Dimmock registered that as it moved away there was no reflected radiance in the surrounding darkness. The car had not put its lights on. That was surely suspicious.

A doctor – Dr Taylor – was called out. An ambulance was sent for. Mrs Jackson, still unconscious, was speeded off to hospital. The police were contacted.

Mr Jackson now provided his version of events. He had, he said, been in bed, half-asleep, when he heard a scream and a dog barking. Alarmed, he had gone to the door. His wife was on the ground, but partly raised up, as if she had been trying to open the door. She seemed to have crawled for a distance of about seven feet. She was bleeding copiously from her head.

The police waited by Mrs Jackson's hospital bedside in the hope that she would regain consciousness and be able to tell them what had happened. The night of the attack was February 4, 1929. By Friday, February 8, Mrs Jackson had recovered sufficiently to say: "They hit me hard." And that was all that she would ever say about the attackers and the attack – except that *they* were after her adopted daughter, Betty, who, incidentally, Mr Jackson believed to be "of titled birth". No proof of any such thing was ever forthcoming. Kate Jackson slipped away on Sunday, February 10, without making the hoped for dying declaration that would point the finger at her killer. That killer, the police had convinced themselves, was, as is usually suspected in these cases, the deceased's husband. The lightless car in the night the detectives now regarded as irrelevant. Henceforth, all efforts were directed towards the entrapment of the grieving widower.

The inquest was opened on February 15. Things began to move. On February 18, the police took away the back-door of "Kenilworth". On February 23, they arrested Mr Jackson and charged him with the murder of his wife.

It was now that strange things began to emerge as regards the dead woman. She had, it turned out, been a witness in a sensational embezzlement case in London in 1927, when the treasurer and secretary of the National Association of Coopers, William George

Harrison, had been found guilty of mulcting the Association's funds. Referred to as Madame X, she admitted receiving between £8,000 and £9,000 from Harrison, whom she had met in London in 1914, at which time she was married and known as Madame Le Grys. Harrison went down for five years' penal servitude.

Indeed, it was in the persona of Mollie Le Grys that, in 1919, his wife to be picked up Thomas Jackson. Himself a fish dealer, he had been busman's honeymooning buying some fish in Lyons' Corner House, Piccadilly, when Madam approached him with the information that he reminded her of her dear, dear friend, Lord Carroll. She had further informed him that he (Jackson) was too ill to eat cold fish, and she had bought him an expensive hot meal. They thereafter spent the afternoon together and, things going from bed to worse, he married her – twice. First, when he called himself, for whatever reason, Captain Gordon Ingram, and secondly, in Cardiff in 1922, as plain Tom Jackson.

Mrs Jackson had confided to a local acquaintance, Mrs Morgan, that she had been born in India, and that she was the daughter of a famous Scottish family. They had left India when she was six, because of a stabbing. She displayed a bad scar on her leg, saying that it had been caused by an Indian servant who attacked her. Back in England, she had fallen in love with her family's butler at their London house in Portman Square, and had eloped with him.

The police discovered that Mrs Jackson had presented herself under a wide variety of names and guises – Mary Kathleen Hamilton, Mrs Amber, Madame Humber, Madame Mollie Le Grys, Mrs Gordon Ingram. This phenomenal nominal protean was a type, a kite-flyer, like Miss Edwards of Liverpool aka Mrs Jane Cannon Cox, the Jamaican widow in the Bravo case. In the village of Frimley, near Ash Vale, Surrey, Kate Jackson fostered the belief that she was Ethel M. Dell, a famous romantic novelist of the period. That she had actually been born Kate Atkinson, the daughter of a labourer, at Wray, Lancashire, on July 26, 1885, there could be no doubt. A deformed thumb was proof. Thomas Jackson was put to his trial at Glamorgan assizes on July 1, 1929. He described his late wife as very well connected, well educated, speaking several languages, and said that they were very happy together until the embezzlement case. Occasionally, she would receive anonymous letters. Apropos, Mrs Morgan testified that she had seen Mrs Jackson receive letters – in at least four different names – containing postal orders or Treasury notes. Once, she had thrown a handful in the air saying "That's what comes of being clever."

The prosecution alleged that Jackson had beaten his wife over the head with a tyre-lever. They cited bloodstains on the back-door of "Kenilworth" as evidence of where the murdered woman's head had touched, and produced a tyre-lever discovered under the "dunny" (lavatory) seat. His motivation? He had a violent temper and was tired of supporting her, was their best effort.

There seems little doubt that, from whatever cause, Kate Jackson was a frightened woman. A letter which she received may shed a little light: "How many more men have you blackmailed until they have to pinch money to shut you up?" Food for thought.

Wright J gave a hostile summing-up. But the jury had their own ideas, and to cheers and clapping brought in a not guilty. Thus was the case officially laid to rest. But, like a couple of those Kelly toys, there are two big question-marks which keep on bobbing back . . .

Murder by Prediction

When I first met Anthony O'Rourke – or Anthony Regan as he was then calling himself – he had already murdered two people. And I knew that he intended to kill again. He told me so.

He was then 39. An ordinary little man – weedy, inconspicuous. He wouldn't even need to be in a crowd to pass unnoticed. Born O'Rourke, he came from a working-class Newcastle family. His father, roots surely stretching back to the Emerald Isle, died in a coal-mine accident. An elder brother lost his life, a wartime casualty, in the Libyan desert in 1942. His widowed mother brought him up, with some difficulty, to be a "God-fearing boy".

His voice was soft, almost a whisper, but it was the things he said, the chill detachment in his deep-set blue eyes, as he said them . . . "I know that I could kill again. Next time it may be Florrie."

And I knew that he meant it.

I did what I could. Made it my business to seek out Mrs Florence Regan. A 37-year-old woman, mother of five, shabbily dressed, but neat and clean, she had the worn look of someone whom life had treated harshly. Although foolish where her worthless husband was concerned, she turned out to be in all other respects quite remarkably intelligent. Mincing no words, I warned her. It came as no surprise. "I know Tony might kill me," she said. "I've known it for a long time. I've lain awake at night listening to him breathing next to me, wondering if one day he'd finish me off. But he's my husband, the father of my children, and, you see, I love him. I know he's done terrible things, but I still love him." That was the last I ever saw of Mrs Regan.

One morning two years later, my telephone rang. A woman's voice told me: "Mrs Regan's been murdered. They've arrested her husband." Before I could ask the woman on the other end of the line who she was, she rang off.

I checked with the police. They confirmed that it was true. Anthony Regan had despatched his third victim.

It was back on November 5, 1949, that Regan first spilt human blood. He was living then with his wife and children at Pickering, deep in the Yorkshire Dales, where he had a job as a railway signalman. Regan's first victim was a 66-year-old Tom Pickering. The Regans had lived in his cottage with him for a few weeks when they first came to the town.

At around 9.15 on the morning of Guy Fawkes' Day, Regan turned up at Pickering's, saying that he had come to collect some things that his wife had left behind. In his pocket was a hammer. Old Pickering was alone in the kitchen, sitting at a table covered with the remains of breakfast.

Regan told me: "We joked like old friends for a while. In the end, he cleared the breakfast things away, got a newspaper and started to study the racing form. I stood behind him, looking over his shoulder, pretending to be interested in the tips he was going over. Slowly I drew the hammer out. I remember his hair was dirty and speckled with dandruff. I sent the hammer crashing down against his skull. I decided that I would say that I'd killed Pickering because he'd made an advance to my wife."

And that was the defence that Regan/O'Rourke put forward when, in March, 1950, he was tried at Leeds Assizes. The jury accepted his plea of self-defence after being provoked into a quarrel by Pickering about Florrie's virtue.

I asked him what was the real reason why he had done it. He told me: "I wanted to commit the perfect murder. All I needed was a good alibi and a suitable victim." He obviously thought that "alibi" meant showing good reason for killing!

Then Regan decided that he had to do a second killing; to show that his first success wasn't just a fluke.

"It was easy to throttle Rose Harper. You see, like Tom Pickering, she thought I was her friend." Rose was a 55-year-old spinster. She lived ten minutes' walk away from the cottage where Pickering died.

The date Regan selected for Rose's demise was May 4, 1951. An early bird again, he called at 8.10 am.

"She invited me in for a cup of tea. She was a lonely soul. I helped her feed the chickens in the back-garden. We returned to the house. She locked the back-door. I was just behind her. I reached forward, crooking my arm round her neck and pulling her to the floor. She gasped. I tightened my grip. She was silent. I removed one of her stockings and knotted it round her neck." Anthony Regan had murdered again.

"I said she'd made amorous passes at me, and that I'd been forced to defend myself before she did me a serious mischief. In the fight, I'd accidentally put my hands on her neck. She slipped, and to silence her oaths, I'd removed her stocking and tried to gag her. But in my panic I'd put it around her neck. It was a simple story."

No, it was the jury who were simple. They believed him. Back in the dock at Leeds, in November, 1951, Regan was given ten years for manslaughter.

He came out of Dartmoor in 1958. The urge to murder came on again in 1960, when he told me all about it. And in March, 1962, he killed the woman whom I had begged to flee from him. He stabbed her with a knife and left her corpse lying for three months in a locked bedroom in their council house home near Slough.

Glib as ever at his trial – he'd made it to the Old Bailey this time – Regan, now 41, produced yet one more simple story. His wife had been having an affair with another man, there was a quarrel in which she (of course) picked up the knife, and in the ensuing struggle he accidentally (of course) wounded her in the chest. This time, however, the jury were not so simple. Found guilty, Regan was duly sentenced to life. He ended up in Broadmoor. The last I heard of him he had driven a long needle right into his heart. But it did not kill him. Anthony Regan/O'Rourke was a survivor. It was those who rubbed up against him who were not. If he is still surviving in Broadmoor he will be an old man in his eighties. Florrie, if only she had heeded my advice, would have been 83. How mad was he? Just about as mad as George Joseph Smith – the Brides in the Bath Murderer.

Mr Furnace's Yuletide Blaze

Christmas, it has to be said, had not that year been a happy one. The season of goodwill had proved singularly lacking in that commodity so far as Mr Samuel Furnace, self-employed builder, was concerned. He had, to be sure, done his best to provide his wife, May, and three much-loved children with a merry Christmas Day at their Crogsland Road, Chalk Farm, home, but as time ticked the Twelve Days of Christmas off the calendar, his troubles mounted and multiplied. January, 1933, loomed bleak.

The root cause of all this anxiety was, as it usually is, if not love, money – or, rather, the lack of it. He had for some years now been battling to scratch a living from the unyielding north London brickland. His business, run from a small yard in Hawley Crescent, Camden Town, faced rising debts and declining numbers of jobs. Life was disastrously out of healthy balance.

At his wits', as well as his purse's, end, Sam Furnace conjured up a desperate scheme. Remembering how, three years before, another desperado named Alfred Rouse had tried to make a human bonfire of his troubles, Furnace decided to do the same. Rouse had given a tramp a lift in his car and set motor and tramp alight, trusting that the incinerated corpse would be taken to be his, thus leaving him free to start a new, *tabula rasa* life. The plan had, as you might say, misfired, and Rouse had hanged. Furnace would profit from his mistakes.

Sam Furnace had a friend, Walter Spatchett. Younger – 25 years to Furnace's 39 – Spatchett made a modest living locally as a rent-collector. Furnace marked him down as his sacrificial victim.

In the dusk of the late afternoon of January 2, 1933, Furnace, on some pretext or other, lured Spatchett to the Hawley Crescent shed, shot him in the back, stuffed his body into the knee-hole of a big desk, and covered it with an old overcoat. He then walked calmly home, had his tea, tucked the children up safe and cosily in bed, and settled down to listen to *Jane Eyre* on the wireless, before turning in for an early night.

Next day he checked over his calculations. Two insurance policies. Their joint yield £1,100 on his death, plus £100 a year for 20 years. That should see the family right. And he could have a second bite at the cherry of life!

Picking up a pencil, he scrawled on a scrap of paper: "Goodbye to all. No work, no money. Sam. S. J. Furnace". He propped Spatchett's corpse up on a stool, splashed oil and paint around the funeral pyre, struck a match, and walked off into the darkness.

It was my old friend Sir Bentley Purchase, the coroner, who smelt a rat. Viewing the charred remains deposited in his mortuary, he spotted bullet holes in the back; wounds so positioned as to rule out self-infliction.

Everything now took on a completely new complexion. Relatives' identifications – Furnace's had said it was Furnace, Spatchett's had said it was Spatchett – had cancelled each other out. In the end it was Spatchett's GP, Dr Clarke, who clinched matters by recognising a deformed tooth in the cadaver's left upper jaw.

The murder hunt for Furnace was on. Meanwhile, the man who wanted to live again, re-born as Roy Rogers, was taking his slippered ease in a lodging-house barely half a mile away, in Princess Road, on the northern fringe of Regent's Park.

Furnace was jolted out of that slippered ease the morning the papers came out with the tidings that Walter it was who had died. He was rapidly up and away, but, for whatever odd reason, his former landlady subsequently received a telegram. It read: "Brother ill. Re-let room. Returning Monday – Rogers". It had been handed in at Southend.

Nor was that the only communication from the reincarnated Furnace. On Monday, January 16, a letter landed on the mat of his brother-in-law, Charles Tuckfield. "I am at Southend," it said. "I want you to come down Sunday. Catch the 10.35 from Harringay Park, that gets you down at 12.8. Come out of the station, walk straight across the road and down the opposite road. Walk down on the left side. I will see you. I am not giving my address in case you are followed." The letter concluded: "Best of Luck. Mine is gone. H. Farmer."

Mr Tuckfield took that letter straight to the police.

The detectives lost no time in identifying the location of Furnace's Southend lodgings as Whitegate Road. It so happened that one of their number, Detective Inspector Kind, was able to play the violin passably well, a circumstance not unconnected with the fact that the residents of Whitegate Road were, that third week in January, entertained by an unusually frequent number of plaintive street-musician renderings of *O Sole Mio*, *The Lost Chord*, and sundry other items from Inspector King's repertoire.

Came Sunday. Tuckfield duly arrived. Paced his way slowly down Whitegate Road. Sure enough, a curtain twitched aside at No 11, and a piece of white paper marked with the black capitals S A M was suddenly manifest for the merest flash behind the window-pane. The front-door swung swiftly open and Tuckfield was whisked into the ground-floor front.

For an hour the two men sat and talked. Then Furnace asked his brother-in-law to slip out for a packet of cigarettes. On his way he was able to tell the police officers that Furnace did not have a gun. Then they moved in. Quietly admitted through the back-door by the landlady, Mrs Shaw, they crept along the hall and burst into Furnace's room. He was sitting reading a thriller, *Traitor's Gate*, by his favourite author, Edgar Wallace. He did not put up any struggle.

They brought him back to London – Kentish Town police station. They lodged him in No 3 cell. It was a bitterly cold night. Furnace asked for, and was given, his great coat.

At seven o'clock on the morning of Monday, January 23, after Furnace had paced his cell ceaselessly all night, the gaoler, PC Partridge, looking through the wicket, saw a medicine bottle in the prisoner's hand. Before he could rush in and wrest it from him, Furnace had taken a good swallow of its contents – spirits of salts. The bottle of deadly poison had been hidden in his overcoat.

Furnace died twenty-four hours later in St Pancras Hospital. His "second life" had lasted just three weeks and a day.

A final touch of irony. Going through Walter Spatchett's papers, the dead man's family came across a Christmas card sent to him that last Yuletide by his good friend Sam. It was an old-fashioned country cottage, its windows glowing red with the radiance of a seasonal log fire.

Grave Waters

It all began with the vanishing of Véronique. She, 21-year-old Véronique Marre, a French agriculture student on a fell-walking holiday in the Lake District, was last seen leaving the Wasdale Youth Hostel one July day in 1983. She was then heading towards nearby Wastwater.

As time passed it was suspected that she had drowned, and local amateur divers began to keep a look-out for her body.

In February, 1984, Nigel Frith, a sub-aqua enthusiast, reported seeing a bundle lying on a ledge, 100 feet down in the icy waters of Lakeland's darkest, deepest, and most sinister lake, Wastwater, haunt of the rare Arctic Charr. And on February 29, Cumbria police frogmen dived, located the bundle, winched it up and took it to Kendal mortuary.

There, under the green slime, were sheets of plastic, tight bound with flex and rope. When the parcel was undone, they found trussed within the naked body of a women.

But it was not Véronique. Who was the lady in the lake? She wore a gold wedding ring. It was inscribed: "Margaret 15.11.63 Peter." A photograph of the ring shown on television brought the breakthrough: a 'phoned in message from a woman in Surrey. "Check whatever happened to Margaret Hogg," said the caller.

Margaret was the wife of airline pilot Peter Hogg, of Cranleigh, near Guildford, in Surrey. He had reported her missing in October, 1976.

Confronted, Hogg admitted having killed – but not murdered his wife. Already divorced, with twin sons, he had married Margaret Hawkins, a flighty air hostess, 11 years his junior. She, too, bore him two sons, but proved continually and flauntingly sexually faithless. In 1973, at a Los Angeles cocktail party, Margaret met a rich international businessman. His home was in Surrey. They became lovers. Then something more sinister – the danger resident in all such lightly embarked upon affairs.

Things had come to a head on Sunday, October 17, 1976, when she returned home after a week's holiday in a country cottage with her lover. There was shouting. Violence. Beside himself, Hogg seized her by the neck, she went limp, slumped. "I was horrified by what happened. I had destroyed a life – unintentionally. But I felt pity and remorse." And the dictates of self-preservation.

On Monday morning he telephoned the headmaster of his son David's boarding-school in Taunton, making an appointment to see him. He drove the 130 miles to Somerset with Margaret's body in the boot of his Alfa Romeo. He kept the appointment and said that, as it was half-term, he would stay overnight and drive David back home with him the next morning.

On the night of October 18–19, Hogg scorched the 325 miles up to Wastwater. He paddled out to the centre of the lake in an inflatable dinghy which he had brought with him, and slid the plastic bundle, weighted with a chunk of concrete picked up at Gatwick airport, silently into the secret waters. Then, streaking through the darkness, drove back to Taunton and, alibi completed, collected David bright and early after breakfast.

Tried at the Old Bailey in March, 1985, Hogg was given four years for manslaughter. He was released on parole in June, 1986, having served only 15 months.

On May 6, 1985, a walker found the body of Véronique Marre on the screes overlooking Wastwater. Cumbria police did not suspect foul play.

But Margaret Hogg was not the only women to be consigned to a watery grave in the Lake District in the year 1976.

In the August of 1997, the body of a young woman dressed in a turquoise-blue, 1960s, baby doll shortie nightie was dredged up from Coniston Water. Her "coffin", too, was of plastic – bin-liners to be precise. It was a quartet of amateur divers who, on Sunday, August 10, 1997, had spotted, 70 feet down, what they thought to be a submerged outboard engine. But when, returning three days later, they managed to drag it to the surface, they made that Wednesday the thirteenth, a sinister discovery. What they had found was actually a human body.

This time there was no conveniently inscribed wedding ring to provide identification evidence. The pathologist, Dr Edmund Trapp, described the remains as those of a well-built 20–30 year-old woman, with short, dark hair, and between 5 ft. 1 in. and 5 ft. 4 in. tall. He estimated that she had been in the water for possibly as long as 25 or 30 years.

Faced with the problem of an unknown woman, the first thing the police did, was to check the lists of the missing. They found there the name of Carol Ann Park, a 31-year-old schoolteacher who had vanished on July 17, 1976, from the bungalow in the village of Leece, near Barrow-in-Furness, 14 miles from Coniston, where she had lived with her husband and three children.

Given a name, several possible identity clinching techniques were available. If DNA could be extracted from the cadaver, it could be compared with that of a blood relative of the suspected identicatee. Again, a skilled "face-maker" – such as the Manchester medical artist, Richard Neave – could reconstruct the corpse's severely battered face into a recognisable lifelikeness. Or the dental records of Carol Ann Park could be checked, and this last was, as it turned out, to prove the fast, direct route to secure identification.

It led, too, to her husband, Gordon Park, a 53-year-old retired primary school teacher, long since remarried to a third wife. When the police went along to interview him, they found that he was away with his wife on a three-week bicycling holiday in France. Members of Coniston Sailing Club said that he was a keen and skilled sailor. He kept a boat moored on Coniston Water.

Like Margaret Hogg, Carol Park had been a faithless wife. Park had a tale much the same as that of Peter Hogg to tell. In the three years before her disappearance, Carol had twice walked out on her husband and her children to go off and live with lovers she had taken.

Her third, and final, vanishing dates from that July Saturday when Gordon took the children on a day-trip to Blackpool. Carol had stayed at home, saying she felt unwell. When the family got back, there was no sign of her.

As usual in such cases, the husband was the prime suspect, and on August 24, 1997, he was arrested. It very soon became apparent that the police had no evidence upon which to ground their suspicions, and on January 6, 1998, his character unblemished, Park was liberated from custody. Re-arrested in 2004, he was tried, found guilty, and sentenced to life imprisonment.

One cannot but wonder . . . How many more errant ladies lie trussed in the lakes, lochs, and tarns of Britain?

Murder Mistaken

The recorded reaction of murderers to the moment of truth when they are arrested are divertingly variegated, but surely that of Richard Brinkley, having the darbies clapped on by Detective Chief

Inspector Fowler for double murder, must be one of the strangest, "Well, I'm sugared," he observed, and added, "That's very awkward, isn't it?"

But Brinkley, I have discovered, was an exceptionally queer character – the unknown mass murderer.

He was born in 1854. The earliest trace that I have been able to find of him is when he was living in Aston, on the outskirts of Birmingham. This would probably have been in the 1870s. By trade a jobbing carpenter, he was also quite a well known fowl fancier, specialising in Wyandottes and Orpingtons.

One night an odd thing happened. Every one of his chickens died. A kindly, animal-loving, bible-quoting man, he shed tears. "I loved every feather on their bodies," he sobbed. It turned out that they had been poisoned with arsenic. It also subsequently turned out that Brinkley was a keen experimenting amateur of venenation.

Let me confess here and now that such is the complexity of Brinkley's woven web that the precise sequence of his murders is difficult to fix, but of their number there remains little dubiety.

Unmarried, although seemingly fond of children, Brinkley is said to have adopted a young girl as his daughter and installed her as his housekeeper. She was, I believe, Margaret Stone, a Hertfordshire farmer's daughter, to whom Brinkley introduced himself as Sir Richard Bradley, experimental soil chemist. She ended up in London, Brinkley moving into Chelsea lodgings with her. Now comes the first likely murder. The girl, only just in her mid-teens died; beside her a cup was found to contain arsenic. Shedding crocodile tears, Brinkley told the coroner she had lately been deeply depressed. Verdict: suicide during temporary insanity.

Brinkley now married a woman, Laura Jane. She gave him a son. Then, with remarkable suddenness, died. Heart failure – or Murder Number 2?

Alone again, fancy-free, Brinkley moved operations to Hammersmith. By her ill-fortune he met there young Ada Turner. Discovering that she had a few hundred pounds, he promptly "adopted" her, and induced her to sign a deed of gift. Surprise, surprise. She obligingly died. Murder Number 3?

With Ada safely underground and her pathetic bit of money in his pocket, our hero sought pastures new for profitable Brinkley-manship.

It is in 1905 that he surfaces again. He is assiduously cultivating a 77-year-old German widow, Mrs Johanna Maria Louisa Blume, who owns and lives at 4 Maxwell Road, Fulham, with her granddaughter of about 21, Gussie. At around 10 am everyday, Gussie would go off to rehearse for the pantomime in which she was appearing and, Box and Cox, as she went out so, three or four mornings a week, in went the ingratiatory Brinkley, to keep "Granny", as he affectionately came to call her, company.

It was in December, 1906 that Brinkley proposed the beanfeast, a springtime outing which he told Granny that he was organising, collecting names of those who would like to come to it. It would do her good. She fancied it? Right! Sign up here – to secure your seat. He presented a folded sheet of paper. Mrs Blume signed it – and her death warrant? Well . . . two days later, December 19, the old lady was on her way to Brompton Cemetery, certified dead of apoplexy – Murder Number 4? – and Brinkley, waving the piece of paper (unfolded now and proving to be a will in his favour to which she had in all innocence put her signature) announced: "I am master here now." Gussie had no choice. She left the house. But she and her mother, Caroline, determined to contest the will.

This put Brinkley firmly on the spot. It had been drawn up and signed, as one of the two necessary witnesses, by Richard Hear, a fellow-villain upon whom he could rely. The other witnessing signatory was an acquaintance, Reginald Parker, whom he had tricked into the signing. He was likely to prove more difficult, having put his name to the folded scrap of paper in the belief that it was his confirmation of requiring a seat for the beanfeast.

Parker was duly approached. Proved, as Brinkley had feared he would, uncooperative. What will? He had witnessed no will. Brinkley came to a swift decision. Very well, he would have to be silenced; made unable to bear testimony.

Parker, an accountant's clerk, lived in lodgings at 32 Churchill Road, South Croydon. Brinkley turned up there that Saturday night, April 20, 1907, on the excuse that he wanted to purchase a bulldog which Parker had for sale, bringing with him as a gift a large bottle of oatmeal stout which he had purchased at the nearby Swan and Sugar Loaf public house – and spiked with prussic acid. But Parker, shrewdly suspicious of the gift-bearing Greek, left the opened bottle of stout untasted on the table while he and his would-be poisoner went off to look at the dog.

During their absence, Parker's landlord, Richard Beck and his wife, Elizabeth, returned home, spotted the bottle on the table and decided to sample it. Their daughter, Daisy, who was with them, also had a sip or two. Mr and Mrs Beck died, agonisingly but mercifully swiftly, of prussic acid poisoning – Murders Numbers 5 and 6. Miss Beck, though sailing close to death, eventually recovered. Parker, realising what had happened, blew the gaff, and within hours Brinkley was safely in custody. On the way to the police station he committed a lethal blunder. He said, "If anyone says I have bought beer, they've got to prove it." Up to that moment no one had mentioned the poisoned bottle of oatmeal stout.

Brinkley was put up at Surrey Assizes at Guildford in July, 1907. Mr R. D. Muir, formidable Treasury Counsel prosecuted. Mr Walter Frampton appeared for the defence. It was a splendid illustrative case of the well established legal principle that if A in attempting to murder B, by mischance or unintentionally kills C, A is nevertheless guilty of murder.

And so indeed it was found in Brinkley's case.

The irrepressible Brinkley made one last-ditch attempt to ameliorate his fate. As he stood in the dock facing the black-capped judge, he flashed out secret Masonic signals of distress. But Bigham J was not a mason. He just gazed in momentary puzzlement at the gesticulating prisoner.

Richard Clifford Brinkley was hanged by Henry Pierrepoint and his assistant, John Ellis, at Wandsworth Prison on August 13, 1907, for the unintended murders of Richard and Elizabeth Ann Beck – his first and final fatal mistake. But there will most assuredly have been other avenged shades gathered about the scaffold that retributory Tuesday.

The Tunnel Vision of Percy Lefroy Mapleton

Striding one June afternoon in 1881 to catch the London train at Brighton Station, young Edward Marshall Hall, the "Great Defender" to be, passed on his way to the platform a youth, white-faced, blood-stained and dishevelled, who had apparently been attacked by robbers on his journey down from town, being solicitously assisted to the station-master's office.

It was one of life's extraordinary path-crossings. The youth's name was Percy Lefroy Mapleton.

On the morning of June 27, 1881, things had come to a head for 22-year-old Arthur Lefroy. An orphan, survivor of a hand-to-mouth childhood, he nurtured high artistic hopes of a career as a writer, but endured poor prospects. Since his return from Australia two years before, he had been lodging – 8s 6d per week B&B – at 4 Cathcart (now Clarendon) Road, Wallington, near Croydon, the home of his cousin and her husband, the Claytons.

A scarecrow-thin, beak-nosed, incipiently-moustached, chinless lad, he had recently changed his name from Percy Mapleton to the, he thought, "sharper" sounding Arthur Lefroy, and squandered his days dreaming in his leafy suburban bed-sitter of success as playwright, poet, novelist, actor, or journalist. Donning each night his most prized possession, full evening-dress, he would go up to the West End, to haunt stage-doors, striving to rub shoulders with real actors and actresses, to several of whom, including the celebrated Violet Cameron and Kate Santley, he had despatched romantic *billets doux*.

His efforts had contrived a few successes; the odd walk-on part, occasional publication of article or short story in some obscurish weekly. But now, his resources dwindled to zero, the time had come for desperate measures. With a few swindled shillings he redeemed a pawned pistol and bought a one-way ticket to Brighton.

On Monday morning, June 27, 1881, Isaac Frederick Gold, 64-year-old retired East London businessman, set out, as he did every Monday morning, from his home in Clermont Terrace, Brighton, for London. There he would collect the previous week's takings from his corn chandler's shop in East Street, Walworth, and any dividends accruing on his and his wife's investments.

Mr Gold was a bit of a miser. "Close, even with me," as his wife expressed it. He suffered – like Miss Gilchrist in the Oscar Slater case – from the phobic burglar-under-the-bed syndrome, locking the bedroom door nightly. He nourished, too, a paranoid fear of the probing talk of strangers. On the train he would ritually avoid conversation by taking off his hat, putting on a skull-cap and pretending, with closed eyes or handkerchief over his face, to be asleep.

On the afternoon of June 27, 1881, shortly before 2 o'clock, Arthur Lefroy was pacing the platform at London Bridge Station, peering into the compartments of the 2.10 Brighton train, trawling for a well-heeled victim. Sitting alone in a first-class smoker was prosperous-looking Isaac Gold. Lefroy, primed with knife and pistol, therein joined him. Gold feigned sleep. He was to awake to a nightmare.

At 3.30 pm the train pulled in to Preston Park Station. That first-class carriage door burst open and out tumbled a wild-eyed, bedraggled, blood-smeared figure, a watch chain – attached to a watch – hanging out of its left boot. It was Percy Lefroy Mapleton aka Arthur Lefroy. Escorted on to Brighton, Lefroy told there a tale of being attacked as the train entered Merstham Tunnel. He had heard a shot, been knocked out by a blow to the head. When he came to, his attacker had vanished. The watch and chain in his boot were his. He always hid his valuables thus on train journeys. He had, he explained, come to Brighton to keep an appointment with Mrs Nye Chart, lessee of the Theatre Royal.

Patched up at the Sussex County Hospital, Lefroy was accompanied back to Wallington by Detective Sergeant George Holmes. But there had been developments. Mr Gold's body, punctured by 14 knife wounds, a bullet in the neck, had been found in Balcombe Tunnel. His watch and chain were missing.

Eluding Holmes, Lefroy made his escape. In the persona of Mr Clark, engraver, newly arrived from Liverpool, he took a room at the Widow Bickers' – 32 Smith Street, Stepney. However, a drawing of him was published in the *Daily Telegraph* and displayed on a wanted poster offering £200 reward for his capture. He also made the mistake of sending a telegram to a man named Seal, who shared his room at Cathcart Road and worked in a City office at Gresham Street, asking for money. Someone somewhere somehow guessed – and whispered. On July 7, the fugitive was arrested.

From Lewes prison he wrote to "My darling Annie," requesting from her a saw-file concealed in a meat-pie, and a tiny bottle of prussic acid, in a cake. Regretfully, Annie told her "Ever dearest Percy" that she was unable to accede.

A cruel contemporary conundrum: why had Lefroy a supreme contempt for money? Answer: Because he threw Gold out of the window and then ran away from the coppers.

Put up at Maidstone Assizes in November, Lefroy's defence line was that of a third man, who attacked him and murdered Gold.

Before his trial Lefroy begged in vain for the retrieval of his evening-dress from pledge that he might wear it in court. Someone however presented him with a brand-new top-hat. The devotion which he lavished upon that hat was bizarre. Each day it was gently deposited upon the ledge of the dock in front of him, and every so often he would pick it up and lovingly polish it with his sleeve, showing more concern for it than for his own fate. So extraordinary was his demeanour that there were many, including his counsel, Montagu Williams, who thought him as mad as a hatter. More seriously, the evidence of his violent mood swings suggests the very real possibility that he was a true psychotic; a manic depressive.

After a fair but lethal summing-up by Coleridge LCJ, the jury pronounced Lefroy guilty. Playing to the last curtain the rôle of the wronged, he bowed and enunciated in his best histrionic mode: "The day will come, Gentleman, when you will find, too late, that you have murdered me." And vanished, bearing his silk-hat tenderly away to the condemned cell with him.

For all his bravado words the thrasonic Lefroy bequeathed to posterity a full confession, his fiat justifying the last rites performed by deft ropesman Marwood.

The Scarlet Woman Murder

It is one of the most celebrated photographs in the pictorial annals of crime. Frozen in the moment of greeting on busy High Holborn, a stoutish man raises his trilby to a diminutive woman. He is Detective Chief Inspector Peter Beveridge. She is Mrs Florence Iris Ouida Ransom. She has killed three people. And this, caught by a *Daily Express* cameraman, is the split-second picture of her timeous arrest.

The human story brought thus to its climax and its close in a sandbagged street in wartime London, had reached its tragic apogee beneath the blue, Spitfire-filled skies of the Battle of Britain Kentish countryside. It is a story straight out of the old Krafft-Ebing box of tricks. Four, seemingly ordinary, petty bourgeois folk are the *dramatis personae* of this domestic tragedy of the Second World War; a tragedy which had its beginning in the gentler days of the 1930s.

Walter and Dorothy Fisher, married in 1913, lived blameless, middle-class, connubial lives in, first, Richmond, and then Twickenham. That was until after the birth of their second daughter, Freda, in 1921. Thereafter, victims of the seven-year non-itch, marital relations dried up. They decided to stay together, but play apart.

Thirteen, lucky for some, years later, Dorothy finally found and fostered a satisfactory sexual liaison with a well-to-do Danish businessman, name of Westergaart. Walter, a lonely man, by now in his mid-forties, cocooned in a sterile marriage, counted himself passing fortunate to encounter, in the mid-1930s, a dazzling red-headed, sexually responsive partner in recently-widowed, 35-year-old Florence Ransom. Back in 1931, Walter Fisher, who earned a most adequate salary as editor of a technical paper devoted to the mysteries of automobile engineering, had splashed out and bought an idyllic, orchard-surrounded, rose-bowered cottage, "Crittenden", at Matfield, near Tonbridge, in Kent, as a weekend place for his wife and two daughters. In Croesus vein, he had laid out again, in 1938, purchasing Carramore Farm, at Piddington, near Bicester, in Oxfordshire.

Then, in September, 1939, came the war. A few months later, Mrs Fisher and Freda – the other, elder, daughter, Joan, had married and gone off to India – evacuated from blitz-threatened London and moved into "Crittenden". And Florence Ransom, assuming the style of "Mrs Fisher", took up permanent residence with Mr Fisher at the farm. Incidentally, three members of this domestic square dance were known to each other by *noms de guerre*: Walter became "Peter", Dorothy became "Lizzie" or "Mrs Kelly", Florence became "Julie" or "Gugsy". Only the Dane retained his rightful nominal identity.

At Carramore Farm, Walter employed a housekeeper, Mrs Guilford, her son, Fred, as cowman, and Fred's wife, as dairymaid. What Walter did not know was that these "servants" were, respectively, his mistress' mother, brother and sister-in-law. Florence Ransom used her skills as a former secretary in the day to day management of the farm.

In June 1940, "Gugsy" asked her brother, Fred the cowman, to show her how his shotgun worked. She wanted to shoot rabbits.

On July 9, 1940, 83-year-old John Leury, from neighbouring Geddes Farm, discovered the bodies of three women scattered about the "Crittenden" pleasances – Mrs Dorothy Fisher and Freda in the orchard, their housekeeper, 48-year-old Charlotte Saunders, beside the cottage. They had all been shot down in their tracks as they tried to escape from the killer.

In the cottage, where a terrified little dachshund dashed, whimpering, from room to room, were all the classic signs of a ransacking robbery. Clothes and documents strewn broadcast, but, interestingly, significantly, money and jewellery remaining untouched.

When Chief Inspector Beveridge of the Scotland Yard Murder Squad arrived, he found a solitary clue: a woman's white hogskin glove, lying between two of the bodies. His attention was caught, too, by a dropped tray and heap of broken crockery on the scullery floor. Pieced together, the fragments added up to *four* cups and saucers. A visitor had come to tea.

Before journeying to Matfield, Beveridge had made two visits. First, to see the Danish Lothario at his luxurious West End London flat; secondly, to interview the bereaved Walter, at Piddington. Both had struck him as genuinely distressed innocent men.

At Carramore he had met, too, Florence Ransom. With her flaming red hair, heavily made-up face, tight-fitting blue "slacks" (as they were called in those days), brilliant-coloured sweater top, and blazing scarlet fingernails, she was . . . well . . . eye-catching, a once-seen-never-forgotten figure. Unfortunately for her! Because some thirteen people had not forgotten seeing her on her way to, from, and around "Crittenden" on the day of the murders.

In a scene reminiscent of Cinderella and the glass slipper, Beveridge proffered the white glove. Smilingly, Florence drew it on her left hand. "It's too tight," she said. But Beveridge had seen that it was a perfect fit.

Having consulted with the pathologist, Sir Bernard Spilsbury, fingerprint expert, Superintendent Fred Cherrill, and completed his own enquiries, Beveridge decided it was time to pull in Mrs Ransom. He arrived at Carramore Farm around dawn, but the equally early bird had flown. Gone to London to see a doctor, he was told. But other "information received" tipped him off that she had arranged to meet Walter at six o'clock that evening at a City solicitor's office.

In the stone forest of High Holborn it was like the meeting of Stanley and Dr Livingstone. Silently, on his rubber-soled policeman's shoes, Beveridge came up to her. Raised his hat. "Mrs Ransom, isn't it?" He should have said: "I presume".

She was tried at the Bailey in November, 1940, before Tucker J The prosecution focused on the overwhelming weight of evidence indicative of premeditation: weeks spent learning how to load, unload, and discharge a sporting shotgun, and the taking of that gun with her to Matfield, showing intent. As to motive – a mystery. That said, the likelihood seems to be that Dorothy and Freda, with both of whom Florence was normally on the friendliest of terms, were the victims of some sudden twisted fantasy evolved in a sick and jealous mind. Charlotte, the housekeeper, was just in the wrong place at the wrong time. That Florence's mind was sporadically sick is attested to by the fact that she had previously been a patient in a mental hospital.

The jury found her guilty, and she was condemned to hang. Sentence was never carried out. She was sent instead to the right place for her – Broadmoor. Reports issuing whence from time to time have indicated that she became something of a star, achieving great heights, and dramatic distinction in the make-believe splendours and miseries of the Broadmoor amateur stage productions – albeit vastly inferior to certain productions of her own enacted beyond those confining walls.

The Great Bournemouth Mystery

For our lofty-minded Victorian forbears the name Spurgeon could have only one possible connotation; it would evoke the pious image of the great Charles Henry, popular sermoniser *par excellence*; he of the City Tabernacle, who filled the well-waxed pews to overflowing with his stirring preaching.

For me, however, at an impious remove from the Stracheyean Great Victorians, Spurgeon calls up the self-effacing shade of Mr Robert George Spurgeon, the gentle Bournemouth schoolmaster who made the appalling discovery of the murdered body of Miss Emma on Southbourne Cliff, on the eastern edge of the town.

The Great Bournemouth Mystery is 98 years old, for it was on February 20, 1908, that Mr Spurgeon, out for a ramble with his party of schoolboys that Thursday morning, had his attention called by one of the boys, who had clambered up an embankment bordering a field hard by the cliff-top path, to "something" huddled in the field. Screwing up his eyes, Spurgeon could just about discern that the "something" was the prone body of a woman. But was she, he asked himself, asleep, intoxicated, perhaps, or, Heaven-forfend, dead. Heaven did not forfend. As he approached the feminine enigma more closely, he saw that she was unmistakably dead.

Help was summoned from the coastguard station, fortunately only a few hundred yards away. On to the scene bustled Chief Officer Laws, accompanied by two other coastguards and a medical man, Dr Facey. The doctor conducted an on-the-spot examination. The woman had, he said, been dead many hours. There was, at first glance, no obvious sign of injury; just some small abrasions on her face and the backs of her hands. Her hair was tidy. She was wearing a hat and outdoor clothes. They were dry, unsoiled and only slightly disarranged. Then came the more worrying discovery: into her mouth had been crammed two white pocket-handkerchiefs. The larger, a man's, lay relatively loose-packed in the mouth-cavity; the smaller, a lady's, had been forced right down into the gullet. On it was written in marking-ink, "E Sherriff". There was neither money nor, with the exception of a ring on the left hand which was too tight-fitting to remove, a single article of value remaining on the body. A plain case of murder for robbery. Or so it seemed. At a post-mortem it became clear that the woman had died from shock caused by internal injuries and bleeding. The whole left side of the chest was flattened and one rib had been broken. The handkerchiefs had nothing to do with her death. They had almost certainly been stuffed into her mouth to stifle her cries.

Now it so happened that, not 24 hours earlier, a young man named John McGuire had reported a Miss Emma Sherriff missing. This McGuire, 21 years old, having recently left the army and embarked upon business on his own as a picture-dealer, said that he had come to know 35-year-old Miss Sherriff when, three years before, serving with the Royal Artillery, he had been stationed at Christchurch. Oddly enough, she, was also an intimate friend of McGuire's mother, who was in service as a cook, just outside Bournemouth.

A retired lady's maid, Emma Sherriff, somewhat frail and of a timid, shy, and nervous disposition, had inherited a little money, some £600, which, invested, yielded a weekly income of 10 shillings, which she supplemented with small sums earned by dressmaking. She lived in rented rooms over a general store kept by the Widow Lane at No 80 Palmerston Road, Boscombe. Hardly a Rothschild, but when you discover that picture-dealing can present a cash-flow problem when solvent art lovers are thin on the ground and your stock is thick on the walls, every little "touch" helps.

Deciding then, for whatever reason, to take up his interrupted friendship – and it was no more than that – with Miss Emma, McGuire, living now in Denbigh Street, Pimlico, had, he told the police, sent a telegram on February 19, telling her that he would call to see her that afternoon. When he had arrived at Palmerston Road, he had found her bed unslept in and no sign of her. Worried, he had immediately contacted the police.

It was on the following day that her body was found and McGuire arrested.

A carefully-crafted case was assembled by the prosecution. McGuire was known to have been short of money. It was thought likely that he had actually arranged to meet Emma at Southbourne on February 18, the day before that on which he had, he said, gone down to Boscombe to see her. He admitted that they had walked together on the cliff path. It was theorised that some sort of demand for financial help had been met with a refusal. Or it could have been that she charged him with having stolen her jewellery – she had a small amount – and some money. He had, the week before, spent a short holiday lodging in the same house as she did, and she was heard to say after his departure: "Have I been harbouring a thief?" For whatever reason, he had turned on her in a fury and battered the little woman to death.

He had then dragged her body from the path, over the embankment to the spot in the field where Mr Spurgeon and his boys encountered it. Not only had the investigating police found drag marks, but a strand of her beads had broken, laying a trail of pearls from the footpath to where the body lay. Having removed whatever portable valuables he could get his hands on, McGuire had boarded the first available train – the 8.49 pm from Christchurch – back to London, and there prepared the setting up of the following day's charade of innocence.

John Francis McGuire was tried at Winchester Assizes in May, 1908. Witnesses were called to testify to having seen him at the material time near the scene of the crime. He said they were mistaken. The defence was denial . . . mistaken identity . . . he was in London that night. The jury, after being out three hours, failed to agree.

Lawrance J sent McGuire back to jail to await a new trial. It was to be a long wait-until the following November.

But, as it turned out, the law's delay was to cause young McGuire small inconvenience, for at the end of June the Crown entered a *nolle prosequi*, and he walked forth to join the rest of us, wondering, from that day to this, whoever could have served so harmless a little woman, for so insignificant a gain, so cruel a fate.

The Goozee and Leakey affair

Goozee and Leakey sound, as the late Ivan Butler, actor and author, astutely observed, like characters in a TV sitcom. But there is nothing remotely comic about the rôles for which Fate cast the two curiously named principals in the story which I am about to unfold. The story of, not Roger, but Albert the lodger – Albert William Goozee, former merchant seaman, subsequent bus conductor, roundsman, labourer, fitter's mate, and general what-have-you.

The year is 1955. The month June. Goozee has just unpacked his bags in the lodger's room at Mr and Mrs Thomas Leakey's well-appointed suburban semi-detached in Alexandra Road, at Parkstone, Poole.

The sedate arrangement started to go wrong within weeks. The fulcrum of impending disaster was an innocent-seeming game of Spin the Bottle, played at the 14th birthday party of the Leakeys' daughter, Norma, on February 4, 1955. The spun bottle pointed first to Goozee, and then to Norma's 53-year-old mother, Lydia, as the pair who, by the rules of this Postman's Knock genre game, had to go outside the room and kiss. The red wine which had flowed, flooding and dousing her normal inhibitions, led Lydia to confess to Goozee, "I've been wanting to do this for weeks." Later that night she came quietly to his room. Later still, came young Norma. Nor, as time ticked on, did this remain anything like a one-off incident.

Predictably, things came to a decided head. Lydia's husband, Tom, it must be explained, was something of an invalid. Seven years before, on medical advice, he had retired on his own to the back bedroom. His healthy and, it must be admitted, frustrated wife, shared the master bedroom with Norma. Big, brawny, dark-eyed and swarthy, Goozee was a startling contrast to Tom, who had lost a leg in the war. Tom, well aware of his own deficiencies in that particular marital department, was nevertheless outraged by Lydia and Goozee's bland misconduct, and in high dudgeon – and low esteem after being hit over the head by Goozee – packed his bags and took refuge at his sister's house at Enham-Alamein, near Andover.

The months went by. The seasons passed. Then, in June, 1956, 18 months after Goozee's first meek entrance, and later warring presence, Tom Leakey hobbled back, and, master of his own semi-detached, ordered Goozee to leave the house, which, without show of violence, he did, as meekly as he had entered.

Goozee betook himself to new lodgings at the home of a Mr and Mrs Pemberton, of Sunnyhill Road, Parkstone. Tom settled happily back in the back room. But all was far from well in the Leakey household. Infatuated mother and daughter were both pining for Big Al.

On Sunday morning, June 16, Mrs Lydia Leakey did something about it. She went along to the Tollard Royal Hotel, on the West Cliff at Bournemouth – that same hotel where the sadistic multicide Neville Heath had stayed one June, 10 years before, and whence he had emerged to murder his last victim, Doreen Marshall – where Goozee had found a job of sorts. Her pleading and cajoling of him to return to live with her meeting stone-wall response, she made her fatal mistake. She attempted blackmail and threatened to reveal his association with Norma. She had put her foot on the accelerator.

Lydia Leakey did not know it, but Goozee's mind had already been in a state of chaotic anxiety before her unwelcome advent. The previous evening he had landed himself in serious trouble as a result of an encounter with a 14-year-old schoolgirl at Bournemouth's New Royal Theatre, and had spent the night in a police cell. Released on bail, he had explained his all night absence to the Pembertons by saying that he had been detained by the police for speeding.

Sunday, June 17, was to be a special day. He was to take Lydia and Norma out in his car, a black Wolseley which Lydia had bought him, for a picnic in the New Forest. He duly called for them at two o'clock, and off they went for a spin. They stopped en route to look at the Rufus Stone, then turned off the road, plunging into Bignell Wood, taking a muddy track to Canterton Glen, quite close to where Conan Doyle once had a cottage.

The preparations for the picnic got under way – a tin kettle of water hanging from a car starting handle over a carefully laid camp fire; a small aluminium tea-pot, a few teaspoonfuls of tea in it, standing in waiting.

Precisely what happened then . . . in what order . . . who did what to whom . . . cannot be said with certainty. According to Goozee, in a frantic outburst of jealousy a green-eyed Norma had seized the axe they had taken with them to chop firewood and hit her mother across the head with it. He had then bundled Norma into the back of the car. Lydia had staggered across and was hunched in the passenger seat. She was holding a knife. As he was trying to take it from her, he slipped. He felt the knife go into his side. "I thought my life was finished, so I jabbed the knife in her. Norma came out of the car and came at me screaming." And then it came trotting out, the old familiar "My mind must have gone a blank." He remembered nothing.

A passing motorist saw a Wolseley parked on the verge of the Cadnam to Brook road. A man was slumped over the mud-guard. He was bleeding from a knife wound. It was Goozee. "There has been a murder in the forest, a fight with two women. I did it," gasped Goozee. "I've a knife in me. Get the police."

Tried at Winchester Assizes, he was found guilty of the murder of Norma Leakey, and was sentenced to death. He did not, however, hang. Reprieved, he went to life imprisonment.

There is a strange appendix to this tale. All the main actors seem to have had a weird premonition of coming doom. In the pocket of a coat which she had left hanging in her wardrobe, Lydia Leakey had tucked a form of will, beginning with the ominous words: "In the event of anything happening to me . . ." The life-loving teenage Norma had told relatives, "Albert will kill us one day." And Albert? He, before doing the deeds, had written a letter to the Chief Constable of Bournemouth foreshadowing the terrible events which were to come to pass. They found it afterwards, unposted, in his blood-spattered car.

So it was that the destinies of three people came to be decided, not by the flip of a coin, but by the spin of a bottle.

The Letter

East of Suez was, for the celebrated author, the late William Somerset Maugham, a dangerous territory in which to point a toe.

Although in the minds of many people he is as closely associated with Malaya as Kipling is with India, if, after his two brief visits of 1921 and 1925, he had ever ventured to return to those parts, he might well have come to serious harm.

The plain truth is that the publication of his collections of short stories, *The Casuarina Tree* and *Ah King*, made him *persona non grata*, for the people who had befriended him and confided in him felt betrayed. He has been roundly accused of having "abused hospitality by ferreting out the family skeletons of his hosts and putting them into books," leaving behind him a trail of angry people marking his passage through Malaysia.

A case very much in point is that of "The Letter". Perhaps Maugham's best known short story after "Rain", it was first published in *The Casuarina Tree*, in 1926, and was subsequently presented, in 1927, as a very successful play, with Gladys Cooper, and, in 1940, as a hit film, with Bette Davis.

The scandal, as seen through the expatriate eyes of the British residents of Kuala Lumpur, was that the Leslie Crosbie of Maugham's story was the undisguised and clearly recognisable Ethel Proudlock, the wife of an Englishman who, in circumstances fault-lessly reconstructed in Maugham's putatively fictional tale, had shot her lover dead.

The shock of recognition emotionally paralysed in their pride the polite society of this colonial outpost of Empire, often described as "Cheltenham on the equator", where suburban snobbery and aspira-tion twinned with gross insensitivity to the native populace over whom they held dominion.

It was the evening of Sunday, April 23rd – all-British St George's Day, Shakespeare's birthday – in 1926, the sixteenth glorious year of the King and Emperor, George V.

The Proudlocks, William, aged thirty-one, acting headmaster of Kuala Lumpur's premier school, the Victoria Institution, and his 23-year-old wife, Ethel, had returned after attending evensong to the smart, verandahed bungalow which they and their 3-year-old daughter, Dorothy, occupied in the school's grounds.

A friend had invited Ethel to join her for dinner after the service, but, thanking her, she had declined, for Will was going to dine out that night. He was to have a meal at his teaching colleague, Goodman Ambler's.

So when, after a brief *en route* visit to the Selangor Club, they got back to the bungalow, they both changed their clothes. She, saying that she planned to spend the evening writing letters, exchanged the pink dress with black spots which she had worn at church for a pale-green, sleeveless tea-gown, with a somewhat revealing neckline.

Having checked that her daughter was sleeping, Ethel fetched a blotter, an ink-stand, and her writing materials, took them out on to the verandah, and settled herself comfortably into a large rattan chair, well provided with cushions, in front of a useful rectangular table.

The day had been rather a miserable one, drizzling much of the time, and now as dusk set in, trying its best to smother the light provided by the single bulb hanging from the verandah ceiling, there was a sudden cloud-burst, the spears of rain filling the Sunday-quiet air with the sound of their vicious slashing.

We will allow Ethel herself to take up the narrative.

She was, she said, halfway through the writing of her second letter when a rickshaw drew up, and a family friend, William Steward, the 34-year-old manager of a local tin mine, appeared all smiles.

She was not expecting visitors that evening and was startled by his arrival. Assuming that he had come to see Will, she told him that her husband was out, having dinner with a colleague who lived on Brickfield Road, a good mile and a half away, and, if he wished, he could find him there.

Steward did not apparently so wish. In fact he showed a distinct disinclination to leave. So she suggested that he should sit down, and they proceeded to make polite small-talk. For something to say, she asked Steward if he had been to church that evening. He replied that he went to church very rarely.

"Then you're like my husband," she said, smiling, "I'll show you a book he's reading."

She walked over to the long bookshelf above the teapoy, and took down a copy of Leslie Stephen's *An Agnostic's Apology*. She was in the act of handing it to him when he grabbed her, saying: "Never mind the book. You do look bonny. I love you. Let me have you. I must have you," and bent down and tried to kiss her.

She pushed him away. "What are you doing? Are you mad?"

His only answer was to seize her right wrist in a vice-like grip, and, with his left hand, turn off the light. He then started to pull up her dress, and he put his hand on what she described as her "person". She grabbed his hand and wrenched it away. He had one arm around her waist and the other on her left shoulder. He pulled her towards him and tried to force her against the wall.

Reaching out to steady herself and to put the light back on, her hand came in contact with a Webley revolver which she had given Will as a birthday present just five days before, and which happened to be still lying on the table. The next thing that she remembered, she claimed, was stumbling on the verandah steps, where Steward lay, blood seeping, six bullets in him. He was dead.

Charged with murder, Ethel Mabel Proudlock was put on trial in the Supreme Court at Kuala Lumpur on June 11th, 1911. Jury trials had been abolished in Malaya and the case was tried by a judge, Mr Justice Sercombe Smith, and two members of the lay public, known as assessors.

Since the time of her arrest many rumours had been circulating about the association between the pretty, blonde-haired, rather baby-faced young woman in the dock and the tall, big-framed, balding, rugby-playing engineer. They had been, it was said, lovers, and the reason that she shot him was because he was having an affair with a Chinese woman with whom he was living, and had come round that evening to tell Ethel that all was over between them.

Certainly there was no medical evidence of rape, or attempted rape, and when the police found Steward he was fully dressed and what were coyly referred to as his "nether garments" – his trousers – were respectably buttoned up and unstained. Her story was disbelieved.

The judge and his assessors unanimously found Ethel Proudlock guilty. She was sentenced to death. That she did not hang was entirely due to the intervention of the Sultan of Selangor. Citing her youth and the circumstance that she was a mother, he granted her a pardon. She returned to England where, it was said, the trial and her time in the condemned cell at Pudu gaol having unhinged her, she died in an asylum.

Not true.

Eric Lawlor, who has made an exhaustive study of the case, has established that Mrs. Proudlock, in addition to being an adultress and a murderess (in that local order of heinousness) was also, and worst of all, (again in the local ordinal) almost certainly Eurasian. And that was what did for her.

He further discovered that, far from dying in an asylum in England, Ethel settled, in 1913, in Portage la Prairie, Manitoba, moving on, in 1916, to New York. She died, on September 22nd, 1974, aged eighty-six, at her married daughter's home in Sunkist Grove, Miami, 63 years after, in far away Malay, a judge, himself long since dead, had donned the black cap and sentenced her to hang.

Caught by the Skin of His Teeth

Seventeen-year-old Gordon Hay was deservedly unlucky in that he was not saved but caught by the skin of his teeth. For the murder of young Linda Peacock was to become a historic case in which the new-fangled discipline of forensic odontology played the central rôle in bringing her killer to book.

It was on Sunday evening – August 6th, 1967 – that the traditional travelling fair arrived at the little town of Biggar, in Lanarkshire, and 15-year-old Linda, a pert and pretty Scots lass with a passion for horses and a good record at the local gymkhanas, was absolutely determined to go along there to ride the hobby-horses and enjoy all the fun of the annual fair.

She lived with her rather elderly parents in a picture-book-pretty cottage about a mile and a half out of Biggar. In the early evening, her parents, albeit a shade reluctantly, yielded to Linda's persuasive entreaties and allowed her to go.

When, by 11 pm, their daughter had not come home, Mr and Mrs Peacock began to be seriously worried, and asked the young man who lodged with them to help. He drove to the fair-ground, searched, but found no trace of Linda. The police were informed.

It was at the break of day, 6.40 am on Monday, that two patrolling constables came upon the body in the cemetery. You expect, of course, to find bodies in cemeteries – but not unburied, slumped against a gravestone, half-hidden by a vasty yew. It was Linda.

There could be no mistaking that murder had been done. Two wounds to the head. The mark of a strangler's ligature around the neck. More marks plainly showing that the wrists had been tied. There was something else . . . an oval area of bruising on the right breast. But no signs of violation.

The ensuing murder hunt, directed by the extremely experienced Detective Chief Superintendent William Muncie, put every conceivable suspect under the microscope, but it was not until the detectives turned their attention to the boarding-school, half way between Biggar and Linda's home, and close to St Mary's Cemetery, that the investigation moved forward. It was a progressive school for maladjusted – not delinquent – teenage lads, and it was unfairly easy to see it as a potential reservoir of sexually awakening and frustrated suspects.

As it turned out, one of them did seem to fit the frame, but a code of silence, every whit as strict as the Mafia's *omerta*, prevailed. Then, a breakthrough. One boy cracked, admitted having lied, covered up Gordon Hay's absence from the dormitory for a crucial fifty minutes – a time that coincided with witness evidence of seeing a girl with a lad at the cemetery, and of hearing screams.

Muncie noted that the glass of Hay's wrist-watch was badly scratched and the winder had broken off. Hay said that he had damaged the watch while polishing the floor of his room. Muncie had a different notion. Perhaps the winder was lying in the cemetery. The Hoover firm in Scotland supplied four specially adapted vacuum-cleaners. For the first time in history a cemetery was thoroughly hoovered. Disappointingly, the contents of the bags disclosed no winder.

In the meantime, photographs of the oval bruise on Linda's chest, which had turned out to be a bite mark, had been sent to John Furness, lecturer in forensic dentistry at the police training school in Liverpool, and a pioneer forensic odontologist. Furness reported that the bite mark showed an irregularity. A cast was taken of Hay's teeth. They matched the bite mark on Linda's body.

Appreciating the – at that time – novelty of tooth evidence, it was decided to call in the complementary dental expertise of Dr Warren Harvey, lecturer to the Scottish Detective Training School.

At Harvey's request dental impressions were taken at Glasgow Dental Hospital from all the inmates, pupils and masters, of the boarding-school. Models were cast and each was marked with a number. To whose identity the number applied, only Muncie knew.

A preliminary examination eliminated all the bite sets except five. A second examination eliminated all except Cast No 11. And Cast No 11 was that of the teeth of Gordon Hay. On the tips of Hay's right upper and right lower canines Harvey found a pit. This he considered to be a rare condition, due to a most uncommon disorder called hypocalcination. He examined the teeth of 342 youths aged 16–17, and found only two exhibiting similar pitting.

There was additionally one mark in the bite cluster on Linda which looked as though it had originated from an exceptionally sharp or jagged tooth. Precisely such a broken tooth was present in Hay's mouth.

Gordon Hay was put up at the High Court of Justiciary, Edinburgh. He pleaded not guilty and entered a special alibi defence, stating that between 9 pm and midnight on August 6th, 1967, he had been in the school.

Professor Keith Simpson testified that in more than thirty years' practice as a forensic pathologist he had never seen a bite mark with better defined detail. Dr Harvey told the Court that he had not previously seen anything like the puzzling tooth marks with a pale centre. However, all immediately became clear when he saw the pits in the accused's teeth.

The Lord Justice-Clerk, summing up on the ninth day of the trial, was at pains to stress the importance of the dental evidence. Of forensic dentistry he remarked: "This is a relatively new science, but there must, of course, be a first time. Scientific knowledge and medical knowledge advance as the years go on, and it is only comparatively recently that fingerprints have come to be accepted." Indeed, and it was as late as 1945 that palm-prints were accepted by a judge in the High Court of Justiciary.

The jury debated for two and a half hours before returning with a guilty verdict against Hay. Because he had been under eighteen when he committed the crime, he was ordered to be detained during Her Majesty's pleasure.

The Hay case was a ground-breaker in the developing new science. Its precedent was an English case, *R.* v. *Gorringe* (1948), in which newly-weds Jack and Phyllis Gorringe were having a hard time adjusting to married life. Their last fight spanned Christmas, 1947, to New Year's Day, 1948, when the battered bride was found dead and tooth-marked in a yard behind the Tunbridge Wells dance-hall where they had been celebrating Her young husband's indisputable bite marks on her right breast established his indubitable guilt. Sentenced to hang, he was later reprieved.

By 1979, when Ted Bundy was convicted in America by bite marks on the buttocks of one of his estimated 23–40 female victims, forensic odontological evidence had become a commonly accepted offering in criminal trials.

The Newent Enigma

There would seem to be something malignant so far as solicitors are concerned in the wind that blows across the Welsh Marches; it appears to be tainted with a distinct whiff of uxoricide.

Twice in the twentieth century members of the profession have brought their marriages to an abrupt end with the illegal aid of noxious potions. In 1919, Harold Greenwood of Kidwelly, and in 1922, Herbert Armstrong of Hay, were both arraigned for having resorted to the unhappy husband's friend – arsenic.

In the case of Greenwood, the alliance went unproven; in the case of Armstrong the illicit relationship was established, and a divorce from life was arranged *per* the Gloucester Prison gallows.

Less well known is the case of a third solicitor from the Cymric borderlands: that of Edmund Edmonds, likewise indicted for wife-murder, although by violence other than venenation, in 1872.

The curtain rises in the autumn of 1871. The scene is the small Gloucestershire town of Newent. Edmund Edmonds, a virile man in the latter half of his fifties, resides in, and practises law from, an impressive town centre abode, the Pigeon House: a generating station of energy every bit as electric as James Joyce's identically named power house on Dublin Bay breakwater.

Behind Edmonds there lay already a slice of history – enshrined in Guy and Ferriers' *Principles of Forensic Medicine* (1888 edition).

In October, 1845, he had married a young widow, Anna Legge. Her husband, Edward, had died in June, 1844, following several strokes. Four months later, Anna gave birth to a daughter, Mary Frances, who became beneficiary to one-third of her grandmother's estate, nearly £4,500.

When Mary Frances died in December, 1848, the money held in trust for her reverted to her guardians, Anna and her new husband, and the legitimacy of the dead child was challenged by the Legge family. Rumours of Anna's adultery with Edmonds had been strong, and it was moreover felt that Legge's medical condition had made him incapable of fathering a child at the presumed date of Anna's conception.

An action at law was taken. The defendant obtained the verdict – and kept the money. And it consequently passed into medico-legal lore that "in hemiplegia there does not appear to be any direct impairment of sexual capacity, and that fruitful sexual intercourse may take place within a few weeks after a well-marked attack of hemiplegia is proved by cases adduced on the occasion of the trial of *Legge* v. *Edmonds*."

The shades grew longer over the marriage of Edmund and Anna. Thirteen children were born to them. The shinings of early romance dulled and passed with the years into the shadows of custom grown stale. Edmund cast a wandering eye, Anna a jaundiced one. The culmination came one February night in 1867.

Edmund had achieved. Purchased the imposing Pigeon House. Advanced in town politics. Adopted a coat of arms. Motto: *Qui patitur vincit*. A reversed prophecy!

Running parallel with Edmund and Anna's decrescent affections, a positively incandescent nexus was prospering between Edmund's 17-year-old orphaned niece, Jeanette Edmonds, daughter of Edmund's deceased brother, who had come to live with her uncle and aunt, and the family doctor, Matthew Bass Smith, an unlikely Lothario of mature years, well married, papa to a respectable quiverful.

In the early hours of February 25th, 1867, Anna died. Cause of death, certified by Dr Smith, apopleptic fit.

Four years went by. Then . . . fearful ructions. Uncle Edmund stumbled upon epistolatory evidence of the Smith-Jeanette liaison. Conveniently forgetting his own adulterous capers with Mrs Anna Legge back in the days when he was a foot-loose articled clerk, he turned furiously upon Dr Smith, who was forced to sell his practice, declare himself bankrupt, and shamble shamefacedly off to London to start up anew. The errant niece was also packed off to London, where she was placed in St James' Diocesan Home, a refuge for fallen women, at Hammersmith.

For some time rumours concerning the death of Anna had been swirling around the huge, ornate, white marble tomb which Edmonds had erected in Newent churchyard. And, indeed, before his departure from Newent, Dr Smith had industriously seeded sinister tattle as to the suspiciously circumstanced death of Edmund Edmonds' late spouse.

So widespread, grave, and loud in their behind hand transit from lip to ear did the uneasy whisperings become, that Henry Christian, Chief Constable of Gloucestershire, felt unable to ignore them. Accompanied by his deputy and Mr M. F. Carter, a Newnham solicitor who was the local coroner, he journeyed to Hammersmith to take a statement from Jeanette Edmonds.

Because of what Jeanette had to say, the Home Secretary issued an order for exhumation, and at 4 am one February morning in 1872, Anna was prematurely resurrected and carted off to the vestry-room of the church for medical examination.

On February 14th, the inquest hearing took place in the ballroom of the George Inn, Newent. Jeanette's statement told how, late on the night of Sunday, February 24th, 1867, she had heard screams and fierce quarrelling between her uncle and aunt, and seen Mrs Edmonds run wildly past her bedroom with her husband in full and angry pursuit. Anna, clasping her breast, cried out that she was dying. Edmund felled her with a blow to the side of the head.

Ann Bradd, the Edmonds' maid, gave evidence that the master and mistress had led an unhappy life together. On the fatal night she had heard the mistress accuse the master of visiting a woman in Gloucester. He had replied angrily, "Damn your eyes, go to bed."

Dr Smith testified that called in at 11.30 pm, he had bled Mrs Edmonds and administered croton oil, but she had died at 1 am.

At the end of that day's hearing Edmonds was arrested, and later charged with murder.

His trial was held at the Old Bailey. The charge was reduced to manslaughter. His counsel, Mr Huddlestone, sought to show that Dr Smith had borne a grudge against Edmonds because he had tried to get him struck off the register of the College of Surgeons, and that Jeanette spoke out of revenge. But the jury took only sixteen minutes to return a not guilty verdict.

This was, though, no "happy ever after" story. In 1878, Edmonds mortaged the Pigeon House and took flight from Newent, settling in

Maida Vale, London. His career as a solicitor came to an abrupt end in 1881. Following appropriation of client funds, he was struck off the Law Society's register.

Thereafter, he vanishes from sight. He is rumoured to have died a pauper's death in a London workhouse. We don't know – but, for sure, the inscription on his wife's Newent tomb is another of his prophecies that went awry: *"Hic sepulchro Edmundi Edmonds et suorum cineres destinantur."*

The Great Swinfen Case

Forgotten – even by lawyers – today, but one of the outstanding sensations of mid-Victorian England, is the remarkable story of the former Bloomsbury parlour-maid, a lone widow, who challenged the might and majesty of the English legal system, daring even to bring a suit against the Lord Chancellor.

Mix in the revelation in court of the scandal of an *affaire de coeur* between a barrister and his client, trace the progression of the widow's cause through the Court of Common Pleas, the Court of Chancery, the Court of Exchequer, and two Assize Courts to ultimate victory, fame, and fortune, and there, in a nutshell, you have the Great Swinfen Case.

In November, 1830, Samuel Swinfen, owner of Swinfen Hall, a fine old mansion, and a 1,243-acre estate, near Lichfield, Staffordshire, decided that he needed to visit his lawyers, Messrs. Dendy & Morphett, of Bream's Buildings, Chancery Lane.

Accompanied by his son, Henry, he put up at Miss Ayres' highly respectable lodging-house in Hunter Street, by Brunswick Square, Bloomsbury. Employed as parlour-maid there was Patience Williams, the 18-year-old daughter of an agricultural worker from Llanfair Caerinion, Montgomeryshire.

Henry Swinfen fell head-over-heels in love with her, and on her Sunday afternoon off – March 6th, 1831 – he was waiting for her on the steps of St George's, Bloomsbury, and the pair were secretly married. After a seven-year "honeymoon", doing a leisurely Grand Tour, and a further six years making a less grand tour of England, Scotland, and Wales, they returned to Swinfen Hall in 1844.

Old Samuel took a great liking to his daughter-in-law, and when, in 1848, he was widowed, invited Henry and Patience to come and live at the Hall. In March, 1852, Samuel made a will. A simple document leaving everything to Henry. One fatal flaw. What if Henry predeceased him?

And he did!

On July 7th, 1854, Samuel made another will, bequeathing all of which he was possessed to his son's widow. Just over a fortnight later he died, and everything passed to Patience.

Old Samuel's father, John Swinfen, had had two families. The deceased Samuel was the eldest son of the first marriage. The eldest son of the second marriage, Francis Swinfen, had married, and his widow was determined that their son, Frederick Hay Swinfen, a captain in the Dragoons, should inherit rather than Patience. But as the estate was not entailed, Samuel had been at legal liberty to make any will he wished, unless – and this was the consideration that Frederick and his mother urged – he had been mentally incapable at the time.

In July, 1855, Captain Swinfen filed a Bill in the Court of Chancery disputing Samuel's will and praying for an issue to try the competence of the testator.

Swinfen v. *Swinfen* came on before Cresswell J and a special jury at Staffordshire Lent Assizes, 1856. Patience's leading counsel was Sir Frederick Thesiger, Q.C. What was on trial was the state of mind of Samuel Swinfen when he made his will. But, Thesiger betrayed his client by, without the agreement of Patience Swinfen, assenting to a compromise whereby she should convey the Swinfen Hall Estate to Frederick Swinfen in return for an annuity of £700 for life. She would be permitted tenure of the Hall until the following Michaelmas . Quite reasonably, she absolutely refused to countenance any such an arrangement.

It was at this juncture that Charles Rann Kennedy, poet, scholar and barrister, whose brother, incidentally, was he of *Kennedy's Shorter Latin Primer*, hove on to the scene. He was to fight tooth and nail through the courts for Patience's rights, fall in love with her, and then, love to hatred turn'd, rend her from limb to limb.

Meanwhile, Captain Swinfen was applying at the Court of Common Pleas for a rule of attachment, an order to impound the property which Patience was still unlawfully retaining. This Crowder

J declined. So did Sir John Romilly in the Rolls Court. While stating that he found no case for specific performance, the Master advised both parties that it would be well to arrive at some sort of compromise, or much of the disputed property would be lost in the litigation.

Turning a deaf ear, Captain Swinfen appealed against the Master of the Rolls – and lost. Kennedy succeeded in persuading Knight Bruce J and Turner J to appoint the issue to be tried at the Summer Assizes at Stafford.

Accordingly, in July, 1858, Patience Swinfen brought a fresh action before Byles J, in which she sought to recover possession of the Swinfen Hall Estate – and succeeded.

One final action remained to be fought. Charles Kennedy, backed – or, rather, fronted – by Patience, proceeded to the Court of Exchequer to attack Thesiger for what he regarded as his abominable, unprofessional conduct in effecting an unauthorised compromise.

By this time Sir Frederick had been elevated, as Lord Chelmsford, to become the Lord Chancellor. No matter. Fearlessly, Kennedy did all he could with wit and eloquence to savage him. Right may have been on his side, but the Establishment ranks held. It was Kennedy who was broken. No one ever employed him at the Bar again.

Worse still, a rift opened up between him and Patience. She – and surely he – realised that there could be no question of marriage. He had a wife and umpteen children. So when an eligible and well-to-do widower, Charles Wilsone Broun, proposed, the Widow Swinfen, grown lonely, accepted him with alacrity. They married in 1861.

Embittered to the very verge of sanity, Charles Kennedy promptly sued Patience, whom he now dubbed "The Serpent of Swinfen", in the sum of £20,000 for professional services rendered. And the jury at Warwick Assizes found for him.

But the pertinacious Mrs. Patience Swinfen-Broun swiftly applied to the Master of the Rolls. The Warwick verdict was set aside. Kennedy, it was decided, should pay all costs, and it was further decided that a barrister could not sue for his fees.

Charles Kennedy died a widower in 1867. His wife had died in November 1863, ironically, only a couple of years after Patience's marriage. Patience died without issue in 1876. The Swinfen Estate passed to her husband. He died in 1883. The property was inherited by one of his sons, Colonel Michael Alexander Wilsone Swinfen-

Broun. He died, childless, in 1948, and the Hall, one-time epicentre of so many quakes and ructions, stood empty and silent.

A ghost was said to haunt its grounds – a man in black, wearing a tall-hat of the kind favoured by gentlemen in the middle of the nineteenth century.

"Could it," asks Howard Clayton, chronicler of the Great Swinfen Case, "be the spirit of poor, tormented, broken Charles Kennedy?" Adding, "If ever anyone was likely to haunt the grounds of Swinfen Hall, it was he."

A Victorian Death Riddle

Among the most celebrated legends of art and literature is that of the sordid tragedy and enigmatic death of the, some say, noble and caring friend of Ruskin, Swinburne, the Rossettis, Burne-Jones and Whistler . . . others say, the vicious, hypocritical blackmailer, Charles Augustus Howell.

He was, the story goes, found early one morning lying in the gutter outside a public-house in Chelsea, his throat cut and a ten-shilling piece wedged tightly between his clenched teeth.

The strange thing, though, is that when, at the suggestion of a friend, I decided to do a little detective work in order to try to bring to light the full facts behind this intriguing mystery, I searched the biographies, autobiographies, memoirs, diaries, letters, and journals of all the friends and acquaintances, debtors and debtees, and avowed enemies of the dead man without finding in a single one of them the faintest breath of a whisper of his having come to such an end. What I did find was Swinburne's description of him (*post mortem* in 1898) to William Michael Rossetti as, "The polecat Howell; the vilest wretch I ever came across."

A similar blank was drawn from a scrupulous searching through the newspapers of the day. Not a hint, not a between-the-lines nod to the *cognoscenti*.

Who, then, precisely was this man Howell? What was his background? It was Anglo-Portuguese. He was born in Oporto in 1840, the son of an Englishman who had been seduced, as so many Englishmen were at that time, by the El Doradoan prospects of the wine-shipping business. For him, opulence proved evasive. Indeed, his son, Charles, was, with his brother, pressed at an early age into diving for gold in the sunken wreck of a Spanish galleon off the coast of Portugal in order to replenish the family coffers. And subsequently Papa Howell had recourse to the teaching of drawing for auxiliary income.

As a 16-year-old Charles was despatched into the care of his uncle, the Vicar of Darlington, and claimed to have been briefly apprenticed to the great civil engineer George Stephenson's nephew, George Robert. One has advisedly to write "claimed" or some such cautionary qualification as regards everything Howell stated, for he was a great romancer, a *grand blagueur – vulgater*: an incorrigible liar. This Münchhausen averred that he had, around 1858, emigrated to Morocco, where he passed day and night in the saddle and became the chief of an Arab tribe. Then, after rendering various sterling services to the Portuguese Government, in recognition of which he had been awarded the decoration of a broad red ribbon which it was his wont habitually to wear on his shirt-front – "Stolen from someone!" laconically observed William Morris – he had returned to England in 1865, and was engaged by Ruskin as his private secretary.

Alternatively, this facile de Rougemont asserted that between 1858 and 1864 he was in his native land, exercising his skill as a civil engineer on the construction of the Pôrto and Badajoz Railway.

By the time, in 1870, he left Ruskin's employ, he had well infiltrated the Pre-Raphaelite world of art and artists, where, for the next, and final, twenty years of his life he was to live on his wits. He became Swinburne's crony and man of business. He established himself as Gabriel Rossetti's agent for the sale of his pictures. He did indeed do far more than that for Rossetti. When, in 1869, Gabriel decided that he wanted to retrieve the manuscript volume of his poems which, in a moment of quixotic grief, he had laid beneath his dead wife's head in her coffin and buried with her, who should he turn to for the grisly aid he sought, but the Pre-Raphaelite factotum, Howell.

Nor did he turn in vain. On the night of October 5, 1869, Howell, attended by the legally required presence of a lawyer, Henry Virtue Tebbs, a proctor at Doctor's Commons – to speak to the real nature of the manuscripts, and, by the light of a fire built beside Lizzie's grave in Highgate Cemetery, supervise the raising of her coffin. In the firelight's glow the dead woman's hair still gleamed its lifetime's golden-copper sheen, and when the little book, grey bound in rough calf, was lifted, there came away with it a single strand of red-gold hair.

As the years passed, the young man who had seemed to Whistler "like a swashbuckling, picturesque rogue out of a book", who had been Swinburne's boon companion, and Gabriel Rossetti's beloved *amanuensis*, redeeming his brazen short-comings by his overweening charm, his sparkling wit, and *contes drôlatiques*, began to emerge in his true false colours.

The tally of his treacheries was reckoned; his devious dealings over the Rabelaisian letters which Swinburne had so injudiciously addressed to him; his "blowing the gaff" about Rossetti's little essay into grave rifling, and his spreading of the romantic lie of Lizzie's hair continuing to grow after death so luxuriantly that it filled the coffin with its gold; his and his artist-mistress, Rosa Corder's, forgeries of Rossetti drawings; his universal thefts from friends. Never doubt, there were those who came to fear and hate him.

Primed with all this background information, I returned to the search for the source of the lurid story of this strange man's strange end. And I found it – in the pages of another man, a man almost as strange as Howell himself, Thomas J. Wise, the celebrated literary forger, exposed in 1934 by the brilliant bibliographical detective work of two booksellers, Carter and Pollard. Wise it was who, in his *Swinburne Library Catalogue* , printed for private circulation in 1925, told, almost certainly invented, the tale.

Just to make sure, I consulted Howell's death certificate. It stated that he, of independent means and living at 91 Southampton Row, London, WC, died of "Pneumonia, Phthisis, Asthenia", in the Home Hospital, 16 Fitzroy Square, St Pancras. Death registered April 25th, 1890.

This does not exclude the possibility that Howell could have collapsed in the street, and a well-meaning passer-by, mistaking his collapse for an epileptic fit, might well have thrust some object between his teeth, as was usually done in such cases. Surely, though, the Good Samaritan would have noticed the cut throat!

Moreover, I find the implication that such an incident could have gone unrecorded by the police, and the fact that the cut throat is unremarked upon the death certificate, unacceptable. I feel absolutely certain that we may regard Mr Wise's account as just one more of the many manipulations of truth of which posterity has found him resoundingly guilty. Investigation completed. Mission accomplished.

Death of a Tyrant

It was the talk of Rome that high Italian summer, the beautiful Beatrice and how she had murdered her father – not, you understand with her own fair hands, but by those of the bloodstained *assassini*. And not, by all tellings, that her father, perhaps the wealthiest nobleman in all Italy, did not richly deserve his fate.

Had it not been for the poet, who presented her story in a magic web of words, and the painter who preserved her likeness in a magic mirror of oils, her story might never have carried *fuori i muri*, beyond the walls of Rome.

That Count Francesco Cenci lived a life of wickedness and debauchery remarkable even for the *Cinquecento*, there can be no question. Choleric, cruel, vice-laden, Francesco was a tyrant within as well as without his home. His spasms of murderous violence and unacceptable immorality had landed him frequently before the *Sacra Ruota*, the Papal Court, and siphoned huge sums in the form of punitory fines from his fortune. A sort of poetic justice really, because the immense Cenci wealth had been derived from depredatory peculations when his father, Monsignore Cristoforo Cenci, had been one of the chief comptrollers and collectors of finance at the Papal Court. These cheatings had added up, *scudi* aside, to two palaces in Rome, as well as properties in the Abruzzi, in the Kingdom of Naples.

For all his ferocity, Francesco seems to have treated his wife, Ersilia, not unkindly. She bore him eleven or twelve children, dying in childbed in April, 1584. He remarried. His bride was a widowy, Lucrezia. She set up home with him and two of his daughters, Beatrice and Antonina, in the Palazzo Cenci, near the Dogana (custom-house).

When, early in 1595, Antonina married, the 17-year-old Beatrice was left alone with her father and stepmother in the gloomy old palazzo on the banks of the Tiber. By this time Francesco's affairs had become perilously Gordian-knotted, and for probably combined reasons of economy and fear of retribution at the hands of his two eldest sons, Giacomo and Cristoforo, he decided to hide himself, his wife, and daughter, away. From a *simpatico*, Don Marzio Colonna, he obtained use of the Castello Petrella in the Abruzzi, a remote, inaccessible, hillside fortress, approachable only by a dizzying mule-track For the two women it was virtually a prison.

Castellan of Petrella was Olimpio Calvetti, in whose charge Francesco Cenci did not scruple to leave his womenfolk. As time passed on heavy wings, Lucrezia and Beatrice grew increasingly unhappy. When, on occasion, Francesco came briefly back into residence, his cruelty, the indignities visited by him upon his wife and daughter, heaped up a pile of grievances which toppled over into a hatred on his head. In the unnatural circumstances of her "imprisonment", Beatrice turned to Olimpio, and was presently bearing his child.

As Francesco Cenci's behaviour intensified in its outrageousness, his two youngest sons, Paolo and Bernardo, united with Giacomo, their sister Beatrice and their stepmother Lucrezia, in the resolution that the only salvation for them all lay in the death of the tyrant. Ways and means were discussed, practicalities weighed. The decision reached was to stifle him in bed, club him to death, and then to throw his body down through a wooden gallery leading to an out-building in the grounds. The cover story would be that the gallery, which was in poor repair, had given way. The deed was to be carried out by Olimpio, assisted by another of the servants, Marzio Catalano.

In the early morning hours of September 7, 1598, Francesco was despatched according to plan. But the murder was clumsily done. The corpse should have been pushed through the rotten planks of the gallery floor. Instead, it was thrown over the edge. Suspicions were aroused; endorsed when a panic-stricken Marzio took flight; further aroused when, very foolishly, neither Beatrice nor Lucretia attended the burial of Francesco; confirmed when, later, bloodstains on the dead man's bedclothes were reported.

The Cenci returned to Rome. Francesco's body lay under the flags of Petrella's church. The gossips began, like hens with teeth, to chatter. Before cock-crow their clucking rumours reached the Papal ear. Beatrice had given birth to Olimpio Calvetti's child. Olimpio himself had been tracked to a mountain hideout near Cantalice, and, on Giacomo Cenci's orders, been beheaded. Now, on the Pope's order, Giacomo was arrested, along with Lucrezia, Beatrice and 18-year-old Bernardo. Paolo was already dead. He had contracted a fever. Giacomo and the two women were put to the torture of *La Corda*, the Rope. As it twisted, rack-like, behind their backs, forcing their shoulders excruciatingly out of joint, all three confessed their guilt.

By the time of their trial the beautiful young Beatrice had become a popular heroine, and her advocate, Prospero Farinaccio, advanced in her defence that her father had attempted to violate her. This may well have been no more than a defence ploy. Certainly, the evidence for it was very weak. All were found guilty. Nothing could now save them except clemency from the Supreme Pontiff – Pope Clement VII. He promulgated his decision on September 10. Giacomo was to be drawn through the streets in a cart, an executioner tearing flesh off his body with hot pincers. Then he was to be struck on the head with a mallet until his soul left his body, which was then to be ripped to pieces and hung on hooks. Lucrezia and Beatrice were to be beheaded. Bernardo, having watched the executions, was to be sent to the galleys for the rest of his life.

On September 11, 1599, in the piazza hard by the prison fortress of the Castel Sant' Angelo, Beatrice Cenci, firm and rapid of step, mounted the scaffold and, without sign of fear, laid her head ready for the axe, housed above in a guillotine-like machine. Thus, saint-like brave, her spirit passed from life into legend.

For more than a hundred years visitors have made pilgrimage to the Roman Palazzo Barberini to view the Guido Reni portrait of Beatrice Cenci. But, alas, there is not an iota of evidence that it is in fact her likeness. Current artistic scholarship thinks it to be the Samian Sibyl of the Bolognese School of Guido, Guercino, and Domenichino. Neither does Shelley's verse-drama, *The Cenci*, written as a result of his being deeply moved by Guido's portrait, truly represent Beatrice, for the ancient manuscript from which he drew his details embodied many falsities. La Cenci, in legend as in life, is not quite what she seemed.

A Wife Too Many

For most men one wife is enough; for some, more than enough. But there does seem to exist a criminal caste for whom a multiplicity of "marriages" – for reasons practical or personal – appears to be a *sine qua non*: the Sailor wife-in-every-port syndrome!

In this quaint hymeneal context there spring to mind such murderous marital voyagers as George Joseph "Brides-in-the-Bath" Smith and fiery Alfred Arthur Rouse. And well up there among the polygamistic charmpionship contenders figures the starred name of Arthur Andrew Clement Goslett.

Born in Cape Town, son of a distinctly well-heeled family, Goslett's exotic mix of English and French blood surely contributed to his hair-trigger romanticism and excessive nuptial enthusiasm.

A well-qualified, highly capable engineer, who had spent his apprentice years working in his father's firm, he seemed set fair for a good, solid career. But there was a dark side to Goslett. He played dangerous games in the West African diamond markets, operating for illicit diamond buyers. Caught out, he had served several prison sentences. At last, disgraced and disowned by his family, he had quit, and made his way to England.

That was in 1914. In the June, he married Evelyn, a widow, at 37 a year younger than himself She had several children. With his new, ready-made family, he settled into a comfortable flat in Armitage Mansions, on Western Avenue, near Golders Green Road, North London.

The following August war broke out. Goslett joined the Royal Naval Air Service and was promptly commissioned. A deep shadow blotted his prospects when he was suspected of being a German spy. Fortunately, he was able to convince British Intelligence that the suspicion was baseless, and promotion to the rank of captain followed.

Less baseless perhaps, although never satisfactorily proved, is the suspicion that he committed bigamy, "marrying" a girl in Devon at the end of 1914.

Handsome, this 38-year-old Lothario was not. Dark, sallow-complexioned, with mean-sized eyes, too small-seeming for the rest of a face which wore a constant scowl. But, then, Casanova was no "looker" either! All was, however, redeemed by the man's bearing.

He carried himself with an air – common to con men and bigamists – most magnificently set off by the resplendent and glamorous uniform of a dashing naval officer.

In February, 1919, calling himself Captain Arthur Godfrey, he went through a form of marriage at Edmonton, North London, with 26-year-old Daisy Holt. He shared with her a modest love-nest at Kew. He told her he was a chief engineer in the Royal Navy. Actually, he had been dismissed from the service, but landed a well-paid position in a Government aircraft factory.

By September, Daisy was pregnant with "Captain Godfrey's" child, and went into a lying-in hospital. It was in the course of what should have been a romantic walk amid the blossoms and blooms in Kew Gardens that the Captain confided the highly unwelcome intelligence that he already had a wife.

To poor Daisy it came as a nasty shock. But, said the gallant captain, this prior encumbrance need not necessarily be permitted to intrude upon and spoil the idyll of their relationship. He had a palliative to hand. Albeit there was a proviso. It was that she would assent to the assumption of the identity of his dead brother Percy's widow. In the respectable guise of his wife's bereaved sister-in-law she could make a home for herself in the Golders Green mansion block with himself and Evelyn.

It was outrageous . . . but it worked.

Then, something even more outrageous. In January, 1920, Goslett contracted a third – or was it a fourth? – marriage. The bride lived in Richmond. Came the spring, the new Mrs G was with offspring. And Captain G was losing the spring in his step. Life had become too complicated, not to say expensive. A drastic reduction in some of his commitments had become vital. Now he saw plainly where the necessary axe, or rather tyre lever, would fall. An instant economy could be effected by the elimination of Evelyn.

On the fine spring evening of May 1, 1920, Goslett asked Evelyn to go along with him to see a house, situated near the river Brent at Hendon, which he was proposing to rent for them. She was walking all trustingly beside him by the river when he suddenly felled her with a murderous blow to the side of the head with a tyre lever and threw her body into the water. He was back home by 10 pm, and went off unconcernedly to bed.

Next morning, a Sunday, a man and his son sailing a model boat on the Brent, were horrified to see the body of a woman floating face downwards towards them in a shallow bend of the river, about 300 yards from the main road. It was Evelyn Goslett, identified through a shop bill.

Her husband, interviewed by the local police, made a poor impression on them. He was detained on suspicion, and within 24 hours charged with murder. After making two statements violently protesting his innocence, he went on to make a further six confessing, in variant ways his guilt.

His strongest assertion was that it was all Daisy Holt's fault. She had threatened that if he did not kill Evelyn, she [Daisy] would give him in charge for bigamy. "I killed the best woman. I am going to have the rope," he said. Thus did he behave like an officer and a (temporary) gentleman to the end.

Goslett was put up at the Bailey in front of Shearman J. He was defended most valiantly by Curtis-Bennett – but to no avail.

Counsel told the court that the prisoner was known at his place of work in the airplane factory as "The Crackpot" and "The Mad Skipper". He attempted to show that an airplane accident which Goslett had been in in Germany in 1913, was the source of serious mental disturbances. For good measure, Dr Frederick Toogood, a specialist in mental diseases, expertly opined that if Goslett had, as he claimed, consumed 20 alcoholic drinks before killing his wife, he might well have been unfit to judge of the "nature and quality" of his act.

None of this would Shearman J accept. "I have never heard of a murderer who was normal," he said in his summing-up. "The defence suggestion that he murdered under a delusion is no defence."

That was virtually the death sentence.

Found guilty, Goslett was hanged in Pentonville on July 27, 1920.

To the very trap's edge he went on voicing his bitterness against Daisy Holt. This inculpation of his of Daisy was, the Scotland Yard officers most vehemently declared, absolute nonsense.

The last person to visit him before his execution was the "wife" from Richmond. She had forgiven him. She was shortly to have his child. Other than that, he left to her such worldly goods as he had to leave. Not a lot.

Poet and Predator

Herbert Leonard Mills was a poet. A literary man. He walked the mean streets of Nottingham, a volume of Keats, Shelley, or Tennyson in his pocket; in his head a vision of himself as the Writer (capital "W") he longed to be.

Herbert Leonard Mills was a 19-year-old, work shy, unemployed clerk, who lived with his father, a miner, and stepmother in Mansfield Street, Nottingham, and got by, scraped an existence, gambling on the gee-gees. But he was not wrong in considering himself unusual – unique, really, as we shall discover.

When he was not reading the works of the Great Poets, or painstakingly composing Great Poetry of his own, Herbert's taste ran, less loftily, more down-to-earthly, to a fascination with crime – fiction, faction, factual, especially murder.

Pondering "Life" in the course of one of those long, long walks he liked to take through the local woods and scrubland, he fell to wondering how he could combine the poetry of the perfect murder . . . with his soaring literary ambition, and come out on the profit side. And he reached a conclusion. He would commit the perfect murder . . . and describe it in perfect prose. It would mean taking a gamble, of course, but, then, he was no stranger to the wager.

He chanced upon his ideal victim in the warm and cosy womb-like darkness of the Roxy Cinema. Her name – perfectly tailored for her rôle – was Mabel Tattershaw. She was 48 years old, a housewife and mother of two daughters. Her husband was in prison for shopbreaking and, to make ends *almost* meet – she took in lodgers at her home in Longmead Drive, Sherwood.

It was, in fact, with one of her three current lodgers, Mrs Lily Wilson, that she had gone to the pictures that Thursday afternoon, August 2, 1951, when she got into whispered conversation with the stranger sitting on her other side in the stalls. Pathetically flattered by the unexpected attention of one whom, taking him at his own manifestly high self-evaluation, she regarded as an "educated" young man, poor, deluded Mrs Tattershaw gladly consented to meet him again, and a date was made for the very next day.

Before sallying forth the following evening, a plainly excited Mabel was to be seen taking unusual trouble over her appearance; lipstick and face-powder, a rare vanity. To be brutally truthful, she was an ill-favoured little woman, commonplace and sexually unattractive. But she dressed up that Friday in her pitiful best; a second-hand plum-coloured floral print dress, a rather shabby old brown coat, and well-worn brown shoes. A final defiant touch, a borrowed necklace of brightly-coloured "poppit" plastic beads. She was to meet her youthful Lothario at six o'clock outside the Metropole Cinema.

Mabel Tattershaw was never seen again – alive.

On the Saturday, her 14-year-old daughter went to the police and reported her missing. Five more days went by. It was at 11.30 on the morning of August 9, that Norman Rae, chief crime reporter of the *News of the World*, received a telephone call. The caller gave his name – Herbert Leonard Mills. He was speaking from a street call-box in Nottingham. "I've found a woman's body. It looks like murder." He hadn't told the police about it. He wanted £250 for the exclusive story.

Rae kept him talking. Had a colleague contact the Nottingham police. "Give me your number and when the money runs out I'll call you back," said Rae, thus identifying the location the call was coming from. Mills was still arguing terms when the detectives came knocking at the kiosk.

At Nottingham Central Police Headquarters he put up a good, if slightly weird, show, telling how the first thing he did after stumbling upon the body was seat himself upon a mossy bank and read Shelley's *Ode to Death*. Eyeing him askance, they let him go.

Rae came to Nottingham and took Mills back to London, where he extracted his story of "How I Met Murder". They didn't want him talking to other papers. They wined and dined him, showed him round the West End, took him to the Festival of Britain, and the theatre to see *King's Rhapsody*, stuffed £75 in his hand and packed him off back from St Pancras.

Home again in Nottingham, disgruntled, Mills rang Rae – "Now I'll give you the *real* story."

On August 24, Rae returned to Nottingham, and booked in at the Black Boy Hotel. There, sitting down at midnight in the lounge, a sheaf of hotel notepaper before him, sipping an orangeade, Mills wrote his confession, which he had every intention of withdrawing once he had pocketed the handsome payment for it he anticipated from the newspaper. He had, he admitted, met Mabel at the

Metropole, walked her to a remote area of overgrown orchard at Sherwood Vale known to local lovers as "The Jungle", and strangled her.

Norman Rae did what he had to do – delivered Mills into the hands of the police.

He came up at Nottingham Assizes before Byrne J in November, 1951. His trial lasted four days. He smiled at the jury as, after 25 minutes, they announced their verdict of guilty. He smiled at the judge as he pronounced the sentence of death.

In Lincoln Jail he passed his three clear Sundays' grace in a fine frenzy of poetic creation, penning such memorable lines as:

> *Though so many would believe*
> *This tale is most untrue,*
> *Who sells the news on Saturday*
> *On Friday that he slew*.

Despite this, and a massive maudlin muddle's output, he was declared sane . . . fit and well to keep his Tuesday appointment with my late friend Albert Pierrepoint on December 11.

He smiled as his grave was dug. He smiled as he asked Pierrepoint to make a good job of it. But when it came to it, the hanging was no laughing matter. The best laid schemes of mice and hangmen gang aft a-gley. Albert broke Mills' spinal column as the law required, but, at the inquest the prison doctor reported that the hanged man's heart had continued to beat for twenty minutes after the drop.

Pit Note. It would appear that this was no unique happening and that judicial hanging was not always the capital form of execution, the clean ending, that its advocates held it up to be.

Professor Sir Sydney Smith, late eminent holder of the chair of forensic medicine at Edinburgh University, who had attended many executions, wrote: "No doubt with the neck broken and the spinal cord severed, death is as nearly instantaneous as may be . . . but when a person is hanged the heart usually continues beating for a longer or shorter time after death; and it has often been debated whether, with blood still circulating, momentary consciousness might be present after the neck is broken."

The Le Touquet Mystery

It was the sort of case that would have taxed – and delighted – the subtle Gallic brain of Chief Inspector Maigret, kept the trays of beer and sandwiches from the Brasserie Dauphine across the way being sent over to his office in the Quai des Orfêvres far into the night.

That long ago Spring of the tragedy, Mr and Mrs Wilson, both of them mighty keen golfers, had come to France on holiday frorn South Africa, and taken the villa "Ma Rose", situated conveniently close to the Le Touquet golf-links.

He, Herbert Wilson, aged 64, was a director, retired, of Cammell Laird's, the well-known steel manufacturers and shipbuilders. His wife, Florence, nine vears younger, was the granddaughter of the firm's founder, Charles Cammell.

Saturday, May 19, 1928. That afternoon the Wilsons, Captain Soanes, manager of the local branch of Lloyds Bank, and some other golfing friends had tea at the Le Touquet Links Club-house. After tea, Mr Wilson and Captain Soanes went on to play a round, but Mrs Wilson declined, saying that she would go on to the Casino and would meet her husband and Captain Soanes for apéritifs at the Café Central in Paris-Plage at 7.30 pm. Some English friends offered her a lift in their car, but she said that she would prefer to walk.

It was about 6 pm when she started off, taking the path through the wood abutting the links. This path was actually the disued track of the old steam tram which used to run between the Casino and the golf-course. Was she hastening to a secret rendezvous?

Mr Wilson and Captain Soanes arrived punctually at the Café Central. By 8 pm there was still no sign of Mrs Wilson. Her husband returned to the villa. Florence was not there. By now thoroughly anxious, he got out his car and did a round of all the hotels which he thought she might be visiting. She was not at any of them. He contacted the police before setting forth with Captain Soanes to search, with a lantern, the entire length of the tram track in the woods. They drew a blank.

It was at 4.30 am that the police found Florence Wilson. Actually, it was an Alsatian dog that made the discovery. Her body was in thick undergrowth close to the track. She lay on her back, her knees drawn up, her clothes disarranged. She had been manually strangled – and stabbed 14 times. With a single exception, all of the stab wounds which, incidentally, had been inflicted after death, were superficial, some barely pricking the skin. The exception was a deep thrust through the carotid artery. There was a distinct possibility that there had been a deliberate staging of an *apparent* sex crime in order to put the police off the scent.

The corpse wore diamonds – rings and a pendant – and a pearl necklace. Nothing had been stolen. Her handbag lay unrifled. This was bizarre.

Arrests followed within hours. Two men. One, a half-witted deaf-mute named Vambre, was only a lad, but he was said to have attacked a woman four years before. The other was a Portuguese pedlar. Both were released.

Next to be questioned was Monsieur Jean Matras, Musical Director of the Le Touquet Casino Orchestra. A handsome man, moulded in the fashionable image of the romantic "Gypsy violinist", after his chilling moment as suspect elect he was rapidly and decisively discharged from the case.

There was one more possibly significant clue, inexplicably seemingly overlooked by the *gendarmarie*. A stone-mason, Celestin Biguet, walking home along the tram track, had passed a tall, well-built man wearing a grey overcoat. As Biguet approached, the man stooped over a bush "as though he were a naturalist examining an object", thus hiding his features. This encounter Biguet timed as between 6.15 and 6.30 pm – about ten minutes before Mrs Wilson was due to pass the spot.

Time passed. The case of the murdered Englishwoman faded: not forgotten, but stowed away among the unclosed files.

A brief false alarm of hope sounded in July, 1930. Sixteen-year-old André Leloutre, arrested in connection with a number of attacks on local women, confessed to the murder of Mrs Wilson. Committed for trial, he was soundly acquitted.

Three more years elapsed. Then, in 1933, an anonymous letter was addressed to the police. The writer claimed that Mrs Wilson's killer was himself now dead, drowned a few months before in the river at Étaples. He had, said the letter, been a contract killer, disposing of Florence Wilson to paid order. But *whose* order? No name was mentioned but the anonymous correspondent stated that the killer had been familiar with Mrs Wilson's every movement, for he had for some time been intercepting her and delivering into her hands letters written by "a certain gentleman" using a "certain café" in the district.

Now it so happened that the police had found – although keeping its discovery to themselves – a letter near the body in the wood, and the handwriting was that of "a certain ex-convict". It was conjectured that this letter could well have been dropped in the course of the fight that Mrs Wilson, a lithe, strong, athletic woman – a rider to hounds, a keen tennis and golf player – put up for her life.

Officially, the police would say nothing about this letter beyond the fact that they had checked with the proprietor of that "certain café", which was actually the very one where Mrs Wilson had had the appointment with her husband and Captain Soanes on the night of her death, and that the *patron* had a clear recollection of a man sitting at a table there writing a letter an hour or so before the calculated time of the killing. The letter had been left in his charge, and he had later handed it, as requested, to a man he knew to be an ex-convict, and who had subsequently been found drowned.

Brave efforts to promote a rational solution to the crime were made by the French press, hazarding that Mrs Wilson was really a member of the British Secret Service, and that she had acted as an espionage "post box", receiving and passing on secret documents. No substantiation of this has ever emerged.

Much more likely, one suspects, is it that she was being blackmailed over some amatory indiscretion. She was well known to have been absolutely mad about dancing, and was certainly in the habit of going to places – such as *thés dansants* – unknown to her acquaintances. Equally well known to the *Sûreté* was the existence of those men who haunt dances in search of victims whom they can blackmail. A case of hunt the gigolo?

But this is mere speculation. The murder of the Englishwoman in the tangled *boscage* of Northern France – with its eerie echoes of the Luard affair of 1908 – is not a satisfactory case. Jules Maigret, one feels, would never have left it like that.

The Veronal Poisoning Case

It began as a shipboard romance: it rapidly escalated into a lethal obsession. Cruising to Australia aboard the *Oratava* in 1906, Hugh Eric Trevanion, a wealthy, eccentric, 21-year-old bachelor, embarked upon a close friendship with Albert Edward Roe, the ship's 28-year-old fourth officer.

Eric was the stereotypic "poor little rich boy". A loner, on uneasy terms with his family, uncertain as to his sexual identity, cushioned – and ultimately destroyed – by the £100,000 legacy from his grandfather, which he had then just come into. And the first thing he did was to move out of his home and into digs as a paying guest at 6 St Stephen's Crescent, Bayswater, the family home of his governess, Miss Geneste.

A frail, willowy, edging on six foot, Beardsley-like figure of the 'nineties aesthete type, there was no gainsaying the oddity of Eric's aspect: dyed hair, painted face, high-heeled white satin shoes, plethoric finger rings, bangles, a diamond-crusted pectoral cross and dangling quizzing-glass. More sinisterly, an addiction to the palliations of drugs and drink.

Roe, in sharp contrast, was of medium height, thickset, built square, clean-shaven, clear-cut features, profuse curly black hair, parted in the middle, sloe-black eyes: an exciting dark presence.

After long, dedicated siege and determined waftings of temptatious financial bait, Eric, little by little, succeeded in seducing Albert – or "Rex", and variantly "Bear", as he pet-named Roe – away from the bosom of the deep, and to his own. Bosom chum, yes, but, more definably, captured into his service as his paid companion.

For a while the affair – and Bear – prospered. From a starting "wage" of £50 a quarter, a speedy move to £300 a year, and thence to an outright gift of £10,000 healthily invested – to make Bear independent, not a servant, as it were – to the final crowning bestowal of the residual legacy of Eric's entire estate; all within a six months of entering into his required duties. For Albert Edward Roe, friendship's road had certainly led, gold-paved, to fortune. Or, rather, *would*, should Eric die. And this, presently, Eric obligingly did, under circumstances of worrying dubiety. In the July of 1912, the two young men set up house together in a luxurious, top-floor flat, overlooking the sea, No 10 Grand Avenue Mansions, Hove. Sumptuously furnished throughout, the irresistible feature of the shared master bedroom was the *lit matrimonial*. The couple were attended upon by a butler, William Joiner, and his wife, Mary, who acted as housekeeper, both of whom would testify to Mr Roe's solicitude for Mr Eric's welfare, and also as to how, by his dominance, he controlled the excesses of his partner's fondness for waking draughts of alcohol and sleeping draughts of veronal.

It was in the high summer of 1912, mere weeks after the setting up of the joyous joint-tenancy, that something – we shall hazard what, later – seems to have imported a sadness so overwhelmingly disturbing that Eric was driven to attempt self-destruction. He tried, with veronal – tbe dangerous hypnotic, diethyl-barbituric acid – overdoses, three times, and failed. The fourth time he succeeded; or did he? He certainly died, but was it suicide or murder?

On the night of September 9, 1912, Eric and Albert dined together at Grand Avenue Mansions. They took coffee in what they called "the den", but which, far from exuding the leather and sporting print atmosphere usual to such male preserves, was described as being more like a lady's boudoir. Then Eric went off to their bedroom, where he had Joiner bring him a half bottle of hock. An hour later he slipped into an unconsciousness out of which he never awoke.

Roe applied to have the body cremated. This request was refused, and Eric was interred in the family vault in Norwood cemetery.

There was an inquest; a verdict of "Death from veronal poisoning by misadventure." This did not satisfy Eric's mother, Mrs Florence Eva Trevanion, who was convinced that her son had been murdered, and agitated for a post-mortem. The Home Office authorised exhumation. Eric's corpse was uplifted and delivered into the hands of Drs Spilsbury and Willcox.

And on January 13, 1913, the Divisional Court granted an application for the holding of a second inquest.

The coroner sat in the Magistrates' Court in Hove Town Hall. The proceedings lasted, with adjournments, for seven days, from January 24 until, some thought appropriately enough, St Valentine's Day.

It transpired that "the boy", as Eric was continually and rather strangely referred to, had somehow ingested the *enormous* overdose of 150 grains of veronal. A fatal dose is 50 grains. The ordinary medicinal dose, packed in a sachet, was seven grains. The 150-grain dose would have meant swallowing 21 sachets.

Dr Willcox opined that the fatal dose must have been taken within an hour of the supervention of unconsciousness. That meant that either the Joiners, Roe, or Trevanion himself must have administered the poison.

If it was not suicide, the one person who had motive, as well as means and opportunity, was Roe. Eric's demise would bring him wealth and freedom. Freedom to marry. For we know that the terrible something which Roe, surely a facultative bisexual, had had to impart that summer, which was so dreadfully upsetting to Eric, was that he intended to get married.

The second inquest jury's verdict was: "That the deceased came by his death by an overdose of veronal. But how or by whom administered there is no evidence to shew."

It could be, though, that Roe, taking advantage of Eric's befuddled condition following his consumption of hock, plus, perhaps, some sachets of veronal, permitted, or even encouraged, him to swallow that huge, lethal dose, saying that it would ensure that he would have a good night's sleep. That would at least explain away the riddle of how the poison, which would have been detectable to taste in the coffee and unabsorbable in a half bottle of hock, was taken.

The coroner, G. Vere Benson, accepting the jury's verdict, made the pointed comment: "My own verdict would not have taken this form."

Mr Albert Edward Roe, the *ci-devant* Bear, left the court stainless, as the saying goes, and to the plaudits of the crowd. The following year he married. His bride was the widow of Mr W. H. Derrick, a Swansea confectioner in a big way of business, who had left her most adequately provided for.

Mr Roe settled down in Swansea to a very comfortable continuance of his life voyage.

Miss Nina and the Anarchists

A fragment of burnt bone and an old, arthritically crippled woman marooned in an attic room in the East End of London: the connection between the two is not immediately obvious.

Permit me to explain.

The charred piece of bone goes back to my medical student days. I remember how, exhausted by the efforts of memory involved in the learning of systematic anatomy, I used to turn away from the potted portions of humanity standing in their serried, glass jar rows on the shelves of the galleries of the old pre-blitzed museum of the Royal College of Surgeons in Lincoln's Inn Fields, and make my way gratefully to the welcome asylum of the small Historical Room or Cabinet to gaze, fascinated, at that fire-blacked upper extremity and shaft of a right femur said to have come from the incinerated corpse of Peter the Painter, the legendary Russian anarchist.

It is exactly 96 years ago since the flames lit up the Whitechapel sky, burning the Siege of Sidney Street into the indestructible pages of history. And it seems incredible that I should have come to know someone who played quite a major part in the affair – Peter the Painter's girlfriend, no less!

The spark that ignited the Sidney Street inferno was struck on the night of December 16, 1910, when strange noises were heard coming from No 11 Exchange Buildings, a small cul-de-sac running behind Houndsditch.

At 119 Houndsditch was the shop of H. S. Harris, jeweller, so situated that it would be possible from Exchange Buildings to knock a hole in the back wall and burrow through to Harris' safe.

And this was precisely what the fund-hungry refugee gang of anti-Tsarist terrorists was engaged in doing.

A neighbour, Max Weil, raised the alarm. There was a shoot-out. The anarchists mowed down five police officers, killing three of them. One of the anarchists, George Gardstein, was accidentally shot by a comrade. Carrying their dying leader with them, the anarchists struggled back to the house – 59 Grove Street – where several of them lodged. Gardstein was left there in the charge of three Russian women associates of the gang – Sara Trassjonsky, Luba Milstein and Nina Vassileva. Gardstein died the following morning.

A hue and cry was raised for the anarchist murderers of the three policemen, and the colourful name of Peter the Painter – actually Peter Piatkow, nicknamed "The Painter" because he used to paint the scenery for plays put on at the Anarchist Club in Jubilee Street – was bandied about.

Before Christmas most of the anarchists had been arrested, but still at large were Fritz Svaars, "Joseph" (William Sokoloff), "Joe Levi", and the talismanic Peter the Painter.

At last, on the morning of January 3, 1911, information was received that two of the wanted men had gone to ground at 100

Sidney Street. A pitched battle ensued. Eventually, the Scots Guards were called out from the Tower of London and the Home Secretary, Winston Churchill, arrived to watch – and supervise – the embattlement of the house in Sidney Street.

All morning shots flickered back and forth. Then, just about lunchtime, a thin plume of smoke wisped up behind a window pane, and shortly afterwards thickening billows, red and black, presagers of a massive, omniphagous shroud of vivid flame, enwrapped the house from top to bottom. In that pyre the anarchists perished.

But *was* Peter the Painter one of the men in the house of fire? The College of Surgeons' bone notwithstanding, legend says not. The inquest officially declared the remains those of Svaars and "Joseph".

And now . . . what of the old arthritic woman of whom I spoke? Large, run to bulk, with white hair, short and straight, and faded blue eyes, she was all that was left of the beautiful young Russian girl, Nina Vassileva.

And, incredibly, when I met her, in November, 1960, she was still living, 50 years later, within a fire-bomb's throw of Sidney Street.

I found her occupying, in poverty, a top-floor front, looking out over London chimney-pots, at 99 Brick Lane. It was a terrible climb up for somebody so disabled.

The room had blue wash painted walls. Furnished with a bed, one hard chair, and a gas-ring, illumined by a single naked bulb, it was a cheerless place. It was also crowded, chaotic, untidy. A Greek Catholic, she had a positive welter of religious objects on display, spilling over everything.

Born in 1891, in Dnepropetrovsk (formerly Yekatorinoslav) in South Russia, she was, she said, the daughter of a chef in the Imperial Palace at St. Petersburg.

We turned the clock back five decades. She told me that she first met the anarchist crowd in the Jubilee Street club long before the Houndsditch affray. It was when she was living in Great Garden Street (now Greatorex Street) that she came into contact with Fritz Svaars and Jacob Peters, who, incidentally were both qualified engineers. They lived upstairs. Her room was the ground-floor back, and the only one that had a fire in it, so they all used to sit in there.

Nina knew Gardstein well, but denied that she had been his mistress. She told me that it was a popular canard that she had been Peter the Painter's girlfriend. She had, in fact, never known him, and her first meeting with Sara Trassjonsky was when they were both in Holloway. She told me that she was not one of those at Exchange Buildings, and denied that she had nursed the dying Gardstein. On the other hand, she had known both Lenin, whom she had found a delightful person, and Prince Kropotkin personally. She maintained that the police behaved very dishonestly towards her, virtually accusing her of murder, but she said that Mr Justice Darling was very kind to her.

She also, most interestingly, confided that it had actually been the fire brigade who had caused the fatal blaze at 100 Sidney Street. They had deliberately set fire to the gas meter, and Churchill had forbidden any attempt to extinguish the flames.

By one of those coincidences which make life bountiful, showing at that very time at a small cinema round the corner was a film, "The Siege of Sidney Street", in which Nina was magically transformed back into the beautiful young woman of half a century before. It was passing strange to watch on the screen a young actress playing the part of the old lady I had just left. I had, in fact, invited her to come with me to see the film, but she did not want to. It had all been so long ago . . . and so sad.

Nina Vassileva died in St Bartholomew's Hospital of myocardial infarction on February 24, 1963. But her heart had been "broken" long before that.

Digging Up a Fortune

The cadaveric enterprise of Messrs Burke & Hare, specialist purveyors by appointment of basic anatomical wares to the Scottish medical profession, is, I think, too well known and widely celebrated for regurgitation, but I venture to opine that the scarcely less flagitious enterprising "corpse" barter conducted over the dead body of Alexander Turney Stewart, American multi-million-dollar department store tycoon, who died in 1876 in his marble mansion on 34th Street, New York – its site now occupied by the Empire State Building – may be satisfactorily unfamiliar.

The Stewart ascent to wealth and power was harsh and slow. An immigrant lad from Ireland, he opened a one-man drapery shop in

Lower Manhattan in 1825, when he was 22. Starting humbly as his own salesman, porter, and errand-boy, he clambered up upon the sole fuel of gritty determination, chasing after cents, and gradually, very gradually, accumulating dollars – by the hundred, by thousands, by the hundreds of thousands, to a death-bed zenith of 30 million.

Penny-pinching, avaricious, as the years mounted over his greying head, Alex T., patting his well-filled money-bags, mellowed. Turning, in the twilight of his days, a no-longer-deaf ear to the venerable religious saw, *Sic transit gloria mundi*, he envisioned his appropriately dignified *post mortem* accommodation in the polygonal, Gothic crypt of the towering Cathedral of the Incarnation, which he was in process of erecting in Garden City, one of the world's first "model towns", which he had built on land purchased on Long Island.

Man proposes, God dispossesses. On April 10, 1876, long before the cathedral dome had burgeoned aloft, Stewart had expired below, and the thwarted merchant prince had to make do with a temporary earthen bed in the graveyard of the historic church of St Mark's-in-the-Bouwerie, at Second Avenue at 10th Street and Stuyvesant, in New York City.

Situated just inside the gate and near the north-west corner of the burying-ground, the vault in which he slumbered was a large, brick-walled apartment, roofed with three marble slabs, and sunken 12 feet below the ground.

Two years went by. One hour after the moist dawn of November 7, 1878, Frank Parker, assistant sexton at St Marks', made a ghastly discovery. Beside a mound of fresh-turned clay a gaping hole yawned. The Stewart resting place had been violated. Grave robbers had chiselled through the leaden coffin shell and crudely resurrected Mr Stewart, well in advance of the Lord's appointed hour.

Not only resurrected, but also kidnapped, what they calculated to be a cadaver worth its dead-weight in gold. The plan, in short, was to hold the return to earth of the spirited away body to ransom.

A nice touch . . . the body-snatchers had carried off, like a sterling visiting-card, the solid silver name-plate on the coffin. They had taken also the coffin's silver knobs and handles, together with a triangular patch of velvet which they had cut from the casket lining.

The next day, Stewart's executor and former partner, Judge Henry Hilton, posted a $25,000 reward for the recovery of the body and conviction of the corpse-nappers. Twelve more months dragged by in silence.

Then, in January, 1879, the bereaved Mrs Cornelia Stewart received a letter from Canada. The anonymous writer made her the offer of a bizarre exchange – a bag of old bones, *aliter* the mortal remains of her, in every sense, departed husband, for $200,000.

The Widow Stewart proved herself every bit as hard and canny a bargainer as her late lamented partner. In a series of flinty communications she not only adamantinely demanded of her correspondent – operating under the *nom de guerre*, Henry G. Romaine, which was patently false and, or so the police theorised, hid the identity of either George Leonidas Leslie, the celebrated bank robber of the time, or that of Travelling Mike Grady, a well known contemporary fence – sterling proof of the authenticity of his wares, but also succeeded in beating the asking price down to $20,000.

The proof which she required was delivered in the shape of the return of the stolen silver knobs and handles from Alexander's coffin, and, final sterling silver proof, the name-plate prised from the top of the whisked-away casket.

With the support of Judge Hilton and her attorney, General Patrick H. Jones, the bargain was struck, and on a dark and moonless night one of Great Aunt Cornelia's grand-nephews set forth alone, as stipulated, in a buggy that rocked and swayed its way to the wild glades of rural Westchester County. Then, suddenly, as the buggy bowled along, a masked horseman came riding out of a thick-wooded copse. By now it was around two o'clock in the morning. He ordered the young man to drive the buggy down a lonely and deserted lane, about a mile along which a waiting wagon blocked the way. Another masked man, or, indeed, for all he knew it might have been the same man dismounted, materialised and, having offered as irrefutable earnest of his *bona fides* a piece of the velvet triangle cut from the Stewart casket, and which was accepted, the bones and "boodle" were duly exchanged.

But were the bones which, speaking both physically and metaphorically, gave off so hollow a rattle when shaken in the gunny sack in which they were handed over, really those of the kidnapped corpse of the merchant prince? We shall never know, for, oddly, perhaps because they had no wish to discover themselves to have been cheated, the Stewart family came firmly down against their being subjected to any authenticating authoritative scrutiny.

It could, of course, be that the ossicular vendors had jettisoned the Alexandrian relics *promptissimo* after their uplifting – they were, after all, hardly the most wholesome and healthful of acquisitions – and traded off later the pickings-over of an anonymous ossuary.

Returned like homing pigeons to New York City, the bones were laid reverently to rest in a zinc-lined trunk and kept under overnight guard. Then, under the pall of the next night's darkness the trunk was conveyed by special freight train to Garden City, where, transferred to a magnificent bespoke casket, they were lodged in their originally intended resting place in the cathedral crypt.

Profiting from experience – and by the advent of electricity – the Stewarts saw to it that an elaborate grave robber alarm system was installed. It was so rigged that when triggered it set a stridency of cathedral bells pealing.

Twice more the eternal sleep of Alexander Turney Stewart was to be disturbed. In 1905, and again in 1908, the bells jangled a clamorous warning. On both occasions the culprit was a short circuit.

Since then . . . the rest is silence.

The Mystery of a Mancunian Growler

In criminal literature and life the homely hansom cab has proved the vehicle of much mystery and mischief.

It was a New Zealand fledgling barrister, Fergus Hume, who, in 1886, published the world-wide bestseller, his Gaboriau-like *The Mystery of a Hansom Cab*.

It was in a hansom, rattling along West Broadway early one June morning in 1904, that Nan Patterson, "the handsome alumna of the 'Florodora' sextette," put finally paid with a bullet to the account of Caesar Young, New York gambler and gay blade.

And the hansom jingles all through the pages of the case books of Sherlock Holmes.

But the great Mancunian exercise in venenation of 1889, was staged, not in a hansom, but in a growler, as four-wheeled, horse drawn cabs were then popularly known.

At 6.50 pm on Tuesday, February 26, 1889, a gentleman accompanied by a youth of eighteen hailed a four-wheeler at Oliver Cromwell's statue, near Manchester Cathedral steps, and ordered the cabby to drive them to the Three Arrows public-house, in Deansgate, where he told him to wait outside.

The oddly-assorted couple emerged some fifteen or twenty minutes later and instructed the cabman to take them to 43 Stretford Road. As they were proceeding at a smart trot down one of Manchester's busiest thoroughfares, a man on the pavement shouted: "A young fellow's just jumped out of your cab and run down Cambridge Street."

Fearful of being bilked, the cabby leapt from the box, noticing as he did so that the nearside cab door was swinging open. Gazing in, he was relieved to see the older man still there – albeit slumped insensible upon the leather. He lifted him up and rubbed his ears to awaken him. In an apparently stupefied state of intoxication, his only response was, "Go away, and leave us alone."

The cabby found a policeman, who examined the flaked-out fare, got into the cab beside him, and told the driver to head for Albert Street Police Station. But on the way there the constable became anxious and said they had better go instead to Manchester Infirmary.

Upon arrival there, the man was found to be dead. Since no marks of violence or anything to arouse medical suspicion were displayed, the house surgeon, Dr Barker, took the view that death had probably resulted from alcoholic poisoning. A post-mortem stoutly confirmed the bull-necked subject's addiction to ardent spirits – the habitual drinker's liver – but it was not until Manchester's public analyst had completed his tests that the cause of death was established. Poison. Chloral hydrate.

That chloroform-related sedative is the nearest thing to the fictive Mickey Finn. A spoonful in a seaman's drink was the "Knock-out drops" used by press gangs shanghaiing sailor-men for the tall ships. In tough seaport pubs the world around, the landlord would have a bottle of chloral behind the bar for slipping into the troublemaker's glass before he could wreck the premises.

The police were called in. The Manchester Force's most celebrated detective, Jerome Caminada, of Italian descent, born in a Manchester slum, knew every inch and character of the city's underworld. First of all, he identified the dead man. He turned out to be a personality well known on 'Change; senior partner in a big Lancashire firm of paper

manufacturers. He was also a Lancashire County councillor and a
Justice of the Peace.

A widower, he had left his house, some distance from the city,
early on February 26, intending to stay a few days in Knutsford. He
had spent the morning in his firm's Manchester office, which he left
at 1 pm, saying that he was going to the Mitre Hotel, near the cathedral, where the sale of a mill was taking place. He was seen there by
several friends, one of whom he arranged to meet at Sinclair's restaurant, Victoria Market, at 7 pm. He did not turn up.

Caminada learned that the deceased was then wearing a watch and
chain worth about £120, and carrying a purse containing gold. But the
corpse had empty pockets and no watch and chain. Clearly, the youth
had robbed him. Upon investigation, No 43 Stretford Street proved to
be a tailor's lock-up shop. The tailor knew neither the older, nor the
younger man. Caminada set out to track the fleet-footed youth. He
managed to cobble together a description of sorts from a selection of
shaky eye-witnesses who had seen the lad and his plucking chicken
together – about 5 ft. 2 in. tall; fresh complexion; no side-whiskers or
moustache; age about 22; dark brown suit; pot hat.

Caminada soldiered grimly on. Found a young man whose appear-
ance seemed to chime, who had visited the York Minster, Higher
Chatham Street. Found the cabby who had driven him thence to the
Locomotive Inn, Oldham Road.

This inn was a noted watering-hole of the pugilist fraternity.
Plugging in to his unique local knowledge, Caminada raked through
in search of anyone of the wanted youth's description who had
connections with the square ring. And came up with Charlie, the 18-
year-old son of "Pig Jack" Parton.

"Pig Jack", a fighting man, retired, had previously kept a beer-
house in Greengate, Salford, resort of dubious ex-pugilists,
racecourse rogues, and a gallimaufry of vagabonds, where, Caminada
recalled, it was strongly rumoured that customers were drugged with
some substance laced into their beer, and, if they had anything worth
the taking, like as not robbed.

Young Parton was duly pulled in on spec. Vehemently he protested
his innocence. Loudly he proclaimed his alibi. He had been in
Liverpool. And that was Charlie's big mistake. It clanged a bell in
Caminada's memory.

The Manchester police had received notification from the

Liverpool Force that a young man was being sought for the theft of a bottle of chloral from a Liverpool chemist's shop. Forthwith, Caminada went to Liverpool and interviewed the chemist. A week to the day before the Hackney Cab Poisoning, a young man had come into his shop asking for 40grs of chloral. Without a doctor's prescription they could not be supplied.

His anguished plea for even 10grs, as his mother was suffering from *angina pectoris*, had succeeded, but while the chemist was weighing them out, the man leaned over the counter, picked up the bottle containing a pound of chloral, and ran off. The chemist subsequently identified Charles Parton.

Put up at St George's Hall, Liverpool, on a charge of murder, young Parton was sentenced to die – he had sacrificed his life for the thin gain of a gold watch and chain and the loose change in a rich man's pockets,

Within a whisker of taking the eight o'clock walk at Liverpool's Walton Gaol, Parton's wavering luck changed. Sentence of death was commuted to one of penal servitude for life.

The April Fool's Day Murder

Not since, factually, Mr George Lusk, of Whitechapel, opened his nice little package from (allegedly) Jack the Ripper on October 16, 1888, and, fictively, Miss Susan Cushing, of Cross Street, Croydon, received, one August day in the late 1880s – as reported by Dr John H. Watson in his account of Mr Sherlock Holmes' case, chronicled as "The Adventure of the Cardboard Box" – her small and gruesome packet, had a more grisly parcel been delivered by post than that which arrived upon the desk of Herr Weitzel, Chief of Police of Vienna, on April 1, 1926.

In Mr Lusk's package, a square cardboard box, glistened half a human kidney, "prasarved" in spirits of wine. In Miss Cushing's packet, a cardboard box filled with coarse salt, nestled two freshly severed human ears. In Herr Weitzel's parcel lay a human finger.

This proved upon closer examination to be the first finger of a right hand. Slender, smooth, uncalloused, with a well-manicured and polished nail, there could be no mistaking the fact that it came from the hand of a middle-aged woman. It had, moreover, been amputated recently, and with obvious surgical skill.

Bearing in mind the date, April 1, April Fool's Day, Chief Weitzel was more than half inclined to believe that he had been the butt of a joker, most likely an over-exuberant medical student or a disgruntled mortuary attendant, either of whom had easy access to such *reliquiae humanae*.

Officially, however, he could make no such assumption. He had to order a serious investigation. His men were accordingly instructed to rake over the lists of missing persons and to do the round of the mortuaries.

While the Chief's men were buzzing busily about Vienna, his ponderings as he sat at his desk were interrupted by the arrival of another personally addressed parcel. He opened it gingerly and not without unpleasant presentiments. They proved only too well justified. It contained another human finger.

This, the third or middle finger, obviously from the same right hand – analysis showed the nail polish to be identical – was to yield a more telling crop of helpful clues.

On the finger was a plain, 22-carat, gold ring. This ring displayed on its underside a series of small marks, minute scratches, tiny indentations, which the forensic scientists readily identified as resultant from the action of a diluted corrosive acid. Experience leading them, the scientists decided that the acid had most probably been used to remove a tattoo.

In order to establish if this was so, it was necessary to peel off the top skin of the finger. At this stage a horrifying discovery was made. Presuming, as they now were, that what they were dealing with was the evidence of a murder, the finger had actually been amputated while its owner was still alive.

The superficial skin cut away, the pathologist could plainly make out the representation of a snake, which curled around the finger in the exact spot that had been covered by the gold ring.

Weitzel's men were forthwith despatched upon another exploratory canvass – to visit all the tattoo parlours of Vienna, and identify that in which the snake had been tattooed on, and that in which it had subsequently been acid stripped off. They failed in their quest. Neither were they able to trace the jeweller's whence the gold ring had originally come.

But enlightenment, albeit of a most disagreeable, not to say nauseous, kind, was close at hand.

A week went by. No more female fingers in the mail. Then, in a swamp on the outskirts of Vienna, the headless body of a middle-aged woman was found. Eagerly the detectives scanned the right hand of the cadaver. Sure enough, the first and third fingers were missing, carved off with a skilfully manipulated surgical instrument.

To everybody's acute disappointment, the torso supplied not the smallest hint as to its identity. The police did make one hopeful discovery, though. In the soft mud close to the body was a single footprint. A plaster cast of it was painstakingly taken, and an anthropologist was called in to see what he could deduce from it. He made careful calculations and announced: "You are looking for a man over six feet tall. He has broad shoulders and long arms." Not a lot – but better than nothing.

Armed with this fresh, though somewhat scanty, information, Chief Weitzel's boys went off in search of a tall doctor, preferably a surgeon. They found several to fill the bill. Then set about eliminating them. Eventually they had narrowed things down to a field of one – Dr Herman Schmitz.

The first thing that they learned about him, checking his record, was that he had been criminally charged with medical malpractice. A jury had, however, brought in a verdict of not guilty. Even so, his practice had suffered; clearly his patients had not all shared the jury's view. Starting again from scratch, he had gradually built up a small but extremely lucrative practice, attending upon wealthy patients who had no notion of his dubious past.

Herr Doktor Schmitz's domestic set-up and extra-marital life were now put under the *Polizei* microscope. There was a Frau Schmitz. There were little Schmitzes of school age. There was, as the cynical detectives had suspected there would be, a mistress. All they had to do now was to find that the lady had vanished. They found, instead, herself – alive and well.

Frustrated but unvanquished, bloody but unbowed, Weitzel's force embarked upon a long and tedious surveillance routine, tailing the doctor, his wife, and his mistress twenty-four hours a day. And it paid off.

It led them to a dress shop where Schmitz's mistress had a charge account. The shopman was questioned. Ah, yes! Dr Schmitz's lady friend. Not a patch on her predecessor, Anna Stein. A pain, in fact. A positive pain. Fräulein Stein had been a much better customer, purchased far more expensive dresses. Her address? He readily supplied it.

The detectives "proceeded" at full pelt to her apartment. No sign of Anna. She had vacated the place all of three weeks ago, they were told. A dragnet operation at her known haunts produced a similar blank result.

Her indisputable whereabouts came to light when they carried out a secret search of Schmitz's consulting rooms. In a small laboratory adjoining, they found Anna's head reposing in a bucket of preservative.

The doctor never stood trial. Attempting to escape from the prison where he was being held on pre-trial remand, he crashed from the roof and died on the ground, but not before confessing his guilt.

The Viennese "mind doctors" wondered, scratched their heads. Whatever possessed Schmitz to post those fingers to Chief Weitzel? The alienists could come up with only one psychiatric explanation: he had never forgiven the police for their investigation of the malpractice charge against him, and wanted to make them appear foolish and incompetent. His retributory catharsis cost him his life.

The Great Defender's First Murder Case

Edward Marshall Hall, generally tagged as a poorish lawyer and gifted exponent of the histrionic school of advocacy, was of 10 years' call and in a fair way of practice when "The Duchess" came into his legal life. His introduction to her was via that most curious, not to say dubious, London solicitor, the subsequently disgraced Arthur Newton, and a brief marked 10 guineas.

The lady's title was a bestowal from her strumpet days in Piccadilly, a tribute to the grandeur and generosity of her manner and modus. She was a creature of considerable attraction, petite and pretty, of the stamp of Dresden china, whose figure, looks, and charming, Austrian-tinged English easily captivated the spruce Victorian mashers who raked the West End coverts for game.

But by the time that Fate delivered her into the professional hands of Marshall Hall, for Marie Hermann the days of wine and roses had long since flown. Although by the calendar's reckoning only 43, too much champagne and brandy, too many romantic vassals that passed in a night, had dissipated her fine looks, etched the hard lines, and spread the cruel patina of harsh wear across her face. Shrivelled now, rather than petite, emaciated, which emphasised a pointed chin, thin, compressed lips, and little beady grey eyes, nature no longer accoutred her as temptress.

Impoverished, too, her "presents" swallowed up in the support of her three children, one of them tragically blind, she had retreated to one of those lost institutions of the Victorian period, a rented room, precursor of the now also vanished bed-sitter.

Marie Hermann's room was on the first floor of 51 Grafton Street, Tottenham Court Road. At 11 o'clock on the night of March 15, 1894, Louise Hutchins and her mother, who lived on the second floor of No 51, heard loud noises, followed by a man's moaning, "Murder! Murder! Murder!", coming from the room below.

In true English fashion, they "kept themselves to themselves". Louise went off to the ball for which she had been dressing. Her mother, afterwards creeping down the stairs, heard a man say: "My five pounds. Give me that five pounds."

Later, there was a very loud crash.

Running to the stairs, Mrs Hutchins heard a woman with a foreign accent saying: "Did you hurt yourself, dear? Speak! Speak! Speak!"

At about 3.30 am there was another great crash. After that, the old house filled up with an almost palpable silence.

Next morning two things happened. Mrs Hutchins found blood in the communal sink. Mrs Hermann told Mrs Hutchins that she was leaving, and a big black trunk suddenly appeared on the scene.

Sure enough, the following day Mrs Hermann departed. An inquisitive and suspicious Mrs Hutchins dogged her to her new quarters – 56 Upper Marylebone Road – and then went to the police.

Sergeant Kane, long acquainted with Marie Hermann, went to her new lodgings, forced the black trunk . . . and inside was huddled the bloodied corpse of an old man.

Mrs Hermann was arrested.

Enter Marshall Hall.

His client had told a tale . . . I picked him up on the Euston Road, took him home. He had no money. She had refused to proceed. He was drunk. There was a struggle. He grabbed her by the throat. Picked up the poker. She wrested it from him and hit him over the head with it.

The dead man was Henry Stephens, retired cab-owner, in his 71st year.

The evidence against the prisoner was formidable. And to make matters worse, Mrs Hermann, who, on March 15 had been hard-up and pawning things, appeared flush on March 16 and 17, displaying gold and notes in her hitherto threadbare purse.

Stephens' son, also Henry, testified that his father always carried money, and had drawn out £50 shortly before his murder.

The prisoner at least harboured no delusions as to the likelihood of her fate. "I shall be hung," she moaned. And no one disabused her.

Hall had but two evidential gifts: a piece of hair found in clotted blood on the mantelshelf, and the prison doctor's testimony of discovering twelve bruises on the prisoner's neck.

Discrediting opposition evidence was the name of the game. He had to undermine the son, who gave his murdered father so glowing a character; Mrs Hutchins and Louise, who reported the overhearing of tellingly interpreted snatches of conversation; Mrs Bricknell, the fellow-lodger, who, said the accused, had helped her to cram the 16-stone corpse into the trunk, and, in obedience to some strange superstition, had thrown in a thimble, all of which Mrs B stentorianly denied. He had, too, to best, or neutralise, the prosecution doctors.

Hall began by establishing the victim as a man of abnormal physical strength and violent temper, known to ill-use women and to be concerned in the affairs of a disorderly house in Albany Street, wherein he lived and of which his wife was the Madam.

The Hutchins's were most respectable, but not necessarily unprejudiced, witnesses. From Mrs Hutchins he elicited the admission that she regarded his client with loathing and abhorrence. Louise was not sure that the word she had heard was "murder". His cross-examination of Mrs Bricknell, whom he led to admit that she had accepted presents from Mrs Hermann and had drunk with her during the night, failed to shake her as regards her part in the packaging of the body, but nevertheless had its intended effect upon the jury.

Next came the prosecution medical witness, Dr Lloyd. Hall

manoeuvred him to agree that old Stephens *must* have seized Mrs Hermann from the front *before* the poker blows were delivered. That disposed of Lloyd's theory that the blows over the right ear were delivered from behind – which would have scuttled the case for self-defence or misadventure. Mr Pepper contended that Stephens was sitting down when he was struck. The prosecution witnesses were disagreeing.

There was no haze of doubt about Hall's crystalline defence submission. The deceased was drunk. He forced the prisoner to the ground. Seized her with both hands around her throat. In her frenzy, her right arm pinned beneath her bulky attacker's weight, she stretched out her left hand, grabbed the poker and delivered six blows in rapid succession on the right side of the head, in self-defence. He was clearly trying for manslaughter.

Finally, his classic peroration – dated but dazzling.

Tears pouring down his cheeks, he told the jury: "Remember that these women are what men make them; even this woman was at one time a beautiful and innocent child." He paused. Flinging an arm in the direction of the crushed and sobbing piece of human wreckage huddled in the dock: "Look at her, gentlemen of the jury. Look at her. God never gave her a chance – won't you?"

It was the first capital case that Hall had conducted on his own.

Marie Hermann's was the first life that he saved from the gallows.

The Murder of "Old Shakespeare"

April, the cruellest month, in the year of Our Sovereign Lady the Queen Victoria, 1891, and the reverberations of yet another Jack the Ripper crime victim, Frances Coles – not really Jack this time, but no matter – are being felt all round the world. In New York, that exceptionally well-pleased-with-himself police officer, Inspector Thomas Byrnes, was trumpeting it about that if a killer of Jack's ilk so much as raised his head, sniffed the air even, in *his* bailiwick, within thirty-six hours at most he'd be banged-up in the Tombs.

Well . . . he was to have his chance.

In the filibustering days of the 1890s, there stood at the south-east corner of Catherine Slip and Water Street, on the Manhattan water-front, a mouldering wreck of a building grandly named the East River Hotel. A squalid drinking-cum-bawdy house, it was the run-down resort of run-down, exceedingly lowly folk.

At nine o'clock on Friday morning, April 24, 1891, Eddie Harrington, the hotel's night clerk, was making his round of the rooms, rapping at doors, rousting out the overnights who had paid their 25 cents and were now overstaying their grudging welcome. In fact, most of the denizens of this unsavoury dive had already picked up their paper parcels and carrier bags and shuffled blear-eyed out into the blinding daylight dazzle sheening off New York's East River. But at the locked door of Room 31 Harrington encountered a problem. He tapped. No reply. He rapped loudly. No reply. Using his pass-key, he opened the door.

Sprawled on the floor next to the bed lay the body of a woman. She had been strangled and slashed, flesh shredded, like a Ripper victim. Into her thigh had been carved a cross. The weapon that had wrought all the havoc – a filed-down cooking knife – was lying there beside the savaged corpse. Pulling himself together, Harrington called in the police.

The murdered woman turned out to be a well-known local character, a raffish sexagenarian (to quote Alexander Woollcott), Mrs Carrie Brown, widow of a Salem, Massachusetts, sea-captain, feeding an alcohol addiction by prostitution. Known to her intimates as Jeff Davis, she was jocosely hailed far and wide as "Old Shakespeare", because of her habit of reciting from the works of the Bard in her cups. She had been an amateur actress in her youth.

Her story was a pathetic one. After her husband's death she had taken to drink, and to avoid local scandal had moved to New York, where she had resorted to street-walking to pay for her liquor.

Next day's newspapers blared the news: Jack the Ripper had crossed the Atlantic. Now the hour had struck for the boastful Byrnes. He had to – and he did – make good his boast. Within the prescribed 36 hours he had his man under lock and key.

His man was a little Algerian, Ameer Ben Ali, known in his haunts along the water-front as "Frenchy". There was but one small shadow of doubt fleetingly blurring the noble profile of Byrnes's exemplary arrest. Witnesses spoke of Old Shakespeare's arrival at the hotel at around 11 pm on the arm of a blond-haired seaman, half her age, who registered as "C Knick", with whom, and a tin pail of beer, she had retired to Room 31.

Several of the hotel hang-abouts had seen him and described him as a "medium-sized, stocky, blond seafaring man." Ali was small and *brun*. Not to be thwarted, the police countered: Old Shakespeare's sailor had left her before dawn. Ali, occupying Room 33 opposite, had crept across to 31 after the sailor's departure, killed and mutilated the old woman, and stolen her meagre earnings.

Evidence? A trail of blood drops on the floor between Rooms 31 and 34, blood marks on both sides of Frenchy's door, on the floor of his room, on his bed, a chair and his socks. Furthermore, two fellow-prisoners of his when he had been serving a term for vagrancy that April in the Queens County Jail, testified to his possession of a knife similar to that used in the murder. Finally, some of Carrie Brown's professional sisters said that Frenchy was one of her regulars, and had occupied No 31 with her only the previous week.

Put up on trial on June 24, 1891, Ali professed to speak no English; only Algerian Arabic. New York was scoured for an interpreter and, amazingly, a man from Ali's native Algerian village was found.

Among the bizarre prosecution assertions was the witness of Dr Formand, of Philadelphia, who testified that in samples of blood found both on the bed and in that allegedly scraped from under Frenchy's finger-nails – one examiner uttered the famous line, "Why, it may be human gore," – he had found that analysis proved that Old Shakespeare's last meal had consisted of corned beef, cabbage, and cheese. Just how he achieved this remarkable forensic result from the finger-nail scrapings he failed to reveal.

Francis L. Wellman, who most vigorously prosecuted, erecting a case built foursquare upon the dubious finger-nail scrapings data, went on to write a bestselling legal classic, *The Art of Cross-Examination* (1903).

Ali was found guilty of second-degree murder, the jury by that verdict making manifest their grave doubts, and was sentenced to serve life in Sing Sing.

But there were those, both in the police as well as out, who were not happy with the verdict. Serious doubts were expressed as to whether there had been a blood trail between Ali's room and the murder chamber when Harrington first discovered the body. Had accident or design placed it there later? Moreover, rumours strongly persisted among New York seafaring men that Old Shakespeare's killer had quietly gone to sea and sailed off to the Far East.

Then, all unexpectedly, a remarkable discovery. It was as if someone had found the veritable room in which Jack the Ripper had indisputably honed his knife and his blood-lust.

It was established that a man answering to the description of Old Shakespeare's tryster had been absent from his quarters in Cranford, New Jersey, on the night of the Shakespearean despatch. His abandoned room had been searched and therein was found a bloodied shirt and a brass key bearing a tag marked "31". Tried in the lock of Room 31 at the East River Hotel, the key opened the door.

Frenchy, released and pardoned after ten years, irresistibly reminding one of the Oscar Slater case, returned to his Algerian village, vowing, understandably, never to set foot on American soil again.

It is pleasant to report that Old Shakespeare recovered in death her life's lost respectability. Her corpse, restored by the mortician's creepy artifice to some semblance of peaceful dignity, was shipped for burial to Salem by her daughter, a respectable matron of that witch-haunted town.

To Meet Miss O'Dare

The old judge – Sir Travers Humphreys, aged 84 – read with considerable interest the paragraph in the London newspaper that September day in 1951.

Headed "The Mystery of Josephine O'Dare", it recounted the proceedings at an inquest held in the Westminster Coroner's Court upon the body of a 50-year-old woman who had died from barbituric poisoning – a self-administered overdose, taken in circumstances not fully disclosed by the evidence. An open verdict had been recorded. The dead woman's name was given as Joan Brookes.

Humphreys J remembered that name: it was the one that the young woman whom he, led by Sir Archibald Bodkin, had prosecuted at the Bailey back in March, 1927, had adopted when she emerged from prison to return to society and start a new life.

The years between dissolved.

We are back in the 1920s, and a very strange story comes slowly into focus. There was at that time a young unmarried woman, self-described as an Irish heiress, who had established herself as a very popular hostess in London Society. Lords and ladies, and some names of the highest birth and repute, flocked to the lavish parties which she threw, in true '20s spirit, at her elegant Mayfair flat.

But there were those – and they included the police authorities – who harboured deep suspicion as to the source of her seemingly boundless wealth.

Time has indeed shown their instinctive misgivings well-founded. For subsequent, closer inspection, of the so-beguiling young heiress' background and credentials has revealed her true identity and station.

Her real name was Theresa Agnes Skyrne, and she was the youngest of the six children of a farm labourer, of Withington, in Herefordshire. Having as a young girl enjoyed no very good repuation in her native rustic environs, it is perhaps not very surprising that when, in her teens, she thrust herself upon the metropolitan scene in her heiress pose, it was initially to consort with the criminal refuse of the Great Wen.

Possessed of considerable personal charm, passing good looks and high intelligence, she had, by judicious application of her qualities, soon settled herself comfortably in fashionable London.

In 1924, by which time she was living in Knightsbridge, Miss O'Dare inserted an advertisement in a newspaper seeking a butler who would be willing to accompany her abroad. In this way she made contact with a Mr George Poole, who, until he had the misfortune to become entangled with her, had been a thrifty, hard-working, and conscientious man. His late employer had left Poole £1,000 in token of his well appreciated loyal and zealous service, and this, together with his life-savings of a further £1,400, made George a plushy bird for the O'Dare plucking. It took her less than six months to relieve the downy one of every last vestige of his plumage.

In the early months of 1925, our anti-heroine moved on to Mayfair. There she rented a luxurious Park Lane maisonette, wherein, it was said, that while entertaining as to the manner born some of the absolute cream of aristocratic London Society in her upper floor drawing-room, below stairs there flourished nothing less than a thieves' kitchen, with Madam equally at home in either domain.

All unsuspected, the elegant Miss O'Dare was actually a member of a six-strong gang of "rapacious parasites", the leader of which was a man named Davis. Like herself, of respectable working-class origin, Davis had come out of the army with an excellent character and blameless record. He had, however, taken to serious crime in civvy street. He had the ability to present himself plausibly as a man of wealth and station and he had successfully passed muster as Lord St Helier and Captain Danvers, DSO.

But the Davis reverse was something very different. There is evidence that he was a dangerous ruffian who treated O'Dare with brutality, and when, in 1926, she was made bankrupt in the sum of £11,000, and possessed nothing, he obtained money for himself by selling to a newspaper a series of articles exposing Josephine O'Dare as the penniless and unprincipled adventuress which, of course, she was.

It was when he had emerged in 1925, after serving a third term of imprisonment, that he picked up the threads of an old association with O'Dare, and the pair, enthusiastically supported by four accomplices, embarked on a fruitful partnership. Their get-rich-double-quick scheme depended upon the pilfering by the accomplices of correspondence from business letter-boxes. All cheques thus acquired were duly endorsed by brilliant Davis forgeries and paid in to a series of modest accounts opened in various branch banks. It was calculated that, in this way, they had netted well in excess of £20,000 – and those were the days when that really was big money.

The fantasy world of Josephine O'Dare came tumbling down in March, 1927, when that cool, cool lady was charged with the forging of a will, on the strength of which she had obtained the sums of £650 from each of two firms of money-lenders. She was accused also of having issued three forged cheques.

The will in question was that of an elderly Birmingham solicitor, Edwin Docker, (whose mistress she had been), and in it she had been left £15,000. As a document purporting to have been drafted by a lawyer and set down in his own hand, and which, incidentally, lacked an attestation clause, it positively shouted "Fraud!"

Put up at the Old Bailey, O'Dare pleaded guilty, and it was decided that she should be called as a prosecution witness against her fellow-accused, Davis, and another, Morton. She was, Humphreys recalled, one of the most convincing performers in the witness-box that he had ever listened to. She had, moreover, the sound sense not to minimise the part that she herself had played in the chicanery. The more vigorously she was cross-examined, the more plainly was it demonstrated that her evidence was, in the main, the simple and unvarnished truth. She neither side-stepped nor sought to avoid frontal attack.

Yes, forging Docker's will had been her idea. She had taken the document along to Davis in a restaurant. No, she had not needed to give him any specific instructions. He knew only too well what it was that was required of him.

Her co-accused, Morton, freely admitted that he had signed as an attesting witness to the will – but only because Miss O'Dare had come to him in great distress, swearing that the old man had been too ill to have had it witnessed.

Her cooperation with the prosecution notwithstanding, the Recorder of London, Sir Ernest Wild, sentenced O'Dare to four and a half years' imprisonment. Davis, because of his record of previous convictions, received 12 years, and Morton three years.

Nearly a quarter of a century was to pass before Josephine O'Dare emerged from the shadows again . . . and then it was only to pass briefly through the light of print into the permanent shadow of an elected premature death.

The Netley Lucas Story

In June, 1940, a man named Robert Tracy was found dead in the burned-out lounge of the furnished house that he had rented at Fetcham, near Leatherhead, in Surrey. The searchers found only one body, but in the smoke and smother there perished also Evelyn Graham, Leslie Graham, Victor Stanley, Lady Angela Stanley, and Mrs Charlotte Cavendish.

The corpse was not that of Robert Tracy, for he, like all the other victims of the flames, was just a name, adopted and used for his fell purposes by the man whose body it really was – Netley Lucas, Class One con man, responsible for some of the most impudent literary frauds of the 20th century, including the first biography of Darling J, and a positive plethora of royal life stories.

Lucas embarked upon what was to be a life of crime – and I don't mean just the writing of a respectable corpus of true crime books – in

1917, at the age of 14. That was when he was expelled from his public school for stealing and forging his housemaster's signature.

Like the dyed-in-the-genes psychopath that he turned out to be, Lucas, unseemly soon, found himself in trouble again. This time it was for obtaining money by false pretences from the secretary of a London club.

Standing, a bright, rosy-cheeked lad, in the dock at the magistrates' court, he was about to be given a first, premature, taste of prison. Having, when arrested and charged, overstated his age as 16, he was accordingly remanded to Brixton. Had he given his correct age, he would have gone to an under-sixteens remand home. Found guilty on his next appearance before the magistrates, he was duly packed off to a boys' home, from which he rapidly decamped.

Re-arrested in the Strand, where he had got in with a particularly low and vicious local group, he was despatched pronto to a reformatory ship. Once again, very little time elapsed before he jumped ship, and thereafter, convicted once more, this time for stealing cheques and obtaining credit by fraud, he was sentenced to a term in the original Borstal Institution, near Rochester.

Released in 1922, still in his teens, he commenced to live a life of boringly regular petty crime – forgery, defrauding young women by offering them bogus jobs, and resorting to plain thieving. He was vintage con man material: good looks, gentlemanly good manners, a cultivated accent. His thievery earned him an appearance, and a ten-month sentence, at the Old Bailey. Back in circulation, he next favoured Canada with his presence, and went down there for running a crooked employment agency, serving his time at Toronto's Gaol Farm. It was now that Lucas took to using his pen for writing instead of forgery, and, in 1925, T. Fisher Unwin brought out his first book, *The Autobiography of a Crook*, fulsomely dedicated: "To those who buy this book, thereby giving the author a chance to start afresh."

Starting afresh, he followed his factional autobiography with a second volume, *Crooks: Confessions*, in 1925, and a further trio of true life crime books in 1926, *Criminal Paris, London and Its Criminals*, and *Crook Janes*, this latter being a study of "the ladies of the under-world". During the writing of it, he had met the notorious gunwoman, Chicago May Churchill, and, in 1928, with his accustomed flair and flamboyance, he announced his engagement to May. When reporters queried: "You know May's over 50?" the 25-year-old Lucas parried:

"Well, she's a blonde, and a man in the toils of a beautiful, fascinating, and unscrupulous woman has no power to control his own actions." Of course it was a put-up publicity job. May was actually 53, when, the following year (1929), she died alone in a Philadelphia boarding-house.

There were, after 1926, no more books by Netley Lucas. However, in 1929, a new author, Evelyn Graham, made his bow with a most impressive "authentic biography" of Darling J, "prepared (for publication) under the personal supervision of Lord Darling". This was followed, two years later, by an equally impressive Evelyn Graham volume, *Fifty Years of Famous Judges*.

It was towards the end of 1930, that a well known London literary agent received a letter from Lady Angela Stanley. She was, she wrote, a former lady-in-waiting to Queen Alexandra, and wished to offer for publication an intimate life of Her Late Majesty, compiled from her experiences at Court. The manuscript was promptly accepted by Messrs Harrap, who, upon inquiring as to whether her ladyship's writings had the approval of the royal family, received a note from Victor Stanley, enclosing a letter of confirmation from Lord Stanfordham, private secretary to King George V.

Now it so happened that, at this precise juncture, there began to appear a series of articles in a national newspaper inquiring pertinently into the affairs of Evelyn Graham, who, in the course of the last couple of years, had made a name – and some £20,000 – for himself as the author of bestselling biographies, including those of the Prince of Wales, Princess Mary, the King of Spain, Queen Ena of Spain, and King Albert of the Belgians. As a result of matters raised by these articles, Chief Detective Inspector Percy Smith of Scotland Yard was called in to investigate. It did not take him long to discover that Evelyn Graham, producer of more than two dozen biographies of royal personages – most of them unauthorised, whatever they claimed – as well as Lady Angela and Mrs Charlotte Cavendish, author of a life of Queen Mary, were all Netley Lucas, and that the Stanfordham letter was a forgery. Lucas had, apparently, put together a stable of skilled ghost writers, who did the literary donkey work.

Perhaps his most audacious exploitation was his pirating of the memoirs of *M*. Alfred Morain, former Prefect of Police in Paris. He had them translated, and then sold them to a London publisher, Jarrolds, and syndicated extracts to a newspaper in New York. Out of all this, Morain never received a single franc.

Smith arrested Lucas, then calling himself Leslie Graham and living with a lady friend at a studio flat at the Fulham end of the Kings Road, on a charge of obtaining £225 – Lady Angela's advance on royalties – by false pretences. Tried at the Old Bailey before Sir Ernest Wild, he was sentenced to 18 months.

When he came out, Lucas wrote under his own name a highly coloured autobiography, *My Selves*. And that would seem to have been his last literary effort, although with so far-flung and multi-nominate an author, it is not easy to be sure before, at the appallingly early age of 37, he went out, as we have seen, in a characteristic blaze of high drama.

Whatever Became of Father Borynski?

It is 53 years this July 13, since the Polish priest chanted the Latin Mass and vanished miraculously into the vast maw of space, leaving the presbytery in Little Horton as empty as the Easter tomb.

The solid facts in this puzzling case are sparse. Here they are.

At 4 pm on Monday, July 13, 1953, the telephone in the priest's house began to ring, and kept on ringing insistently. His housekeeper, Mrs Irena Beck, answered it. A man with a strong foreign accent politely asked if he might speak to Father Borynski, who was the Roman Catholic chaplain to the thousand-strong Polish community which, since the war, had settled in this quiet suburb of Bradford, and the priest came from his study to take the call. As Father Borynski put down the receiver, Mrs Beck heard him say: "Now this has come. I go." Seizing his hat and a light overcoat, and with only 10 shillings in his pocket, he went briskly out of the house without another word.

Watched by his housekeeper, he walked up the road, turned right past a hospital, and was lost to view. He was seen a minute or two later at a street corner a 100 yards away from his home, but from that moment to this he has never been heard of again, alive or dead.

As the tally of days of inexplicable absence mounted, a thoroughly worried Mrs Beck telephoned the local Bradford City Police. They viewed the 42-year-old priest's disappearance extremely seriously. Both Scotland Yard and MI5 were called in. Misgiving increased manifoldly when, upon investigation, it was discovered that the vanished priest had left behind him his missal, the prayer book containing his divine office, his crucifix, his certificate of ordination, his wallet, all his clothes, and £300 in his bank account.

The local community, Father Borynski's parishioners, harboured not the least doubt about what had happened; their priest had been kidnapped and murdered by the Communists, whose agents were widely supposed to be present and festering in the Bradford of the time. The good father had ever and obdurately opposed them and their atheistic doctrines. The text by which he preached was always that of the urging of his parishioners, all of them exiles from Poland, never to return home to live as victims of the dictatorship of a Stalin-backed regime. Doubtless, his corpse had been cunningly disposed of, carefully concealed somewhere remote upon the bracken-covered Yorkshire moors that swept down to the very town's rim of Bradford.

There were other theories, though. That he took his own life at some lonely spot. That he had returned secretly, of his own volition and free will, to his home in Poland. Questions were put in the House of Commons. Captain Henry Kerby, Member for Arundel, a Russian speaker who was well known for his practical experience in the Russian Baltic Provinces and an acknowledged authority on Polish and Lithuanian affairs, met the stone-wall response that "it would not be in the public interest" to make full disclosure.

Descending from the heights of international espionage and such like significant skulduggery, the suspicion was bruited abroad in Bradford that Borynski's predecessor, Father Boleslaw Martynelles, bitterly resented his replacement by his young, active, dynamic successor, and he had undeniably moved over into retirement amid communal rancour and jealousy. This led to an ill-feeling split between the Poles and the Lithuanians, a rift so serious that it built up into a rapidly escalating feud which threatened to destroy the entire community. The theory was born that, activated by jealousy and profound dislike, Father Martynelles had eliminated his rival.

Logistically, this was a non-starter. Martynelles was old and in failing health. He quite simply had not the physical capacity in his infirmity to have disposed of the 6 ft, 14-stone cadaver.

Martynelles was in no ignorance of cruel rumour's accusations. "The police think I murdered Father Borynski," he told reporters on August 11, 1953. "1 did nothing of the sort." Just under five weeks later, on the following September 12, he was dead of a thrombosis.

Curiously, not long after Borynski's disappearance, Martynelles had claimed that he had been attacked, and that he had found, spelled out in matchsticks on his table, the cautionary message, "Be silent, priest." He subsequently came to think that he could in his nervous state have imagined the attack, and that he might have unconsciously laid out the matchstick message himself.

The kidnap by Red agents theory proved no more persuasive to substantiation, although sightings of Father Borynski, looking "grey with fear", were reported from Oldham, in Lancashire, and from Glasgow. He was said to have been in the company of "sinister men". These men had also been seen hustling him into a big, black car, which had drawn up near the presbytery and been driven off at speed, heading in the general direction of London.

It was said that when, two days later, the Russian vessel *Gribojedov* sailed for Leningrad, two mysterious extra passengers had been swiftly smuggled on to her. One of these men was, it was claimed, a professional assassin, who, working for the Polish Communists, had liquidated, with cyanide pellets fired from a gas pistol, two important Russian refugees attempting to make their escape to Germany. The other was Father Borynski, who was murdered by the professional assassin aboard the *Gribojedov*. His body had been cut up into tiny pieces and fed through the coin-sized holes that opened into the ship's boilers.

By 1959, even the most optimistic members of Father Borynski's flock had abandoned their long-cherished hope, if not belief, that their priest was still alive somewhere, and, presuming him to be dead, a solemn Requiem Mass was said for the repose of his soul.

But there remains another possibility. Had Borynski, said by his friends to have admitted being fed up with Bradford and thoroughly upset by the strife among the congregation resulting from his appointment, voluntarily decided to find his own way back to the homeland which he had left in 1939 to join the Polish Free Forces?

Interestingly, perhaps significantly, on July 26, 1953, 13 days after the vanishing of Father Borynski, a letter arrived for him. It came from a village near Cracow. It was from his 72-year-old mother. "Please tell me," she wrote, "why are you silent this long time? I am old and sick. What has happened to you?"

The old peasant woman never wrote again.

What are we to make of that? Does it mean that, old and sick as she confessed to being, she may perhaps have died? Or could it have been that Hendrik had come home after all? It would be nice – and possibly naïve – to think so.

A Grisly Game of Haydn Seek

Any man may lose his head, even the wisest, but to have it stolen is, under whatever circumstances, a most curious as well as undesirable tribulation!

This is precisely what happened to Franz Joseph Haydn, the "Father of instrumental music," from whom Beethoven took lessons. I tell the tale as I heard it. Minor inaccuracies may have crept in over the centuries, slight chronological discrepancies and distortions, but the story is in the main unquestionably correct.

Haydn died, aged 77, at his Viennese home on May 31, 1809. The time of his dying was one of great political upheaval in Austria. Napoleon's soldiery was knocking at Vienna's city gates. This meant that instead of the grand state funeral that so great and popular a musician might normally have expected to have been accorded, Haydn's burial had to be a rush job, with little pomp or ceremony. He was interred quietly in the city's Hundsthurm Cemetery.

Now at this time the great Viennese fad was phrenology, a pseudo-science devised by Dr Franz Josef Gall, indulged in as much by the doctors as by cranks. The locations of a man's cranial bumps were believed to provide relief maps, as it were, of his direction and inborn talents. It was a cabal of these bump-fanciers that sought venally the capital advantage of hands-on examination of the maestro's cranium, and to that end bribed Joseph Rosenbaum, secretary to Prince Nicolaus II Esterhazy, who had been Haydn's patron.

Thus it came about that in the black of a May night, four men carrying spades and a shaded lantern, moving silently through the Hundsthurm's ranks of buried dead, stole up to Haydn's new-turned grave, swiftly dug up his corpse, sliced neatly from it his head, and bore it stealthily off into the swallowing darkness.

Such was the beginning of a *post mortem* odyssey, which was to last 145 years.

The severed head was duly delivered to Johan Peter, superintendent of two prisons in Vienna and an avid head-hunter. He reduced it to a skull, composed an intricacy of exact cranial measurements and calculations, and pronounced Haydn's "bump of musicality" well developed. He then returned the skull to Rosenbaum.

The gruesome relic was ecstatically received by that gentleman's wife, a lady who did most zealously use music to raise herself in the social scale. In high delight, she visualised Haydn's head as striking just the right note to make her musical *soirées* the talk of the town. She commissioned, no expense spared, the construction of a magnificent glass and ebony case, wherein the head would, like a Victorian stuffed bird, be displayed.

It was when, in 1820, the Duke of Cambridge came to stay at Eisenstadt Palace as Esterhazy's guest, that he reminded his host of a plan the Prince had long ago hatched to bring Haydn's body from its humble grave and re-inter the great musician more fittingly in a magnificent bronze casket in the Esterhazy family church at Eisenstadt. And that was when, as they lifted the headless body from its plain wooden coffin – horror of horrors – the capital theft was discovered.

A positively apopleptic Prince summoned the *Polizei*. Johan Peter, in panic, begged Rosenbaum to return the skull to Esterhazy. He was willing. Frau Rosenbaum was not. Stubbornly, she refused to part with her status-symbol trophy. When, following a tip-off, the police searched the Rosenbaums' house, they found nothing. The good Frau had hidden her osseous treasure under the mattress of the sickbed to which she had betaken herself with feigned illness.

Prince Esterhazy offered a reward. Rosenbaum could not resist the bait. His wife could. Her frustrated husband tried to palm off another skull, obtained from a Vienna mortuary, upon the Prince. The ploy failed. Shrewd Esterhazy had it examined by an anatomist. It was pronounced to have belonged to a man of no more than 20 years of age. Rosenbaum delivered a second skull, this time that of a man of the correct age group. It was accepted and buried at Eisenstadt with due pomp and reverence.

The years passed over the greying heads of the Rosenbaums. Mrs Rosenbaum died. Then, Josef. On his deathbed he sent for Johan Peter and passed to him the controversial glass-and-ebony-cased *memento mori* of his original ordering. Peter kept the skull until his death in 1852.

What exactly happened then is not historically established. *Either* his widow made a present of it to the doctor who had attended Peter in his last illness – *or* he purloined it. Whichever way he obtained it, the doctor subsequently sold it to a noted Austrian professor, who, in turn, bequeathed it to the Pathological Museum of the University of Vienna.

It was then somehow discovered that Rosenbaum had actually willed the skull to the Vienna *Gesellschaft der Musikfreunde* (The Society of the Friends of Music – also sometimes known as the Academy of Music) – and when the *Gesellschaft* heard of this, it began a legal process which eventually succeeded.

Haydn's head remained on exhibition, a prime tourist attraction, sitting in its glass case on top of a piano in the *Gesellschaft's* museum from 1895 to 1954. Throughout all those 59 years the Esterhazy family continued doggedly to press its claim, arguing that Joseph Haydn should be accorded a better fate than to he headless in his tomb, his pilfered skull shamelessly exposed, a titillation to the gruesomely curious.

Two World Wars were fought. The Austro-Hungarian Empire was dismembered. There were occupations by the Nazis and the Soviets. Civilisation itself almost became a museum-piece. In the end, it was the Society of Friends themselves who resolved to bring about the termination of the ceaseless wanderings of the dead composer's head.

For decades, the Vienna Council had been powerfully advocating the permanent exhibition of the skull in Vienna's Historical Museum, but at the Second World War's end, the *Gesellschaft der Musikfreunde*, active once more, set to work to persuade the new Vienna Council to renounce their claim and permit the skull to be returned to its rightful place . . . in the sarcophagus at Eisenstadt. And they capitulated.

On a summer's day in 1954, Haydn's head was formally handed over to the officials of Burgenland, the province in which Eisenstadt was situated. Placed in an urn decorated with laurel wreaths, it was carried in procession for 30 kilometres through streets hung with flags and resounding to the iron-tongued music of church bells. Then, taken from the urn and gently laid upon a cushion, it was lowered to its right and proper position in the new copper casket wherein the exhumed trunk already lay.

Haydn was whole . . . himself again. There was surely great rejoicing in the spheres.

The Forest of Dean Murder

Christmas was only days away, but the atmosphere of festivity was sadly lacking at Fetterhill Farm. Harry Pace was seriously ailing again. "The Pain" had first come on after lamb-dipping. That was back in July. Now it had returned, as bad, worse, than ever, a twisting, burning agony in his guts.

Pace, a quarryman and part-time sheep-raiser, lived near Coleford, in Gloucestershire, on the lip's-edge of the Forest of Dean.

The Forest, as it is always called in those parts, is a strange, secretive place. A realm within a realm. Its native inhabitants are an isolated, clannish collection of "Forest folk", said to have been given to interbreeding and, in the old days at least, rural incest.

It is a place that brings to mind the late Mr Sherlock Holmes' stricture that: "The lowest and vilest alleys in London do not present a more dreadful record of sin than does the smiling and beautiful countryside."

It was here, then, in a lonely country cottage, that there existed a very unhappy hidden household – Harry Pace, his wife, Beatrice Annie, and the surviving five of their 10 children.

If his wife's evidence is to be believed, Harry Pace was a brute. His temper was maniacal. He beat her. He savagely killed her pet dog. On Christmas day, he had risen from his sick-bed, come downstairs, struck violently at her with a pair of fire-tongs, then threatened to cut the throats of the whole family.

If these things were true, I believe that – not that the law takes cognisance of any such sentiment – if anyone ever did, he certainly deserved to die.

And die he did, in very considerable pain, on January 10, 1928. As a result of representations made by the dead man's brother, Elton Pace, the coroner's officer halted the funeral cortège as it left the Paces' cottage. A post-mortem, conducted upon the coroner's order, revealed that death was due to arsenical poisoning.

After a protracted series of inquest hearings – 22 extending over four months – the jury's verdict was rendered against "some person or persons other than himself." The proceedings were then turned, by the coroner's insistence upon the naming of someone, into "Trial by Coroner", and led, incidentally, to subsequent curtailment of coroners' powers in this respect.

The jury named Beatrice Annie Pace, and the 36-year-old widow was arrested on the coroner's warrant.

The case presented against her at Gloucester Assizes in July, 1928, seemed pretty formidable, until her counsel, Norman Birkett, set to work to demolish it. His plain objective was to implant elements of doubt in the jury's mind. There were 9.42 grains of arsenic, over four times the minimum fatal dose, to be accounted for.

The question of administrative opportunity reduced the suspects to two: the ill-used wife or the husband himself taking his own life.

The vehicle of the poisoning, it was generally agreed, was sheep-dip. Sheep-dip, it must be borne in mind, consists of 65 per cent. sulphur, and when the powder is mixed with water the arsenic is easily soluble, whereas the sulphur is not. Since no sulphur was found in Pace's remains, this argues that the arsenious fluid, which would appear as a colourless liquid, was drawn off – something a would-be suicide would be unlikely to bother to do. If sheep-dip had been swallowed suicidally *as sheep-dip*, you would necessarily find in the body about three times as much sulphur as arsenic. They found none.

In cross-examination Birkett elicited from the Paces' 10-year-old son, Leslie, that he remembered his father asking him to bring up to him in his sick-bed the sheep-box, and saw him removing from it "something wrapped up in paper".

What was in that box was a packet of half-used sheep-dip, screwed up in paper.

From the dead man's mother, Birkett extracted the information that she did not know that an illegitimate son of hers had committed suicide, and contrived to expose Harry's brother, Elton Pace, as showing great. animosity against his sister-in-law, who he suggested "went with men". Playing Elton Pace gently, like a fish on a line, Birkett demonstrated that this brother-in-law was a potentially violent and massively prejudiced witness.

From the Pace family doctor, Birkett drew the opinion that the prisoner had appeared to him to be "a devoted nurse and wife".

Cross-examining the prosecution's big gun medical witness, Sir William Willcox, Birkett established that arsenic might find its way into the body through the mouth and broken skin, and that there was a realistic risk of chronic arsenical poisoning to those engaged in sheep-dipping.

The case for the Crown closed just before the luncheon adjournment on the fifth day of the trial. Immediately the Court reconvened, Birkett was on his feet submitting to the trial judge, Horridge J, that there was no case to go to the jury on the indictment.

He proceeded then to make, and get away with, the distinctly dubious statement that: "The scientific evidence is consistent with administration of the poison by the deceased equally with any other theory." The Crown, he said, had not, as they must, excluded the fact that the quantity of arsenic found in the body, and its effect upon the organs, were all consistent with self-administration. Understandably, he made no reference to absence of sulphur!

The judge, apparently agreeing with Birkett, and opining that it would not be safe to ask the jury to proceed further, instructed them to return a formal verdict of not guilty. To almost universal acclaim "The Tragic Widow of Coleford", as the newspapers hymned her, was acquitted. A strong hint that all was not perhaps quite so straightforward as the rejoicing, sympathetic multitude believed, is dropped in the biography of the celebrated medical analyst, Sir William Willcox. Doubt is there cast upon Harry Pace's actually being the cruel blackguard that – with mitigation in mind? – he was depicted as at the trial.

Some confidential documents submitted to Willcox in October, 1928, revealed that repeated poisonings with arsenic had extended over a period of three years, and that the final dose was administered 33½ hours before death. Sheep-dip was used, mixed with butter, in cornflour, in beef sandwiches and in brandy. There was suspicion (not proof) of participation in the crime by hands other than those of Mrs Pace.

The hands suspected were those of Leslie Sayce. A neighbour, he was a poultry farmer and eggler, who delivered eggs – and, said local gossip, more besides – to Mrs Pace. He is alleged to have made a post-trial confession that he had helped her in the despatch of her husband.

Jack the Ripper, I Presume?

But it *is* always presumption. The latest gentleman to extend his hand in questionable greeting is "Dr" Francis Tumblety.

Forget stereotypic Jack – twirling moustachioed Victorian villain figure, Phantom-of-the-Opera-like cloak, black Gladstone in black-gloved hand, shuffling through shadowed East End court and passage.

Visualise instead the travelling herbal doctor-showman, as patented by itinerant patent medicine man "Dr" Tumblety, American pill-pushing quack He rides astride a white horse, a brace of hounds slipped behind, laying siege to country fairs and market-places of smalltown, backwoods America.

He glitters in the rainbow-coloured raiment of the out-to-dazzle mountebank. The drum beats, his self-blown trumpet blares the fanfare of his triumphant salvatory crusade, coast to coast, across the States.

Purveyor of a whole pseudo-pharmacopoeia of salves for all the ills to which sad human flesh is heir, he is a frank extravert, the antithesis of shadowy Jack, the skulking silhouette of East London.

Such is the Whitechapel murderer conjured forth by a long lost letter discovered in the last decade of the twentieth century by Ripper historian Stewart Evans. Dated September, 1913, it is addressed by Detective Chief Inspector John George Littlechild, former head of the Secret or Special Branch at Scotland Yard, to a well-known journalist of the day, George R. Sims, author of, among many other books and poems, the famous ballad, "It is Christmas Day in the Workhouse".

In a pregnant paragraph, Littlechild writes: "In connection with the Whitechapel murders . . . amongst the suspects, and to my mind a very likely one, was a Dr T . . . He was an American quack named Tumblety."

Evans and his co-researcher, Paul Gainey, set to work to find out all they could about this brand-new Ripper suspect. According to Littlechild, he was a frequent visitor to London, "constantly brought under the notice of the police", and what the Inspector calls a "*Sycopathia* [*sic*] *Sexualis*' subject." Tumblety was apparently a resolute homosexual, trawling New York's Old Post Office Building for susceptible young clerks, rather as in London the Cleveland Streeters went trolling after such telegraph boys as Thickbroom, Swinscow, Newlove, and Perkins, of the St Martin's-le-Grand Post

Office. He is said to have harboured massive mysogynistic feelings, consequent upon an early marriage to an older wife who turned out to be a still-practising prostitute.

Ingeniously piecing together the elusive message of a wide scatter of often conflicting-seeming newspaper reports, Evans and Gainey constructed a convincing scenario in which Tumblety could well have been a bloodstained American who was said to have lodged at No 22 Batty Street, in the heart of Ripperland, sought but not found by the outwitted constabulary.

Francis J. Tumblety was born, the youngest of 11 children, in 1833 in Canada, but not long afterwards his family moved to Rochester, New York, that same city where those other mountebanks, the finger-and-toe-cracking Fox sisters, set spiritualism tapping its way to a thumping success.

At the same time as the girls were selling their new religion, 15-year-old Frank was turning a fast buck peddling pornographic books and papers on the local canal boats. His first taste of medical practice was doing odd jobs as a teenager for the highly dubious Dr W. C. Lispenard, specialist in various varieties of sex nexus afflictions.

Tumblety, his "medical student" days over, struck out on his own in the early 1850s. Following in Lispenard's disreputable medical footsteps, he had, by the time he was 24, built up a reputation as a herb doctor and an abortionist. There were deaths and brushes with the police, but Tumblety was a survivor. He side-stepped trouble with remarkable agility, and his fortune grew.

His first descent upon the Old World would seem to have been in 1869, when he visited Ireland and England, staying in London at the rather splendid Langham Hotel. He was back again across the herring pond in 1874, setting up business in Liverpool. It was in his rôle as herbal doctor that he met in that city the young Hall Caine, later to become a celebrated author, and a Uranian relationship blossomed between them.

Throughout the next dozen or so years, Tumblety was constantly back and forth between England and America. On Friday, August 31,1888, when Ripper-shed blood fell on the setts of Bucks Row, he was assuredly in London. That was the day that he committed an offence of gross indecency there with one Arthur Brice. Twice more he was similarly caught out, on October 14 and November 7, when he was arrested. He appeared before the magistrate at Marlborough

Street on November 16, was remanded on bail, and fled from England, sailing on November 24 from Le Havre to New York. Supporting the theory that Francis Tumblety was the Whitechapel murderer, Evans and Gainey have discovered that when he reached New York, two American detectives shadowed him to his lodgings. And in December, Inspector Walter Andrews, one of the original three Ripper hunters, arrived in Manhattan. If his trip was in quest of Jack the Ripper, nothing came of it.

Tumblety lived on for another fifteen years. In 1901, he was in Baltimore. It was there that he, the allegedly vitriolic hater of prostitutes, made a will bequeathing $1,000 to the Home for the Fallen Women of Baltimore.

He died on May 28, 1903, a Roman Catholic, ultimately groomed and garnered for salvation by the nuns who ran the institution where he breathed his last – St John's Charity Hospital, St Louis.

Was Dr Tumblety Jack the Ripper? Evans and Gainey are persuaded that he very likely was. But what of the official police conclusion in the matter? Littlechild wrote to Sims that there was a "large dossier concerning him [Turnblety] at Scotland Yard."

Here is the oddest thing of all. There is a total absence of the name of Francis Tumblety, not only from the English newspapers, but also from all the official documents. Not a single mention in the police files, nor in those of the Home Office. There is nothing even in the highly confidential progress reports which were supplied regularly by the police to the Home Office. Moreover, Evans and Gainey combed the Public Record Office files in vain. Drew a complete blank. The large dossier of which Littlechild spoke has simply vanished into thin air.

Tumblety's name exists nowhere amid the acres and acres of bureaucratic paperwork. Does that, perhaps, savour of a significant conspiracy of silence – a shroud for the Ripper?

Sherlock Doyle and the Manor Place Holocaust

Conan Doyle had, in 1893, disposed of Mr Sherlock Holmes over the Reichenbach Falls – "murdered" him as some angry devotees of the *Strand Magazine's* great detective expressed it. Nonetheless, Doyle had signally failed to abate his own interest in crime and criminals, and more particularly in the study of criminal psychology.

A case which fascinated him, and one about which he wrote in the *Strand*, in March, 1901, was that of William Godfrey Youngman.

Youngman was just that – a young man of 25. His father was a journeyman tailor, and William had started out in life apprenticed to the trade. He disliked it, nurtured far grander, although unspecified, ambitions.

His first upward, as he saw it, step was his securing of a situation as under-footman to a Dr Duncan, of Covent Garden. Reports vary as to how he fared. One says that he served with credit for some time, but finally resigned his post. Another strongly hints that his departure from that office followed upon the discovery of certain articles of clothing in his box which actually belonged to his master. Whatever the truth, he was presently back home, living with, and on, his parents at No 16 Manor Place, Walworth, South London. There, loafing, lying abed as late as they would allow, his idle thoughts turned to scheming criminous short cuts to relative riches.

And that is where Mary, the daughter of a prosperous farmer of Wadhurst, in Sussex, Samuel Streeter, came into his villainous plans. Since Wadhurst was a mere 40 miles from London, Mary, who had friends there, often came up to town. One unlucky day she was introduced to William Youngman. Spotting potential prey, he paid her assiduous attention, even went down to Wadhurst to meet, and successfully ingratiate himself with, her father.

A dab hand with a pen, William wrote tender love-letters to Mary. The one thing about them that irked her a little was her suitor's continually repeated reference to her taking out insurance – £100 was the sum mentioned – on her life, himself, her affianced, to be the nominated beneficiary. This he eventually persuaded the simple country girl to do.

Youngman's next ploy was to invite his sweetheart to come up to London to meet and stay with his parents. In his letter of invitation he included the odd instruction regarding his previous letters to her, "Bring or burn all your letters, my dear girl. Do not forget." In fact, she did forget.

William was there on the platform, bright and sharp, when, at 9.45 on that Monday morning, July 30, 1860, the train bringing her from Wadhurst steamed into London Bridge. They took an omnibus, straw-strewn, horse-drawn, to Manor Place, arriving there at 11 o'clock.

William's father, John, was away at work. His two young brothers, Thomas (11) and Charles (7), were at school. Only his mother, Elizabeth, was there to greet the pair. She made dinner for the three of them, after which the lovers set forth to see something of the city.

We do not, save for one incident, have any record of where the happy couple, death hovering above one of them in the fickle sunshine, betook themselves that day. We do, however, know that at one stage they called in at the Green Dragon in Bermondsey Street, whose genial host, Edward Spicer, happened to know Mary and her father. Her country pink cheeks blushing pinker still, she shyly introduced her intended to the publican.

Imagine the poor girl's embarrassment when, an opportunity presenting, the innkeeper drew her aside and whispered that it would be better for her to take a rope and hang herself in his skittle-alley than to marry such a man as that. God alone knows what warning signs Spicer thought to descry in Youngman's face, what sense of malignancy in his character or bearing switched on an alert at the back of his brain.

In the evening, the pair went to the theatre to see one of the celebrated tragedian, William Macready's, plays – for sure, howsoever dramatic, a pale imitation of the reality which was now drawing horribly near.

It was eleven o'clock before they were back once more at Manor Place. The entire family and their visitor supped together.

It is necessary here to explain the division of the Manor Place household. Those were the days before English architects had embraced the idea of flats, but residences were nevertheless divided. As a rule the division was planned thus: the tenant of a three-storey house, the landlord, occupied the ground floor, and sub-let his first and second floors. At No 16, Mr James Bevan resided on the ground floor, Mr and Mrs Beard on the first, and the Youngmans on the second.

After supper, family and guest retired to bed – mother, Charles, and Mary in the front bedroom; father, Thomas, and William in the back.

At 5 am John the tailor rose, 20 minutes later crept quietly down the stair, and closed the front-door softly behind him.

Shortly after 5.30 am Mrs Beard on the floor below was awakened by the sound of what she took to be the Youngman boys romping. She nudged her sleeping husband, and as they both sat up in bed they heard a terrible gasping cry and the dull, soft thud of a falling body.

Beard and Bevan, whom he had aroused, crept up the creaking staircase and in a blaze of golden July morning sunshine they beheld the incongruous horror of a confused huddle of white-clad figures littered over the landing and passage. They heard a stirring, someone moving in the bedroom. Then framed suddenly in the doorway stood William Youngman his white nightshirt brilliant with streaks and smears and blotches of bright blood.

"Mr Beard, for God's sake fetch a surgeon. I believe there's still some alive yet," he cried. Then, as they turned and ran downstairs, he called after them: "My mother has done all this. She has murdered my two brothers and my sweetheart, and I in self-defence believe that I have murdered her."

Youngman was tried at the Old Bailey before Williams J. The only motive seemed to have been poor Mary's £100. Significantly there was lunacy on both sides of the family. Youngman's father's father, his father's brother, and his mother's mother had all been confined in asylums. Found guilty, he was hanged before a crowd of 30,000 at Horsemonger Lane Gaol.

"Do not leave the world with a lie on your lips," the chaplain implored him. "If I wanted to lie I'd say I did it," was the tart retort.

Doyle concludes: "And so, with the snick of a bolt and the jar of a rope, ended one of the most sanguinary, and also one of the most unaccountable, incidents in English criminal annals. That the man was guilty seems to admit no doubt, and yet it must be confessed that circumstantial evidence can never be absolutely convincing, and that it is only the critical student of such cases who realises how often a damning chain of evidence may, by some slight change, be made to bear an entirely different interpretation."

One is tempted to add: "My dear Watson".

The Windham Lunacy Case

Let us begin with a vignette. It is the small hours of a September morning in 1861. Ancient Felbrigg Hall, three miles from Cromer, lies awake and alert under the wide East Anglian sky, awaiting the home-coming of the young squire and his bride.

As the battered old Windham family coach debouches its party of eight travellers, the joy of expectancy fades from the faces of the welcoming servants lined up in the lamp-lit hall. They do not like what they see.

Resplendent in the latest Parisian crinolines, Agnes, the bride, and Thirza, her sister, sweep superciliously in. Behind them, the bride-groom, William Windham, grubby, soot-begrimed, as of old. Behind him, a Frenchwoman – Agnes' lady's-maid – clasping a tired little girl, Agnes' other sister, by the hand. And, bringing up the rear, three sinister-looking men – Agnes' solicitor, doctor, and former whore-master.

The outstanding figure in the group, the one around whom this strange story revolves, is the groom, who, coming of age on August 9, 1861, had married, three weeks later, and most unsuitably, one of the celebrated "pretty horsebreakers" of Rotten Row, Agnes Willoughby.

From this point forward, young Windham embarked upon an extravaganza of folly so excessive as to cause those who had the family welfare at heart – notably his uncle, General Windham – to entertain grievous doubts as to his sanity.

The truth is that William Frederick Windham's conduct had always been distinctly bizarre. Removed from his preparatory school and later from Eton, he had in his teens refused *de rigueur* induction into his peer group, Norfolk county society, preferring the company of his social inferiors. Although fond of the company of men-servants, footmen, and the like, his absolute favourites were railway porters, engine-drivers, and guards. By dint of princely tipping, he was able to indulge a fancy for the fantasy of "playing trains", adult version.

Rigged out, full fig, as a guard, he would parade the platforms of the Great Eastern line, passenger-herding and whistle-blowing to his heart's content. He even bribed his way on to the footplate and would return delirious and soot-covered after such adventures as driving the night mail between Norwich and London. Another little eccentricity was his habit of dressing up as a police constable, and setting forth for the Haymarket at midnight, where he would round up the ladies of the night as they emerged from the various drinking places, and order other policemen to cart them off to the police station.

Having come into his inheritance, the Felbrigg Estate and an immense fortune, he felt in a position to make serious advances to Agnes. She accepted him – at a price. Born Agnes Rogers, daughter of a Hampshire village sawyer and former nursemaid, who could neither read nor write, the 21-year-old girl had, under the harsh tutelage of James Roberts, pimp and smart Piccadilly gambling hall proprietor, come a long way. Wearing a scarlet riding-habit, mounted upon a huge black Belgian mare, cantering in Rotten Row, she, with her pale, heart-shaped face, deep blue eyes and cascade of light gold hair, was a seductively attractive sight.

That attractiveness had brought her two St John's Wood villas, a house in Paris, a £2,000-a-year allowance from her current protector, and an £8,000 lump sum from the errant Vicar-General of Canterbury, as well as sundry further satisfactory "wages of sin"!

"Mad" Windham's contribution to her resources was to be, literally, ruinous. Her mulcting of him was utterly cynical. At no time did she make the least pretence of caring, let alone loving. In his very presence she told her solicitor: "I feel a repugnancy for him. I will marry for a good settlement."

She settled for £800-a-year for seven years, and thereafter £1,500 *per annum*. Additionally, she had him redeem £400-worth of antique jewellery for her from Attenboroughs, the pawnbroker's. She led him to a Brook Street diamond merchant's, where he bought her £13,000-worth of jewels. This was followed by a further £,4,500-worth of diamonds and emeralds.

The wedding took place at All Saints' Church, St John's Wood, on August 30, 1861. The honeymoon was 10 days in Paris. Then, in the first week of September, that early morning return to Felbrigg Hall; "Mad" Windham, soot-drenched after riding, as usual, on the footplate of the train.

On Sepember 23, Agnes bolted. She had gone to Dublin to join Signor Antonio "Cherub" Giuglini, an internationally celebrated Italian opera singer, who was the courtesan's *amant-de-coeur*. For Windham, this was the beginning of what was to be the incredibly protracted end of his one-sided romance.

Meanwhile, his uncle, the General, had for some time been watching with mounting alarm the dwindling of those family estates to which he, if his nephew died without issue, was in entail. In fact, "Mad" Windham had arranged for the execution of a deed whereby the entail was barred. Now, if young Windham could be proved to be of unsound mind, his disastrous marriage, the barred entail, all the mischief could be undone. The state of affairs, he determined, called for a *Commission de Lunatico Inquirendo*.

The enquiry opened on December 16, 1861, in the Court of Exchequer, at the Westminster Sessions House, before the Master in Lunacy, Samuel Warren, QC, author of the very popular novel, *Ten Thousand a Year*. The jury found "Mad" Windham of sound mind, but he was saddled with a decidely disturbing £20,000 costs.

Yet even that was not sufficient to curb his ingrained *folie d'extravagance*. There was a costly final flaring dalliance with Agnes before his total collapse into engulfing bankruptcy. Every last penny had been fiittered away, and Felbrigg sold.

For a time he took a job as coachman, driving one of the old yellow four-in-handers that plied between Norwich and Cromer. At the end of ten months he had lost enthusiasm and came to blows with the coach proprietor.

By now virtually a pauper, lodging in a Norwich pothouse, subsisting on General Windham's charity, which measured out at one pound per week, his star of fortune was in terminal decline. The end came on February 1, 1866. That was when he set out with a gaggle of local youths on a round of the Norwich pubs. Fourteen hours later, and indubitably out of his senses "Mad" Windham staggered back to his pothouse pallet, lay down, and died.

Agnes had produced a son. She tussled her way indomitably through the courts to prove that he was, as she had had him baptised, Frederick William Howe Lindsay Bacon Windham, son of Frederick. She succeeded, vanquishing the General's cast doubts. She ended her days the strait-laced Lady Bountiful of the Windhams' Hanworth Estate – happily married to the agent.

The Duke and the Dead Draper

On a December morning of biting wind and cutting sleet the lid of the old merchant's coffin, resurrected from the family vault in Highgate Cemetery, creaked stiffly open to reveal . . .

Such is the beginning – and the end – of what the late Dr John H. Watson would surely have called the Bizarre Affair of the Baker Street Bazaar, or the Mystery of the Duke and the Dead Draper.

The whole extraordinary business had started when a little old widow woman, Mrs Anna Maria Druce, relict of Walter Druce, the son of Thomas Charles Druce, self-made proprietor of a flourishing London drapery emporium, announced: "My husband, Walter, was the rightful Duke of Portland."

Mrs Druce's interesting proclamation could be held to be a shade tardy, for it was all of 17 years' since William John Cavendish Bentinck-Scott, fifth Duke of Portland, had laid his coronet aside and taken up residence in Kensal Green Cemetery. And ever since, a distant kinsman had ruled as sixth duke at Welbeck Abbey, controlling the purse-strings of the £16 million Portland estate.

An awkward fly in the ointment for Mrs Druce was the fact that the fifth Duke had died a bachelor. She squashed it promptly. "Rubbish! He led a double life." Elaborating, she said that about the year 1835, the duke had donned a false beard and eyebrows and adopted a false identity. Calling himself Thomas Charles Druce, he began a prosperous career as a Baker Street shopkeeper. Then, in 1851, he had married a Miss Annie May Berkeley, and the first fruit of the marriage was a son, Walter Thomas Druce. She had married Walter, and borne him a son, Sidney George Druce.

Another inconvenient fly: the fifth duke had died in 1879, but Thomas Charles Druce had been dead since 1864. The self-styled duchess was not to be deposed by a trifling detail like that. Resorting once again to her favourite word, "Rubbish!" she explained that the duke, wearying of life as a tradesman, had arranged Thomas Charles Druce's "death", and a mock funeral from Baker Street. The coffin in the Druce family vault at Highgate had contained only a man's weight in lead.

Sheer fantasy on the part of a woman who was obsessed with the idea of becoming a duchess and the mother of a duke? There was only one way to find out. Open the coffin. Legal permission was sought.

And refused. For a couple of years old Mrs Druce went on pestering the courts. Then, in February, 1899, something happened that knocked her sideways. An excavating reporter on the *Weekly Dispatch* dug up evidence that Thomas Charles Druce had been married before he had taken unto himself Miss Annie May Berkeley. In 1816, he had put the ring on the finger of a Miss Elizabeth Crickmer at Bury St Edmunds, and from this union there had been male issue. And to top it all, in came long lost George Hollamby Druce from Australia. That did it. The "duchess" retired to a mental home. Concerning her the rest is silence.

But the ball, once set rolling, did not stop. The claimant from down-under, a carpenter in quest of ducal robes and the cash that went with the coronet, was unquestionably the grandson of Thomas Charles Druce's first marriage. Taking over where her late putative Grace had left off, he went about matters with a much more cunning hand. Going to law costs money. He floated companies to finance his £16 million fortune hunt. Speculators greedy to share a piece of the fiscal action when his coronet came home, shelled out liberally.

Thus primed with the necessary funds, George Druce began his legal battle, setting to work to prove that Anna Maria's brother-in-law, Herbert Druce, who swore that his father, Thomas Charles Druce, had really died in 1864, was a liar. In October, 1907, at Marylebone Police Court, he brought a charge of perjury against him.

Robert Caldwell, an elderly Irish-American, stated that he had been introduced to the duke by the well-known physician, the late Sir Morrell Mackenzie. He had known His Grace at both Welbeck and Baker Street. He had himself bought the lead, ordered the coffin, and arranged the bogus burial.

A Mary Robinson, claiming high birth, brought all the way from New Zealand, testified that she had met Thomas Charles Druce in 1862, and knew that he and the Duke of Portland were the same man.

Mrs Margaret Hamilton swore that the duke had proposed marriage to her. She had known him as Druce,

Things were looking good for the claimant and his investors . . . until the opposition lawyers got to work. Caldwell was shown to have a shady reputation in the States, where he was known as "the great American affidavit maker". Sir Morrell Mackenzie would have been a 16-year-old boy at the time of the alleged introduction to the duke. Mary Robinson was forced to admit that her father had actually been a Mortlake policeman, and her dead husband had served the duke as a shepherd. Neither was Mrs Hamilton so high born as she would have the court believe. She was the daughter of a flax manufacturer.

The name "Scott", by which she said she used to address the duke, had not been adopted by him at the age of their alleged courtship. The hue of George Hollamby Druce's case was now decidedly less rosy.

It was at this stage that the Court decided that it might now be advisable to sanction the opening of the Druce grave.

On a December morning of biting wind and cutting sleet the lid of the old merchant's coffin, resurrected from the family vault in Highgate Cemetery, creaked stiffly open to reveal . . . surrounded by shroud and sweet-scented sawdust, the well-preserved body of Thomas Charles Druce.

To this day no one really knows how the classic Druce-Portland false claim, another Tichborne, was conceived, let alone allowed to snowball and spread confusion through the courts. What seems most likely is that the whole fantasy was erected on the basis of a delusion that took hold in a crazed woman's brain, and that others, sane and scheming, tried to turn it to advantageous reality.

The Lady Was For Burning

The trouble is that, searching for the killer of Evelyn Foster, who died one bitter January night 75 years ago, we have not a single substantial clue to the manner of creature that he was. He is said to have been a dapper little man. He wore a bowler-hat. He materialised like some evil northland boggart out of the blackness of the winter's night, importing with him the lethal Will-o'-the-Wisp flame with which, cruelly and senselessly, he incinerated a harmless young woman . . . and then melted back into the shrouding darkness whence he came. The mystery has been exhaustively investigated by my friend, Jonathan Goodman, in his book, *The Burning of Evelyn Foster*, which provides the full-length, classic account of the case.

Tuesday, January 6th, 1931. Twelfth Night. The dead end of Christmas. A clear, star-flecked sky, like a cold sarcophagus lid, was gleaming over the sabre-toothed northern heights of Northumberland. Chugging and steaming across rough, tussocked moorland, frozen stiff as corrugated iron and magpied with great splotches of frost that glittered grittily in the cold blaze of moonlight, the little country bus was returning, shortly before 10 pm, from Newcastle to homebase, Foster's Garage, Otterburn.

There were no passengers aboard, only the driver, Cecil Johnstone, and his conductor, Thomas Rutherford. They had just passed through the small sliced crag of moorland backbone known as Wolf's Nick when they saw the eerie orange glow. Drawing closer, they spotted the source of the fire. A burning car. Johnstone recognised it. The Hudson Super-Six, TN 8135, belonging to his boss' 29-year-old daughter, Evelyn Foster. Then, from somewhere out of the smoky darkness, came a kind of thin, rustling moan. It was Evelyn Foster . . . transformed into a human torch . . . burning against the ice. They wrapped the poor charred body in an overcoat and carried her gently to the bus. Over and over again she kept whispering: "It was that awful man. Oh, that awful man."

The girl had a strange tale to tell. She had, she said, been hailed by some people in a stationary car as she was passing through Elishaw on her way back to Otterburn after having driven three passengers to the village of Rochester in her hire car.

A man got out and came across to her. He had, he explained, had a lift as far as Elishaw after missing the Newcastle bus at Jedburgh. He could, he understood, pick up a Newcastle-bound bus at Otterburn.

No, said Evelyn, it was now about 7 pm, and the last bus from Otterburn had long gone. What she could do was take him to Otterburn and on to Ponteland, where he would get a Newcastle bus.

Reaching Otterburn, she had dropped the man at the village inn, the Percy Arms, while she went to the garage to fill up. He was waiting for her by the bridge beside the Percy Arms, clambered into the front seat next to her, and off they went. They reached Belsay, six miles from Ponteland. "Turn here and go back," suddenly ordered the man. He was creeping along the seat towards her. He seized the steering-wheel. She protested. He dealt her a stinging blow to the eye, shoved her roughly over to the side of the car and, pinioning her there, headed back in silence in the direction of Otterburn. At Wolf's Nick he stopped. Then began to attack her – hitting, kicking, finally knocking her into the back of the car, where, as she told her mother, he interfered with her. She lost consciousness. She awoke to find him pouring the contents of a bottle or tin over her. Then . . . a great swoosh of flame . . . and she was burning. At half-past seven the following morning, in her own bed, Evelyn Foster died. Her last words were ""I have been murdered, Mother, I have been murdered." With every confidence, the Northumberland police began combing the frost-bound wilderness for the man in the bowler-hat. But clue after clue melted away like ice-water. The barman at the Percy Arms swore that no stranger had come in that Tuesday evening. Professor Stuart McDonald, the pathologist, said that he had found no indication of the dead girl's having been raped.

At the inquest, held in Otterburn's War Memorial Hall, where, mere weeks before, Evelyn had attended a Boxing Night dance, the coroner sought to impose his view that the girl had set fire to herself. But the jury would have none of it. Steadfastly, bleakly, they returned a finding of wilful murder against some person or persons unknown. The villagers greeted the verdict with cheers.

The case of the burning girl had been concluded – but not resolved.

The mystery is still alive. So many questions remain, glowing unanswered in the grey moorland air.

One among half a dozen theories pleads a special consideration. Formulated by Jonathan Goodman, it would fix the guilt of the burning of Evelyn Foster upon a man named Ernest Brown. He was a 35-year-old groom, working for Frederick Morton at an isolated farm, Saxton Grange, near Tadcaster, Yorkshire. Between Brown and Morton's wife, Dorothy, there developed a passionate liaison which, on her side, turned sour, and on his, escalated into a frenzied jealousy. One September night in 1933, Brown murdered Frederick Morton, by shooting him and incinerating his body in a car. What possible linkage could there be between the Lothario of Saxton Grange and the pyromaniacal killer of Wolf's Nick? Briefly: both Evelyn Foster and Frederick Morton were variantly accused of self-immolation. Evelyn testified that her assailant had an accent like that of Tyneside, and Brown had spent part of his childhood in Newcastle. Brown used to attend horse and cattle sales around the country, so could well have been in the vicinity of Otterburn. Finally, as Brown stood, pinioned and hooded, on the scaffold at Armley Gaol, Leeds, he spoke three muffled words – "Ought to burn." Or was it perhaps one – "Otterburn"?

Whatever, time has not bulked out the killer of Evelyn Foster. He has remained what he was then, the invisible man, his entire existence encompassed in a few flame-lit hours around Otterburn – all that remains to mark his terrible visitation, a black marble stone in the graveyard of St. John's Church, and a clutch of rapidly thinning memories.

The Liverpool Lodger

For numberless weeks he had been roaming the streets. When he saw the little white card in the window, he knew his prowlings were at an end.

It was some time during the latter part of the year 1848, that Captain John Henry Hinrichson, master of a sailing-ship plying between Liverpool and Calcutta, and his wife, Ann, decided to purchase No 20 Leveson Street, in the downtown quarter of Liverpool. By the beginning of the following year, the Hinrichsons, together with their two sons, Henry George, aged five, and John Alfred, a three-year-old tot, and a maid-servant, Mary Parr, had settled into their new home.

Finding the place just a trifle large for their requirements, the captain and his wife decided to let a couple of furnished rooms. The money, together with what Mrs Hinrichson earned by teaching the pianoforte to a number of pupils, would help considerably towards household expenses. Accordingly, a neat card was placed in the front-parlour window – "Furnished Apartments to Let".

At about 4 pm that day, a well-dressed young man of some 26 years presented himself at the door and inquired in an engaging Irish brogue about the lodgings. He gave the name of John Gleeson Wilson. It wasn't his real one. He was Maurice Gleeson from Limerick. He was shown a back-parlour and a bedroom on the second floor. Telling Mrs Hinrichson that he was a carpenter employed by the Dock Estate, he said that he would take the rooms.

He then left the house. He returned at about eight o'clock that evening, and around 10 pm sent out for a pint of ale before going up to bed.

Those were the days before "Dora" had come to put a curb on the Englishman's drinking habits, and at half-past seven the following morning Wilson was in a nearby public-house having a breakfast glass of ale. Calling over to the woman behind the bar, he asked if she could supply him with a wafer to seal an envelope. She brought him instead a stick of sealing-wax. Telling her that he couldn't write, he asked if she would address the envelope for him – "John Wilson, Esq 20 Leveson Street, Liverpool."

Wilson then left the pub and, beckoning a passing youth in the street, promised him a few coppers if he would deliver a letter for him. "Watch me go into a house in Leveson Street, wait a few minutes, then knock and ask if John Wilson lives there. Tell whoever opens the door you have a letter for Mr Wilson from his employer."

The servant, Mary Parr, answered the lad's knock. Wilson, who was hovering in the hall, took the letter ostentatiously, making sure that Mrs Hinrichson also knew what was going on, and bore it off to his room. It had been a pantomime, staged to impress the household with his status as a respectably employed respected employee!

Shortly after 11 o'clock, Mrs Hinrichson told Mary that she was going out to do her shopping. She went first to the greengrocer's, and ordered some potatoes. From there she went to a chandler's and bought two jugs. Both these purchases were to be delivered to her home by errand-boys.

The boy with the potatoes arrived first. The door was opened by Wilson. About twenty minutes later, the second boy turned up with the crockery. He put his basket down on the step . . . rang the bell . . . whistled a popular tune while he waited . . . rang again . . . still no reply. He tried the effect of a thunderous assault with the knocker. The door remained tight-shut. Putting his eye to the keyhole, the boy peeped into the hall. What he saw gave him a fright – a pair of woman's legs lying across the passageway. Curiosity aroused, he clambered on to the handle of his basket and, perching himself precariously on the area railings, peered in through the parlour window. The scene in that room drained the colour from his cheeks. There lay the blood-drenched body of Mary the maid, beside her, his head battered, was little Henry George. With a shriek of terror, the chandler's boy took to his heels and never stopped running until he helter-skeltered into the arms of a passing policeman.

When, later, the authorities embarked upon a thorough search of the premises, they found 29-year-old Mrs Hinrichson, who, by the way, was shortly expecting a third child, lying mortally injured in the lobby. Down in the cellar, was three-year-old John Alfred. His throat had been cut. Upstairs in Wilson's room was a bowl of bloodied water in which the murderer had evidently washed his hands. But of Wilson himself there was no sign. Mary Parr, with anxious police officials watching beside her hospital bed, lived just long enough to falter out her story of the horror that was enacted in the old dark house in Leveson Street.

Meanwhile, Wilson, a human tiger, prowled the drab jungle of the streets of Victorian Liverpool as the hunters set to work casting a drag-net to snare him. Wilson had a wife living at Tramnere, over the water on the Birkenhead bank of the Mersey, and he spent the night with her. Next morning, ignoring the hue and cry, he took a ferry-boat back to Liverpool, and made his way to the shop of Israel Samuel, a Great Howard Street grocer, who also had a nice little side-line dealing in watches. Wilson showed him a gold watch – plundered from Mrs Hinrichson's – saying that he wanted £6 for it.

But the shrewd Mr Samuel smelt a rat and refused to make an offer before calling in a policeman to confirm that the watch was not one that had been notified as stolen property. Even when so reassured, Samuel remained suspicious. He told Wilson that if he accompanied his son to this other shop in Dale Street he would be paid there. And he told his son, in Hebrew, "When you're passing the police station, collar this fellow and give him in charge". The son did as his father told him and so surprised was Wilson that he had been bundled inside the bridewell before he could muster the slightest resistance.

Staunchly maintaining his innocence when put up at the Liverpool Assizes, Wilson showed no hint of remorse, and heard the guilty verdict with a seeming brutal indifference. He was hanged outside Kirkdale Gaol on September 15, 1849, in the approving presence of an estimated 30,000 spectators. Excursion trains, packed to suffocation, were run to the execution, the railway companies advertising, "Reduced fares for this occasion only." A one turn off, you might say.

The Shakespeare Birthday Murder

April, says the poet, is the cruellest month . . . and it was just that for a 45-year-old midwife named Olive May Gardner Bennett. It was in "Shakespeareland" – Stratford-on-Avon – and, indeed, upon the very day of the quarter centenary of Shakespeare's birth that Nemesis overtook her.

Friday, April 23, 1954, saw Stratford determinedly celebrating, as it does every year, the birthday of its most illustrious son. On this 400th anniversary people had come from far and wide to mark the occasion, among them the diminutive nurse – only 4 feet 11 inches tall – from the Monroe Devis Maternity Home, in the village of Tiddington, a mere mile-and-a-half north-east of Stratford.

Set on having a good time, Miss Bennett could scarcely wait to get off duty that night. So eager was she to be away to Stratford, that she could not wait even to eat her supper, but, pulling on her brown tweed coat, dragging her floppy felt hat well down to hide her greying hair, she rushed out shortly before eight o'clock to catch a bus into town, shouting over her shoulder, "I won't be back until about two o'clock."

She did not return at 2 am – or ever.

Early on the morning of Saturday, April 24, Tom Anderson, sexton-gardener at the Avonside Church of Holy Trinity, Stratford, walking to work along the riverside was suddenly halted in his tracks by something which, caught by the spring sunshine, was glinting in the grass. It turned out to be a pair of gold-rimmed spectacles. His eye now raking the ground, he found next a set of lower jaw dentures, a woman's brown shoe, and a pigskin glove.

He saw, too, alarming evidence of malfeasance amid the trimmed grass of his graveyard demesne. The footstone, weighing all of 56 lbs, of the grave of one Robert Adams, *obit* 1875, had been wrenched from the Warwickshire clay, dragged towards the river wall, and made away with.

Below that 15-foot churchyard wall, floating in an eddy of the river that lapped it, he spotted a woman's brown felt hat. Anderson had seen enough. He immediately contacted the police.

From the river they brought out the body of Olive Bennett. Near it was the footstone; it had been flung in on top of her in an unsuccessful attempt to pin the body to the bed of the Avon. A post-mortem established death by strangulation.

Searching for a possible motive for the murder, detectives, including my old friend Superintendent John Capstick, well nicknamed "Charlie Artful", called in from Scotland Yard, set to work to piece together all they could about the victim, her history, and her way of life.

Born in Edinburgh, on May 23, 1908, Olive, who had ambitions to become a teacher, had enrolled when she was 19 as a student at Edinburgh University. Unfortunately, she failed to do well enough on her course there, so, abandoning the idea of teaching, she decided instead that she would take up social work. No more successful in this, she had ultimately enlisted as a probationer nurse, and in 1939 achieved her qualification as a State Certified Midwife. Then, in 1945, she went to Southampton, where she spent three years training for, and obtained, her SRN.

Returning to her first love, midwifery, Olive got a post at Shrub Hill Hospital, Worcester, and it was there, in the summer of 1953, that, the detectives learned, the quiet, respectable, inoffensive little midwife had begun to show gross signs of an extraordinary personality change. She had, as one of her disconcerted colleagues put it, "suddenly gone mad".

Night after night, after spending ages and ages titivating and getting her make-up just right, she would be off down into the town, where she would do a vast round of the public-houses, sipping innumerable sweet sherries, chain-smoking, and picking up, or being picked up by, any foot-loose male who should happen to stray within flirting distance.

It was a change of life style that cost her dearly too. She was now regularly drawing sizeable sums of money out of her Post Office Savings account, rapidly diminishing the fruit of years of providence. Once adopted, it was a course of conduct that set in. It complicated things.

On the Birthday evening that became Olive's death-day, her movements proved at least partially capable of reconstruction. She had been seen at the George Hotel, in Bridge Street, and again, between 9 and 10.30 pm, when she was sitting in the corner window-seat in the bar of the Red Horse Hotel, off Bridge Street. On both occasions she had been on her own.

Thus far Olive had adhered to an accustomed pattern of behaviour. But hereafter, as the celebratory fireworks fade and the darkness grows thicker and the crowds thinner, all becomes an obscure haze of unknowing.

There is, perhaps, just one possible glimpse, a tantalising *aperçu*: a hotel porter, cycling home, had seen a couple embracing in Holy Trinity churchyard. The description which he gave of the woman seemed to fit Olive. His sighting of the man was less satisfactory. All that he could say of his appearance was that he was tall, or tallish, was aged, at a guess, around 35, had bushy fair hair – that was surely the best clue – and wore a belted gaberdine raincoat.

Searching Olive's room in the nursing quarters at the maternity home, Capstick had found a number of letters addressed to her by various men. He had also come upon a diary of hers which contained the names of a great many men with whom she had apparently had dealings. All the names, all correspondents, were tracked down and rigorously investigated. An enormous tally of work – and, disappointingly, nothing came of it. Her killer remained as much a mystery as the force which drove her into his clutches.

All of her first 44 years, Olive had lived a sheltered and eminently respectable life. Her mother, Calvinistic by persuasion, had been a stern, unbending parent, perhaps psychologically damaging her daughter, inclining her to, in resentment, choose, when freedom came, to embrace a diametrically opposed path, showing herself both willing and available to strangers.

Alternatively, there is firm medical evidence that Olive was latterly suffering from congenital degenerative disease of the brain, which could account for bizarre behaviour.

As to the reason for her murder, the sole feeble offering of motive was that she was blackmailing some specific man of her too intimate acquaintance. But there is not the slightest supporting evidence for this. Far more likely is it that she had the misfortune to encounter a wanderlusting serial killer.

All that can be said for certain is that, in her pathetic search for a late in life romantic excitement, poor Olive Bennett kept her appointment in Samarra, but met a false lover and an inglorious death among the tombstones and under the ancient yews of the burying-ground of Shakespeare's church.